MY ENEMY, MY LOVE

MY ENEMY, MY LOVE

Women, Men, and the Dilemmas of Gender

Judith Levine

ANCHOR BOOKS
DOUBLEDAY
NEW YORK   LONDON   TORONTO   SYDNEY   AUCKLAND

AN ANCHOR BOOK

PUBLISHED BY DOUBLEDAY

a division of Bantam Doubleday Dell Publishing Group, Inc.
666 Fifth Avenue, New York, New York 10103

ANCHOR BOOKS, DOUBLEDAY, and the portrayal of an anchor
are trademarks of Doubleday, a division of Bantam Doubleday Dell
Publishing Group, Inc.

My Enemy, My Love was originally published in hardcover by
Doubleday in 1992. The Anchor Books edition is
published by arrangement with Doubleday.

"Apology for Husbands," copyright 1941, 1969 by Phyllis McGinley from *Times Three*
by Phyllis McGinley. Used by permission of Viking Penguin, a division of
Penguin Books USA Inc.
"Damn, Wish I Was a Man," copyright © 1987 Starbitch Music. Lyrics used by permission.
"Wild Women Don't Have the Blues." Words and music by Ida Cox, copyright 1924 by
Northern Music Company. Rights administered by MCA Music Publishing. A division of
MCA Inc., New York, NY 10019. Copyright renewed. Used by permission.
All rights reserved.
"Trying to Talk with a Man," by Adrienne Rich from *The Fact of a Doorframe: Poems Selected
and New, 1950–1984.* Used by permission of W. W. Norton & Company, Inc.
Excerpt from article in *New York Woman* by Marcelle Clements, copyright © 1987.
Used by permission of the author.
"Bath," by Kimiko Hahn. Used by permission of the author.
"You left me—Sire—two Legacies" by Emily Dickinson from *The Complete Poems of Emily
Dickinson,* edited by Thomas H. Johnson, copyright © 1988. Used by permission of
Little Brown and Company, Inc.
Reprinted with permission of Macmillan Publishing Company from *for colored girls
who have considered suicide/when the rainbow is enuf* by Ntozake Shange.
Copyright © 1975, 1976, 1977 by Ntozake Shange.
"Looking at My Father," by Sharon Olds, from *The Gold Cell,* copyright © 1988 by Sharon
Olds. Used by permission of Alfred A. Knopf, Inc./Random House, Inc.

Book design by Tasha Hall

Library of Congress Cataloging-in-Publication Data

Levine, Judith.
My enemy, my love: women, men and the dilemmas of gender
Judith Levine.—1st Anchor Books ed.
p.   cm.
Includes bibliographical references and index.
1. Women—Psychology.   2. Misandry.   3. Stereotype (Psychology)
4. Interpersonal relations.   I. Title.
HQ1206.L455   1993
305.3—dc20   92-32703
CIP

ISBN 0-385-41080-8
Copyright © 1992, 1993 by Judith Levine
All Rights Reserved
Printed in the United States of America
First Anchor Books Edition: March 1993

1   3   5   7   9   10   8   6   4   2

TO DEBORAH TANZER

Acknowledgments

WRITING THIS BOOK HAS ENLISTED the practical help and emotional support of so many people that I'm as daunted as I am delighted by the occasion to thank them.

I am most indebted to the eighty women whose thoughts and feelings form the backbone of *My Enemy, My Love,* but whose names I promised to hold in confidence. An interview of such intimate nature, conducted with a stranger, cannot help but stir anxiety on both sides. I often felt it was my subjects who put me at ease, and not the other way around.

I thank the many people who scoured their address books and coaxed friends, family, and coworkers to talk to a nosy New Yorker. Theresa Ghilarducci and William O'Rourke, Marcy Darnovsky and her housemates, Jesse and Carol Epstein, Jan Pickard and Ann Harvey, and Elizabeth Lide and Paul Kayhart also put fresh linens on their guest beds and set places at their tables for me. Their hospitality is much appreciated.

The Blue Mountain Center and the Cummington Community for the Arts offered me serene time in beautiful places. The Writers Room, under the firm but loving administration of Renata Rizzo, has rescued me and many a writer from the fate Jack Nicholson suffered in *The Shining,* undoubtedly making New York a safer place. Thanks, too, to the Barnard Center for Research on Women, the Women's Herstory Archives at Northwestern University, and the music department of the New York Public Library for the Performing Arts.

The personal in my life truly melds with the political and intellectual; I find it hard to distinguish between those who nurtured me and those who nurtured my work. Over the last seven years, I have received no less than a higher education in thinking from Ann Snitow and the members of the Sex, Gender, and Consumer Culture seminar at New York University's Institute for the Humanities. The erudite therapists in the seminar on Psychoanalysis and Sexual Difference helped me summon the chutzpah to advance my own theory about fathers and daughters, then helped me get it as right as I'm able to.

My group kept me honest; my comrades in the National Writers Union keep me brave; and my feminist coconspirators in No More Nice Girls keep me bad, in the best sense of the word.

Charlotte and Ted Levine taught me to question everything and struggle for what I believe in. I hope this book does them proud. Because of them, and the greater Levine-Zimmerman-Rappaport-Rosenthal clan, I have never felt alone in the world.

But I do live alone, without the Tom, Dick, or Sally so often acknowledged in pages like these who removes the coffee cups, corrects the footnotes, and generally acts as emollient to the irritations of book writing. I have, therefore, been dependent on the kindness of friends—in alphabetical, but not affectional, order, Pam Black, Larry Bush, Vanalyne Green, Susie Griss, Cindy Karasek, Myra Leysorek, Leonard Nakamura, and Jonathan Tasini.

Brett Harvey deserves special gratitude. She has been with *My Enemy, My Love* from the start, calming my considerable fears, discussing ideas, craft, and everything else, and reading the pages with care at every stage. Particular thanks, Brett, for putting me up and putting up with me and my competitive cooking in Craryville. Marcy Darnovsky and Paula Diperna also took time from their very busy schedules to give the final manuscript their astute and generous attention. Stuart Math extended technical assistance with competence and graciousness, as he does most everything.

Diane Cleaver's contributions to the survival of both *My Enemy, My Love* and its author give new meaning to the sentence "Don't worry, I'll take care of it." More guardian angel than agent, Diane fed me innumerable Japanese meals, took every panicked phone call, and shepherded this perennial orphan through a record number of editors until it finally found a home with the enthusiastic and very capable Sallye Leventhal and her excellent assistant, Arabella Meyer. Also in the Beyond-the-Call-of-Duty Department: Susan Moldow, who, with one foot out Doubleday's door, nonetheless applied her trenchant intelligence to a thorough reading of the manuscript.

Abundant thanks to all, but to none even a morsel of blame.

JNL

Contents

Foreword

ONE OF THE CURIOUS, sometimes unnerving, experiences in writing a book is the discovery of what the book is about—after it's been published. You talk about it and people talk to you about it. Critics get it wrong or they get it right, and you gripe or rejoice—but in the end you have to accept that the ways people read a book are half of what it is: what *you* mean and what *it* means are variations of the same hue, but they are variations. An author is lucky if the shades others find in her work enrich the original picture rather than clash with it.

Because *My Enemy, My Love* is about many things, it offers many surfaces to color. But the hardback subtitle, "Man-hating and Ambivalence in Women's Lives," laid out the primary themes, and the palate. "Man-hating" was bright and garish, challenging; "Ambivalence" would, as it does in life, shadow man-hating and bring it subtlety, complicate it, second-guess it.

Some readers responded as I would have wished. They took the challenge of man-hating, then were pleased to find how multifaceted and multifarious that apparently solid lump of a feeling is. Others, rather than being intrigued, found the very word *man-hating* too extreme—threatening, repulsive, embarrassing, indeed opaque. A question one might have asked about the book became, too frequently, *the* question, and it was often posed belligerently: "What do you mean, hatred?" "Do all women really hate men?" "Are you saying *I* hate men?" "My wife? You mean my wife?" I found myself having to climb over the word, again and again. For these readers, or potential readers, my brash colors had painted the door shut.

There were readers who were blinded by the word, I think, and read the book with blood in their eyes. I received a skewering review and a terrifying hate letter from men in this crowd, which I only hope is small. And those who told me they had overcome their aversion, and read on, concluded that the subtitle had misled them. They said the book is really about ambivalence, as well as feminism, power, relationships, families, and popular culture. Hating is a relatively small part of it.

Who's right? Who knows. What I do know is that these reactions confirmed my contention that man-hating—women's categorical, undifferentiated hostility toward men—is terrifying even to think about. But my aim is to get people, women and men, to think about it, talk about it, and maybe figure out ways to overcome it. A title should invite readers to share in the author's project, and some readers obviously did not feel welcome.

I do not intend to disown *man-hating*, although that is every woman's desire, including mine. In fact, how and why these feelings are repressed and suppressed is largely what *My Enemy, My Love* is about. Still, I have changed the subtitle to "Women, Men, and the Dilemmas of Gender." I want not only to be more inclusive of those rejected or rejecting readers, but also to take in a fuller range of the book's subjects.

As I traveled around discussing the finished book, what kept working its way to the foreground, and what held my own interest after umpteen interviews, was not hatred but gender—the social definitions of masculinity and femininity—and the quandaries women encounter as these definitions change. Women want change, and they also want to prevent change—and they invent stereotypes of men that militate for the former while surreptitiously helping to guarantee the latter. The word *dilemma*, suggested by a dear male friend, seemed perfectly to sum up not only the ambivalence women feel but the situations they are in.

Since I started this book in the mid-1980s, women's situation has changed dramatically. During those years, masculinity and femininity were quietly undergoing all sorts of metamorphoses, from gender-bending fashion to the acceptance of female firefighters to the robust new culture of fathering. But the deliberate effort to push for those changes—that is, a feminist movement—was pretty stagnant.

Fatigued by the combat of the 1970s, women seemed to be wishing that the battle of the sexes would just go away. They were ready to try cooperation, even renewed conciliation, with men, and in some cases, the ceasefire became a satisfactory peace. Perhaps for the first time in history, a large number of Americans accomplished egalitarianism in sexual relationships, families, and workplaces.

Mostly, though, male-dominated business went on as usual, and outside certain pockets of female progress, the feminization of poverty hurried forward, while rape, domestic violence, and sexual harassment showed no signs of abating; some believe they increased. By 1990, the Senate had two women in it, and the Constitutional foundation of women's right to make their own reproductive choices had been whittled to a splinter. Long before feminism's utility had been worn out, the media grafted a "post" to its front end, and there were few organized and constructive outlets for women's justified anger.

Meanwhile, women kept trying to smile and be nice. But an inchoate subterranean man-hating boiled, surfacing in women's magazines, film, art, pop psychology, and propaganda of all stripes.

Then, in the fall of 1991, shortly before the release of this book, an African-American female lawyer accused a Supreme Court nominee of sexual harassment, and he was confirmed anyway. While women were still smarting from that blow, two prominent men, William Kennedy Smith and Mike Tyson, were tried for date rape and the white defendant acquitted, and the year came to a close with the near death of *Roe v. Wade*.

Suddenly, the women's movement stretched and yawned, and laced up its sneakers and started running, full speed. Established feminist groups like NOW and the National Abortion Rights Action League started getting calls and checks—lots of them—and the Job Problems Hotline at 9to5, the National Association of Working Women, was overwhelmed with reports of sexual harassment. Susan Faludi's unapologetically feminist *Backlash* stood proudly on the bestseller list for months, along with the latest book of a pioneer and longtime soldier of feminism, Gloria Steinem.

New activism sprang up all over. The hip and fearless Women's Action Coalition took New York's breath away, growing from 100 to 1,500 members in a matter of months. Black women, stirred by the Thomas-Hill hearings to right sexism both outside and within their own communities, launched African-American Women in Defense of Ourselves with a full-page ad in the *New York Times* signed by over 1,600. Hundreds of young women climbed on buses to take a "freedom ride" across the country, registering pro-choice voters. Unprecedented numbers of women ran for office on every level of government, from school board to Senate, and Emily's List, the pro-choice Democratic fund-raising organization, called in more than $3 million to support their campaigns. At this writing, the odds are excellent that this year voters will seat the first African-American female Senator.

The Grand Old Party was strained by female revolt, as pro-choice women drilled their party to chop anti-choice from its platform and withheld support from those who wouldn't speak up for women's rights, while other formerly loyal female Republicans crossed party lines to vote for those they could trust. Even that most macho of macho institutions, the United States Navy, was so riven with revelations of sexual harassment that its chief, Secretary H. Lawrence Garrett III, was forced to resign.

From such a short distance it is hard to limn the role and gauge the influence of man-hating in this "new feminism." Surely, man-hating did not disappear. In fact, the slogan that arose from Hill-Thomas and launched a thousand women's campaigns—"They just don't get it"—is vintage man-hating, pure Us against Them. *They* don't get it, and, the slogan implies, they never will. Only women can be relied on to represent women.

While I fervently endorse women representing themselves, not only in Congress but in court, in advertising, or at the dinner table, a slogan like "They just don't get it" does not serve women's interests. Typical of man-hating generalizations, it represents men as almost constitutionally deficient, in this case politically learning-impaired. Instead of demanding that men understand women's disadvantaged position in the workplace (and stop exploiting it), or demanding that they notice there is dust in the corners (and vacuum it), or demanding that they know No means No (and respect it), it leaves men just where they are. "They just don't get it" not only writes men off, it *lets them off the hook*. If they can't, then they don't have to try to be different.

Where does that leave women? In the short run, man-hating can cement female solidarity and propel women into action. It did in the last wave of the women's movement, and it may do so in this one. In the long run, it can leave women feeling morally and emotionally superior, but still burdened with taking care of men, cleaning up after them, or fighting them off.

At the moment (I am writing during the 1992 electoral campaign season), women are feeling their power. Many men were surprised and shaken by the outpouring of female response to Anita Hill, and in this year during which gender issues have dominated the news, they have begun to listen, genuinely listen, to women. Male candidates are running scared of a potential retaliation from women voters and are scrambling over each other to promise to fight for child care, pay equity, remedies for sexual harassment, and women's right to choose.

The difference between this political season and previous ones, perhaps, is that this time women *expected* to be treated as fully powerful players from the start, instead of hoping for it, asking for it, or even demanding it. That posture has put women in an unprecedented position of influence, and at the same time, seems to have instilled great confidence in themselves and each other.

Women will do best expecting men to "get it," and if men don't, seeing to it that they do. This doesn't require loving all men blindly or tolerating them sentimentally, but it does preclude hating them indiscriminately. Women will achieve equality by expecting it—by expecting, while extending, respect.

JNL

Prologue: Man-hating

IN THE SPRING OF 1987, a friend gave me six photocopied, stapled-together pages from a group calling itself A Southern Women's Writing Collective: Women Against Sex (WAS). It was a manifesto, written in hermetic language and tortuous syntax, as if transcribed from a middle-of-the-night brawl between pixilated philosophy students. But its tone was ferocious, and the world it depicted was one of terror and rage, male conquest and female surrender.

In WAS's world, men's sexuality is mean and violent, and men so powerful that they can "reach *within* women to fuck/construct us from the inside out." Satan-like, men possess women, making their wicked fantasies and desires women's own. A woman who has sex with a man, therefore, does so against her will, *"even if she does not feel forced."*

There are no boundaries between affectionate sex and slavery in this world. Distinctions between pleasure and danger are academic; the dirty-laundry list of "sex acts" itemized in one paragraph includes rape, foot binding, fellatio, intercourse, autoeroticism, incest, anal intercourse, use and production of pornography, cunnilingus, sexual harassment, and murder.

There's no mutuality of interest between bedmates, either. Sex has but one purpose: male arousal. "The practice of sexuality . . . [is] animated by an eroticized dynamic of male domination and female submission . . . If it doesn't subordinate women," the collective concludes with tautological certitude, "it's not sex."

The Women Against Sex do not sign their names, but urge others to action. Become "sex resisters," a politicized form of celibate, they exhort, and "be part of the process of transition that will dismantle the practice of sexuality."

I read the manifesto over several times with fascination, not so much for its ideas, which alternately appalled and amused me, but for the feelings it evoked. I recited the litany of sex acts, the words *compulsory, humiliating, dependencies, murderous, disorientation,* and *violation* that crowded the text.

The piece was a feminist madeleine. Tasting it in the benign eighties, I was taken back to 1971, to the wild childhood of the women's movement and to an Oriental-carpeted boardroom on the second floor of the administration building at a college in western Massachusetts. Our small Women's Liberation group called this room the Men's Room, because it was hung all around with stern portraits of the Founding Fathers. But no name was further from apt. The room functioned as Command Central, where along with more conventional political activities, our Gang of About Twenty carried on a Lysistratan guerrilla war. At one time or another, we placed practically every man we knew—including our own boyfriends and husbands—on a sexual blacklist. If John Smith or Tom Greenburg had committed a crime of piggishness against women, he would lose his privileges. Until he reformed, his wife, girlfriend, or any member of Women's Liberation would refuse to have sex with him.

Needless to say, the deployment of this tactic turned out to be impossible. Our troops couldn't quite muster the discipline (I still have a *National Enquirer* headline of that vintage tacked to my bulletin board that reads: "WOMEN'S LIB HAS DESTROYED MY LIFE"), and anyway the struggle wouldn't be won with one stroke—or lack thereof. But we carried on methodically and almost gleefully. In the war between Us, the women, and Them, the men, our methods felt justified and necessary. If sex or relationships were bad, men were the culprits. This was a brilliant, if vastly oversimplified, discovery of the moment: it, whatever *it* was, wasn't women's fault. Men were the ones bollixing up the harmonious functioning of heterosexuality, so banishing them from our bedrooms—even our lives—could only be for the better.

Reading the WAS paper in my sunny little Brooklyn apartment, with nearly twenty years between me and the Men's Room, I found myself feeling more and more unsettled. At first I rejected the thing out of hand. I was distressed at the authors' self-punishing eschewal of sexual pleasure. I was convinced that their "line" represented the remotest edge of an already marginal politics, and certain that most women who read their manifesto would think it was nutty. I was repelled by their portrayal of the all-powerful Enemy, grotesque as an agitprop puppet.

But the crazy words of this missive began to mix with a voice of my own, a voice scratchy from disuse, holding back some long unacknowledged feelings. I realized that a part of me still looks at the world as I did back in 1971—as Us and Them. It feels as wounded by men as the WAS women do. It fears men and is threatened by their bodies. It suspects that heterosexuality is a golden trap, a pleasure compulsion somehow conditioned against women's better interests.

I feel what they feel: man-hating, that volatile admixture of pity, contempt, disgust, envy, alienation, fear, and rage at men. It is hatred not only for the anonymous man who makes sucking noises on the street, not only for the rapist or the judge who acquits him, but what the Greeks called *philo-aphilos,* "hate in love," for the men women share their lives with—husbands, lovers, friends, fathers, brothers, sons, coworkers.

What's different and shocking and impressive about WAS, what consigns them to fringe lunacy, is not that they *have* such feelings, or even that their feelings are so extreme. It's the loudness, the pride—the *certainty*—with which they express man-hating. These days especially, such words are not shouted from mountaintops, not painted in primary colors on billboards.

Man-hating is everywhere, but everywhere it is twisted and transformed, disguised, tranquilized, and qualified. It coexists, never peacefully, with the love, desire, respect, and need women also feel for men. Always man-hating is shadowed by its milder, more diplomatic and doubtful twin, ambivalence.

A project like this must involve a healthy measure of self-suspicion. On one hand, we all accept that men and women are locked in combat. It's a platitude, a truism, affirmed by James Thurber and Alice Kramden, Tracy and Hepburn, Thelma and Louise.

But hatred? Do women *hate* men? Wouldn't it be more reasonable to conclude that this is *my* problem, or at the very least the women's movement's?

I don't believe it is either. Or rather, it is both mine and the women's movement's—and also everyone else's. Man-hating is an emotional problem inasmuch as it creates pain and hostility between women and men. But it is not an individual neurosis, à la "Women Who Hate Men and the Men Who. . . ." Man-hating is a collective, cultural problem—or to refrain from diagnosing it at all, a cultural *phenomenon*—and men, as the object of man-hating, are part of it too.

Feminists have been accused of hating men all along, and in some sense rightly. What makes this chapter of feminism different from previous ones is its discovery that "the personal is political," which means figuring out how the big hand of Oppression feels when it comes sharply into contact with one's own person. To recognize oppression is to be infuriated, and to recognize it right here at home is to be infuriated *at someone,* someone you know—sometimes, in fact, to hate him.

Man-hating isn't a function of feminism; it's a function of the *reasons* for feminism. Feminists did not invent man-hating. Women of all politics and circumstances carried these feelings into the 1970s and have lugged them around ever since, at times conquering them, at times conquered by them, but always negotiating with them. If man-hating is mine, and WAS's, it belongs too to my next-door neighbor, my mother, and to the woman standing in front of me on line at the post office.

Feminists did not invent man-hating, but they gave it a name and a voice, and in that sense made it a problem to contend with. Once you know something, you cannot unknow it—you can't sign up for consciousness-razing groups, a friend noted—but neither does the new knowledge erase the feelings that preceded it. Now you can hate, but what do you do if you also love the hated person, need him emotionally or depend on him materially, if you feel compelled to placate him or fearful to disturb him? A powerful unspoken theme of post–World War II feminism—and women's lives since feminism—is the struggle with the enormously disquieting ambivalence accompanying the fury of recognized oppression.

• • •

Putting on a pair of admittedly mud-colored glasses, I began seeing man-hating all around me. I inquired, I eavesdropped. And with shrugs, with fervor, with wariness, with laughter, with anecdotes, women confirmed my thesis. Men are babies, I heard. Men are impossible, men are beasts, men are irrelevant.

"Women have the curse of knowing," Paula says over drinks. "We know men too well. So we know how inadequate they are."

"Their brains are between their legs," a woman on the subway says to her companion. The companion nods, goes back to her magazine. Pause. First woman: "Well, not all of them. Not always . . . Anyway, not Michael." Raised eyebrows from companion. First woman: "Okay, Michael too."

A thirty-nine-year-old environmentalist and former steelworker, waitress, hospital kitchen aide, and secretary says the men she's worked with—laborers, tradesmen, businessmen, or professionals—all share one trait:

> *Last week, I had to go to this meeting. I look around the table and I count fifteen men. A lot are older, beefy, and stupid, and I listen to these men discussing this issue and I can't help thinking, "How is it that men are so stupid and so proud of it?"*

Man-hating comes out in dismissive trickles, or in anguish. "It is a love more intense than any I have ever known," Carole tells me about her feeling for her teenage son. "But at times, I feel he is so alien, so strange, so *male,* that I can barely even like him. It's as if he could be my enemy—can that be?" Or it bursts forth in scattershot fury. Roslyn recalls a walk with another woman. They approach a site where men are drilling up the sidewalk with pneumatic drills, causing the two to take a short detour. Suddenly the friend, a softspoken married person, shouts, "MEN! It's men that do this to us!"

Still testing the ground, I started paying a new kind of attention to women's jokes, songs, films, novels, and advice books, to politics from feminist to conservative. Cards and letters came in the mail. A chain letter, on which my friend the sender had scrawled, "Manhating!!! PERFECT ambivalence!":

> *Just send a copy of this letter to five of your friends who are equally tired and discontented. Then bundle up your husband or boyfriend, send him to the woman whose name appears at*

*the top of the list, and add your name to the bottom of the list.
When your name comes to the top of the list, you will receive
16,877 men . . . and one of them is bound to be a hell of a lot
better than the one you already have.
DO NOT BREAK THE CHAIN!!!!!!
HAVE FAITH!!!!*

A birthday card: "Birthdays are a lot like men . . . The more
you encounter, the more you want to scream!"

Comediennes from Paula Poundstone to Reno seemed to be
ganging up on the guys. Performance artists Karen Finley and Holly
Hughes were standing onstage declaiming, "I HATE MEN!!"

I thought again of women's writings about men, of the disdain,
pity, and hatred there. Of Edith Wharton's seductive dodgers, Edna
O'Brien's alcoholic louts, the slight fools who disappoint Doris Les-
sing's women, the rapists and batterers in Alice Walker, the sexual
flops and users in Jackie Collins.

I perused women's magazines, edited, written, and read almost
exclusively by women. These took a common tack: present a com-
pendium of male flaws ("Seventy Telltale Signs that Men Are Still
Boys"), then reassure women that not all men are that bad. Should
the reader fail to find a good one, offer a few easy steps to reform the
one she has. In *Glamour* there is "Love Lessons Learned from
Creeps, Cads, and Snakes." In *Cosmopolitan,* "All Men Are Not
Gray in the Dark" humorously describes a handful of sexual losers—
The Stopwatch, Jack Be Nimble, etc.—and counsels patience and
good-natured help to make them winners.

Lurking behind these cheerful admonitions is the hostility at the
heart of the troubled heart of heterosexuality. Behind the take-
charge practicality is a bleak view of The Way Things Are, or rather
The Way Men Are: silly or overserious, unemotional or overly volatile, comically transparent or tragically inscrutable.

Interviewing women—single, happily and unhappily married,
straight and lesbian, black, white, and Latina, homemaker, steelworker, and lawyer—I heard man-hating too, from mild condescen-
sion to character assassination. Some women spoke without qualifiers. "I can't see how any contemporary woman who wasn't
absolutely brain dead could not be ambivalent about a close relationship with a man," said Anne Rivers Siddons, the novelist.

Michaelene Varda, a New York artist, seethed as she described the difference between her chaotic life—day job, artwork, child care, housework, social organizing—and her husband's far more relaxed and ordered one. "The whole thing can make me hate men and the whole man-made world," she said. "In the dark hours, it makes me hate him."

Women described their fathers, from just not there ("My father? You mean that guy in the suit who slept in my mother's room?"), to there but not there ("We kids got the impression that he was interested in our lives, but he couldn't talk directly to us," said a Chicago schoolteacher with chilly equanimity. "It was kind of the best he could do"), to too much, too intrusively there ("My father was a drunk, bigoted, mean son of a bitch. Some part of me loves him—I think").

Most often in my interviews, women were circumspect, fastidiously fair, fearful, it seemed to me, of naming negative feelings, resistant to going public, even anonymously, even in a room alone with me.

Anticipating this, I had stressed ambivalence rather than hatred when contacting potential subjects; if you're going to say something bad, I reassured, don't worry, you can say something good too. That wasn't a misrepresentation; I didn't intend to lay a benign-looking trap, catch unwilling victims, then force lurid confessions out of them. Ambivalence *is* what interested me most. But where I'd girded myself for repression, I hadn't bargained for the surprising and varied methods of repression I came up against.

One sixty-nine-year-old Californian who owns a photocopy shop with her husband was polite and straightforward in answering my queries. But she volunteered little without encouragement, as if she felt her comments couldn't possibly be of value to anyone, as if, in modestly disowning all authority ("This is just little me. Don't mind anything I say"), she could also disown any threatening emotion ("Nobody said that").

I asked her one of my standard questions: When the waitress in the coffee shop sighs and says, "Oh, men," and all the women know what she means, what does she mean?

She laughed and paused. "She's impatient, I guess."

"Impatient about what?"

Pause, then: "Their stupidity." Immediately she laughed again, and took it back: "Not really stupidity" (more laughter). "Their lack of awareness, um, about women."

Later, much later, in our conversation she said, "They never listen, men. They don't feel they have to. They're . . . I was going to say they're like little children . . . This guy that works here, he's thirty years old. He needs a pat on the back for everything he does. Everything! Look what I did, Mommy! All day long. It drives me crazy." Then, again, the softening: "He's a little dense, anyway. He works hard."

Feminists—most likely to be accused of man-hating—had different, though no less effective, methods of avoidance. As a group, they had spent so many years sorting out, like so many stones in a field, what they had learned from the culture, what feminism had taught them, what they expected of themselves, what they expected of men, what they believed was fair to expect, what was emotionally honest and what was politically correct, what was idiosyncratic and what generalizable, that these rational categories now lay in massive heaps all but burying any primitive, long-ago-immediate feelings.

"I don't hate men as such," said one feminist art critic. "They embody this terrible fix that we are in, which has such powerful social and political histories that have served a view of life that I won't subscribe to anymore."

View of life: it was a phrase she used a few times in our talk. I envisioned her on a hillside, surveying a city through binoculars. From up there, the ugly and the dangerous, even if discerned in detail, were safely distant. One could plan a strategy before descending.

Not that she or other feminists—or any other women, for that matter—do not struggle to descend, to tell the dark side of their feelings. In the interviews, these feelings revealed themselves in vivid sentences, knifelike phrases.

From the critic: "It can make you kill," ". . . how penetrating is this profound antagonism . . ."

From the copy-shop owner: "A psychologist asked me to respond to words immediately. He said, 'Men.' And I laughed. I just laughed."

Or, from a woman in my exercise class: "If I didn't work out this much, I'd be in a fury." About what? "Oh, you know. My husband, my son, the housework, my husband, the subway, money, my husband. Life." Laughing, she says, "I'm so physically exhausted by the end of the day, I don't have the energy to be anything but nice."

As for myself, having once proclaimed the existence of man-hating, I must have thought I was above denial. Yet as I proceeded, I began to find out just how deep ambivalence runs, and just how difficult is the acknowledgment of man-hating in one's own heart.

For a while, I managed not to mention my book to any casual acquaintance. But in New York, where "What do you do?" follows immediately upon "How do you do?" exposure was inevitable. So when people, especially men, asked me what I was writing about, I'd disclaim any personal association with the topic. "It's about, uh, man-hating," I would allow, then rush ahead with "It's not an endorsement, just an exploration." When asked *why* I was writing about man-hating, I'd insert another arm's length between it and me, answering with something like "The subject seems intellectually rich but commercially viable"—more sales pitch than self-revelation. The first statement, "not an endorsement," was true, but somewhat suspiciously quick and emphatic. And the second? I don't think I was trying to be evasive; rather, I didn't know why, and didn't feel I needed to find out.

At that time, Women Against Sex surely would have counted me among the enemy's collaborators. I was in a long-term relationship with a man. He was my friend; sex was nothing like the gruesome torture they described. We fought, yes, but our fights were usually finished fast and constructively. We biked in the country on weekends or spent Sundays at the aquarium with his son. We cooked dinners together; he was a good cook.

In the safety of loving and being loved, I could talk about man-hating all I wanted. Like a sure-footed circus performer dancing on the back of a tiger, I could control it. Man-hating couldn't hurt me.

Then my boyfriend and I split up, and with him disappeared my nimble confidence. Suddenly, I could no longer skitter around my own fear of man-hating—of thinking about it, talking about it, having anything personal to do with it. Did *My Enemy, My Love* cause the rift between my boyfriend and me? I wondered. (The answer is no, but the doubt nagged anyway.) Were the two pursuits —loving a man and dragging every living germ of man-hating back to my lab for testing—irreconcilable? (No again, but that would take far longer to understand.)

And what did going public mean, now that I was stripped of the social pedigree of Coupled Heterosexual? For one, I suspected I had lost my objectivity, or the appearance thereof. Single, I was no longer dispassionately *discussing* man-hating. I might easily be accused of *practicing* it. Given my situation, "I hate men" could turn, without my consent, from a mere expletive to a veritable political platform.

When *Esquire* ran its regular summer feature, "The Women We Love and the Women We Don't," I spent a long weekend poring over it. It was no comfort to find in the latter category Shere Hite, who had ventured to expose women's disappointment in their marriages, nor to notice that the editors had unearthed the only bad photo ever taken of her.

Shere's face was distorted, her hair wild, Medusa-like. But this being real life and not myth, she had not turned men who gazed on her to stone. Quite the contrary: they'd gotten her, humiliated her, turned her image stony—hard, unloving, unlovable, *hateful*. I imagined myself on the list of *non grata* a few years hence. A friend suggested that making *Esquire*'s Most Unwanted List might be considered an achievement, like getting on Nixon's enemies list, but it was a while before I could agree, or laugh.

These imagined retributions were not completely unrealistic, but my experiences talking to men about the book had shown me they were vastly overblown. Many men, in fact, were intrigued. They took for granted the "why" of my writing such a book: man-hating exists but it is hidden, and therefore it would be interesting and fruitful for women and men to expose it and analyze it. These men had friendly questions, anecdotes to contribute, and—most of them—a sense of humor about the whole thing. Why, then, was I waking up in the night with visions of sexual exile?

Here, I see now, was my own method of denial. By focusing on men's opinions of me and not on what I was discovering about women's opinions of men—some of which I shared—I could cast off the excruciating burden of ambivalence onto men. Just as women experience desire in the passive voice—instead of "I desire," they long to feel "I am desired"[1]—I was disowning the dangerous act of rejecting by anticipating my own rejection. Before speaking about

hatred out loud, I could imagine myself hated—and, mercifully, silenced.

Many psychologists, noting that both sexes have trouble with anger,
have observed that where men tend to be too ready to express anger,
women aren't ready enough. It's not that women don't fight—they
do—but in trying to circumvent negative expressions they often end
up "fighting dirty," using indirect and manipulative tactics like guilt-
tripping, or surrounding their attack with so many tears and self-
recriminations that it loses its credibility and force. Just as often,
women turn their hostility inward, where it becomes self-blame,
sadness, and loneliness.

"When I reviewed my clinical practice, I was impressed with
the observation of how frequently the phrases 'hurt feelings' and
'afraid to hurt their feelings' and even the word 'hurt' were used by
women and how rarely I heard these same phrases from men,"
writes psychoanalyst Martin Symonds. "This observation seemed
more striking when these phrases seemed to be used as equivalents of
anger, resentment, or even rage."[2]

Why do women pull their punches, especially when their
grievances are justified?

There are, to start, two enormous facts of female life. One is
women's economic dependency. Whether a battered wife who fears
murder or starvation if she leaves her husband or a low-paid academic whose mortgage payments, haircuts, and children's summer-
camp bills come out of her husband's corporate salary, a woman feels
men's financial power deeply. Sociologists Pepper Schwartz and
Philip Blumstein found that in heterosexual couples, a person's relative decision-making power rises with the amount of money he or
she contributes.[3] It makes sense that the person—almost always the
female person—who brings in less and has less earning potential is
more likely to fear speaking up, and to defer.

Then there is the fact of men's violence, a floating threat
wielded, if not carried out, by every man over every woman. The
woman who flies into anger is especially vulnerable to this threat, so
deep are the myths that women "bring on" the harm done them.
Batterers experience themselves as provoked by their mates; rapists
commonly believe a woman, just looking at them or walking down

the street, silently taunted them to attack. When a woman expresses unbridled rage, particularly physically, she feels as if she had broken the contract. No longer is the man required to check *his* rage at women, which women suspect is there, boiling not far from the surface.

Carol Tavris, in *Anger: The Misunderstood Emotion*, stresses social status rather than internal or unconscious inhibition as the deterrent to women's aggression. Women don't feel anger any less, she argues; they simply express it less because they're likely to pay more dearly for speaking up.

> Because women on the average occupy the lower rungs of the social and economic hierarchy, they find themselves more often than men in situations in which either sex might have an "anger problem." Most people have difficulty expressing anger to others of higher status, especially when those others have the power to administer raises, pink slips, tickets or contempt-of-court citations.[4]

Tavris believes that in the privacy of their homes women are just as likely as men to let their anger rip. But she doesn't consider the question of what women must first achieve before winning the "right" to this expression, and what effect that expression has. If a woman feels she must consolidate her status in relation to a mate or certify his emotional dependency on her before voicing dissatisfaction, she is likely to become more reluctant as time goes by to "break the spell" of sweetness and accommodation. The stereotype of the woman who metamorphoses into a harridan the day the couple returns from the honeymoon is not entirely invented. When and if the change takes place, both partners may find the eruption of her anger even scarier for its novelty.

Men's resistance to women's demands in the family is strong, especially now, when male backlash is socially permissible and even chic. For every New Man there are plenty of the Old variety. These are the men longing for a *Good Housekeeping* "New Traditionalist," who, according to the ad copy, was "searching for something to believe in" and found "her husband, her children, her home, herself." They are the men who patronize a lively trade in mail-order brides imported from Asia for their docility and subservience; and, a less extreme example, those chuckling over *Esquire*'s "Owner's

Manual" for husbands, which described, as if this were innocent kitsch, the mysteries of a wife's underwear and the contents of her handbag.

Even when women are courageous in confronting their husbands and the husbands do change, men's acquiescence doesn't necessarily mean surrender, or peace. One study showed that couples with a high degree of egalitarianism in child care and housework also reported a great amount of conflict.[5]

Still, while financial inequality is the rule, total financial dependency is rare—in only 13 percent of American married-couple families do men bring in all the bacon.[6] And while emotional and physical battery is alarmingly widespread—according to the New York Coalition Against Domestic Violence, it is a regular occurrence in 20 to 30 percent of marriages—most men do not keep their wives or lovers in violently enforced subjugation. Yet women's status is still inferior, and the battle cry against this state of affairs seems progressively less audible, or is so coded and couched that it loses its ferocity almost before it comes out.

To suggest that women play a part in perpetuating their own oppression is not to deny the many ways men keep women involuntarily in their place. As interested parties from Hegel to the members of the Eulenspiegel Society have shown us, domination is not always an act perpetrated by one person or group upon another. It is an *interaction;* wherever the enslaved are not literally in chains they are in some way complicit—they get something from subordination. After all, as Michel Foucault said, if power "never did anything but to say no, do you really think one would be brought to obey it?"[7]

It may be argued that lots of women simply aren't angry about what their defenders (usually other women) think they should be angry about. For one thing, the benefits of dependent, second-class citizenship often outshine the cloudy and seemingly unattainable promises of freedom. This troublesome fact has not escaped even the most fervent liberationists. The late-eighteenth-century feminist Mary Wollstonecraft contended that women were degraded and spiritually and intellectually stunted by having to please men in order to attain any station in life. Yet she saw women clutching tight to the constraints men had created for them. Women, she wrote, "have chosen rather to be short-lived queens than labour to obtain the sober pleasures that arise from equality."[8]

The dangers of independence may speak louder than the comforts of dependence as motivation for women to keep their mouths shut. But neither these, nor the fear of male retribution, can explain why women stay in highly compromised situations with men if they have the means to get out. Neither can explain the deep, deep reluctance of women to be aggressive.

Some psychologists have advanced the theory that what women fear in their own anger is an incalculable destruction—of self, of the other, of everything. This terror, largely unconscious and shared by men and women, may be even greater than the fear of men's violence. That we should fear women, who bear, nurture, and protect the species, rather than men, who are largely responsible for violent crime and war, is too huge and profound a part of human culture to be trivialized with the word *irony*. It is, as Dorothy Dinnerstein postulated in her influential book, *The Mermaid and the Minotaur*, a central organizing fact of gender, of domination and submission, of, it might be said, the human condition. "The deepest root of our acquiescence to the maiming and mutual imprisonment of men and women," writes Dinnerstein,

> lies in a monolithic fact of human childhood: under the arrangements that now prevail, a woman is the parental person who is every infant's first love, first witness, and first boss . . . The initial experience of dependence on a largely uncontrollable outside source of good is focused on a woman, and so is the earliest experience of vulnerability to disappointment and pain.[9]

Mother is the very means of survival, her body is the source of sustenance, comfort, sensual pleasure; she also requires the first submission, she metes out the first rejection, inflicts the first punishment.

Men have dealt with the fear of this great power in one way, says Dinnerstein: to make a very long story short, they have built the entire patriarchy, which both mythologizes the mystery of female power and guards against it. "Man's dominion over what we think of as the world rests on a terror that we all feel: the terror of sinking back wholly into the helplessness of infancy."[10] When the forces of darkness, of death, of destructive sexuality, of Otherness, are constructed as female—from Lilith to the Glenn Close character in *Fatal*

Attraction—then misogyny and male violence against women are defensive, justified.

Our families, which shape us as men or women in our culture, perpetuate both this sexual enmity and the male prerogative of domination. Boys, becoming men, separate from their first love, Mother, and identify with Father. To do this, they must repudiate all that is "feminine" in themselves, including the dependency that they cannot really escape. These qualities they learn to revile and fear, abetting the practices of women-hating and the enforcement of a sexual hierarchy.

And how do women deal with this terror of the person who they themselves become, or are already—the mother, the adult female? They incorporate it and disown it at once. Women feel this power within themselves and learn that if they were to unleash it, the sky would fall—nothing less. To avoid this seemingly inevitable pain to themselves and others, women act "feminine."

"The definition of 'normal' female is kept in force by continuous warnings about the danger of becoming one of the frightening and despicable stereotypes which depict women as ferocious, envious, vengeful, or 'castrating,' " writes psychologist Teresa Bernardez-Bonesatti.[11]

The fear is not one-dimensional, however, and the repression not complete. And so women make these stereotypes real. Writes psychologist Harriet Lerner:

> *The envious, castrating, "man-hater" venting her rage and resentment against men[;] the passive-aggressive housewife who bitterly dominates and controls her husband from behind the scenes[;] the infantile, irrational, "hot-tempered" female who hurls pots and pans from across the kitchen and carries on like a hysterical bitch. These familiar images are more than just cruel, sexist stereotypes. They are neurotic positions that real women adopt when intrapsychic and cultural pressures combine to inhibit the direct and appropriate expression of legitimate anger and protest.[12]*

Not surprisingly, there is one exception to the law against female aggression: mothers are not only justified in being, but are expected to be, fierce in protecting their young and avenging those who do their little ones harm. Our welfare system, for instance, encourages men to abandon their children while it routinely inflicts poverty and humiliation on mothers and children—making maternal heroism almost a prerequisite for receiving "benefits." By the same token, when a woman fails to be a lioness in defense of her child, we are horrified. Only under extraordinary circumstances do we even question this assumption, as in the case of Hedda Nussbaum, whose abusive lover had so thoroughly broken her that she may have been incapable of saving their child from his killing blows. Not even systematized torture, as in Nussbaum's case, exonerates a woman, however.

Because female nurturing extends to adult men, saying a negative thing against a man is a perversion of this "good" aggression, and thus devastating to the woman's "victim." At the same time, because women are dependent on men, expressing anger poses a major risk: overstepping the boundaries of her prescribed roles, she fears male punishment—loss of love, abandonment. The challenge and threat of women's anger goes so deep that it not only disrupts the balance of sexual power, it upsets the very equilibrium of the gendered self as she knows it.

"Women are reared to be connected, to seek affiliation with others, to provide nurturance and support," writes Bernardez-Bonesatti.

> Much of women's sense of usefulness and self-value is attached to this [function, whose loss] is threatened when anger or protest is expressed . . . In anger, the person establishes automatic aloneness and makes herself temporarily separate from the object of the anger. This loss of connection, happening when negative feelings are openly expressed, is so feared by many women that frequently the expression of anger is accompanied by tears, expressions of guilt and sorrow and a cluster of responses that contaminate the . . . anger or nullify it altogether. In this complex response the woman appears to be expressing her anger, her conflict and fear about it, her sorrow at the loss of a relationship, the sadness at her own self-betrayal and her impotence in making herself clear, all at the same time.[13]

To express man-hating, which itself comprises anger along with other emotions, is an angry act. And just as anger often disguises itself, so does hatred of men. And as guilt, sorrow, and fear cannot quite suffocate anger, the pulse of man-hating, though denied, keeps pounding in the temples. Internally, prohibitive emotions mix with prohibited emotions to yield nothing more comforting than ambivalence. But externally, dissembling is often effective. In my researches I was struck by how self-evident the idea of man-hating was to women—"Wow, of course," "Yes" were the usual responses—whereas men were frequently surprised to be informed about it. One male editor who read my proposal said he felt he was being let in on a secret.

Still, women's talent at placating and prettying up is only part of the reason man-hating is so palpable and at the same time so indiscernible. Feminine self-censorship plays its role, but it is masculine censorship of the most fundamental nature that eradicates an entire spectrum of female experience from apprehension and comprehension. Man-hating has no tongue.

Women speak as foreigners in men's language, as interlopers in men's forums. "We loiter outside of trade and speech," writes the word-and-image artist Barbara Kruger, "and we are obliged to steal language." In that language, man-hating cannot even recognize itself, the psychoanalyst Jacques Lacan might say: in the male world of definitions and laws, where to be named is to exist, man-hating does not even officially exist. Except for the lately coined, little-used *misandry,* there is no word for it.

In fact, flouting the First Commandment of Writing—Thou shalt not start a composition with a dictionary definition—I set off on the first day of my research to the Main Reading Room of the New York Public Library to find the word *misandry* in the dictionary. As far as most lexicographers are concerned, there is no such word. *Misandry* is not in any of the Random House dictionaries, not in the American Heritage Dictionary of the English Language, Collin Cobuild, or the Chambers Twentieth Century Dictionary. Webster's Ninth New Collegiate and Webster's New World Dictionary do not see fit to include it. When I finally found it, in Webster's New International, I realized that even where the word is acknowledged, what it means is not. "Dislike or disesteem of man by woman" is Webster's International's mealy-mouthed offering. Compare that to the straightforward and unapologetic definition of the word's cited antonym, *misogyny:* "hatred of women." Only Funk and Wagnalls New Standard Dictionary of the English Language and the newest edition of the Oxford English Dictionary call misandry "hatred" of men or males, respectively.

Withal, man-hating remains not an action but a reaction, not a power but a subversion of power. In a patriarchal world, woman-hating is built into every institution. Patrilineal families expunge women's names and rights, religions define women as sin, laws make female victims criminals, and workplaces consign women to low-status jobs and low-end wages. If misogyny is the Establishment, man-hating is no more than a counterculture. If Woman is the Other, her hatred must also be other, outside. When it emerges, it is called everything but what it is. It is a petulance, a means of seduction: "You're so cute when you're angry." It is spiritual possession: witchcraft. It's a sexual aberration: lesbianism. It's penis envy, maladjustment, frigidity.

Practically languageless, gagged by self-censorship, how does man-hating express itself? An illegal alien ever in exile, where does it live, how does it dress and behave? Part I of My Enemy, My Love, "Images of the Enemy," explores these questions within a taxonomy of man-hating, a collection of women's negative and ambivalent stereotypes of men. My aim is not to judge the accuracy of any of these types, not to ratify any representation as "truth"—for, being stereotypes, none is altogether accurate or truthful—but rather to examine what they look like, what they mean, and how they function.

Some of these portrayals are almost protective of men, others no less than mutilating. Often, as I've suggested, the uglier aspects of hatred are cosmetically improved. Pity takes on the veneer of compassion, ridicule dons the finery of affectionate amusement, and sexual rage is neutralized into romantic sparring or polite indifference. Together, the stereotypes are a babble of competing, often opposite, female claims as to what men are like. Their very anarchy is evidence of women's ambivalence.

Demonstrating that man-hating exists, even describing how it works, does not entirely explain why it exists and wherein it originates. Part II looks for the seeds of man-hating and ambivalence in the nuclear family. Where psychological theory has recently focused on the child's relationship with the mother (and for a long time, psychologists have tended to blame the mother for everything), I propose that men—fathers—and the patriarchal structure of the family may be largely held to account for women's anti-male feelings. In the Western family, Father is absent, and as inaccessible as he is to his sons, he is that much farther from his daughters. Yet each family idolizes Papa as the patriarchy idealizes men in general; meanwhile, each mother subtly undermines that idealization. This section's first chapter, "Daughters and Fathers," explores how these and other processes work within the family's larger project of gendering its children to produce daughters who continue to long for perfection, and also expect deficiency, in men.

If man-hating germinates within the daughter-father relationship, eventually it pushes out of the hothouse of the family, and the period of the 1960s and 1970s was a time it did so with remarkable vehemence and consequence. Part II, Chapter 5: "Sisterhood and the Patriarch," examines how political and social forces cross-fertilized with personal, familial feelings and spread, as modern feminism, across the landscape of American womanhood. How did man-hating invigorate the early years of the movement, how did it impede progress? How did the daughters create a feminist sisterhood self-confident enough to dare to topple the father, the patriarch?

And how, now that the sisterhood is fractured and far-flung, do women live with the undeniable consciousness of man-hating? Part III travels from the sizzling sixties and seventies into the present to answer that question. Today feminism is not gone, but it is changed. While a great many of even its most radical principles have been internalized into "mainstream" thought, it has also encountered backlash and undergone revision since those early years. Moreover, the generation of women who lived through its birth have grown up: they have husbands and ex-husbands, lovers, jobs, and children.

Part III, "Living with Ambivalence," is based on eighty interviews with women of varying ages, races, classes, sexual orientations, and marital and parental statuses.* It portrays thirteen of these women up close, dissecting their strategies for living with love and man-hating, cooperation and rebellion, intimacy and alienation, and

---

* Throughout the book, I have changed the name and some identifying details of anyone speaking about the personal details of her life. People talking in their public capacities as psychologists, writers, activists, etc. are identified by their actual names.

all those other ambivalent pairs (and triads, quadrangles, etc.) of feeling that relationships are made of.

While there are strategies here I'm partial to and others I wouldn't promote as a program, I don't submit that any is a be-all, end-all "solution" to man-hating. In this highly psychologized time, it is tempting to pose women's problems as purely individual, to construct man-hating as a "dysfunction," a symptom of Loving Too Much, fear of intimacy, codependency, or the fallout of a Foolish Choice. Prospecting for the sources of man-hating and ambivalence in the family threatens to reinforce such a tendency; if the problem started in a one-to-one relationship, presumably it could end there too.

Now, I am all for understanding, communication, and whatever form of therapy works, but if there is a solution to the problem of man-hating, it must be in a movement—a feminist movement—that recognizes power in its most concrete as well as its slipperiest unconscious forms. Even feminism's maxim, "the personal is political," can, as historian Alice Echols points out, "encourage a solipsistic preoccupation with self-transformation,"[14] with "lifestyle" rather than social change.

As I think this book will make clear, I don't lend greater weight to material, or structural, forces like economics or class than I do to the less apparent, less quantifiable phenomena of the unconscious—desire, sexuality, and infantile memory. I don't hew to any trickle-down or trickle-up theory of social interaction, don't think events on one "level" cause reactions on another. Power resides in family and sexual relations, from the giving and withholding of kisses or money to dishwashing or domestic violence. It resides too in the world of newspapers and advertising, of salaries and Star Wars. The family is both a psychological place and a social institution, a microcosm of a larger world, fundamental to and dependent on a vast and complex patriarchal structure. Neither can change without the other, and the hatred bred in sexual inequality and rigid gender definitions must be routed everywhere, from the hidden crannies of home to the forums of politics, economics, and war and peace in the world community.

Or rather, communit*ies*—and there lies the last of the tenets that shape my thinking. I began my work with an idea about Women, and about How Women Feel. I traveled around the country, assembling a small but demographically representative sample of interview subjects. In sifting through the troves of culture, I looked for the graffito as well as the national magazine, the folk song as well as the rap song, the voices of women not heard as well as those heard round the world.

As I proceeded, I became more and more aware of the perils of representing Women as a uniform category that feels or thinks or even suffers unanimously, and of the problems inherent in positing a universal American Family from which those feelings flow. I did discern patterns in what I saw and heard; these are essential to any cogent thesis, any narrative integrity. Yet at the same time I had to remind myself constantly that the more generalized or homogenized, the less nuanced, ambiguous, and untidy my patterns appeared, the more they came to resemble "mainstream"—by definition, inaccurate—pictures of the world.

Inaccurate because in order to exist, the so-called mainstream must erase differences among people, whether those are the inherited differences of race and class, the baggage of upbringing and temperament, or the affiliations of ideology or sexual orientation. Even in dividing the world between the "majority" and the "minority," I would collaborate in creating an Other whose case was "unusual" enough to be consigned to a margin, tabled for later consideration, or forgotten.

I am certainly guilty of some of this exclusion, for just as every author inevitably depends on what others have considered before her (including all the prejudices invisibly written there) she must also table a great deal for later consideration. *My Enemy, My Love* aims to be neither encyclopedic nor definitive, both suspect notions to begin with. In a long and ongoing conversation, this book is one sentence, which ends not with a period but a question mark.

PART I

Images of the Enemy

Naming the Enemy

THE TASK OF MISOGYNY, and of stereotyping women, is maintenance. Men both magnify woman's threat and devalue her to justify keeping her under the boot. Women have a tougher lot: they want to lift the boot from their necks, or, failing that, make sense of the fact that they can't. They may need or want to sweeten the unacceptable notion that the boot feels good there; at least it's warm and secure. It is to these ends that women's stereotypes of men work.

Gender stereotypes enforce a cultural status quo. They originate from, and live for, the culture's assignment of certain exclusive traits to each biological sex. Rather than constructing masculinity and femininity as phenomena that are continually thrashing against, readjusting to, and recuperating from the fluxes of history (as I believe they are), stereotypes are *essentialist*. They are born out of the assumption that the ability to diaper or to drive a nail, the drive to nurture or the willingness to kill, come in the same package as testosterone and estrogen, penises and vaginas—that the collections of traits we call masculinity and femininity are twisted into the DNA, static, immutable.

Stereotypes act as a shim, holding a space between the genders by reifying sexual difference, but that shim is squeezed into unexpected new shapes as the two sides of the gender divide crush and grate upon each other. Today, boundaries between the two spheres of influence—men's in the outside world and women's at home with children—are crumbling. But while men are striding onto women's turf (most vigorously in the heralded areas of emoting and fathering, least vigorously in the degraded area of household drudgery) women are having a far harder go at penetrating men's. Feminism, one may ruefully note, has been good to men.

The emergence of modern negative and ambivalent male stereotypes and the persistence of anachronistic ones reveal women's anxieties about these shifting frontiers, as well as their frustrations when the borders are closed tight.

Among the Infants, for instance, the Bumbler, or domestic incompetent, has for centuries been a figure of fun, a benign symbol of women's dominance in the household. Yet as the Happy Homemaker loses prestige and the Unhappy Homemaker goes crazy trying to cajole her husband into sharing the shitwork, the Bumbler's charm wears thin, and he skulks into the gallery of hateful types. The Infants represent a sense of female superiority and necessity: men, the poor dears, are so babyish (Mama's Boy and the Babbler), inept (the Bumbler), or emotionally or physically vulnerable (the Invalid) that they couldn't live without women. Belittling men, women at least symbolically redress an imbalance of power and hold off displacement from their only realms of certain authority: the home and the heart.

With the tricky new partnerings in the dances of courtship, sex, marriage, and divorce, a new gang of male stereotypes stride forward: the Betrayers. In our cultural and emotional heritage, seduction and abandonment are vices consonant with the primary law of gendered sexuality—man is active, woman passive; men do, women are done to. Yet recently women have begun to challenge the exclusivity of male sexual prerogative and question men's presumed strength and domination in the contests of romance and the battlefields of marriage and divorce. At the same time, other women are reinstating themselves as the Betrayers' victims, reequating sexual and familial irresponsibility with maleness, and fidelity and commitment with femaleness.

In the new sexual landscape, the classic male Betrayers are harder to locate. The cool Seducer just can't lose his embarrassing sidekick, the Slave, who is reduced to slavering obsequiousness by the littlest hint of female attention. The Abandoner, closely resembling his eighteenth- and nineteenth-century forebears, is making a comeback, but the deserting father has a wicked new trick. Rather than disappear forever over the horizon, he remains menacingly present: the Abductor is a kidnapper with an illicitly procured writ of custody that guarantees his paternal rights but blacks out his spotty record at fulfilling parental obligations. He is an embodiment of women's anger and hurt at being forced to relinquish one of the few privileges that accompany the burdens of motherhood—uncontested custody—with no commensurate prize forthcoming.

Images of the Beast confront the male body, its attractions and its threats. While the Prick and the Pet indicate a raised eyebrow (and a raised skirt) toward "animality," the Brute and the Killer embody women's detestation and terror of male violence. As they reinforce female solidarity and mobilize militancy, representations of an implacable and ruthlessly violent male sexuality also alleviate women's guilt for conciliation in their own subjugation. If, as Susan Brownmiller suggests, men are all potential rapists, or, as Andrea Dworkin proposes, in every act of heterosexual lovemaking a man tears a woman's integrity to shreds, then men are both so loathsome and so strong that any female response, from pusillanimous abjection to a campaign of mass castration, is justifiable.

Stereotypes defend the borders of gender, but they can't effect separation between the sexes. Masculinity and femininity may stand on either side of a mile-high wall, yet women and men share beds and homes, histories and children. So while racial or ethnic stereotypes are fueled by segregation and prohibit familiarity (the picture of the Jew with horns and a tail is concocted by someone who has never known a Jew well, much less well enough to inspect the part where a tail might be attached), sexual stereotypes are formed in intimacy. This is what makes them unique, and uniquely troubling. "The attempt of the sexes, in the intervals between copulation, to study each other is human, and accounts in turn for the singular capacity of human beings to experience attraction and animosity simultaneously," comments the literary critic Mary Ellmann. "The profound trial of having always not only to deal with, but to think about, those who are different from themselves, combining with the elusive nature of this difference, produces a large body of opinions which, if it is no more precise, is certainly more irritable than other bodies of opinion."[1]

Intimacy itself is difficult, and the very irritability of our opinions of the other sex—our negative stereotypes—may in fact be the tool with which we handle it. We want to be known, but we don't want to relinquish all privacy to a Big Brother, no matter how well meaning. Survival in intimacy involves separation and distancing—milestones in children's growing up are marked by new secrets kept from their parents—as much as merging and sharing.

If to love is to know—that is, to discern uniqueness—then to hate is to attempt to homogenize, deracinate, and obliterate, to willfully not know. "Truthfulness anywhere means a heightened complexity," writes Adrienne Rich.[2] But to stereotype is to move in the opposite direction, toward simplification, and then oversimplification. A stereotype dismantles a complex subject and reassembles it "as a discontinuous series of gestures and poses," says the art critic Craig Owens.[3] It blinds us so that we may perceive the elephant only in parts—that is, misperceive it.

This not-knowing experienced as glib knowing is a way for women to maintain boundaries. If men are all Standard Issue they are that much easier to comprehend, to "have," as one "has" a language. An early feminist newspaper ran a sort of geological survey of the "Four Types of Men": stone, chrome, silver, and clay: "The following represents a condensed picture of four types of men we have had to deal with and have loved," wrote the group of authors. "We have already found it to be a useful tool in discussing what we hope men are and what they turn out to be in fact. So we thought other women might like to try and use it as a systematic shorthand for the same purpose."[4] At the same time, such shorthand, by implying the sameness of vast quantities of men, makes each one opaque, indistinguishable, only superficially knowable.

The allure of heterosexuality is difference, and the frisson of difference is mystery. It is one of the irreducibly sad ironies of marriage that the same familiarity which fosters trust also engenders boredom: as many a married person complains, sex and romance suffer. If familiarity can breed a measure of contempt, the assumption of an irreducible measure of strangeness can have the opposite effect. Strangeness promises surprise, or at least supplies a distance that requires bridging.

Negative stereotypes can thus play two roles in alleviating the suffocation of heterosexual intimacy: by asserting difference they provide the distance that protects each partner's separateness. And they can pry two people apart in a way that makes them want to work to get back together again—to meet each other again, to relearn the other's uniqueness as well as their commonality. In this paradoxical way stereotypes aid intimacy—but intimacy in turn makes negative stereotyping that much harder to ratify. As the servants of love, the stereotypes are fickle employees. At hatred's behest, they are a ready army.

1

The Infant

I once asked a man what sorts of things he wanted a woman to ask him to make him feel loved. To my surprise, the first thing he said was, "Are you hungry?"

Toni Grant, Being a Woman[1]

[The] infantile needs of adult men for women have been sentimentalized and romanticized long enough as "love"; it is time to recognize them as arrested development, and to reexamine the ideal of preservation of "the family" within which those needs are allowed free rein . . .

Adrienne Rich, "Husband-Right and Father-Right"[2]

Mama's Boy

LIKE THE WEARY MOMS OF TERRIBLE TWOS, women trade stories of manipulating and being manipulated by, doing for and being done in by their big male bundles of needs, demands, and expectations. Yet women are exasperatingly eager to take the rap for these bad boys: if men are babies, guess whose fault it is?

"Men are babies," said Rosalie Angel, thirty-four, a secretary in a large New York corporation and the divorced mother of two.

"They're dogs," corrected her coworker, Michelle Washington, twenty-five, single and childless, and very much in the market for a man.

"Baby dogs?" I suggested. "Puppies?"

"Too cute," answered Michelle. "Too good."

"Right, but admit it," said Rosalie resignedly. "They're cute, immature, impossible dogs—and we baby them."

Why do "we" baby them? Woman after woman told me, as if reporting an incontestable and inevitable fact, that they have little choice. Mothers spoil their sons, guaranteeing that these boys will never truly grow up—and the next generation of women simply has to make do.

One story in Gloria Naylor's *The Women of Brewster Place* is almost a cautionary tale for mothers tempted to baby their boys. Mattie Michael lives only for her son Basil, in return, she believes, for his unwavering fidelity. At five he is still sleeping in her bed; her rationale is that he's afraid of the dark. As he grows older, she makes more excuses for him:

> *Irresponsible, his counselors had said in school. High-natured, she had replied in her heart. Hadn't he said that they were always picking on him; everyone had been against him, except*

her. She had been the refuge when he ran from school to school, job to job. They wanted too much . . . She had demanded nothing all these years, never doubting that he would be there when needed.[1]

Predictably, Basil grows up to be a no-account sweet-talker. He can't even take time between girlfriends to mow the lawn for his aging mama. Then he is arrested on murder charges, and Mattie makes his bail by mortgaging the house she has sacrificed her life for —so that he could have "a yard to run in, a decent place to bring his friends." Basil takes her money and skips town, and she is left homeless.

Kaila Lacrosse, a twenty-five-year-old journalist in Cleveland, referred to Naylor's story when telling me about her aunt who supports her son's drug habit; she thinks the aunt is afraid of the man's rejection—or worse, his violence. Kaila's friend Tania Peters, at twenty-four a well-paid personnel manager of a small company, chimed in that it was her mother's fault her own two brothers are "a waste of time"—one on the street, the other almost thirty and still comfortably at home. "Black mothers raise their daughters and love their sons," she concluded.

That statement, other sources indicate, can hardly be confined to black mothers.

"You just simply expect at all times in your life that you have things coming to you, that someone has made a deal on your behalf —and that person is usually your mother," a self-confessed Jewish American Prince told the writer Marcelle Clements.

"Every bruise is kissed, every cry is heard. Every doubt's cast out with a soothing word," sing the French-Canadian McGarrigle Sisters about the First-Born Son. The same might be said for the second, third, and all the sons born thereafter. "I can see that I am making the same mistake with my son," said Michaelene Varda, a forty-year-old artist, after describing the way her mother-in-law accustomed her husband to seamless caretaking.

[My son] never in his life has taken the wash out of the hamper, sorted it and put it in the washing machine, then sorted it and folded it and put it back in his drawer. So now he opens his drawer and there they are in a pile. I don't think I would treat a

daughter that way, even though I like to think I'm beyond those distinctions.

Michaelene's analysis of why women coddle their sons goes beyond the usual one that they're irreversibly habituated into servitude by their mothers. This may be true, she says, but the underlying cause is a vicarious grasp at power.

There's a deep reason why mothers spoil their sons: a secret desire that my child would end up like a little king—because women themselves don't have that access. I'm fascinated by men who get away with that. When I see men who say "Hop to!" and get people to behave that way, I don't like it, but on some level I'm in awe of it; it's so opposite of the way I behave in the world.

It's almost like fathers want to teach them how to repair things. You wish to pass on these basic survival skills to your children . . . You can be giving your child a deadly pill that will explode in his face and leave him in a terrible place, where he neither has the social skills to effect that nor the survival skills to take care of himself.

[But] maybe women secretly understand that for boys it's an important skill to be arrogant, demanding, and have high expectations of the way people will behave toward them. Women want their sons to be powerful, and believe they're giving them a powerful arrogance.

Not all women believe male infantilism is rooted in childhood nor see it as a condition handed down to sons like a recessive gene through generations of mothers and daughters. A school of cultural conservatives, harking back to a historically unspecified Golden Age of the Family, contend that when women were women, men were also men—grown-up men. It's feminism's fault, according to these critics, that men are throwing tantrums; even if they *want* to be mature, the New Woman won't let them. Here is Dee Jepsen, an antiabortion activist and a liaison to women's organizations during the Reagan administration:

Now if the husband is stripped of any meaningful position in the family, and if the wife is also working, partially filling the provider's role, where does it leave that man? What is left but

for him to flounder, like a little lost boy, or to rebel in some way
—not sure just who he is, or what his purpose is?[2]

Conservative and Christian marital advisers counsel women to
restore their men's mature masculinity by submitting to his biblically
ordained "headship" without protest or resentment. A wife must
never criticize or even advise her husband. Instead, she must love
and admire him, warts and all. *She,* not he, should act the child.

Ironically, however, these counselors exhort women to cosset
men as if they were babies—because, they imply, they *are* babies.
The Boy-Man must not be crossed, not only because the Bible tells
women to obey, but because he's too fragile to hear a discouraging,
even a challengingly constructive, word without feeling cut down.
"Save your lectures," instructs Marabel Morgan, the bestselling Total Woman. "He needs your ear, not your mouth. One man hid
behind his newspaper for 13 years to avoid a face-to-face encounter
with his wife. He was afraid she'd tell him what to do."[3]

Always build him up, even if you suspect he's a bit lowly, says
Darien Cooper in *You Can Be the Wife of a Happy Husband.* Despite
the book's woman-deprecating title, its descriptions of men hint at
even worse deprecations. This passage on uncritical acceptance bears
an uncanny resemblance to Mattie Michael covering for her disso-
lute son:

> *It might be comforting to realize that [his] negative traits are*
> *distorted positive traits. If negative traits can be modified or*
> *channeled in the right direction, they can become strengths.*
> *Stubbornness can become perseverance. Cowardice can be*
> *turned to gentleness. Tactlessness can be turned to frankness.*
> *If you trust Jesus Christ to take care of your husband's prob-*
> *lems, and fix your mind on his assets, you can help him turn*
> *bad traits into good ones.[4]*

Cooper's exercises in wifely acceptance and attentive listening
sound like a course in child rearing; their rewards might just as well
be promised by a handbook for the parents of troubled teenagers.

> *Even if [he] is talking about something you don't understand or*
> *feel interested in, give him your undivided attention. You'll*
> *learn a lot about him. You will begin to detect how he feels*
> *about people and situations. You will even discover noble, ma-*

*ture dimensions in his character that you never knew were
there.*[5]

For many women, treating a man like a boy in order to bring
out the man in him is just too roundabout, and dubious, a tactic.
Stuck somewhere between resignation that men's development is
permanently arrested and a sort of cautious optimism, these women
attack the problem head on. "A good man don't just happen,"
Roseanne Barr lectures her coworkers in the lunchroom. "They're
made by us women. A guy is a lump, like this doughnut. First
[*dusting off the sugar*], you gotta get rid of all the stuff his mom did to
him. Then there's the macho stuff he learns from the beer commer-
cials [*takes one bite*]. Then there's my favorite, the male ego." In a
few large mouthfuls, she dispatches the whole thing. An interesting
image: "making" a man by devouring him—precisely what men fear
from women.

Roseanne, in this segment, shows considerably more relish for
the doughnut itself than for the job it represents—training a man to
manhood. And in other women's discourses, the task inspires as
much fatigue as cheery excitement (if there's any of the latter), as
much impatience as tolerance. Black women's blues and literature,
for instance, often suggest African-American women's ambivalence
toward nurturing men. Themselves forced into sexual and economic
independence by slavery, poverty, and migration, black women have
felt sympathy and solidarity with men who are toughened and at the
same time culturally infantilized by racism. In this historical context,
there are painful reverberations beyond those of gender when a
woman calls a man "boy."

Still, any woman gets fed up when a man takes without giving
enough back. Chippie Hill, in "Charleston Blues," rids herself of
one ungrateful "baby," while caring for two or three others.

> *I'm going back to the fish house, baby, and get me some
> shrimp.*
> *I'm going back to the fish house, baby, and get me
> some shrimp.*
> *I gotta feed, baby, two or three hungry old pimps.*
>
> *Now, I knowed you baby, when you did not even know
> yourself.*

I knowed you baby, when you did not know yourself.
Now, you trying to give me the jive, baby, but you got
to help yourself.

Other cultures breed other ambivalences. A similar major-minor modulation runs through *On Loving Men,* a late-1970s nonfiction book by Jane Lazarre, a white feminist raised as a Jewish communist. Recounting a conversation in which she asks a friend how she feels when men act needy, Lazarre alludes to the lures of male dependence, as well as to the revulsion it inspires.

> *Judith shuddered. "I resent them. I hate them. Even if I love them, even if I would like to answer their need."*
> *"My father used to ask like that," I said.*
> *[Judith's nursing baby fusses, monopolizing her mother, and the conversation stops.]*
> *"My father too," Judith said, her attention released again, and then—for the symbolic vignette had just been drawn for us—suddenly she smiled.*
> *"Well, he was like Emma in a way, like an infant. It's that same quality of absoluteness. If you agree to give to me, he seemed to say, you must give everything. No half-hearted attention will do, not even to my small needs. Give to me! I want you totally. And if I responded to him at all, it was like I do now with the children, with total attention. Energy is drained from everything, but everything else. They devour you.[6]*

Men, fearing Mother's devouring mouth (Does the huge and domineering Roseanne, beyond her doughnut routine, represent that fear?), turn to their women and devour *them* in neediness. It's an interesting turn, typical of the many ambivalences—for men and for women—that surround the Infant.

The boy-inside-the-man is irrefutably a charming, disarming figure in the collective libido. He is the guileless Jimmy Stewart, the gullible Henry Fonda, the blubbering drunken genius Jack Kerouac. He is the incorrigible Bruce Willis of "Moonlighting" and Ted Danson on "Cheers." He's the brat-packer, now graduated from junior high and moving into leading-man status though he's scarcely within worrying distance of his twenty-fifth birthday, or the literal thirteen-year-old inside the *Big* hunky body of Tom Hanks. He is the ever-randy rock star and the baseball player, that sandlot kid with full-grown muscles and fuller-grown genitals, which he is forever drawing attention to by scratching, hefting, and fondling on the field.

But the irresistible Infant also meets resistance, and where man-baiting turns to man-hating Mama's Boy becomes a user, an irritation, and, finally, an unnecessary burden. "I'm divorced and it's hard to be alone, but I have enough to do without taking on any more projects," a Detroit hospital worker complained to an interviewer in 1970. "And men are projects. I don't want one just hanging around."[7]

The Babbler

PART OF THE PROJECT OF BRINGING UP BABY BOY is teaching him to understand and articulate his feelings. The first step, women say, is alerting him to the fact that he has feelings. "Women do hold up things, very much so," said Mary Louise Finnegan, a freckle-faced thirty-three-year-old Irish-Catholic sales manager, who spoke with me on an unbearably hot summer night in Chicago.

> *In personal relationships . . . the woman's got to pull out of the man what is wrong. You've really got to work at it to keep the communications open. The man would be more than happy to sit back and dummy up, until maybe he walks, or a really serious situation occurs.*
>
> *A woman is attuned to picking up, this is happening, that is happening, I need to address this. But the man, you need to hit him with a brick.*

Men are silent; men talk all the time but say little; men don't listen; men are forever blowing up or withdrawing but never come out and say what's bugging them; men want you to intuit or interpret their feelings—these are among the complaints that add up to the stereotype of the Babbler, an Infant just barely capable of emotional speech.

"Men are emotional amateurs," says a painter.

"Practically preverbal," says a recent divorcée, describing her ex-husband exactly as a mother would describe a toddler. "He had a few words. *I, want,* and *no* were big."

HUBBY GIVES WIFE THE SILENT TREATMENT—FOR 30 YEARS!! screams a tabloid headline, in characteristic fashion hinting at a home truth via massive hyperbole. The story, in which the man finally breaks his verbal abstinence with a trivial comment about the food, was probably based on the women's joke about the man who for years utters not a word to his wife, leading her to believe he is mute. Then one morning, several decades into their marriage, he announces, "This oatmeal is cold." Astonished almost to speechlessness herself, his wife manages to ask, "Why haven't you said anything before this?" "Until now, everything was okay," he replies.

The related themes of emotional deaf-muteness and insensitive, self-centered blabbering run through contemporary women's art. One of the ominously sweet little tales accompanying a series of 1947 prints by Louise Bourgeois goes, "Once a man was telling a story, it was a very good story too, and it made him very happy, but he told it so fast that nobody understood it." The series is entitled *He Disappeared Into Complete Silence*.

A Barbara Kruger image of a man's face shadowed by a fedora, his finger to his lips in a gesture of shushing, is bannered "Your comfort is my silence," suggesting the complex relations between suppressed speech and intimacy. Another American artist, Nancy Grossman, constructed male figures, entirely corseted, chained, and zippered into skintight black leather, their heads hooded to cover eyes, ears, and mouth, "effectively trapping them in a state of sensory deprivation—unable to communicate or respond to stimulus," wrote Sarah Kent. "Grossman's drawings and sculptures offer a frightening glimpse of a world in which sexuality and aggression are inextricably linked, where communication is irrevocably blocked and frustration rules.[1]

Grossman implies that men are frustrated by bound affections and gagged speech. But some women contend that this frustration is a female invention, that women project their own exasperated desire to communicate onto men, who are actually quite happy to "dummy up." In her book *Mantalk*, writer Irma Kurtz comments that when women accuse men of emotional blankness, they are actually condemning men for not being more like women.

> What are these "feelings" men are denied and women want them to recognize? Feelings of incompleteness, of emotional vulnerability, of boundless tenderness, and of bitter blame. In other words, what it feels like to be a woman.[2]

But even Kurtz, who extends little esteem to what she sees as a female propensity to "inflict" feelings on others, believes men withhold their true emotions. And, she says, they do so out of egotism. "In fact, the male has his feelings even though women do not recognize them, because they are not usually expressed or extroverted; they are protective and used to shield his dearest part, his ego, against real or imagined attack . . . *in extremis* [the male ego] will even cut the man off from himself and try to cut him off from women who are emoting at the top of their lungs and nagging him to listen." Fortunately, Kurtz assures, "this is a rare condition . . . less common than touchy women suppose."[3]

Cathy Guisewaite's comic strip alter ego "Cathy," indefatigable toiler in the mines of heterosexuality, frequently makes stabs at transporting emotions across gender lines. After years of surviving the Man Shortage, Cathy has hooked up with Irving, a nice but nerdy fellow. In one strip, which takes place early in their romance, Irving is sitting on the couch as Cathy emerges from the kitchen. "Anything I can do, Cathy?" he asks. "No, I ordered dinner and drinks by phone . . . movies and popcorn are being delivered later . . . and I called a maid to come tomorrow and clean up . . . For once I want a whole uninterrupted evening to just sit and catch up with you, Irving." In the next frame, they are sitting side by side, grinning nervously. The last frame shows Cathy on the phone: "To whom do I speak about having some conversation sent in?"

At the other end of the temperamental scale from Cathy is Tina Turner, the sexually red-hot yet emotionally cautious rebel in a musical genre that practically celebrates male cheatin' and mistreatin'.' Turner, the survivor of wife abuse who sang, "Who needs a heart when a heart can be broken?" sends out similarly fed-up signals, this time about men's lack of feeling, when she asks, "Should I be fractured by your lack of emotion? Should I?" Her refrain hints that she fears she might be; it is as beseeching as it is belligerent: "You better be good to me."

Informing this mixture of combat and surrender, of dogged effort and intimations of failure, is the idea that men and women speak two distinct languages, the concepts and assumptions of which are as different as Chinese and English, and between which there is no interpreter. Communications are not only frustrating, they are treacherous and possibly futile, as Adrienne Rich suggests in "Trying to Talk with a Man."

> *. . . walking at noon in the ghost town*
> *surrounded by a silence*
>
> *that sounds like the silence of the place*
> *except that it came with us*
> *and is familiar*
> *and everything we were saying until now*
> *was an effort to blot it out—*
> *Coming out here we are up against it*
>
> *Out here I feel more helpless*
> *with you than without you . . .*[4]

Sociologists, anthropologists, and sociobiologists have lots of explanations for the two-language phenomenon, extrapolating it from the mating habits of the gorillas and swans or comparing it with ritual chanting in hunter-gatherer societies. In general, current commentators view the gap as a result of social learning. For example, Jean Barko Gleason, a Boston University psychology professor who studies gender and the learning of language, has found that parents speak differently to children of different sexes. "Both parents used more inner-state words, words about feelings and emotions, to girls than to boys," she told a *Newsweek* reporter. "By the age of 2, girls are using more emotion words than boys."[5]

By the age of, say, thirty-two, the "emotion words" in a man's vocabulary are no more abundant, and when forced to speak them— say, in therapy—he is likely to be about as articulate as a Topeka businessman asking for directions in Hong Kong. "She was Anna Freud," said one man humbled by couples counseling, "and I was a bear." This man's feeling of inarticulateness might have been worsened by the therapist herself. Mental-health professionals, who contend with psychologically tongue-tied men daily, have been found to favor female patients because they can more facilely "talk the talk."[6] (Wouldn't you know that the place women are more welcome than men is in the shrink's office?)

A lucid analysis of the two languages has been set forth by Georgetown University psycholinguist Deborah Tannen in *You Just*

Don't Understand: Women and Men in Conversation. Tannen too sees gendered styles of communicating as the results of social learning, but puts a slightly different spin on the phenomenon. Girls get used to talking about feelings as a way of forming intimacies, she says; it's how they play. Boys, brought up in the rituals of hierarchy, learn to do, not to talk, and their aim is to establish those hierarchies in all situations. If they talk at all, it is to further the competition, not alleviate it. Where women focus on connection through sameness and sharing, men focus on status through maintaining difference. Where women get close by "matching" problems—Tannen calls it "troubles talk"—men are attuned to pick up slights or compliments, perceiving them as cues to who's "one up" and who's "one down." For men, troubles talk feels like an admission of defeat. Confronted with emotional problems, men are likely to run from what women would call sharing and gravitate toward solving, their strong suit. To the women, this often feels like insensitivity, dismissal, or rejection.[7] So entrenched is this perception of men's inability to express emotion communally that a caring man becomes, to some women, an oxymoron. "I'm looking for a man who's compassionate, a man who's a good listener," a female stand-up comic quips to a mostly female audience. "I guess I'm looking for one of my girlfriends to grow a penis."

Tannen might find the comedienne's conclusion distressing. In fact, she contends, men can feel "like women" and women can solve problems instrumentally "like men." If each sex would learn to give voice to some of the other's lingo, she says, there'd be a lot less voice-raising. She's right, I think—but not entirely.

Because after entreating and hectoring men for years to be more expressive, women don't always approve when men do begin to talk from the heart (or its vicinity). "Next year at 2:00 P.M. men will start talking about their feelings," divines a fortune-teller in a Nicole Hollander cartoon. "And at 2:05 women all over America will be sorry."

There are exceptions, of course, men like Dante, Donne, and Marvin Gaye, who are accepted and credentialed feelings-speakers (poets and musicians are almost by definition feminized). In general, though, when women hear words like *vulnerable* coming from male mouths, they often cut the speaker off by turning toward more "androgynous" topics, like a male car mechanic who refuses to engage in conversation with a woman who takes the word *carburetor* in vain, or a Frenchman not so subtly insulting an American stumbling in his language by replying in equally stumbling English.

For one thing, women suspect men of employing the vocabulary with dishonorable intentions. Where the old-fashioned man might have talked a woman into bed by professing undying love, his modern incarnation drops a few well-chosen, preferably women's-libbish, feelings. Not that the ruse doesn't work; even the tough-cookie cartoonist Mimi Pond instructs men in its proper application. In "Conversation Tips," under the heading "DON'T SAY" she has drawn a stooped-over goof with crazed eyes opining, "They say every man is capable of rape. It's kinda sick but I guess it's true, huh?" (Ice cubes form in the snarling woman's talk-balloon.) But under "DO SAY" a chap with hand to heart croons, "You know, sometimes I lie awake at night thinking about how wrong the double standards we were raised with are . . ." "You do?" replies his smitten prey.[8] Speaking the "female" vocabulary of feelings, or expressing a repertoire of ideas sympathetic to women, is not a bad way of getting girls.

Or of getting attention, without necessarily offering any in return. In the words of one female wag: "A man who cries is in touch with feelings—his own."

Women's slowness to draw men into the circle of emotion is understandable. Society doesn't exactly confer high status to the role of expressing feelings. Rationality is prized far above emotionality, movers and shakers above lovers and caretakers. (Compare a stockbroker's or an engineer's salary to a daycare teacher's or housewife's if you doubt this.) Still, a kind of power resides in nurturing, loving, civilizing, peacemaking, and articulating emotions, and women experience challenges to the wide acceptance of female domination in this domain as encroachments on their limited power. Like the man whose skills at cooking and bottle-washing begin to equal the chief's, a new emoter is a competitor. Adding emotional expertise to his already established arsenal of sexual and economic advantages, he comes to the contest better armed than the woman does.

"I begged him and begged him to go into therapy," a friend, who calls her husband the Male Expert, recounts. "After about a hundred years, he did. Biggest mistake I ever made. Before, he knew how to make salad dressing, how to run my computer, how to drive, how to do everything better than me. Now he even knows how I *feel* better than I do."

But the emotionally mature man, the man who wants to express his feelings and probes to understand a woman's, is an invader in an even deeper sense, a sense that goes beyond competition. All intimate relationships involve a constant pushing and pulling between the desire to merge and the need for separation. The psychologists Susie Orbach and Luise Eichenbaum discuss how partners, heterosexual and homosexual, trade off roles in vying for closeness and separateness. As one steps forward, the other steps back, then the other moves forward and the first moves back, and on and on in a continual "cha-cha" of dependency and independence.[9] Most psychologists, including these two, agree with Nancy Chodorow, who argues in *The Reproduction of Mothering: Psychoanalysis and the Sociology of Gender* that heterosexuality and the traditional family exaggerate the polarization of roles in the dance: women more often advance, while men retreat. Women, who have retained their identification with the first love-giver and receiver, Mother, feel more comfortable with merging and are more fearful of isolation. Men, who have had to reject the mother in order to assert a masculine identity, tend to keep apart in fear of engulfment, even to the point of loneliness.

Still, each sex yearns for and fears both merging and separateness. Women can feel suffocated too; men can feel isolated. A number of lesbians have described to me how two full-time mergers in a couple can be unbearable. "God, the minute-to-minute updates, the how-are-you-feelings and what-are-you-thinkings!" a lesbian neighbor once exploded after a difficult phone conversation with her lover. "Give me a man! Give me an animal! Give me singleness! But please, leave me be for just one moment!" She sounded, I told her, like a sitcom father swatting away his family to defend the stronghold of his easy chair.

Woman's resistance to man's attempts at greater intimacy, and her insistence that he is congenitally autistic, are the marks of a strong desire less openly acknowledged than the inclination to merge —and that is the desire for privacy and for separation. The stereotype of the Infant reinforces the possibility of that separation. One can love a baby passionately, and every mother knows a baby demands attention of the most constant and intense nature. But between adult and child there is always a space; an adult can be "alone" with a child. Young children often ask when they will "catch up" in age with their parents. The assurance that they cannot is both disappointment and comfort.

This ambivalence is one meaning of the story of Peter Pan. When Peter returns, still a boy, from a sojourn in Never-Never Land, he meets Wendy's children in the nursery where she slept as a child. Peter Pan, as the tale's name connotes, is his story, the story of a boy who refuses to grow up. But it is the story of Wendy too, who chooses *to* grow up, and is wistful but not regretful about her choice. *Peter Pan* is about the rewards and perils of maturity, but it is also a fable of gender difference: girls grow up and boys do not.

For what if men could "catch up" with women? What if they could close the distance between the sexes, advance across the age-gender divide, and enter woman's space, chattering all the while in the secret female language? What separation would heterosexuality afford?

As sexual difference enters an era of greater contestation, the Babbler stands guard at the border between the genders. Amateur at intimacy, he is the protector of privacy. Refuser of merging, he is the savior of separation.

The Bumbler

MAN AS PRACTICAL INCOMPETENT IS PERHAPS the most affectionate, the most "grown-up" of infantile types, and until the housework wars of the early seventies, the most gently indulged by women. This characterization is less an indictment than a chiding, a cuffing on the nose of a large, unruly, but endearing dog whose wagging tail has a tendency to knock over ashtrays and whose happy barking wakes up the neighbors' children. He messes, but he doesn't plunder. His offense is obliviousness and perhaps dullness, not viciousness. He is a big goofy golden retriever, not a Doberman pinscher.

The Bumbler is a husband, not a lover, embodiment of men's domesticability as well as its limits. He may be a Great Man absorbed in More Important Things—Einstein leaving the house in his stocking feet, Nelson Mandela unable to locate his shoes or his tie.[1] Or simply, exasperatingly, an ordinary man—"Isn't that just like a man?" says a female voice with a sigh—in the normal course of things upsetting the order that women bring to the world.

This inept, silly (and not infrequently full-of-himself) fellow is the stock character of women's domestic humor, of the comic strip, of the situation comedy and its condensed and expanded versions, the TV commercial and a certain stripe of slick, flip Hollywood movie. He is primarily a figure of fun, but that fun verges on derision; beneath the cute exterior, the Bumbler is not altogether amusing. "When I met your father he was an insensitive boor," a sixty-nine-year-old woman tells her daughter, always with a smile. "Now he's a sensitive boor."

Stumbling blindly from front door to dinner table (perhaps tripping, like Dick Van Dyke, over a skate or toy), from table to easy chair (then immediately hidden behind evening paper or zombified by the TV's glow), and from chair to bed, where he is no less clumsy, the Bumbler represents both women's conciliation with traditional marriage and, more subtly, more cautiously, a resigned dissatisfaction with gender roles within it. On the new frontiers of conflict between women and men—the egalitarian home and the sexually integrated workplace—the Bumbler is coming under angrier and more explicit criticism. Even where he, and attitudes toward him, appear most benign, his image is a kind of revenge at the inflation of male privilege and the consignment of women to the invisibility of domestic or sexual servitude at home, and to obscurity and subordination at work.

The "housewife humor" of such writers as Phyllis McGinley, Peg Bracken, Jean Kerr, and Erma Bombeck garners bestseller status by puncturing the ideal of the Happy Housewife and defending women against cultural depredations of their character and abilities—not infrequently by taking jabs at the family's little dictator. Spiked with negative observations about husbands, housewife humor is rife with odes to wifely and motherly love and caveats of the I-love-him-but variety. Regarding marriage as a given, without alternatives, its little insults are like peppercorns in a heartwarming stew of domestic satisfaction: they're a bit disturbing to bite into, but ultimately enhance the good flavor.

Housewife humor revolves around Mom, the disorganized general, womanfully leading her ragtag army through a jungle of quotidian perils (power failures, toilet stop-ups, measles) and battling the loony guerrillas (intransigent pets, eccentric extended-family members) along the way. In fact, General Mom has more than enemy forces to contend with: she can never quite predict when her own troops will mutiny. Yet cynical as she may get, her loyalty to them never flags. Much of what is funny in this work is the screwball ways in which the woman is vanquished in battle—but her failures don't severely discomfit either her or the reader. In a world without divorce, the war can never really be lost.

Self-deprecating heroism is common to many species of comedy. S. J. Perelman remarked that humorists thrive on adversity, which was why he lived in a hotel in New York City. Among comics, though, the housewife humorist is closer to, say, the early

Eddie Murphy than to Perelman: she does not feel she is where she is entirely by choice. She sees her situation, like Murphy's blackness, as inevitable and inescapable. There's considerable self-defense in both these self-lampooners, but there's a difference between them: African-American comics don't defend their white tormentors; housewife humorists do defend traditional marriage—and their husbands.

In 1946, Phyllis McGinley wrote this "Apology for Husbands (In answer to a friend's observation that they're 'more bother than they're worth')":

> *. . . I grant the Husband in the Home*
> *Disrupts its neat machinery.*
> *His shaving brush, his sorry comb,*
> *Mar tidy bathroom scenery.*

A recital of his other liabilities and assets concludes:

> *What gadget's useful as a spouse?*
> *Considering that a minute,*
> *Confess that every proper house*
> *should have a husband in it.²*

Of course, in 1946, when the GIs were just returning home, every proper house did want a husband in it. Domestic humor would install one, immovable and implacable as a boulder, and playing the same roles: to impede wifely progress beyond the home and provide the social stability the war had disrupted.

The Bumbler and his faithful wife are staples of postwar radio, comics, and early television: Lorenzo Jones' inventions make him the laughingstock of town, but his wife Belle believes in him to the last; on a moonlight canoe ride, Fibber McGee uses the wrong end of the paddle, and then when he loses it employs his mandolin instead—and with all that, Molly still finds him romantic and sexy. Dagwood is continually being undone by toothpaste tubes, tin cans, puppies, and squalling babies, but Blondie's alarm never exceeds a few ink dashes of surprise around her head. On "The Honeymooners" not only does the tough-talking but ever-patient Alice shrug off Ralph's threats and temper tantrums, she comes to his rescue in every scrape and ends every episode hugging and kissing her over-grown-baby husband.

In creating the likes of Fibber, Dagwood, and Ralph, their mostly male authors had hit a certain female attitude toward men approximately on the head. Yet it is hard to look at these hypertolerant wives as much more than male fantasy. In the end, their stories may reveal more than anything else male discomfort with the changes family relations were undergoing—men's chafing at being redomesticated after wartime adventures and their wishes to suppress women's resentment at being shuttled out of well-paying, important jobs and back into the kitchen.

If the Happy Housewife and her Bumbler husband were enshrined in 1950s popular culture (early TV is almost unimaginable without them), clues soon began emerging that life with Riley, Ozzie Nelson, or Ward Cleaver wasn't as much fun as the (male) sitcom writers said it was. In 1963, Betty Friedan's *Feminine Mystique* met a roar of female approval. As the 1970s opened and Sue Kaufman's Mad Housewife was entering the details of her deterioration in her diary, Pat Mainardi penned the landmark essay "The Politics of Housework." Translating through feminist analysis the canon of male excuses for not sharing household responsibilities, she scrawled women's dissatisfaction across the "Home Sweet Home" sampler the media had stitched. "We used to be so happy," says He, vexed by a new regime of domestic egalitarianism. "Meaning," writes Mainardi, "I used to be so happy."[3] In the mid-1970s, Ann Landers found out that indeed, women were not so happy. When she asked her readers whether they would marry their current spouse if they had it to do over again, 70 percent of thirty thousand respondents, mostly women, said no. Of these, 190 said "HELL, NO!" prefiguring Shere Hite's scientifically dubious but altogether credible findings a decade later that women were widely dissatisfied with their husbands and male lovers.[4]

By the time Archie Bunker was bellowing his bigotry and sexism, the series' writers felt the need to provide an antidote to the ditsy solicitude of wife Edith in the far less tolerant feminist person of daughter Gloria. The networks came up with Cagney and Lacey and Kate and Allie, competent, independent women who, to the delight of loyal audiences, regularly took potshots at machismo.

The domestic humorist keeps chirping her wisecracking yet

complacent song, with only minor variations. Divorce rages all around her, single mothers live down the block, Geraldo and Oprah feature incest survivors and teenage runaways every other Thursday, but in her home things are as chaotically unruffled as ever. In "The Family: 1987" Bombeck pauses to reflect:

> *Sitting there I thought about how the years have challenged families in a way no one would have thought it possible to survive. They've weathered combinations of step, foster, single, adoptive, surrogate, frozen embryo, and sperm bank. They've multiplied, divided, extended, and banded into communes. They've been assaulted by technology, battered by sexual revolutions, and confused by role reversals. But they're still here—playing to a full house.*[5]

Begging the question of what "family" is still here, and whether, therefore, "it" has indeed survived, Bombeck reasserts that "it" is indestructible. The challenges she lists have the ring of history, as if the family had been through a rough patch, like a temporary marital estrangement, and now could be expected to return to its former self.

Bombeck's household is disrupted—her kids have grown up and moved away—but, it turns out, only superficially so. They regularly descend on her, dropping their towels on the floor as they go. As for the Bumbler, he's still very much in residence. The New Man might have moved into the families described in the slicker women's magazines, but he does not live here yet. In fact, now the Old Man is literally old, and underfoot twenty-four hours a day: "Retired men like Jim bring efficiency to the home. It is cheaper to make your own tea bags than to buy them ready-made," writes Bombeck, gamely facing the next chapter of happy marital disharmony.

The always unspoken paradox in the Bombeck household, of course, is that in real life Mom is substantially, if not totally, supporting the family. With Dad retired, he's not even contributing to the kitty, and knocking around at loose ends, he's become a pretty pathetic character: "Jim used to run and jump and chase clients. Jim stays home now. He has a new watch. He will tell you what time it is even if you don't want to know." Jim is "busier than ever" (whispered behind the hand: *'keeping* busy'"), while Erma's busy as ever, doing the meaningful drudge work of family-tending.

Housewife humor poses as nonfiction, but the reader is at least subliminally aware that the stay-at-home mom on the page is actually a hard-working bestselling author. This contradiction might seem at first to create an unbridgeable credibility gap, but in fact the humorist's dual personality may serve to enhance her popularity and credibility. She is truly Superwoman: the well-coiffed professional leaning over her typewriter in the dust-jacket photo disguises herself, inside the book, as a spreading-hipped matron in frumpy mumu. But Bombeck isn't the independent single gal with the Nautilized body making eyes at one's husband over the water cooler, the divorcée whose pain and poverty loom like a bogey. If the working woman is portrayed in other media as a threat to the family, Bombeck is no such thing. She is loyal to the matron, not the professional, and her choice of allegiance is informed by broad experience. She's both lovable and authoritative.

Barbara Ehrenreich, in *The Hearts of Men,* points out that as the companionate marriage, founded on affection, replaced alliances based on economic need, ideological supports for the institution became that much more important.[6] And Pepper Schwartz and Philip Blumstein found that as a wife's financial dependency wanes, her personal and sexual expectations increase. The two factors—her ability to be economically independent and her greater demands of the relationship—make two-earner marriages more unstable.[7]

Ideologically and emotionally, a woman like Bombeck, who is financially capable of walking out on the rampaging kids and the vestigial Jim but stands by them through thick and thin, provides a role model for women who feel their commitment to female familial self-sacrifice wavering—women who straddle generational notions of marriage (i.e., they fantasize leaving their husbands but don't believe in divorce) or are exhausted by the struggles of working and mothering. When one foot threatens to stray out the door, the housewife humorist draws these women back to the kitchen table and offers them another cup of coffee. There, as she joins in a round of griping, she gives them permission to feel dissatisfied but guarantees that she won't push the issue too far. Domestic humor reassures the reader that her lot is not so bad as it seems, and that the Bumbler is an extra reason to stay put. It relays the message that the man who looks like a lazy bum or a sadistic torturer is really a sad sack himself. The poor dear would be lost without Wifey.

But there's a certain hypocritical, almost traitorous, aspect to the doubleness of these writers' lives. Many domestic-humor newspaper columnists have proposed pay for housework, for instance, yet their humor (and maybe their success) depends on the improbability of ever getting it. Their own homebound personae must be victimized to be funny, after all, not so much happy as hapless homemakers. In this regard, these well-respected and well-remunerated working women both lionize the homemaker and write her off. Putative champions of the trapped woman, they can't truly advocate liberating her. They rock, but won't capsize, the boat.

No matter how bad things—or husbands—get in this genre, divorce is not an option. An episode of "Maude" about a sorority reunion has Maude's friend Vivian deciding to leave her husband, Arthur. After calling him a jerk, Maude has second thoughts: "All right, just for argument's sake, let's say he is a jerk. That's still no reason to leave him. I mean, what kind of country would this be if every woman got a divorce just because she was married to a jerk? We'd have seventy million women dancing with each other . . ."

The Bumbler's dependency is an antidote to the negative self-image that such complacency evokes, and is an implied plug for marital longevity and perseverance. Phyllis McGinley's "useful gadget" was so handy he was practically indispensable, but Erma Bombeck's tea-bag maker is a nuisance. Why keep him? There is no justification but love, and the love of family.

Like many other stereotypes, the Bumbler depends on a world in which women and men occupy separate spheres—his, the workplace; hers, the home. Today, however, these lines are dissolving and in the border skirmishes casualty figures show women suffering greater losses. As hostilities escalate, the Bumbler is losing his appeal and Bumbler-bashing is getting more vicious.

The family Erma Bombeck conjures is going the way of the convection oven: both husband and wife work in almost seventy percent of married couples in their prime earning years,[8] and most mothers work outside the home. Media suggestions to the contrary notwithstanding, women planning their futures do not appear to be longing to return to the home. In a 1988 survey of the career aspirations of two hundred thousand freshmen at four hundred colleges, only 1 percent of the women named "full-time homemaker."[9] As Arlie Hochschild explores in *The Second Shift,* negotiations—or, as often, battles—over housework and child care have become one of *the* barometers of marital happiness. Over eight years of study, she closely observed fifty-two couples in which both partners worked and found that "whether they were traditional or more egalitarian in their relationship, couples were happier when the men did a sizable share of housework and childcare."[10] On the other side of the coin, Hochschild quotes a study of six hundred couples initiating divorces in which "the second most common reason women cited for wanting divorce—after 'mental cruelty'—was 'neglect of home or children.' " Comments Hochschild, "Since women traditionally care for the home, it is striking that so many women considered men's lack of care for the home such an important source of their unhappiness."[11]

Different couples manage to share family work to different degrees—in Hochschild's sample only 20 percent of men shared equally. John P. Robinson, a demographer who reviewed the recent literature on the subject, concluded that while men perform more household chores than they did twenty years ago, they still do on average only about one fifth of the daily tasks of cleaning, cooking, and laundry. And even in those families where men perform housework or child care, almost none are responsible for what one study called "remembering, planning, and scheduling." Of 160 fathers in this study, 150 were responsible for no "feminine" home chore, and eight were responsible for one, two, or three.[12]

To accommodate their "gender ideologies" and wishes to the realities of their arrangements, Hochschild says couples construct "myths" of equality or inequality, which often serve to prop up marriages in trouble. In one couple, Nina Tanagawa has made sacrifices in a valued career to be more present in her children's lives, but both she and her husband, Peter, agree that this makes sense, since she is "naturally" better at child care and housework. In another home, Evan Holt responded to his wife Nancy's demands that he do more around the house with a drawn-out campaign of incompetence and neglect. His chores just didn't get done, and he won the battle by attrition.

Both of these men could be considered Bumblers, but Peter Tanagawa is closer to the housewife humorists' version than is Evan Holt. The Bumbler, after all, is incompatible with the ideal of household egalitarianism: if women want men to do housework, they have to believe men *can* do housework. If the man doesn't do it anyway—either he refuses outright or, like Holt, avoids it by silent subterfuge—one way of living with his failure is to reconceive of him as a Bumbler, to tell oneself that he tried but couldn't make the grade. For the woman like Nancy Holt, who starts out expecting a man to be more responsible and then meets insurmountable resistance, the readjustment of his image from capable to incapable requires a certain amount of deliberate delusion, whether conscious or unconscious. Needless to say, the swallowed resentment that accompanies telling oneself lies (not to mention living with a man who shirks his household duties) also takes its toll, on a woman and on a marriage.

Today's Bumbler is not the lovable old pup who cohabits with the Happy Housewife. He's not welcomed home each day so much as taken in, like the family member in Frost's poem, whether he deserves it or not. In most cases, women don't fully give up on reeducating him, and he doesn't drop out of his studies either. Indeed, many current images of bumbling center around a man's clumsy attempts at doing housework, and his need for reminding, guidance, and congratulations. A New York newspaper editor who is fond of saying, sarcastically, that certain female skills (the ability to see dust in the corners, for instance) "come with the genitals," tells the story of how she taught her boyfriend to iron fourteen years ago. "He still comes in every morning holding up his shirt and says, 'Look, Deb. Didn't I do good?'"

As Hochschild points out, couples that share housework pretty evenly are in general happier than those who don't. But there are other aspects of equality and inequality—financial status is only the most obvious—affecting relationships, and it is the rare couple that has achieved parity all around. When other things are unequal, the stereotype of the Bumbler can step in to "even the score" for a woman whose power or self-esteem is suffering. In my interviews, interestingly, I often observed this going on where men had made moves toward participating in household work.

Said one fifty-five-year-old homemaker:

Leo will say, in an evening, "I'll make my own dinner," and I'll say, "No no no, I'll do it." And I don't mind doing it, because I know it will be better than what he's prepared. I really think that he eats better when I cook. Men don't do things as well as we do. They really don't care about doing things precisely or accurately . . . in my case anyway. I'm more of a perfectionist.

Along with insisting on her superiority in matters domestic, this woman implied that she is smarter and better equipped to deal with the world in general than her husband is. Yet he has made all the major decisions in their lives. He has, for example, made investments she firmly opposed and moved the family across the country against her will.

In relationships of greater equality, it's not uncommon to hear women express mixed feelings about the Man Who Does Everything. "I've realized that we have such an egalitarian marriage that there is nothing I have final say about," my friend Joan told me during a month her husband was out of the country. "Whenever I cook, he comes in and tastes and gives suggestions about a little more salt or a little oregano. We discuss *everything*—which plumber to call, what cereal to buy, even the goddamn vacuuming. I'm exhausted having the kids by myself, but it's also been kind of a relief."

Many parents and child-development professionals have noticed that women monopolize their newborns, leaving fathers who are eager to care for the baby feeling isolated and useless. In a 1987 study of 1,100 mothers, two out of three "seemed threatened by the idea of equal participation" by fathers. These women usually want their husbands to help more, but not to "overshadow" Mom, say Louis Genevie and Eva Margolis, who analyzed the survey, but the writers see this reaction as one of uneasy compromise:

It may be that being "number one" in the family gives women a sense of security and stability that compensates for the inadequate support they receive from their spouses . . . [However,] the fact that women generally do not expect their husbands to split the work equally, that they are content to do more than half, only adds to [their] feelings of resentment.[13]

If ridiculing the Bumbler-in-Transition may undermine his full participation in housework and child care, it also registers anger when that participation is too little too late, or fear that he might take power on that turf, as has happened in "female" occupations like nursing and social work, where there's been an influx of men.

Men, after all, have not exactly relinquished power to female competitors on their turf. In contrast to the male nurse who quickly moves into an administrative position, most women still work among women and in a small number of job categories; about half work in occupations that are at least 80 percent female.[14] Even those who reach relatively high places in "men's" occupations are mostly limited to feminine spheres—personnel, sales, customer service, and the "helping" roles and professions in general. An interesting working out of women's frustration at this situation can be seen in popular representations of the battle of the sexes, and the Bumbler, at work.

"Trapped in the kitchen" in the workplace, women level the same criticisms at men that they might at home: the Worker-Bumbler is having a hard time doing his job, but he fails in ways women do not—managing the "feminine," personal side of working. Anchorman Ted Baxter on "The Mary Tyler Moore Show," and his later reincarnation Jim on "Murphy Brown," are derided as much for their inability to relate to their workmates as for their stupidity about the news. Emotionally, managerially, they're Bumblers.

The same is true of the boss, Mr. Hart, in the movie *9 to 5,* written by Patricia Resnick. The three secretaries, our heroines, are portrayed as crackerjacks in the office and dynamos at home, good at everything from fixing garage doors to driving their men wild in bed. Hart is a parasite professionally and a tyrant in dealing with his subordinates: "You're a sexist, egotistical, lying, hypocritical bigot," Judy, played by Jane Fonda, informs him.

The women's revenge is a kind of forced sex change. First they threaten to castrate Hart—"I can turn you from a rooster to a hen" with one pistol shot, says Dolly Parton—then abduct and imprison him, like a woman, in his own home. Meanwhile, they take over the department by "feminizing" it—instituting day-care and flex-time and lifting the injunction against the secretaries prettying up their desks. When the avuncular chairman of the board is pleased with the changes the women have made, Hart tries to take credit and is found out and censured. His disgrace is brought on not only because he is a bad and dishonorable business*man,* but because he is a Bumbler at womanly things—incapable of office "homemaking," including nurturing the workers.

Other media portray Superwoman giving the old Bumbler a run for his money, not only at home or on the job. One breakfast cereal commercial shows a man playing tennis with his wife. He's a total klutz and she's a champ. He even gets hit on the head with the ball—all because he's constipated and, presumably, is ignorant of prunes or laxatives. In the comic strip, the eponymous Luann and a girlfriend give the "male expert" some of his own medicine. Looking under the hood of a boy's car, the friend says, "Hm, I dunno . . . I think you need to detonate the cylinder head torque injector divot ratio and realign that upline intake pre-vapor infiltrator." She confides to Luann, "I love to do that," as the two walk away, leaving the befuddled boy gazing blankly into the car.

Where once the image of the Bumbler was a symbolic defense of women's traditional sphere, he now represents female anger, revenge, and fierceness to compete in men's spheres as well.

If women can do some satisfied smirking at the domestic Bumbler and his complement at the office, there is a kind of male incompetence that offers women cold comfort at best, and this is sexual incompetence. Not that women haven't gleaned solace from making fun of men's overinflated sexual self-images. "How come women are so bad at math?" goes an old one-liner. "Because they've always been told that this [indicating a space of about two inches between thumb and forefinger] is ten inches."

"Your carburetor's rusty, your gas tank's empty, steering wheel's wobbly," sang Virginia Liston in "Rolls-Royce Papa," one lyric among many invented by women of the 1920s and 1930s to razz men about their sexual inadequacies. Twenty years after the sexual revolution, many women are still singing, and laughing through, the same blues.

"Usually the subject for laughter is men's boasts, failures, or inadequacies, 'comeuppance for lack of upcommance,' as one of my aunts would say," writes Rayna Green in an article about rural Southern women's humor. "Hilarity over tiny or nonperforming 'tallywackers' or the foolish escapades of drunken, impotent men form a body of material over which women vent their anger at males and offer alternative modes of feeling to female hearers," she continues. Letting the little boys listen to the women in the kitchen "is just a tiny act of revenge on the big boys out by the pickup."[15]

And speaking of revenge, the British comic Jenny Lecoat describes this sexual encounter: He, laboring away, pauses to ask, "Are you nearly there?" "It's hard to say," says she. He plunges on. "If you imagine it as a journey from here to China, where would you be?" She considers. "The kitchen."

The more practical-minded of women have set out to solve this problem through education and propaganda. A friend of mine hatched a plan to air-drop annotated illustrations of the vagina and clitoris over the major cities. Cynthia Heimel, whose *Sex Tips for Girls* comments more obliquely on men's foibles, offers this as a last resort for indicating a desire for cunnilingus: "Get into bed upside down."

But the gallons of earnest ink the women's magazines pour on male sexual ignorance and dysfunction suggest that for many women this is no laughing matter. Wives do not find the Bumbler in love as attractive as the lovable Bumbler. In fact, the domestically inept guy is considered manly; one who's searching around a woman's body the way he searches for the mayonnaise in the fridge definitely is not. Moreover, his incompetence in matters domestic offers her at least the dubious prize of competitive superiority. Yet making love with a clod has no such consolation; in fact, it is likely to make her feel worse about herself—not only neglected and unloved but inadequate and guilty. As Lillian Rubin pointed out in *Worlds of Pain,* women who do not reach orgasm often experience it as their own failure—and as a disappointment to their husbands, whom they have recently been told won't feel complete pleasure unless they do. His inadequacy or her failure to climax are both "her fault."[16]

Such dark feelings have little place in the cheerful homes of the domestic humorists, who approach the bedroom to discuss matters no more intimate than men's obtuseness in matching a tie to a shirt, their habit of dropping their underwear on the floor, or—most risqué—their snoring. The Bumbler may be a little boring in bed, but that is the worst of it; impotence and other bona fide sexual problems simply are not a part of the fictional world he inhabits.

These are only some of the real griefs that do not exist in housewife humorists' marriages. In its effort to uphold the last vestiges of female domination over homely things—with all the burdens and ambiguities that powerless domination entails—domestic humor must present a family whose crises are surmountable. So even as resentments accumulate like unironed laundry when he refuses to do his share or ambivalences collect around his agreement *to* do it, the Bumbler is a figure who deflects real strife. He's teased, but rarely taken to task, and never to court.

While the housework wars rage and office sexual politics reach new heights of complexity and conflict, the old Bumbler remains perched upon the patriarchal throne, no matter how foolishly he may wear its crown. Ridiculed but respected, privately torn down but publicly propped up, he is a comfortable deflation of men in a world that makes them by definition the Foremost Authorities.

A woman whose worst complaint is that her husband doesn't know his elbow from elbow macaroni is a secure woman—secure in her authority, and, ultimately, in his. The freedom to condescend is a privilege of the unendangered wife, of whose healthy survival women's domestic humor seeks fervently to reassure its readers. The Bumbler can't be counted on to bring home a ripe cantaloupe or even to fix the bathroom sink, but as a steadfast member of a disappearing nuclear family, he is reliable as the housewife's day is long.

The Invalid

WOMEN MISTRUST MALE DISABILITY; they often regard it as invented or exaggerated. But they also pity it, revel in it, and imaginatively they inflict it. The Invalid, afflicted in body, mind, or sexual spirit, is, like the other Infants, a man reduced and weakened. He is a man of small stature, smaller than his nurses, his saviors. For centuries, female writers and artists maimed male characters to bring them eye to eye and heart to heart with their heroines. In our time, when women stand taller, they continue both in tenderness and derision to cripple men, symbolically to diminish—and to punish—them.

Women did not invent the icon of the mutilated man, nor did they alone eroticize him. His archetype in Western culture is of course the pierced, bleeding Christ, though dead looking like a man who has just made love—languid, undefended, exhausted, and serene, cradled in the Virgin's arms, guarded by the good whore, Mary Magdalene. Still, "invalided" men, as art critic Rozsika Parker calls them, particularly those invalided by women, have populated women's art and domestic craft since the seventeenth century. "They stitched cream-colored satin with Jael hammering the tent peg through Sisera's temples, and in delicate white work embroidery they depicted Judith decapitating Holofernes."[1]

On his slack and pained face unmasculine, the Invalid exerts a strong emotional and sexual pull. "Before, he was always a pain in the ass," recalls Viola Jackson, a thirty-five-year-old community organizer, of her mother's feelings toward her father.

> So now my dad's health is failing—he's had three strokes in the last year . . . He's becoming an invalid so my mother's becoming more at peace with who he is now. And taking care

of him—I've never seen her take so much joy in taking care of him, now that he's unable to take care of himself.

A lapsed-Catholic nurse cackled scandalously as she confessed a girlhood fantasy: "I used to sit in church and think about taking Christ down from the crucifix—and laying him on the floor and fucking him."

Women's pulp novels of the eighteenth and nineteenth centuries were heavily populated by maimed and sickly men. In the novels of the early-nineteenth-century writer Caroline Lee Hentz, a Cincinnati matron and friend of Harriet Beecher Stowe, for instance, hardly a man is whole and hearty. Fathers, brothers, suitors, and husbands are "imbeciles . . . moral cripples, violent, untrustworthy and jealous," writes literary critic Helen W. Papashvily. Or dead: they die in war, in foreign lands, or, in Hentz's *Linda,* "obligingly . . . at sea."[2]

De rigueur in these novels is the sickbed scene in which a woman nurses a man, who may or may not recover. Many critics have interpreted these as the maudlin portrayals of a sentimentalized feminine virtue and have condemned the genre as pious and silly. But in these books—which were written and read almost exclusively by women and enjoyed popularity comparable to the Barbara Cartlands and Jackie Collinses of today—other critics have discerned the thinly disguised anger and revenge fantasies of ambitious women imprisoned by the custom and economic strictures of a male-dominated society. Men's sickness and death free the heroine from passivity, often to adventure and feats of daring. But she may also be forced by simple male irresponsibility or incompetence to undergo dangerous trials. In the enormous seller *Queechy,* by the Civil War–era novelist Susan Warner, the protagonist's

ordeals are caused by defective men who shirk their duties and abuse their authority in a system that gives them all the economic power and responsibility. Men shrug off the responsibility on women while retaining the power, leaving women to struggle for bare survival, with no hope of achieving financial comfort or security.[3]

Those men who aren't literal Invalids might be disabled by moral lassitude, or they're emotional cripples.

Few sentimental novels of the eighteenth or nineteenth century propose anything like a feminist-inspired sexual equality, although those ideas were being loudly proclaimed right outside the authors' writing rooms. In almost every story, in fact, the heroine is eventually reunited with a chastened, and newly appreciative, lover or husband. Registering protest against the social order and convicting men as the cause of women's problems, these novelists nevertheless saw happy marriage as the only plausible end to a woman's trials.

Literary critics Sandra Gilbert and Susan Gubar suggest that women writers, the great authors no less than their pulp-market sisters, were compelled to wage a rear-guard battle of the sexes, sidestepping direct contests between women and men by dropping accidents into the plots, felling the male characters by Nature, not confrontation. When Mr. Rochester is blinded, "his power dropped," wrote Charlotte Brontë, and Jane Eyre's "Soul grew straight." In the long (and, some say, protofeminist) poem *Aurora Leigh,* Elizabeth Barrett Browning blinds Romney and strips him of his patrimony, allowing Aurora to triumph and to love. George Eliot drowns some inconveniently nasty male characters, for instance, in *Daniel Deronda.* In each of these stories, say Gilbert and Gubar, "an outright battle between hero and heroine [is] evaded, almost certainly because both the author and her protagonist assume that a directly antagonistic sexual confrontation would only issue in defeat for the woman."[4]

The word *castration* leaps to mind, and many critics see in these female fantasies of blinding, crippling, and maiming symbolic emasculation. Rozsika Parker, however, argues that invalided men are not emasculated, they are feminized—a gentle act, erotic rather than desexualizing. The prone Christ, the weak and suppliant patient: "Soft, sweet, spiritualized, who do these sick men resemble, if not women? In order for men to appear desirable they have to resemble *the* objects of beauty and desire in our society—women."[5]

The man feminized by disability not only resembles a woman, he is also brought to power parity with her. He can empathize with women and can be loved without fear. The connection between invalidism and a reassuring sexual passivity has been made more explicitly by modern writers, such as Marilyn French in *The Women's Room.*

She knew he would never approach her sexually. Because of his limp, probably: he was in college by virtue of a scholarship given to poor children with disabilities. Biff had had polio. So, bright as he was, attractive as he could have been if he'd had enough to eat, he never made the first move with women. And because she felt safe with him, she could afford to love him.[6]

Parker's idea of the Invalid as feminized and lovable, rather than emasculated and punished, can be seen in franker contemporary fiction, whose writers have dispensed with the metaphors of blindness, war wounds, tuberculosis, and vague spiritual ailments and created a male character who is literally impotent. But this sexual Invalid is not exasperating, angering, saddening, or confounding, as he is in real life. On the contrary, he's sexy.

The erotic blockbuster of the early seventies, Erica Jong's *Fear of Flying,* introduces Isadora Wing as an eager new player in that formerly male sport, the pursuit of the "zipless fuck." Her first mark, a furry, ass-grabbing Englishman named Adrian Goodlove, turns out to be impotent. From the start, Isadora's expressions of affection feminize him. She alludes to Yeats' poem for Anne Gregory: "Adrian wanted to be loved for himself alone and not his yellow hair (or his pink prick)." And she is intrigued by his girlish reticence: "It was rather touching actually. He didn't want to be a fucking machine."

Lying in bed, Isadora contemplates the sexual superiority of women, the inadequacy of the temperamental male organ compared with the "wonderful all-weather cunt . . . always there, always ready." Adrian rises, rhetorically if not physically, to the occasion.

"When you finally do sit down to write about me, you won't know whether I'm a hero or an anti-hero, a bastard or a saint. You won't be able to categorize me."
And at that moment, I fell madly in love with him. His limp prick had penetrated where a stiff one would never have reached.[7]

The sexual Invalid, unlike the absent-minded Bumbler in bed, is emotionally vulnerable, spiritually deep, lovable.

In the film *Coming Home* (written by Nancy Dowd and Walter Scott) the cripple also gets the girl. The disabled Vietnam veteran

Luke (played by John Voight) seduces Sally (Jane Fonda), who has never before been unfaithful to her husband, Bob (Bruce Dern), an officer on duty in Vietnam. Where Bob has rank, Luke does not; where Bob is hard, Luke is literally soft. He is without stripes and, in effect, without a penis—paralyzed from the waist down and confined to a wheelchair. Yet it is his very softness that appeals to Sally. Her husband, macho, emotionally constricted, and inarticulate, pumps away at her in bed, leaving her to glare stoically at the ceiling. Luke fastidiously removes his colostomy bag in the bathroom, hoists himself from his wheelchair, then makes slow love to Sally. He brings her to her first orgasm, the way a woman would, by cunnilingus.

For the popular advice mongers, conjuring improbably accidents or aiming a kick to the genitals may be overly radical, but they have their own strategies of crippling men: they deploy medical and scientific "evidence" to prove that men are the infirm, perhaps the inferior, sex. Dr. Joyce Brothers' *What Every Woman Should Know About Men* starts with the male embryo, its little testes laboring to pour out testosterone, pitifully struggling to assert its masculinity, not sure which way it's going to swing; meanwhile, its calm and dignified sister is assured of her femaleness from the moment of conception, with "none of this dithering."[8] Through the life of the "fragile sex" we go with Dr. Joyce, braving the perils of greater neonatal death and vulnerability to adult diseases (Legionnaires', gastroenteritis, etc., etc.). We pant for his second-rate endurance (you remember, women make better astronauts) and weep upon his earlier grave. Go easy on the guys, we infer. They can't take the heat like we can. A piece in *Cosmopolitan* about genetic differences between the sexes is previewed on the cover: "Why Women Are Better, Stronger, Smarter than Men."[9]

Conservative advisers, ministering to the suffering nuclear family, also fret over its sickest patient, Father. Constructing a medical equivalent to the Bumbler, who would suffocate in his own unwashed laundry if his wife didn't cart it away, they portray a man so spiritually and sexually reduced that he needs a woman to nurse him, full time, to health. Unlike his nineteenth-century predecessor, whose male pride was enfeebled only as his body succumbed to disease, however, this Invalid exhibits ego wounds as the first symptoms. Indeed, prostration of masculinity is the disease itself.

The trick for women, therefore, is to administer the emotional equivalent of the candy-coated baby aspirin, to cure the patient without letting on and further indisposing his delicate pride. If he has a real infirmity, seize the opportunity. An "appropriate way to exercise the maternal aspect of personality with a man is when he is physically ill. At these times, a woman may be extremely solicitous and nurturing without fear of smothering him," advises Dr. Toni Grant.[10]

Conservative pop shrinks observe vast numbers of men vitiated by the disease of gender confusion and the opportunistic viruses of impotence and marital discord. "The case of a man seriously split off from his masculine side and identity was at one time a pathological rarity, a condition to be met with only now and them," writes Leanne Payne, president of Pastoral Care Ministries, in *Crisis in Masculinity*. "Men, affirmed as men by their fathers and the men of the community, were by and large free to mature as husbands, fathers, and leaders . . . Now, however, what was once the exceptional psychogenic factor [of the absent or inadequate father] has become, unhappily, a ruling feature of the culture at large."[11]

Like missionaries swarming over the bodies of ravaged plague victims, Payne and other right-wing fundamentalist Christians fly to the sides of men writhing in the throes of passivity, immaturity, homosexuality, "addiction" to pornography, and the compulsion to perform unsavory sexual acts (even with animals!). These healers appeal to God the Father to reinstill the lost souls with the strong masculine identities their human fathers neglected to cultivate. The wife, meanwhile, is exhorted to abet God's work by being as "womanly" as she can, among other things submitting meekly to all her husband's wishes, including sex, whether she feels like it or not.[12]

The prescription sounds almost like penitence: if woman has (even unconsciously) avenged her dissatisfaction by emasculating man, she must now embrace femininity with equal vengeance, sacrificing herself to nurse him back to healthy manhood.

Nowhere do man-hating and female self-blame collide with more violence and more consequence than in the fields of "addictionology" and "codependency." Hundreds of books—85 percent of whose readers, like most of their prominent authors, are female—broadcast an emergency of sexual disease and emotional injury. In them, the man who might once have been indicted as a Don Juan, male chauvinist, or philandering bum is now a "compulsive woman-izer," a "sex addict," gripped with "Jennifer Fever" or "commit-mentphobia." Wandering the pages in hospital greens, he is not a victimizer but a victim, a sufferer himself.

The diagnosis of men's ill health is welcome to women in one way. Many were getting sick of being blamed for the dearth of reliable, monogamous, grown-up men, sick of being told they'd brought the alleged Man Shortage on themselves by pouring too much energy into such selfish pursuits as getting Ph.D.s and law-firm promotions and not enough into building white picket fences. The proliferation of pop-psych titles that begin "Men Who . . ." still indicates that women are, or are being reminded that they should be, preoccupied with the other sex. But it also rechristens a social problem, this time with a masculine name.

There is vindication in being told that the Problem is not only woman's, it's men's too. But popular psychology does not hand out (to women) absolution clean, unaccompanied by guilt. Couched in the new therapeutic-medical language of "addictionology," and hawking the twelve-step recovery program (modeled on Alcoholics Anonymous) as a panacea, these books also send women an old message: even if it's not women's *fault,* it's their *responsibility* to do something. Like alcoholism, "compulsive" sexuality is constructed as a disease that the sufferer may successfully manage, but over which he will forever be powerless; he neither caused nor can he ever really "cure" it. *Women,* if they want to be happy with men, must either heal these Invalids or heal themselves. Men, one infers, won't do it.

In a contradictory morass of advice, women are either (or both) implicated in men's "addiction" by being "codependent" ("addicted to his addiction") and "enabling" his behavior, or told to lose the bum. They are both asked to sympathize with the patient and told that too much sympathy is their own "disease."

Codependence, it seems, is a problem of pandemic proportion. Says writer and fellow sufferer Melody Beattie, trying to put a finger on just what it is, "Some therapists have proclaimed: 'Codependency is *everything,* and *everyone* is codependent.' "[13] Her *Codependent No*

More contains a nine-page list of behaviors codependents may manifest, from "try[ing] to please others instead of themselves" to "feel[ing] harried and pressured" to "talk[ing] too much." If you don't find your symptoms—"pick nose when nervous" and "sweat in elevators"—you may still not be in the clear. "The preceding checklist," Beattie warns, "is long but not all-inclusive."[14]

The alleged ubiquity of this condition, and the marked femininity of its major symptoms—low self-esteem, putting others first to the detriment of one's own best interests—might lead a person to call "codependence" a problem of society, caused by (oh my god, here comes the S-word!) sexism. To eradicate it, one might prescribe that now-controlled substance, feminism. However, while the twelve-step primer in every codependency book's appendix aims to empower the sufferer, it requires first that she admit to being "powerless" over her addiction. Don't organize, mourn.

Only then can the addict free herself of her fix, the alcoholic, substance abuser, or "sex addict," who himself is powerless over his addiction. It's hard to say who's sicker, but the sex addict is definitely in bad shape. Anne Wilson Schaef in *Escape from Intimacy* calls sex addiction a "progressive, fatal [!] disease."[15]

Just as all women might safely be called codependent, so are all men commitmentphobic. "We call it the Cold Feet Syndrome, and it is an epidemic," write Drs. Sonya Rhodes and Marlin Potash (both women).

> *Every man in our society suffers from it, at least to some degree. We won't pull any punches. Not only are men different from us, but they are amateurs at intimacy. Men in our society have not been trained to be intimate—and for the first time in history, commitment means emotional connection, not just financial responsibility.*[16]

Carol Botwin, in *Men Who Can't Be Faithful*, terms womanizing an addiction and limns a horror-film-like specter of Bad Men pouring over the hills like giant, woman-eating worms:

> *Most wives—at least 35 million women—will share, at some time, the heartbreaking experience of having been sexually betrayed by their husbands—some of them repeatedly . . . The figures on adultery, of course, don't account for the additional*

millions and millions among the 41 million single women today who also have to cope with men who can't be faithful.[17]

Botwin's advice is in one way incompatible with the codependency-mongers': she believes women must make an issue of the man's philandering. For, unlike the Invalid crawling into bed, this patient wants to go back outside and play.

A man will only see his fear of commitment as a problem if you see it, name it, and insist on it. Otherwise he will be all too happy to blame you for the fact that the two of you just can't "get it together," and he will set the terms of your relationship.[18]

A number of these books counsel women to perform a sort of triage: separate out the terminal commitmentphobes (whom Rhodes and Potash call the "Good for Nothing Guys") and steer clear; diagnose the borderline cases ("Good Guys Today/Gone Tomorrow") and the curables ("the Good Enough Guys"); then sympathize with and ultimately coax the best possibilities into commitment. Some coaxing takes the form of self-effacement: Margaret Kent, in *How to Marry the Man of Your Choice,* tells women to let the man do all the talking.[19] Some marshals self-regard: Rhodes and Potash advise women not to have sex if "the man has become withdrawn, controlling, sadistic, or just mechanical."[20]

Botwin's discussion of What to Do About His Infidelity mixes the contradictions of the "treatment" into one sweet and sour stew: maintain your dignity, she says—"Don't grovel, beg, or become hysterical"—while you figure out how you've "colluded" in his adulteries.[21] Get mad, but not so mad that you'll make him mad. "You have every right to feel angry and let it out, but don't let the tirades continue beyond a week or two, because your goal is to put things back together again."[22]

As presented by the advice-givers, the process of curing the womanizer dovetails happily with its aim: a joint marital project, like starting a small business or raising Akitas, it brings the couple closer together, thus rewarding the man who refrains from straying and encouraging him to remain faithful, which in turn rewards the woman. For the man, the proposition is win-win. Not only is he pardoned for neglecting or betraying his wife, he gets extra attention for it. For her, it is more ambiguous. Faced with a sick, rather than a bad, man, she is expected (and expects herself) to be sympathetic rather than spiteful, to give rather than get even.

In the name of female self-respect, pop therapists suggest responses that look suspiciously like old-fashioned self-sacrifice; in the name of marital egalitarianism and maturity, the "cure" requires of women the simultaneously obsequious and superior role of coddling a grown-up who by all rights ought to take care of himself. If the codependency literature encourages women to get out of bad relationships and almost forbids them to try to change their men, it too is a form of capitulation: whatever happened to demands? The cure, in all cases, calls for women to do, to change, to psych out and work out.

This genre is so hugely popular because it taps into a rich vein of female self-blame at the same time as it allows women to blame men for bad relationships. It draws on the comfortable, if bleak, notion that biology is destiny—in this case, that infidelity is a sex-linked trait, like baldness or color-blindness (although the *New York Times* has now revealed that practically every animal in the kingdom, male or female and including such reputed faithfuls as swans, engages in "extrapair copulation").[23] With all this, it also addresses women's need and desire to preserve long-term intimacies, to forgive and forget—and to deal realistically with scarcity.

These books may save relationships, who knows—there's no data correlating high consumption of psych pap with marital longevity—but if so, it is at the cost of sexual equality. He is not held responsible because he is sick; she (who may also be "addicted") can and should make things better. The Invalid embodies the maddening paradox at the heart of man-hating: he is supposedly weaker, but simply by virtue of maleness wields more power. The woman restores her Invalid to health. But as lay doctor, does she heal herself?

There are women, of course, who are fed up with Men Who Lie Around in Bed, demanding chamomile tea and sympathy. Alongside the stereotypes of the ailing man as involuntary liberator of women, as deserving victim, or lovable object of pity lurks another Invalid, this one the emblem of women's impatience, cynicism, and resentment. Where women no longer see any advantage in playing Florence Nightingale and refuse to feel guilty about allegedly making men ill ("I don't get ulcers," said the TV journalist Linda Ellerbee, with unapologetic pluck. "I'm a carrier"), enter the Hypochondriac.

Unlike the bona fide Invalid felled by a war wound, a rare jungle parasite, or something else equally manly, the Hypochondriac is a little boy who doesn't want to go to school, so he comes down with a mysterious affliction, hijacks Mommy to his bedside, and forces her to administer the love he feels he's not getting enough of. There is little that is cute, sexy, admirable, or in any other way appealing about this faker. He is compelling by sheer force of perseverance. At best he manages to be funny, albeit in a pathetic way. Mainly, the Hypochondriac, with his invented pain, is a pure pain in women's ass.

In fact, the Hypochondriac is renowned for coming down with whatever he's going to come down with precisely when it is least convenient for his woman. "I had to go to Denver for this giant sales conference," a businesswoman told me, "and I was going to book a million . . . maybe it would mean a promotion. So I'm rushing around getting ready and Joe starts coughing. He says he absolutely can't leave the house. He can barely budge from the bed to make himself a cup of soup." She goes on, "Or we play tennis—and I think this happens mostly when I'm winning. He gets this cramp in his calf which causes him to fall to the ground yowling like a stuck cat, then he limps off the court."

No more Ms. Nice Guy, women are implying in the snide discourse that has grown up around the Kleenex-draped image of the Hypochondriac. Even the wife who still agrees to standing vigil by her ailing husband gets off a few good ones. "Of course, Leonard was never able to stand pain," says an Erma Bombeck character. "When he suffered a paper cut in '59, I never left his bedside. The doctor said it was my strength that pulled him through."[24]

Tina, in *Diary of a Mad Housewife,* feels guilty for not bearing up better under her husband Jonathan's vague complaints, but her creator, Sue Kaufman, obviously has less patience. On Thanksgiving Day, while Tina scurries around preparing a gourmet dinner and taking the kids to the parade, Jonathan skulks from bed to bathroom and back in his robe. "I know it isn't possible, but I think I'm getting that Thing again," he moans. When she declines "a little ole roll in the hay" to make him feel better, he manipulates her into delivering second-best service.

> *"Do you think you could at least manage to bring me some breakfast on a tray? I think if I take it very easy all day I'll be all right . . ."*
>
> *"Of course I'll fix you a tray." I was so guilty I was near tears. "What would you like?"*
>
> *"My usual Sunday breakfast. Juice and coffee, two four-minute eggs, two toasted scones—but without butter today—and some Damson Plum preserve."[25]*

Kaufman lets us know who's driving whom mad.

If each of these examples illuminates one face of the Hypochondriac, there may be in modern letters no exegesis on the subject more thorough than the journalist Marcelle Clements' diatribe against the Jewish American Prince. I take the liberty of extending her description to all Hypochondriacs, for the author herself does. After introducing her subject as "infantile, exhibitionistic, manipulative, tyrannical, insanely competitive, whiny, greedy, spiteful, paranoid, cowardly, choleric, terminally neurotic, [and] grandiose," she steps back: "But, you might ask, isn't that true of all men?" Yes, she answers, and barrels on.

Here is Clements on finding the way to a (Jewish) man's heart: "not through his stomach but through his symptoms":

> *Study ulcers, shingles, and perpetual back problems. Bone up on asthma. Learn to use words like prostate and epididymis conversationally. If you're looking for a specialty, concentrate on the alimentary canal, starting with the impacted molars and ending with spastic colons. Don't forget lethal dyspepsia. Sleep disorders is a required course. Learn first aid: a small cut on the finger can always lead to tetanus. Be prepared for mysterious ailments: I know a Jewish man whose tongue hurt for two years. Be sure to take an interest in every orifice. Understand from the start, however, that you don't have the tiniest, tiniest chance of ever beginning to match a Jewish man's interest in his own symptoms.[26]*

Clements took a beating from Anti-Defamation League types for the perceived anti-Semitism of her attack (a Jew herself, she apologized in advance). But could their outrage have had a little to do with the man-hating in her savage refusal to take the blame for men's afflictions?

A few women go further than rejecting blame. In reality or in fantasy, they deliberately hurt or sicken men, even unto death. Blueswomen show little sympathy for the "sex addict" running around with other women. "I cut him with my barlow, I kicked him in the side. I stood there laughin' over him while he wallowed round and died," sang Bessie Smith.

But their savageness is often softened by remorse or regret. For, partly because of its rarity in reality, the idea of women doing violence to men is always compelling—and, as I've said, scary to both sexes. Few women in the classics or the Bible kill their husbands, fathers, lovers, or male enemies. Even now, with the growing sexual egalitarianism of violence, when women take up the gun or the knife the event is newsworthy—though her motivation often is not. One study of spousal homicide in Canada found that all the female killers had been abused by their husbands. A pretrial study of women charged with homicide in Missouri discovered that 75 percent had been abused. A third study found that at least 40 percent of women who commit murder do so in self-defense. Myriad statistics suggest that wife battery—a tragically common violence—is a precursor of murder, although few abused wives actually kill their assailants. For these women, murder is a last resort, a final "escape" from victimization.[27]

Women who exact revenge by causing illness or those who torment weak men are interesting and repulsive in the same way women who neglect or abuse their children are: they are flouting the sacred female duty to nurture and protect, turning it nauseatingly on its head and defiantly owning women's reputation as moral or sexual infectors. They are Eve, Typhoid Mary, Lizzie Borden.

If the dirty deed is done with poison (as, at least in fiction, it often is) femininity is further transgressed, this time by perverting the image of one who expresses love by feeding. Shakespeare's witches work their evil by stirring up a nasty brew. Mexican women tell of female black magicians who administer the herb *toloache,* or jimsonweed, to errant lovers, causing the victim to lose his memory of everything but the woman he has betrayed.

In mystery, a genre known for its preponderance of female writers, murderesses are commonly poisoners. A recent newspaper item about a seemingly nice old Massachusetts matron who allegedly poisoned her lover and two husbands alludes, not surprisingly, to *Arsenic and Old Lace.* The appeal of that play to high school students and their drama teachers must have something to do with the chaste frisson of this gender reversal. The mystery writer Ruth Rendell adds a delightfully unsavory dollop to the story in "Means of Evil," wherein a health-food gourmet tries to wreak revenge on her ex-lover and his new wife by donating some decidedly unwholesome mushrooms to a vegetarian casserole he cooks from her recipe. These fixes are far from the homeopathic remedy prescribed by the pop shrinks—a dose of intense love at home to cure the "disease" of too much loving scattered abroad!

One of the darkest contemporary novels of invalidism and revenge is *Mrs. Munck,* by Ella Leffland. A young, unmarried virgin, Rose Davies is raped by, then falls into an affair with her boss, Mr. Leary, who is more than twice her age. She gets pregnant, and he denies paternity and fires her. When, nearly penniless, she asks him for fifty dollars, he comes to her house to taunt her with his refusal. "I'll kill you someday," she says. A violent fight ensues, during which her baby is killed.

Twenty-three years later, Rose, now the widowed wife of Mr. Leary's nephew, takes him into her home, putatively to care for him. He is an Invalid, half-paralyzed, wizened and whimpering. She plots to kill him, but not without a protracted period of torture and humiliation first. Paying for his own crimes, cardinal among which is his assumption of invincibility, he entreats Rose to extend a hand in help. Graciously she may deign to, and reap his gratitude. Or she may leave him to suffer. Either act is sweet, sickly sweet, revenge.

In the end, Rose decides to keep Mr. Leary alive, takes him to the desolate farm where she grew up and deposits him with her old, broken mother. She does not drive away unburdened, though; there is only a sliver of implication that her life is to begin anew.

Unlike sentimental fiction, wherein the Invalid returns to his lover's bosom on the final pages, unlike popular psychology, which sends the reader forth fortified with therapeutic resolve, *Mrs. Munck* offers neither relief nor hope, promises neither romance nor recovery. What linger instead are the pitiless disgust, the methodical cold-bloodedness of Rose's revenge, her glee at her victim's cowering terror. What echo are the struggling breaths of the Invalid and his nurse in "frantic battle," man reduced by age and sickness, woman empowered not by compassion but by hatred.

2

The Betrayer

... for man to man so oft unjust,
Is always so to women.

Byron, Don Juan

Trust no man, trust no man
no further than your eyes can see.
He'll tell you that he loves you and swear it's true,
Then the next minute he'll turn his back on you ...

Ma Rainey

The Seducer

THE INFANTS EARN WOMEN'S ATTENTION, and their disdain, by not doing—by needing and whining, rolling over and playing dead, or in some cases, dying. They haven't grown up, and won't. At best, women put up with them; the Infants suffer, and women suffer them.

At the hand of the Betrayers, women suffer. In the intrigues of love and the contests of marriage and divorce, these con men are ample matches for their female adversaries. Liar, cheat, trickster, manipulator, no-account charmer, roué, womanizer—the Betrayer changes his aliases daily, but his crimes are sickeningly predictable: seduction, betrayal, abandonment (and a new crime, we will see—abduction).

Samuel Richardson's Lovelace is the archetypal Seducer:

> *a man born for intrigue, full of invention, intrepid, remorseless, able patiently to watch for [his] opportunity, not hurried as most men by gusts of violent passion, which often nip a project in the bud, and make the snail that was just putting out its horns to meet the inviter withdraw into its shell.*[1]

In Byron, Don Juan's "manner was perhaps the more seductive, / Because he ne'er seem'd anxious to seduce; / Nothing affected, studied, or constructive / Of coxcombry or conquest . . ."[2]

Such disinterest is a form of treachery, for seduction is actually the antithesis of nonchalance. The Seducer's "whole character is trapped in the moil of domination," writes Elizabeth Hardwick, "and [he] drudge[s] on, never satisfied, never resting, mythically hungry."[3] The Seducer is not what would be called compulsive, acting on irresistible orders from the unconscious. Never rash, never impulsive, he is an experienced hunter: sober, methodical, undeviating, disciplined. He is nevertheless a man obsessed.

The combination of cool exterior and hot interior makes the Seducer seem the perfect lover. Nothing dampens a woman's ardor like a pursuer's desperation, but nothing piques it like the knowledge that he is thinking about her all the time. Yet his obsession to prevail, ironically, makes him subservient. As long as he must work hard to dominate, he is enslaved. The Seducer wears a woman's resistance down, but the fact that she resists bespeaks more than the social prohibitions against her succumbing. It calls into question *his* worthiness—does he deserve her? She is, or will be, his *mistress:* in our time the word implies the second-class status of other-womanhood, but it literally denotes superiority, ownership, mastery.

Domination and submission; conquest (which is about force and associated with rape) and persuasion (which involves a coy but willing participant): the tensions between these pairs ensnare the soul of the Seducer and convolute women's fantasies of him. Women do, of course, know a real rape when it's happening to them. Indeed, consent or its absence is the only determinant of the criminal act; only the victim herself can tell. This definition of rape, which is increasingly becoming law, is one of the true victories of feminism.

But where the unconscious is concerned, the distinction between rape and seduction blurs. So as stereotypes, as figures in the imagination, the Rapist and the Seducer sidle dangerously, confusingly, close to one another. In that murky place where cultural myths, subjective experiences, and fantasies mix, women are struggling to define a female sexual agency, to name coercion and consent, to act rather than be acted upon.

It is self-evident that men use power to get sex. In the sexual hierarchy, all men are of a higher "class" than all women, and because men control most of what's worth having—money, property, jobs to give out and take away, academic credentials to dispense—they don't even always need physical force to extract sexual favors from a women. Survival—at school, at work, in marriage—is an offer women can't refuse. Susan Brownmiller was one of the first to name this manipulation of power *rape*.

The women's folklore of rape—cases that seldom, if ever, reach a court of law—is an oral history of abuses by men in positions of authority. The therapist who applies his personal kind of sexual therapy, the doctor or dentist who suddenly turns a routine examination into a physical overture that the bewildered patient feels helpless to halt, the producer who preys on a starlet's ambition, the professor who twists to his advantage his student's interest in his field of scholarship— these are examples of what men would call seduction since the sexual goal may be accomplished without the use, or even the threat of physical force, but the imposition of sex by an authority figure is hardly consensual or "equal."[4]

The enforcement of that power, and not sex, is the "goal" of rape, says Brownmiller. The rapist—and the Seducer—is aroused by making a woman bend to his will; his sexual pleasure is inextricable from the exercise of power.

Jacob Barker, the eponymous Professor Romeo of Anne Bernays' novel, thrills as much to power as to sex as he plies his skills on a vulnerable young student:

Barker felt the twin engines—sex and power—surge along bur- ied pathways and come out on his face with an intensity most girls were unable to resist . . . He told her she was one of the smartest students he'd seen in seven years of teaching. "You have a grasp far beyond your years," he told her, mimicking [his mentor's] style . . .

Patty lapped it up, a kitten at a saucer of sweet cream. It almost made him feel guilty, the ease with which he fed her.[5]

Barker, whom Bernays portrays with a combination of revulsion, compassion, and humor, has little affection for his marks, or for any woman. He idealizes and infantilizes those he "loves," fears those he cannot manipulate, and objectifies, often despises, those he desires. Indeed, after power, he lusts most after lust itself—"the ardent chase, the quickening pulse, the verbal foreplay, the heightened fantasies."[6]

Constantly crashing headfirst into the evidence that he is a tinhorn Machiavelli of sex, Barker persists in thinking of himself as a great lover. Even when his students bring charges of sexual harassment against him, he can't admit that they were not greedy for his charms, slain by his "bedroom" eyes. By his own definition Barker is a Seducer, an artful persuader; by Brownmiller's, he is a rapist. Bernays makes him both.

While not polemical, Bernays' novel is in a sense ideological; it is one of the few literary explorations I know of this subject in which the Seducer-Rapist's female victims are in no way implicated. They may use an unfortunate situation (a lecherous teacher bribing them with academic favors) to best advantage, but none enjoys having sex with this puffed-up has-been.

Other women's representations of coercive seduction are less clear-cut than Bernays'. Rape—violent from start to finish, or miraculously and instantaneously metamorphosing from brutal to gentle— figures large in women's narratives from *The Story of O,* Pauline Réage's* classic of sadomasochistic pornography, to the bestselling novels of Rosemary Rogers and Jackie Collins. In these stories the heroines' passions are roiled not by the dependable, devoted, steady suitor with a good job and a respectable family, but by the icy, imperious rapist-lover. Why?

Theories as to why women fantasize rape are myriad. Psychoanalysts, most notably Helene Deutsch, found in these fantasies "proof" of an inborn female masochism. Other Freudians have posited that women (and men) dream of rape because it offers sex stripped of agency, and therefore of guilt. More recently, post-Freudians have associated sexual submission with a desire to return to infantile states of helplessness and boundarilessness.[7]

Rejecting a psychological approach wholesale and applying a strictly political analysis, Brownmiller argues that being raped is just about the only heterosexual fantasy available to women, who are brainwashed by an all-pervasive "male ideology of rape" that constructs rapists as heroes and women as willing victims. Either women rebel against this ideology by reducing their dream lives to nearly nothing, or they dream the dreams men script for them, says Brownmiller. "[W]hen women do fantasize about sex, the fantasies are usually the product of male conditioning and cannot be otherwise."[8]

---

* Pauline Réage is a pseudonym, but the author has been identified almost without dispute as female.

Neither the psychoanalysts' claim of masochism nor Brownmiller's of coercion suffices to explain rape fantasies. Film and literary critic Tania Modleski, who analyzes the Harlequin romances, modern gothics, and soap operas, synthesizes a Freudian analysis with an understanding of "real world" power. She sees these narratives of the magnetic Seducer-Rapist as representing the "complex strategies women use to adapt to circumscribed lives and to convince themselves that limitations are really opportunities."

In the Harlequins, the hero is cruel, haughty, mocking, disrespectful, and impenetrable. His advances are more like demands: he grabs and kisses the heroine, traps her in his arms, in his room, wherever. The heroine is constantly "drawing herself up," recovering from his insults, holding back tears of humiliation, trying to interpret his half-smiles and silences, and rebelling (usually without success) against his control over her. If there is an explicitly sexual relationship, the first encounter is almost invariably a rape.

During all this she both consciously hates him and is addled by his magnetism—hopelessly in love. Pride and fear make her spurn him, and eventually this rejection, no matter how artificial, begins to torment him. By the novel's end, needless to say, he wins her. Still a little mysterious, a little rash (no Molly-and-me-and-Baby-makes-three here) he is nonetheless revealed as a *mensch,* his heart of gold beating hard for her behind his steely exterior.

In the gothics, this good-bad guy has a mirror image: a bad-good guy, the heroine's legitimate lover or husband. The antithesis of the felon with an innocent heart, this fellow acts gentle, protective, and "normal"—but, the heroine senses, there's something weird about him. He has odd sleeping habits, off-limits rooms, and untouchable subjects of conversation. Of course, the heroine's instincts are correct: he turns out to be a lunatic, murdering members of the household one by one, and homing in on her.

Modleski believes these marauders represent women's fears of men, whom they often find emotionally opaque and unpredictable—intimate strangers. As well, she says, these narratives offer an explanation—latent, troubling love—for men's seemingly inexplicable brutality, much like the mother who tells her daughter that the boy who is teasing her really has a crush on her. Modleski reads the heroine's breaking the heartbreaker's heart (at least temporarily) as a revenge fantasy and an expression of female "longings for power."

But "it is crucial to understand the double-edged nature of women's revenge fantasies," for none of these rationalizations and fantasies is without contradiction. The heroine suffers as much as, if not more than, the hero. She is humiliated, tossed upon his whims, not to mention taken by force.

> *As long as resentment is accompanied by self-denigration, Harlequin Romances can hardly be said to perform a liberating function. However, once it becomes clear how much of women's anger and hostility is reflected in (albeit allayed by) these seemingly simple "love stories," all notions about women "cherishing the chains of their bondage" becomes untenable. What Marx said of religious suffering is equally true of "romantic suffering": it is at the same time an expression of real suffering and a protest against real suffering.[9]*

The Seducer and his would-be lover are embroiled in a highly nuanced contest between women and men, the contest over body and emotion: which gender is to own each, whose are they to take, to give or withhold, to deploy as weapons, to surrender as the spoils of battle?

Traditionally, the Seducer wants the woman's body, and he gets it via her emotions. Not only is this the sole route available—short of assault, only love will persuade a lady to lift her petticoats—but to conquer her virtue, to seize her integrity, he must plunder her emotionally as well as physically. The skillful Don Juan never lets his own feelings get in the way.

The intrigues of romance develop when the Seducer unwittingly becomes emotionally involved. At first, he is "captivated" by the heroine. He savors this sexual attraction, frothy with affection, like a skim of cream on strong coffee. He savors too his control. But if she wends her way into his heart, he becomes her captive: she controls him. "What was it about this woman that seemed to arouse such uncontrollable emotions in him—feelings and urges he had no desire to feel?" wonders the Seducer in *Takeover Man,* a Harlequin romance by Vanessa Grant. "He was a rational man who prided himself in planning, analyzing."[10]

It is only at this point that he begins truly to suffer. By the time she shows signs of giving in sexually, he can no longer coldly take her body, for he is, confessedly, in love. As if he had not been forcing his kisses and caresses on her for a hundred pages or so, he insists that they remain chaste until they exchange vows. The seduced has domesticated the Seducer.

For her part, the woman desires love and uses sex as bait. But neither is she "pure" in conscious or unconscious motivation. In the Harlequins, she feels drawn to him, but unschooled in recognizing the signs of lust or prohibited from acknowledging them as such, she conceals and interprets them in the language of love. Modleski suggests that the heroine's confusion over her feelings for the brutish hero is a working out of women's fears of men. I'd add that it is a way of naming lust in a universe where female lust is impermissible. If she feels this way, she must be in love—but how can she love such a bastard? The only resolution to the dilemma is to make him lovable after all.

Male and female "turfs" in the Harlequins are rigid. His is the overtly, aggressively physical:

> *His arm flashed out and caught her shoulder. She jerked away, only to find herself suddenly imprisoned as both his strong arms encircled her.*[11]
>
> *He grabbed her arm as she made to pass him.*[12]

The romance heroine deploys her sexuality strategically too, but is "active" only insofar as she resists—a sort of passive aggression, if you will.

In the more sexually explicit glamour novel, the stakes are escalated and modernized. Where once the heroine carefully doled out kisses, now she goes all the way, considerably complicating the Seducer's task and its consequences.

The Seducer still scopes the scene thoroughly, and his assessment of the women on it is as contemptuous as ever (as contemptuous, by implication, as the author's is of him). "This little number was for him, for his pleasure, a fuck-toy for his frequent business jaunts to L.A.," muses one of the bad guys in *Rich Men, Single Women,* by Pamela Beck and Patti Massman.

He never used to tell them he was married. But now he generally did. It wasn't the obstacle it used to be, so why bother with lying? With the proportion of single women to single men so unjustly balanced, women appeared to have a whole new mindset.[13]

The Seducer has more weapons at his disposal. He can reel in a woman with real sex, and not just burning kisses (although there are still plenty of those. Some scholar of dentistry might write a thesis on the explorations of the oral cavity contained in these novels).

When at last she reached the moment she hadn't dreamed existed and madly, unknowingly screamed his name, he thrust his middle finger a few inches inside her so that she would remember, forever after, who was her master, so that she would be branded by his touch and would never forget him, for that was the ultimate pleasure he had been so determined to secure.[14]

But with both body *and* soul to maneuver, so does the woman have a more subtle and stubborn, and less scrutable, means of resistance: now she withholds her love, not her lust. In Rosemary Rogers' *Love Play* Sara tells herself to "accept the fact that her body seemed to want this impossible, hateful, arrogant man. There was no emotional involvement of course. How could there be? . . . [S]he *did* hate him—black-hearted, unscrupulous bastard that he was!"[15] While temporarily perplexing to the Seducer, this female emotional distance evaporates sooner or later. Needless to say, Sara does not hate her black-hearted bastard, and the two confess their love on the last page.

Still, this less charted romantic territory, somewhat leveled by sexual egalitarianism, confuses the Seducer: he is both aroused by and resentful of women as they move in on his once exclusive prerogatives. And as things get more emotionally complicated, female authors have a new demon with which to torment him: guilt.

In *Glitter Baby,* Alexi seduces Belinda, his friend Errol Flynn's lover. Like his Harlequin forebears, Alexi is irked and stymied because she has gotten under his skin: "No, winning her love did not frighten him. It was the power she gained over him that was so terrifying." Unable to control himself, he starts to rape her. But her protests, and then his conscience, stay him. Alexi views his disloyalty and lust as wrong—even though at bottom he believes his transgression is her fault: "As he stared into the quiet darkness, he wondered how he could have let himself fall so foolishly in love with a woman half his age . . ."[16] He marries Belinda, and, as if to make the hot seductress of his courtship a virgin bride, forces her to wear a white cotton gown and panties on their wedding night, and to wipe off her makeup. But he cannot restore her innocence with these rituals: she is pregnant by Flynn. When Alexi finds out, he banishes her to a convent, and if that weren't enough, tries to appoint himself lord of her virtue forever: he refuses to divorce her.

Alexi inaugurates his relationship with Belinda in guilt. To assuage it, he marries her. Then he becomes obsessed with what he sees as her sin—as well as his jealousy and desire to punish her. Still, by prohibiting a divorce from the woman who he feels has tricked him, he shall be linked to her in mutual guilt forever; his penance will almost equal hers.

New sexual rules make the rape-seduction a different kind of risky business than it was before. Intact hymen or no, young women flirt shamelessly. They unsteady the Seducer's aim: he's not sure if he's preying on girl or woman. Female virginity, once the Seducer's trophy, is now more like a booby prize. Discovered too late by the unsuspecting casual lover, it becomes a moral shackles for the man, if not a compulsion to marry. A sexually experienced woman is still unrapeable by definition in this fictional universe. But if virgins walk in whores' clothing, and the Seducer is capable of suffering guilt, rape becomes a potential trauma to the rapist as well as to the victim.

The themes of virginity and rape, the reassignment of guilt, and the renegotiation of gender roles are especially compelling to women. Perhaps this is because full female sexual agency is still such a relatively novel phenomenon. As Barbara Ehrenreich, Elizabeth Hess, and Gloria Jacobs argue in *Re-Making Love,* the sexual revolution was a revolution for women: women could finally define, as men had always done, when, with whom, and to what purpose they would have sex.[17] The first wide availability of contraception coincided with a receptive social climate to make this possible—a mere twenty years ago.

Many women now feel like adult sexual subjects, but collectively the sex might still be considered adolescent. With women just "coming of age" as a gender, stories of girls' sexual awakening and first sexual experiences are more than intriguing, they are also especially problematic. Molly Haskell, in discussing the popularity of boys' coming-of-age films like *Stand by Me* and *Big,* notes that boys *have* rites de passage while girls *are* rites de passage. Even if a boy is guided into sex by a kind, experienced, older woman, a maid or neighbor (I'm never sure whether this is a male wish or a common real-life occurrence), he feels his first sexual experience as a "taking" —taking the woman, and more symbolically, taking on the mantle of masculinity.

But if first intercourse is the big stride into manhood, menarche traditionally has symbolized becoming a woman. He is an initiated lovemaker, she a receptive vessel, a potential babymaker. Because the culture defines women reproductively, and women are just starting to define themselves sexually—and trying to sever the automatic equation of the two—abortion, with its connotations of both pain and adulthood, may have become the modern female rite of passage. Indeed, a four-year study by the Johns Hopkins School of Hygiene and Public Health of teenage girls at a birth-control clinic found that those who had abortions did better educationally and emotionally than those who had borne children, and better even than those who were not pregnant at the beginning of the study. "Clearly, the abortion experience is not setting these kids back," said Dr. Laurie Schwab Zabin. "If anything, it's probably giving them some sense of control over their lives so they can move on and do the things that are important."[18] Making a big decision about the course of one's life is empowering.

But abortion is a *rite manqué* at best, a sexual coming of age by default. First intercourse may not be much better. I have spoken to teenagers who wistfully recall first experiences of sexual touching, which proceeded at their own pace, sometimes involved another girl, and were propelled by mutual desire. When it came to doing It, however, the boy "took" and a girl, no matter how eager, "gave."

By definition the loss of virginity is feminine and passive. Men often don't call their lack of sexual experience virginity, probably because of the word's feminine connotation. A male friend refers to a man's first time in extremely active, if pleasingly silly, terms, as "shooting the silver bullet." But a woman *is deflowered*—there is no active verb for it. Even the expression *to lose one's virginity* (or—remember this?—*to lose one's cherry*) has a ring of absentmindedness, as if the woman had unintentionally misplaced something. Worse, something has been subtracted from her. "The moment women . . . 'have sex' . . . it is lost as theirs," writes Catherine MacKinnon. "To have it is to have it taken away."[19]

A fascinating and subtle exploration of the confusion between active and passive, between being swept away and consciously becoming, between the sweetness of wanting and the sweet terror of being wanted, is the film *Smooth Talk,* made by Joyce Chopra from a story by Joyce Carol Oates.

Tired of girlish flirting with the boys at the mall, Connie, a pretty, giggly fifteen-year-old (played by Laura Dern), and her friend cross the street to the bigger kids' hangout—and Connie symbolically crosses into sexuality. There she meets the boys with whom she begins tentatively to make out and pet. At home Connie struggles with her disapproving mother, her emotionally absent father, and her jealous older sister, June. But in the boys' cars, in their arms, all is lovely.

> *It's not what you think—I'd never do that [she tells June, who has never had sex]. It's just the boys are so nice to you when you're together. I never knew it was going to be so nice. Did you ever have a boy hold you close . . . and sing to you? . . . Oh June, don't you know how that feels, just to be held like that?*

Then her deliciously slow initiation into adulthood accelerates abruptly and horribly. One Sunday afternoon while her family is at a barbecue and she is alone in the isolated house, Arnold Friend and his creepy accomplice, Ellie Oscar, arrive in Arnold's gold-painted car. Arnold, played with brilliantly sexy menace by Treat Williams, is a man of about thirty who has seen Connie at the hamburger place marked her as a victim, and spied on her. Arnold will rape her, and he will soak his assault in a syrup of politeness, spike his seduction with the acid of violence.

He recites the names of her friends and family, a litany of omniscience and omnipotence, and presents her fate as ordained: "I'm your lover, Connie," he says.

"You're my what?" she says, scared and incredulous.

He answers, in a kind of prose poem of rape-seduction:

> *You don't know what that is, but you will. I know that too . . . Hey, it's real nice. I'll hold you so nice and tight you won't need to think about it or pretend anything and you won't even wanna get away, even if you're scared. Everybody's scared the first time. That's why I'm so 'specially nice. I'll come inside you where it's all secret and I'll whisper sweet things . . .*

"Stop," says Connie, shaking. "You're crazy."

But Connie cannot stop him; it is as if she cannot stop the inevitability of adult sexuality.

> *Connie [he says], the place where you came from ain't there anymore. The place where you had to go is canceled out . . . This place you're in now, inside your Daddy's house, is just a box. It's just a cardboard box. There's nothing for you.*[20]

Languidly, without resisting, Connie opens the screen door of her father's house and strolls into Arnold's clutches. She is his victim, but she is also victim to her own lack of agency or will—to what the literary critic Ann Snitow called "the emptiness of a girl" waiting to be filled by a man.

Here Oates' story ends, but the film continues to an ambiguous conclusion. Leaving Ellie to rifle through the house, Arnold drives Connie to a field in the hills; the viewer sees only his parked, empty car but understands what is going on. Afterward, he drops her off at her driveway. She tells him never to come back—a pathetic, too-late assertion of will. Her family has returned—they don't see him—and she gives herself back to their embrace, the embrace she had been extricating herself from as she discovered her body as a source of independence and connection with the world beyond them. Her mother apologizes for slapping her that morning. Later, she dances with the sister who hates her for the pleasures boys give her.

Does Connie want to return to childhood? Or is she, irrevocably older and wiser, seeking temporary comfort? Has she been made to pay for her unabashed pleasure, for her "rush" into adulthood? Is the gingerly delight of early sex, and sexual confidence, just a fleeting girlhood dream—and is Arnold Friend the emblem of the real, grown-up thing? Is Connie raped or does she desire sex and have it willingly?

The answers to all of the above are yes. For adolescent girls—and for women—sexuality is an ambivalent prospect. Throughout female lives, the knell of sex's dangers sounds louder than its pleasures. Don't don't don't, says one voice of the culture. Do do do, another one says, demanding here, cautiously whispering there. Do have sex, don't have pleasure. Do give, don't take.

The sexual initiator, the first Seducer, looms large as a symbolic messenger of these contradictions. He is a mystery man with a familiar face: when Arnold shows up, Connie recognizes "that slippery friendly smile that all the boys used to get across ideas they didn't want to put into words."[21] The Seducer's face is lit with permission, invitation, insight, promise, and desire; it is shadowed in prohibition, coercion, omniscience, and terror.

The Slave

OUR CULTURE KNOWS THE FEMALE SEDUCER and aban-
doner, but she is the exception, the transgressor. She is not a girl
who just wants to have fun; she wreaks havoc in her exploits. Ulysses
and his men would have been home safe by supper if not for the
treacherous enticers they met along the way. The African goddesses
Oya and Yamaya and the Hindu Kali were not exactly tractable
companions and good citizens. Nor were Potiphar's wife, Lot's
daughters, Salome, Eve, or Delilah.

The femme fatale, embodiment of the profound fear of
women's sexuality, is an invention of men. Men imbue her with
irresistible power, then whittle away at it and ultimately punish her
for it. If men suffer for succumbing, the true price is paid by the
seductress herself. Emma Bovary and Anna Karenina, unlike their
lovers, are tortured by remorse. Emma pines for the lost ardor of her
straying lover, Anna for her child. Both find a kind of absolution
only through horrible suicides. In the film noir of the 1940s, the
seductress is either jailed or killed in the end.

A particularly vicious update of this theme is the blockbuster
film of 1987, *Fatal Attraction,* by the coed team of director Adrian
Lyne and producer Sherry Lansing. Glenn Close's Alix gazes upon
the man as object, then becomes the active sexual agent to Michael
Douglas' ever more passive victim. A sex-maddened beast, immoral
and psychotic, she preys not only on the man but also on the sancti-
fied Family; the pet-bunny-boiling scene alone wins *Fatal Attraction*
its place in the Horror Film Hall of Misogyny. Of course, Alix must
be destroyed.

The power of the comic femmes fatales, bombshells like Marilyn Monroe and Mae West, is undercut in a different way. These
women "slay" men with their charms, employing their beautiful

faces and bodies to full advantage, but their games tend to be innocent and their intentions honorable. They're calculating, but not
ruthless; sport-seducing is governed by the rules of emotional fair
play. They may be after a man's money (analogue to a woman's
virtue, the literal "currency" of marriageability), but they also desire
lasting love. "I really do love Gus," a wide-eyed Marilyn Monroe
tells her fuming father-in-law in *Gentlemen Prefer Blondes* (cowritten
by Anita Loos). "There's not another millionaire in the world with
such a gentle disposition. He never wins an argument, always does
anything I ask, and he's got the money to do it with. How can I not
love a man like that?" Marilyn was revered as a tigress, but she was
loved (and pitied) as a kitten. In that sense her sexuality did not
present a challenge; vulnerability made her manageable—it guaranteed her femininity.

The threat of other lustful man-killers is diminished by intimations of their androgyny; they aren't "real women" but male imper-
sonators. Mae West looked all girl but her style was decidedly butch.
"It's [men's] game," she says with trademark smarminess of her mul-
tiple, casual seductions in *She Done Him Wrong*. "I happen to be
smart enough to play it their way." Marlene Dietrich in tux and top
hat is also both hyperfemme and *faux homme,* a man in drag in drag.

While these representations of the sexually aggressive woman
construct her as dismissibly masculine or subjugably feminine, death-
dealing or death-deserving, they also suggest a complementary male
stereotype who is a commonplace of women's lore. The femme
fatale's victim is antipode to the Seducer. Instantly and completely
undone by a sexy woman, he is the Slave.

In the Slave, women replay the myth of the fatal woman, this
time glorifying her and denigrating her dupe. Here is Shulamith
Firestone:

> Love is the underbelly of (male) culture just as love is the weak
> spot of every man, bent on proving his virility in that large male
> world of "travel and adventure." Women have always known
> how men need love, and how they deny this need. Perhaps
> this explains the peculiar contempt women so universally feel
> for men ("Men are so dumb"), for they can see their men are
> posturing in the outside world.[1]

One very beautiful African-American woman in Chicago put it more succinctly: "Men are weak. They are weak for women."

The same observation, turned slightly askew, can be an explanation—you might say a rationalization—for sexism. "Don't you think the Beastie Boys' act puts down women?" a journalist asked a young fan at a concert by the rock band, which has been accused of misogyny.

> Actually I think they're really worshipping them. Even though they have them in a cage, they're up there on stage, and they have all these songs about looking for girls. I mean it's what they live for—beer and women. It seems like they can't live without us.[2]

The Slave's single focus is also his undoing. "They can't see beyond the end of their thing," said a woman who described herself as a "former Southern belle." In Zora Neale Hurston's story "Spunk," Spunk Banks and Joe Kanty are so obsessed with Joe's wife Lena that they both end up dead. Spunk kills Joe (". . . Spunk wants Lena. If Joe was a passle of wile cats Spunk would tackle the job just the same. He'd go after *anything* he wanted the same way"[3]) and Joe's ghost returns to get him back (". . . the dirty sneak shoved me [says Spunk dying] . . . he didn't dare come to may face . . . but Ah'll git the son-of-a-wood louse soon's Ah get there an' make hell too hot for him . . ."[4]) At Spunk's wake, "[t]he women ate heartily of the funeral baked meats and wondered who would be Lena's next."[5] Hormones render men not only blind, say women, but stupid. "Nature played a cruel trick on men," says Marcy, in an episode of the sitcom "Married . . . with Children" that was written by a woman. "She gave them a source of pleasure, but the blood has to leave the brain before it can work."

The animal kingdom seems to provide women much compelling data to support the above thesis. If my interview subjects are any indication, the mating habits of the black widow spider and the praying mantis are common knowledge among American women. During intercourse (or whatever you call it between insects) the female mantis bucks and twists and bites off the male's head; without his brain, his ardor increases. After about a half hour (a long session for bugs), fertilized and sated, she eats him. A joke going around plays a variation on the theme that for males, fucking leads to a cessation of thinking.

> *Did you hear about the baby born at St. Luke's Hospital*
> *with the characteristics of both sexes?*
> *It had both a penis and a brain.*

Women aren't altogether unhappy about this defect, however: like other male weaknesses, it is exploitable. In *Rich Men, Single Women*, Paige, on the prowl for a millionaire husband, weighs the pros and cons of using the man who is thoroughly besotted with her.

> *Being Nicky Loomis's wife had nothing to do with sharing her*
> *life for love, building a future together, becoming a partnership*
> *greater than any other partnership.*
> *Marrying Nicky was more like accepting a job.*
> *Title—Mrs. Nicky Loomis.*
> *Job description—hostess-slash-whore.*
> *Salary—high.[6]*

To her regret, Paige finds that the "job" requires kickbacks of a spiritual, emotional kind as well. Financially dependent, she cannot entirely master her Slave.

The Slave, like the other Betrayers, is psychological compensation, born of wish and envy: the wish that women could express desire openly and the envy of men's privilege to do so. "Damn, wish I was a man," sings the folk-rocker Cindy Lee Berryhill.

> *I'd play the field for nothing but fun.*
> *Lord, if I was a man,*
> *They'd say she'd gone bad and I'd have a good*
> *   reputation.*

Berryhill's is the wish of a woman in her twenties, who came of age when the sexual revolution had already won its victories. Yet women whose coming-of-age straddled pre- and post-revolutionary times suspect that they can't get away with playing the victor to a male sexual victim. Even in women's fantasies, as Judith Rossner's mid-seventies bestseller *Looking for Mr. Goodbar* reveals, the seductress pays the price.

Rossner's protagonist, Theresa, takes the sexual revolution to heart and to body. She prowls the singles bars with the same bleak hunger that drives her to drink, drugs, and shopping. In fact, this Doña Juana only *thinks* she's after sex; what she's actually seeking (or running away from) is love or self-love, but on her joyless joyride she does not find herself, and connects with no one else.

Unable to be affectionate or faithful, Theresa drives away the man who would marry her, cools to the lover who is as unreliable as she is, and sinks into a depression from which she will not emerge. She spends New Year's Eve alone, desultorily considering various strategies of self-improvement, meanwhile numbing herself with sleep and wine. Back at Goodbar's, she picks up a stranger after a short conversation and takes him home. The sex is rapelike; it turns her on immensely. When she asks the man to leave, he becomes violent. He fucks her again, ferociously, and in the act murders her.[7]

Though not a teenager, Theresa is like Connie in *Smooth Talk:* she seeks sexual pleasure to fill up some inner emptiness. Connie, we surmise, may yet fill that void, but Theresa doesn't get the chance. *Smooth Talk* is ambiguous about the pleasures and dangers of sex outside of commitment. *Goodbar,* whether intentionally or not, darkly cautions against it, implying that female promiscuity is more than a recreational drug, it could be a fatal narcotic.

And what about Theresa's men? They are a sorry lot of Slaves —dull, weird, or crummy lovers. The suitor, James, is a prig and a sexual washout (although Theresa's inability to respond to him may be *her* problem), and Tony, her working-class Priapus, is jittery, shady, and practically aphasic. All are easy to snare and not that hard to leave. She drags them down into her hell; they cannot rescue her —in part, because they are as "easy" as she.

Women whose class, race, or milieu permits some transgression against bourgeois standards of female propriety don't get off scot-free either. Blues and pop singers and comediennes, for instance, have long celebrated the rewards, but also lamented the costs, of openly seeking sex.* Bessie Smith is known for making no bones, so to

---

* I'm not suggesting that similar values don't exist in the African-American community. Speaking of the blueswomen's message, Daphne Duval Harrison writes: "[S]ince men cannot be depended upon to be faithful, then a woman would be foolish to act like an angel in order to keep one." Such behavior was "counter to the prevailing norms in the black community—monogamous relationships, fidelity, temperance, family, home, and health, yet illustrates the urge for self-determination and expression." *Black Pearls: Blues Queens of the 1920s* (New Brunswick: Rutgers University Press, 1988), 110–11.

speak, about a hot sex life. Still, in "Young Woman Blues" she's clear that women can't eat their cake and be guaranteed of having it for long.

> I got no time to marry, no time to settle down.
> I'm a young woman, and I ain't done runnin' round
> . . . Gonna drink good moonshine and run these browns
>   down.

Not every "brown," however, consents to Bessie's running:

> Woke up this morning when chickens were crowin' for day,
> On the right side of my pillow my man had gone away.
> On the pillow he left a note,
> Reading: "I'm sorry. You got my goat."

Men in the blues don't always just up and unceremoniously leave. They may beat, mistreat, rob, and even kill women they suspect of cheating. Moms Mabley, whose comic persona is a very sly, very randy, and very very old lady, tells it this way: "My boyfriend was mean, you know. Oh, he was mean to me. He walked in one day and knocked me down. 'What you hit me for?' He said, 'On gen'ral principle.' I knew he was lying—I hadn't see Gen'ral Principle for years!"[8]

In the late 1980s and 1990s, women's pop music suggests that younger women have worked through some of their ambivalence about Seducers and Slaves. Today's performers' mothers were women of extreme passions and passionate extremes: in the 1960s Janis Joplin proffered morsels of her heart on one concert stage while Nancy Sinatra ground female abjection (and men) into the boards of another. But with the exception of a handful of hard-driving teenage girl rappers, eighties and nineties female performers seem born to be mild. Many affect a ho-hummish, wait-till-I-finish-filing-my-nails pose and a girlish, airy, uninflected sound reminiscent of the 1950s girl groups.

This stance may be more stylish than substantive, however: the lyrics make it clear these women have not regressed to fifties sexual subservience. It's as if they don't have to announce sexual egalitarianism; they take it for granted. There's an easygoing symmetry between the Waitresses' "I know what boys like, I know what boys want" and Cyndi Lauper's "Girls just wanna have fun." The Bangles, enticing a boy young enough to live in his parents' house, promise, "I'll teach you everything a boy should know . . . in your room." Even the goody-two-shoes Debbie Gibson has taken a course in assertiveness training. "This time I'm not asking you what you think," she announces. "I'm telling you: We're stayin' together."

The apotheosis of the "postfeminist" femme fatale—and of all the contradictions embodied therein—is, of course, Madonna, who professes to be a sexual agent with unmitigated self-determination. "I'm in charge," she frequently tells those who accuse her of collaborating in her own sexual objectification. Yet she has adopted many of the conventions of clothes and body language that signify traditional female sexual passivity—the lacy lingerie and porn-star postures that say "Come get me" rather than "Here I come." She refuses to be confined to type, she says, and has spun through an ever-changing repertoire of identities—tongue-in-cheek "Boy Toy," forties Glamour Girl, and nineties Amazon are only a few of her serial selves. But no matter how inventively she interprets them, these identities are circumscribed within a repertoire of received cultural types. And while she professes to be ever "in control," her videos portray this control as if the real strictures on women's bodies and lives didn't exist. "Papa Don't Preach," in which a pregnant teenager "rebels" against parental authority by deciding to keep her baby, was criticized for sending a message to her young fans that having a child is not only cool, but without consequence.

And yet, as she acts out these female stereotypes, Madonna simultaneously destabilizes and transgresses them. The peep-show dancer of "Open Your Heart" is positioned as the object of the viewer's gaze, yet the patrons within the video are geeky and pathetic Slaves, slavering in their little booths behind the glass. And in the end, Madonna leaves the porn palace, changes into little-boy's clothes, presumably packing away the myriad "feminine" meanings along with the black corset and stockings, and skips away down the road, an unencumbered androgyne. In the video of "Justify My Love" (which was banned by MTV and went on to record-breaking sales on its own) Madonna is dressed as a soft-core sex goddess, yet she is the desirer, the composer, orchestrator, and conductor of all the sex scenes, themselves overstepping accepted boundaries by suggesting bisexuality, voyeurism, group sex, and transvestism.

All this sweaty, supercharged stage sexuality notwithstanding, Madonna the person remains humorously, professionally "above" the heterosexual fray. Her followers have long been mostly female and under the age of fifteen (with semioticians of both sexes running a close second). Opinion had it, she was just too aggressively sexy for the males of the Clearasol set to deal with. And although her videos feature plenty of men and her lyrics are as love-and-lust-filled as any, male response has appeared relatively unimportant either to her career or to her personal life. When her erstwhile husband Sean Penn got too rowdy, she dispensed with him and started hanging around with the comedienne Sandra Bernhardt. If she was going to get attached to a man, it seemed, he would have to prove his worth, "justify [her] love." In the end of the video of that name, in fact, she leaves the overheated room and runs down the hall, stumbling, giggling, sated, but alone.

The man's job is to satisfy her needs: in this way, Madonna's male partner is a Slave. Yet her independence and relative indifference free him too: she can't be bothered keeping him chained down.

Madonna's new hardened, sculpted body complicates her image, and its implied relationship to men, even more. Now she represents both a literally muscular take-charge sexuality and a growing obsession with the body as object. But is it a *sexual* object? Her fans, who may once have identified with a fresh-mouthed, fleshy girl who could easily be imagined making out at the corner video arcade, now aspire to a sleek feminine abstraction created by advertising and pornography. Madonna is ever less a quirky personality and ever more an unattainable ideal—one which, it seems to me, has little to do with actual sex. Ironically, as she becomes less and less accessible to her female fans, she may be more approachable to the males in the audience, who may insert her into culturally convenient fantasies precisely because she is distanced by "perfection."

If Madonna's young imitators long for a body like hers because they believe it will win them male love and passion, Madonna herself seems to move further from such concerns with each rep on the

Nautilus. The body as object of male desire is more significantly her own object of desire and obsession—and of hard work. Indentured to "it," Madonna labors for pleasure in accomplishment and fame, in self-regard—an attenuated form of eroticism perhaps, but an autoeroticism in any case. Men, enslaved or not, are irrelevant.

This aggressive gonna-take-it coupled with a decided could-live-without-it is perhaps the most striking quality of new women's music in general. The pre-sexual-revolutionary female prerogative to pick and choose men was only a means to an ordained end: the woman ended up with some man or another, or she had a definite problem. In the eighties and nineties if there is no number hot enough, she can simply go dancing with her girlfriends on a Saturday night. Even the hyperheterosexual Janet Jackson can dismiss the drooling horde of Slaves with a wave of her long-fingernailed hand: "Oh, you nasty boys don't mean a thing."

Far more fundamentally threatening than bored straight women, however, are lesbians, and it is a mark of feminist-won female sexual agency that women-identified women have moved out of the noncommercial margins and closer to the commercial spotlight. In the twenties and thirties, some important female musicians were known bisexuals or lesbians—"Went out last night with a crowd of my friends / Must've been women, 'cause I don't like no men," sang Ma Rainey. But segregation silenced this music, at least to white audiences and producers, and sexism confined most of the lesbian sisters to the closet. In the late 1960s and 1970s, white lesbians created a separatist musical culture—"wimmin's music"—but its themes usually stuck to a correct-line love and fidelity, abetted by the community and, if one was lucky, the Goddess. Eighties punk, most of it not only heterosexual but baldly misogynist, offered little berth to lesbians, but a substantial minority of female musicians in New Wave and pop are plainly uninterested in men. The success of Tracy Chapman, whose politically and sexually radical album hit Number One in 1989, proves that a lesbian can be "out" and still hold the loyalty of straight fans.

The Slave, whom his female rocker-lover once would rather have died than lived without, is being thrown over—even if women's offhanded put-downs and mild-mannered indifference resemble the election of a Democrat after a Republican more than a violent coup d'état. Still, boredom can be a mask for anger, and the delectably sexy female singer whose open lips signify a yawn rather than a sigh of ecstasy is inflicting a certain pain and humiliation on that formerly indispensable man.

Perhaps it's no accident that many female rock star–seductresses get themselves up in leather. For where still unfulfilled wishes of sexual freedom intersect with new assertion and anger, seduction becomes a fantasy of revenge and the Slave a literal victim.

Judy Tenuta, a comedienne whom critic Laurie Stone described as "a fey dominatrix," creates a tense humor by careening between a camped-up nightingale-voiced girly-girl and a gravel-throated sexual taskmistress. Prancing and stomping across the stage, referring to herself as the Love Goddess or Petite-Flower-Giver-Goddess and to men as love slaves, love squids, and dancing studs, she's Big Nurse dressed as Disney's Cinderella, with more tit showing. Not altogether kind to women, Tenuta is downright cruel to men, who have but one function: to serve and amuse her.

> *He's not really my boyfriend. He's more like this thing I sit on . . . when I can't find a chair. One day he wanted me to prove my love by lifting up an entire Pontiac . . . I parked it on him for a reason!*

Tenuta is fond of ordering male audience members to take the gum from her mouth.

Tenuta won't be a link in anybody's chain of fools. "They want to possess me," she growls with the inflection of a vampiress in a grade-B horror movie. "They can-not pos-sess me." This va-va-voom body dressed in frills is no approval-seeking sex kitten. In fact, she uses sex to distance men: they can "have" her maybe, but they can't own her.

Hers is the classic dominatrix's stance, and she assumes it quite literally. One evening, she called a tweedy, middle-aged, mustachioed fellow onstage, aptly dubbed him "Mr. NYU Professor," and ordered him to kneel (which he sheepishly did). Producing a shopping bag and from it a bullwhip, she climbed astride her Slave, raised the leather, and brought it down beside him over and over and over—"whipping" him, and men, into submission.

If Judy Tenuta is a tongue-in-cheek dominatrix, the heroines in Jackie Collins' novels are not kidding. In her stories the themes of male sexual slavery, seduction as revenge, and symbolic castration appear with remarkable frequency and clarity. Unlike most of the genre, there is almost no love in these tales. Few characters find happiness, sex is rarely an expression of affection, and marriage is an economic arrangement or a trap.

Men and women both are amoral, vicious, mercenary, and self-obsessed—but the men have the added deficit of sexual weakness. They will do anything to get into the panties of a beautiful girl (those who wear panties, that is), yet they often can't measure up once they get there: they suffer impotence, ejaculate prematurely or can't come at all, have tiny penises and even tinier amatory talents. The women pretend to enjoy fucking with fat, old, or ugly partners who can pay them with movie deals or penthouse apartments, and they sexually torment or punish those who cross them. "Most of the sexual athletes of this world were users. They bargained with their bodies. She should know—she had done it herself," says a character in *The Bitch.*[9] Many of Collins' characters are sexual athletes; almost all are users.

An especially vicious example of this truism about sex and exploitation is Collins' *The Love Killers,* the story of a group of women and one man who set out to avenge the murder, by Mafia capo Enzio Bassalino, of a feminist antiprostitution crusader, Margaret Lawrence Brown. Margaret is, variously, a friend, sister, and (to the man, Dukey) lover. Dukey's goal is simple—he wants to kill the whole Bassalino family—and eventually he succeeds. The women have more baroque fantasies: "Their plan was to grab Enzio Bassalino's three sons by the balls sexually and mentally, destroying their lives, and by doing so reduce the old man to a wreck."[10]

This irreligious crusade is only temporarily foiled, and morally leavened, by the falling-in-love of one of the conspirators, Lara, with Nick Bassalino (who is killed in the end). Otherwise, the story is 294 pages of nearly uninterrupted male sexual humiliation and mutilation.

His face was a mask of seething fury mixed with surprise. "You dumb cunt!" he yelled.

She shot him between the legs, aiming at his crotch.

He screamed out in agonizing pain.[11]

Recoiling from the weight of his body, she shut her eyes as he pushed her legs apart. And then she felt him, and the tension slipped away and she almost smiled.

Frank Bassalino was endowed with no greater gift than a ten-year-old boy.[12]

[Angelo] mounted [Rio], and before he knew what was happening, she stretched her long legs straight out, trapping him inside her, and with one movement she twisted her pelvis up, and the pressure was so great, so incredibly tight, that he came at once.

She started to laugh, loud, mocking laughter. The whole thing had only taken a few seconds.

"Hey, baby, baby," she crooned. "What are you—a rabbit?"[13]

[Mary Ann] giggled and began fiddling with [Enzio's] clothes.

He closed his eyes and sighed as he felt the erection beginning.

His mouth was full of her when she shot him precisely and silently straight through the heart.[14]

Jackie Collins is no lunatic-fringe man-hater. She is one of the world's most popular authors. At this writing, there are more than 100 million copies of her books in print worldwide.

The Slave reverses the Seducer's tale in every way. The Seducer was a man, now she is a woman. He manipulated emotions, bribed with wealth, and exerted power to conquer her virtue and vanquish her body. She employs her body, jettisoning virtue, to horn in on his wealth and appropriate his power. He considered himself a lover; she knows she's a hater. He saw lovemaking as a prize after long pursuit, and a celebration. To her sex is bait, trap, and weapon. His world was a vast sexual playing field; injuries were inevitable and not always intentional. But her bed is a killing field; what is made there is nothing like love.

The Abandoner

WITH FEMALE VIRGINITY DEVALUED, pregnancy prevent-
able, and seduction edging toward androgyny, sexual abandonment
has been emasculated. To love and leave is no longer an act defined
solely as the male exploitation of female innocence. In personal relationships and law, rape is more and more forcefully defined as sex
that takes place against the woman's wishes, be it in a dark alley, on a
date, or between husband and wife.* As "no" is increasingly understood to mean "no," the woman who says yes takes on commensurate responsibility for her actions. Most people assume that women
enter sexual liaisons of their own free will, cognizant of the risks, and
that they may be held accountable for what happens to them.

This morality has its material side: economic self-sufficiency is
expected of women of all classes, despite the fact that sex discrimination and wage inequities often mean that what she manages is more
like economic self-*in*sufficiency. Still, our culture now views the
financially dependent woman as lazy, lucky, or whorish, and her
male supporter as generous, rich, or chauvinistic. Theirs is considered an intentional, private, old-fashioned, even somewhat suspect
arrangement, not a cultural institution. If a man withdraws from
such a pact, her luck or his generosity may have run out, but he is
hardly considered to have committed an impropriety; he may, in
fact, be viewed as correcting one. An unmarried childless woman of
sound mind and body is not "abandoned"—not in the U.S., not in

---

* According to the National Clearinghouse on Marital and Date Rape in Berkeley, California, as of
1990, eight states still have laws on their books exempting a husband from prosecution for raping his
wife unless they are living apart, legally separated, have filed for divorce, or the woman has obtained a
protection order. See Diana E. H. Russell, *Rape in Marriage* (Bloomington, IN: Indiana University
Press, 1990), 23.

the 1990s. It is getting harder even for a woman with children to claim she has been deserted.

Meanwhile, as marriage regains ideological, and loses actual, sanctity and the postwar baby boomers embark on their own baby boom, abandonment leaves the realm of romance and takes up firm, if uncomfortable, residency in the family. And as the definitions and expectations of that institution change, so too does the Abandoner. Clothed in new garb, he also wears his predecessor's. And like all "retro" looks, his is both modern and anachronistic.

While some men are becoming more responsible to their children, many others still see little or no relation between begetting and supporting. Among women and men both, marriage is no longer a requisite for childbirth and child rearing, and high divorce rates mean that most kids won't live with both their parents all through their childhoods anyway. Gone is the overt moral opprobrium or social ostracism of the single mother. The women's magazines, once manuals of marital longevity, now consider the difficulties of her single sex life, advise her on applying for bank loans, and offer her quick and freezable recipes. She's a regular on the TV screen (though not as regular as the single dad) in the chipper straight-arrows Kate and Allie or the brilliant, lovely doctor, with son in tow, on board the Starship Enterprise in "Star Trek: The Next Generation." Apparently, the show's writers envision a future where single mothers will be as common as computer-driven androids. We read about single mothers on the style page, meet them in films and novels. In practically everyone's family or circle of friends, there is a single mom.

These women struggle, but they're not tragic figures. They may be iconoclasts but they're not oddities, unhappy but not failures. Historian Linda Gordon suggests that all this social acceptance of the single mom may not help her much on the practical side. In the nineteenth century, the single mother was almost by definition tainted with immorality. "Preserving [her]respectability required angelic behavior and luck . . . [But] paradoxically, in some ways the turn-of-the-century assumption that single motherhood was always a misfortune and never a choice made that condition easier. There was pity for the widow and the deserted wife and a sense of dignity attached to a mother struggling alone with children which has diminished since the mid-twentieth century."[1]

Today, respect for women's sexual, reproductive, and marital self-determination—concretized in "no-fault" divorce law—also serves subtly to absolve men of responsibility for their part in problematic pregnancies and, ultimately, fatherhood. As we will see in "The Abductor," divorced women are no less vulnerable than they were before, only differently so.

Mainstream (that is to say, mostly male-produced) images of the Abandoner reflect this nonchalance about paternal absence. Not around to do much harm, he's almost benign, less a villain than a Missing Person. Although research shows that the children of Abandoners feel wounded and enraged at their fathers ("When I see him, if I ever see him again," a twelve-year-old child told the *New York Times,* "all I want to do is beat him and spit on him and then laugh when I'm done"),[2] the divorced kids on TV—say, Kate's and Allie's kids, the prepubescent son of Alice the waitress, or the child of the Annie Potts character on "Designing Women"—are more likely to be world-weary and glib about their dads, who if not altogether gone are pretty much forgotten, mere walk-ons in the family drama. Beyond the occasional pissed-off quip, little rancor strays Dad's way, suggesting that gone and forgotten, he's forgiven as well.

The Abandoner who doesn't benefit from this broad pop-culture absolution is black. Journalism especially, which has for decades regarded African-American men as a social problem, and lately (with disturbing animal-behaviorist overtones) as an "endangered species," defines him as an outlaw member of a "typical" black family: single mother, children, and him, on the lam.

Although there are today proportionately more African-American single mothers than white (in 1986, 42.8 percent of black households were female-headed, compared with 12.9 percent of white),[3] this has not been true for most of African-American history. Slavery exerted myriad pressures on them, but slave families organized themselves in nuclear units and strove to stick together.[4] As late as 1970, more than two thirds of black fathers were living with their kids[5]— suggesting that the domestic and economic policies of the allegedly pro-family Reagan administration may have been more devastating to the black family than many of the assaults it had suffered to date.

Current statistics of black paternal absence may be misleading. As Barbara Omolade of the Sisterhood of Black Single Mothers has pointed out, the lack of a wedding band, or even of cohabitation, doesn't mean a woman is estranged from her baby's father. Many unmarried African-American dads (like many white fathers, undoubtedly) contribute to the family household with groceries, Pampers, and rent, babysitting and companionship.* If the mother is living in subsidized housing or receiving Aid for Dependent Children, the arrangement is compulsory; his presence would threaten those much-needed benefits.

Once married and divorced, African-American fathers don't leave their children in the lurch at significantly greater rates than do whites. In one study, 60 percent of black divorced fathers had not seen their children in a year; 47 percent of white fathers hadn't.[6] Where child support payments are concerned, there are scofflaws of every race, but about alimony many black men don't even get the chance to be remiss; whereas few women of any race receive alimony, black women are about half as likely as their white counterparts to be awarded it.[7]

Neither history nor African-American cultural values universally support paternal abandonment, yet when the media represent black fathers, the Abandoner's old incarnation as careless lover marauds across the scene. While popular magazines and tabloid television train their admiring cameras on white celebrity single moms, thundering their spunk and (depending on the mother's preference) trumpeting or politely sidestepping the question of the sperm's origin, commentators both white and black damn young black men as parasites and con artists and their girlfriends as immoral, passive, and stupid.

Where religious moralizing has been bleached from most mainstream discussions of the (read: white, middle-class) Family, preaching is front and center whenever African-Americans are the subject —way beyond acknowledgment of the important role the church plays in the black community. A TV special on the black family, hosted by Bill Moyers, had community leaders sermonizing that a return to the church and its values is the only hope for the black family. The Reverend (but, one thought, politically astute) Jesse

---

* Omolade's contention is supported, at least historically, by Elliot Liebow's famous "Tally's Corner" study of black "streetcorner men," which showed a range of fatherly relations to children, from wholesale denial of biological paternity to affectionate attention within an extended-family setting to loving and continuous relationships with a child of a live-in lover. *Tally's Corner: A Study of Negro Streetcorner Men* (Boston: Little, Brown, 1967).

Jackson, then running for President, pontificated against the social evil of "babies having babies." And while he did imply that the family is an economic, as well as a social, institution by proposing jobs for young black men, he seemed not to consider the same for women. (Nor did anyone mention the extended-family/community systems of support that African-American women and their kids rely on.) Studies show that teenage fathers tend to marry if they can support their families, and don't when they can't.[8]

But if, as the pundits implied, instability in the African-American community comes down to personal spinelessness and sinfulness, and if the only solution to the poverty of single-mother families is to get black men to work and marry, then the viewer concludes the main problem is black men—shirking their responsibilities.

Toni Morrison's *Beloved* is a masterful exploration of the ways human love and desire are perverted by brutality, the way slavery smashed friendships, sexual relationships, and families so thoroughly that for its victims long-term commitment becomes a quest, a prize, sometimes an impossibility.

> *Anybody Baby Suggs knew, let alone loved, who hadn't run off or been hanged, got rented out, loaned out, bought up, brought back, stored up, mortgaged, won, stolen or seized. So Baby's eight children had six fathers. What she called the nastiness of life was the shock she received upon learning that nobody stopped playing checkers just because the pieces included her children.*[9]

In Paul D, Morrison paints an Abandoner fighting with all his might, against the claims of history, not to abandon the woman he loves. A former slave whose body and soul have been battered by bondage and the postbellum African-American diaspora, Paul D has been deprived of the opportunity, and almost lost the ability, to commit himself to anyone.

> *During, before and after the war he'd seen Negroes so stunned, or hungry, or tired or bereft it was a wonder they recalled or said anything. Who, like him, had hidden in caves and fought owls for food . . . who, like him, had buried themselves in slop and jumped in wells to avoid regulators, raiders, paterollers, veterans, hill men, posses and merrymakers . . .*
> *Move. Walk. Run. Hide. Steal and move on. Only once had*

it been possible for him to stay in one spot—with a woman, or a family—for longer than a few months.[10]

Sethe, his lover, has also been harrowed by sadness and violence. She lives day to day. From men she expects nothing—except abandonment.

> *Another woman might have shot him a look of apprehension, pleading, anger even, because what he said sure sounded like part one of Goodbye, I'm gone.*
> *Sethe looked at him steadily, calmly, already ready to accept, release or excuse an in-need-or-trouble man. Agreeing, saying okay, all right, in advance, because she didn't believe any of them—over the long haul—could measure up. And whatever the reason, it was all right. No fault. Nobody's fault.*[11]

Nobody's fault, Morrison implies, but their white slavemasters'. Like Sethe starved for "rememories," he is also starved *by* them—starved of healthy desire, of self-love. And he is defeated by a memory: Beloved, the ghost of Sethe's child whom she killed rather than relinquish to the master's posse, drives him from Sethe's bed.

But Paul D is a man of courage, introspection, and sweetness, "the kind of man who could walk into a house and make the women cry."[12] Which he does, again, returning to Sethe years after he has left. This time he will stay (and here, Morrison turns wishful, romantic), he will rescue her from despair—wrestle down history.

> *"Sethe," he says, "me and you, we got more yesterday than anybody. We need some kind of tomorrow."*
> *He leans over and takes her hand.*

Paul D is an Abandoner, but one created by oppression, not fated to dissolution by personal frailty or the inborn "deficiencies" of race or gender.

Other fictional representations of the African-American Abandoner more nearly fit the stereotype of the sweet-talking runaround, the ruthless parasite. The searing penultimate scene in Ntozake Shange's choropoem *for colored girls who have considered suicide / when the rainbow is enuf* is the story of Crystal and her children's father,

Beau Willie Brown, who, having abused and neglected them all for years, returns.

> *crystal had gone and got a court order saying beau willie brown had no access to his children / if he showed his face he waz subject to arrest / shit / she'd been in his ass to marry her since she was 14 years old & here when she was 22 / she wanna throw him out cuz he say he'll marry her / she burst out laughin / hollerin whatchu wanna marry me for now / so i can support yr ass[13]*

Beau Willie pleads, cajoles, and threatens, finally tricking Crystal into letting him hold the children. Snatching them up, he dangles them from the fifth-story window, shouting to the frantic people on the street below, "You gonna marry me!"

The narrative, reflecting Crystal's paralysis and final loss of hope, falls off with a whimper.

> *i stood by beau in the window / with naomi reachin for me / & kwame screamin mommy mommy from the fifth story / but i could only whisper / & he dropped em[14]*

The men in Shange's choropoem are fly-by-nights, liars, and brutes, and the playwright was skewered, mainly by male critics, for bad-mouthing the brothers.

But the play is less about men than about women. There are no male actors onstage, and the play's theme is a celebration of women's relationships. In the writing of Morrison, Alice Walker, or Terry McMillan, or the work of younger playwrights like Suzanne Lori Parks, mothers carry on with or without men. The literary critic and anthologist Mary Helen Washington points out that the absence of men in African-American women's stories does not necessarily signal sexual enmity.

> *Being loved is not regarded as the urgent business in the quest for identity. In [critic Hortense] Spiller's words, "male absence or mutability in intimate relationship is not the leading proposition of a woman's life, but a single aspect of life issues."*

If the Abandoner is not the absolute undoing of black female characters, that's not because he is uncritically tolerated, however.

Rather, the heroines are frying bigger fish. "These women are not stalking lovers," says Washington.

> They are laying claim to the freedom and triumph that were forbidden little black girls in this century, and in the process, springing from their own heads, full-grown.[15]

White writers, whose history is one of economic dependency on men, are only now starting to create characters who can get along after the Abandoner packs his bags. But, rather than transformative, the tone of this work is often resigned and listless. The characters survive, but they hardly triumph. Romantic love and marriage are disillusionments, but nothing has quite yet taken their place. "How old were you, three or four, when your dad left?" the grandmother asks the protagonist, Ann, in Mona Simpson's *Anywhere But Here*.

> He came and went a couple of times—Adele gave him money to fly back and forth from Egypt, they thought he could get money from his parents, but I don't think that ever came to much. Then, the last time, he charged up all those bills. That time he went to California. I guess he thought he could get famous there. He was a handsome man. For a long time, I watched for his face on the television.[16]

If this grandmother's narrative of the father's desertion is placid, Ann's is nonexistent. Her passionate, if deranged, relationship is with her mother. Men are interlopers in their all-engulfing folie à deux, temporary fellow travelers in their peripatetic life.

In Alice Adams' "1940: Fall," Caroline's husband leaves her and her three girls gradually. At first she is pained. After a while, she is "managing considerable detachment." And eventually, stoicism turns to "a large sense of relief," almost pleasure. Finding out her husband won't be home for Christmas, she sighs.

> Oh good, is what she thought. I won't have to make a lot of Christmas fuss—or not Arne's kind of fuss. No big parties, and I won't have to try to look wonderful all the time. And worry that he's drinking too much and making passes at undergraduate girls. I can just do the things I like, that he thinks are dumb. I can bake cookies, maybe run up a new formal for Amy . . . I

can read a lot, she thought. And I'll go for a lot of walks in the snow."[17]

Rather than a burden, her children are allies, comforts. Her husband, already, is extraneous.

Now, as she peacefully crooned to the milk-smelling, half-asleep fair child, she thought that this time even if Arne decided to take off for good, she would really be all right, she and her three girls, who themselves were more than all right—they were going to be great women, all three. She could cope with the house, the good big lakefront place bought so cheaply ten years back. They would all be perfectly okay . . .[18]

It is interesting that the fiction of abandonment is not a lot angrier. For in reality, most abandoned women are not perfectly okay, and it is a cruel irony that efforts toward fairer treatment in divorce have resulted in legal practices that drag women deeper into the hole. "No-fault" divorce, a response to demands that women not have to prove they *deserve* support, enforces a kind of get-tough egalitarianism whose underlying principle is that women are as able as men to support kids. Able they may be, as people, but *enabled* by social and economic conditions they are not. Still, judges determine support payments with the expectation that women will soon start holding up their end, even if they have been homemakers for decades.

Alimony payments, once won as a kind of emotional and moral reparation, met a real economic need, but only for a minority of ex-wives. Now, as before no-fault, at least four fifths of divorced women rely on child support payments to supplement their earnings and keep their kids fed and clothed. But these are almost always insufficient and frequently irregular, if they're paid at all. Of the 1.2 million kids whose parents are divorced each year, 30 percent receive no child support from their fathers. According to the 1987 census, the average monthly award is two hundred dollars, grossly inadequate for the majority of divorced mothers, and only half of men ordered to pay comply fully. "Federal statistics show that about $18 billion of owed child support is unpaid," the *New York Times* reported in June 1990.[19]

Harvard sociologist Lenore Weitzman, in her influential 1985 book, *The Divorce Revolution,* postulated that no-fault laws have exacerbated the economic fallout of marital breakup for women.[20] Stephen Sugarman and other sociologists and demographers, without disputing her claims that women are economically worse off after divorce and that they fare worse than their ex-husbands, are now challenging Weitzman's findings that no-fault law is the culprit. Reviewing her data, for instance, Sugarman shows that only 2 to 6 percent fewer women received alimony payments after no-fault than before.[21]

In either case, if "no-fault" divorce law has removed the guilt of divorce from both men and women, current divorce practices both legal and extralegal continue to exact economic punishment from women.

In part because divorce is so devastating to women, political responses to the Abandoner are not so passive as current fictional representations might lead one to believe. Feminist or culturally "liberal" women may feel uncomfortable with nineteenth-century-like images of the deserting father skulking out of the kitchen while weeping wife and children huddle around the dying embers in the stove. But the stereotypes that people "pro-family" rhetoric, with its undisguised anxiety about the dissolution of a once-dependable nuclear family, markedly resemble old incarnations of the Abandoner.

Where these ideologues basically see nurturance as female and the inability or unwillingness to nurture as male, they have found ways to understand these "essential" concepts as mutable. And while their deepest rage is at men, they take the safer tack of blaming women for sending men back to their uncivilized state of sexual irresponsibility and thus destroying the Family. Women who have sex or babies without love or commitment are behaving "like men," they feel; those who support legal abortion and other feminist demands are accessories to the Abandoner's crimes. But the only way these women see to prevent male flight is to surrender to traditional roles, in hopes that female subservience will reinvigorate a waning male enthusiasm for protectiveness and, failing that, a sense of inescapable duty.

In her early-1970s campaign against the Equal Rights Amendment, Phyllis Schlafly, the mother of the "pro-family" movement,

unabashedly proclaimed her opinions on the evil of male desertion—
and what should be done about it. Repeatedly stressing men's propensity to run off, she warned that the amendment would *"invalidate
all the state laws* [her italics] which impose the obligation on the
husband to support his wife, [laws that] give the wife her legal right
to be a fulltime wife and mother, in her own home, taking care of
her own babies." As it is now, "love may go out the window, but
[men's] obligation remains, just as the children remain. The ERA,"
she admonished, "would remove that obligation."[22]

Advanced in a newsletter which through the years has been
graced with an American eagle and Phyllis' own continually updated
photograph (she gets older, but her hairstyle is always ten years behind the times) Shlafly's analysis stands as the pro-family prototype.
Framing "pro-family" as antifeminist, it directs much of its vitriol
not at men but at their female "collaborators" in the women's
movement.

"In the ideology of American antifeminism," writes Barbara
Ehrenreich, "it is almost impossible to separate the distrust of men
from the hatred of feminists, or to determine with certainty which is
the prior impulse."[23] If men are instinctively irresponsible, feminists
are encouraging that instinct, against women's best interests. The
"antifeminist analysis of male irresponsibility stops short of question-
ing the structural insecurity of marriage," Ehrenreich continues.
"Distrust of men takes the socially more acceptable form of resentment directed at the would-be independent woman, who, in her
selfishness, would undermine other women's fragile privileges."[24]

Independent women are more than coconspirators, however.
Conservative ideologues argue that in buying into "male" values
these modern women are *becoming* like men. Here is Notre Dame
English professor Carson Daly:

> *Even more disturbing is the choice of the militant feminists to
> imitate the very kind of masculine behavior which they con-
> demned in the past and which, ironically, contributed to the
> rise of feminism, [such as] no standard [of sexual conduct and]
> neglect of wife and family for the job . . . Feminists . . . ar-
> gue that since society has traditionally been lenient on men
> who committed these sins, society should now encourage
> women to misbehave similarly.[25]*

Women who have abortions, "by seeking sexual pleasure for its own sake, material gain and self-aggrandizement at the expense of others, or eschewing motherhood, are acting in culturally male terms," observes anthropologist Faye Ginsburg in her study of pro-choice and antiabortion activists in Dickinson, North Dakota.

Unlike Ehrenreich, Ginsburg sees close parallels between the philosophy of the right-to-life picketers she met and their opponents on the other side of the abortion clinic doors. Although not always self-consciously, both groups critique aspects of the capitalist market-place as it "penetrates" the female domain and threatens "female" values of altruism and nurturance, Ginsburg says. The antiabortion-ists find in abortion an "unraveling" of the "natural" chain of events linking female sexuality with pregnancy, marriage, and a legally en-forced male obligation to the economic security of women and chil-dren; their antiabortion sentiment "is rooted in a desire to reverse the social causes and consequences of this unraveling, which they attribute to a increasing materialism and selfishness" and which they gender as male.[26]

The overlaps between these two worldviews can be seen in a curious pro-feminist, antiabortion polemic published in *To Rescue the Future,* the 1983 volume of Right to Life's annual anthology.

> *Feminism hopes for more equitable marriages, workplaces that recognize and make concessions to the obligations of parents, and men who are more willing to accept an active role in the rearing of their children.*
>
> *Legal abortion threatens every one of these goals. Acces-sible, socially acceptable abortion gives reluctant employers more leverage to resist demands for a working environment that recognizes the needs of working parents. Abortion is eas-ier and cheaper than accommodation. A society that promotes abortion is not likely to aggressively seek positive solutions to the problems of pregnant women and working parents.*
>
> *At present, the fathers of unborn children have absolutely no right to participate in the abortion decision . . . Men whose rights as fathers have been so severely curtailed are not as likely to be enthusiastic about accepting the responsibilities of fatherhood.*[27]

The author, Rosemary Bottcher, seems to agree that men and women should share responsibility for children, yet she argues that women, not men, are making this impossible by breaching a more fundamental family covenant.

> *Women are free to abandon their unborn children, but if they decide to let their children live, men are given no option but to recognize their obligations to these children. Women who think they can't be equal without their abortions forget that the law expects and requires that a man provide for his children, even though doing so may cause him much inconvenience . . .*
>
> *Though men have certainly abused their power over women, they have never done so to the extent that women have abused their power over unborn children. This is the grotesque hypocrisy of the feminist demand for unfettered abortion.*[28]

Where other women complain (rightly) that men abandon, leaving women to hold the bag, Bottcher sees *women* as the Abandoners, though they do it prenatally, by having abortions. Men want to father, she thinks, and law, gently reinforced by a female-encouraged sense of fair play, can gently hold them to the task. (She conveniently neglects to mention how little paternity law is obeyed or enforced.) Culture, not Nature, makes the man.

Or the woman, say antiabortionists, according to Ginsburg. Dickinson's activists define womanliness not so much in the possession of a female body and reproductive capacities, but in a person's *stance* toward these biological traits, she says. They see themselves as embracing femaleness, in spite of ambivalences they may have; therefore they are feminine. Because antiabortionists reject it (and because pro-lifers, like practically every other Western-born person, divide the world into opposites) these women must be "masculine."

Femininity belongs to those who choose it, "regardless of the shape of [their] body," comments Ginsburg. "The right-to-life position rests, paradoxically, on a view of gender that is both essentialist and radically cultural: the category 'woman' is produced by but also disconnected from the female body."[29]

This hybrid view, when applied to men, serves well in reconciling one of the major ideological and emotional dilemmas that pro-family and religious-fundamentalist women face: how to endorse the traditional biblically ordained family structure in which men rule and women submit, while at the same time gendering the behaviors that undermine family stability—selfishness, irresponsibility, and sexual impulsiveness—as male.

The solution can be found in humanly willed activity: religious practice, a hard discipline that ultimately frees a man from the destructive urges of biology and offers him consolation, calm, and stability in family and Christ. Just as women may embrace or deny their "natural femininity," so may men renounce those aspects of themselves that are controlled by the baser male instincts. In this, the Christian woman must be his helpmeet.

Pam Brady (whom you will get to know better in Part III, Chapter 10, "Withdrawal") is the daughter of the pastor of a black Pentecostal church in rural Mississippi. She explained to me, irony inserted, the church's teachings on this subject.

> JL: *Seems like a contradiction in the role of the man. Here he was dating girls and he was just going to love 'em and leave 'em, then once he gets to be married and the father, he's going to suddenly be this upright person worthy of other people's obedience. Was there any process that he would have to go through?*
> PB: *Salvation* [she laughs]. *Through Christ. Through being saved, born again. This was basically what would keep a man in line . . . And because men would fall in line at that point, then women should also fall in line and do the things that are prescribed in the Bible. The Bible was the plan to keep everybody in line.*
> JL: *But in their natural unsaved state, men—*
> PB: *Heathens. Heathens!* [Laughing] *Just wild, would do anything! No morals, no ethics, you know. It's funny, because that's what they were communicating . . . that until you get saved, you're basically hopeless. It threw responsibility for the self out the window. You really weren't responsible for yourself, and until you got saved and put God in control, you really had no control over yourself.*
> JL: *Was that true of women and men?*
> PB: *It felt like it was true for men. Because the bottom line, it was up to us as women and girls to say no, and to keep them in their place.*

The wife's task is a delicate one. She must accept the wanderlust in her man—yet she must humbly work to eradicate the Abandoner in him. She must be aware that men may not be naturally trustworthy, yet she must entrust her body and soul, and those of her children, to the institutionalized man, the Husband. Subtly playing nurture off against nature, she must declaw and domesticate the Abandoner, feminize but not castrate him. She must keep him fundamentally masculine, but not too male—a tom who doesn't prowl.

The Abductor

"I'm just calling to warn you." His voice was flat, had gained a higher pitch. "I'm keeping her."

"What do you mean?"

"She's staying with me. With me and Brenda. She's not coming back to you."

. . . "Brian," I said. I could hear the fear in my own voice. I felt I was trying to conjure the Brian I knew, that this was some nightmare version I don't know how to talk to. "Tell me what you mean. Tell me what you're talking about."

There was a silence. Then he said, "Right. You've got no idea what I'm talking about. Right?"

"That's right," I said.

"Well, then, Anna, I'm calling out of a sense of fairness. I've filed papers, there'll be a hearing, you'll get a subpoena fairly soon. I'd get a lawyer if I were you. Lots of people wouldn't even have warned you, but I still have some feelings, I still have a sense of what we . . ." his voice caught, and I waited. He didn't go on.[1]

MANY MOTHERS READING SUE MILLER'S NOVEL *The Good Mother* feel fear in their own hearts as Anna hears her ex-husband say those fateful three words: "I'm keeping her." The short phone call is like the premonition of a nightmare, one from which she will not awaken. In the end of the story, Anna loses custody of her daughter, Molly.

The red heat of pain and rage, the gray blankness of a child suddenly whisked away, the leathery green and brown of the superior economic, social, and legal power at a man's disposal should he choose to use it against a woman—all these emotions color the political landscape of divorce and child custody, reproductive technology and surrogate motherhood. Stealing across this terrain is a new stereotype of men, the Abductor.

The Abductor is a Seducer who selfishly uses women not as lovemakers but as babymakers, an Abandoner who makes off not with a woman's heart but with her next-nearest, her child. He may be husband, judge, or doctor, a Neanderthal or a New Man, but he is woman's enemy. His shadow darkens feminist visions of a society in which adults of all ages and relationships freely share affection and responsibility for children.

Like other stereotypes of men, the Abductor is not cut from whole cloth. After all, fathers have hardly honored the role of parenthood: the worst are abusive, the best-meaning are often emotionally absent from their children's day-to-day lives. At the same time, women put up with male doctors, social workers, and judges who interfere with their pregnancies, advise them on the best ways to mother, and when they do it "wrong," deem them unfit and seize their children. Fathers, once passive bystanders in much of this, are now using the law to win and protect "paternal rights" over fetuses, and, of course, kids after divorce. These developments are part of the positive trend in which fathers are taking more and more interest and responsibility in raising their children. While women say they welcome it, as we saw in other chapters, they also feel threatened by a perceived male intrusion on a once-exclusive female turf.

In response to these threats, a vocal faction of women is taking the position that men have no right to compete with mothers for children. Biology and centuries of social learning make women better—and more deserving—parents than men, they say. The position is one of high moral posturing, but also of rage. Ironically, that rage is often directed at the very men who are, or might become, the good fathers women wish for: divorced men seeking to share custody, sperm donors who want to know their offspring, gay or straight single men who want to adopt, and the professionals (usually assumed to be male) who help them. The women say these men are motivated toward increased involvement with children by envy and misogyny; they see their actions as trickery.

"The men's right activists [are] only interested in postmarriage fatherhood as it reflects their personal power," writes Canadian journalist Susan Crean. "Yet [they are] having an insidious influence on the ideology and actions of the mainstream . . . an influence which threatens to make fatherhood just another word for patriarchy."[2]

Until the mid–nineteenth century, patriarchy was, literally, the power of the fathers. Common law gave fathers all custody rights over their children (who, before restrictions on child labor, were economic assets to a family), including babies nursing at the breast. Men already had uncontested legal, economic, and physical control over their wives, and this gave them emotional control as well. Fearing for her children's health and welfare, many a woman stayed under a man's roof, suffering cruelty and domination of the worst kind. Court records of the period show that the authorities regarded this threat positively—it safeguarded the status quo. If women could leave men and take their children with them, one barrister asked the judges in British court, what would remain to hold marriages together?

In the latter part of the century, feminists began to strike blows against the absolute power of the patriarch. Their campaigns, among which were the outlawing of wife abuse and the liberalization of divorce law, combined with an opposite-moving trend, an emergent cult of domesticity that idealized motherhood and women's "special" bond to children, and family law began slowly to change. Increasingly, judges awarded custody, especially of younger children, to their mothers, although older children, in particular boys entering the workplace, were as likely to be placed with their fathers. Two principles of modern divorce law were developing: the "tender years" doctrine, which presumes that little children need a mother's touch; and, more generally, the idea that the court's first duty is to protect not the rights of the parent, but the "best interests of the child."

As industrialization solidified gender roles in the family and the influence of psychological and public social-welfare establishments grew in the twentieth century, two assumptions—the saliency of maternal care, and the economic dependency of women—took hold in divorce law. By mid-century, mothers were being awarded child custody almost automatically, fathers got visitation rights and were ordered (sometimes) to pay alimony and child support. The arrangement, and the principles it was based on, lasted until very recently, and is a mixed blessing for women: motherhood is a huge burden and divorced motherhood an even greater one, but it is also a source of power and gratification. And even though most twentieth-century fathers hadn't been that involved in their kids' lives, the threat of restricting men's access to children was a card women could play in marital conflicts where they had little other leverage.

In the last two decades, it is well known, the picture has changed radically. Along with incremental progress on this front, the 1980s and 1990s have witnessed a virtual promo campaign for the "new fatherhood." Many social-scientific studies find that men's attitudes and wishes toward more active parenting are ahead of their actual behavior. Perhaps this is why *Vogue* is still so romantic about the "love affair" between men and their children and *Esquire* pronounces fatherhood "a state of being, a triumph of instinct, and above all, an opportunity for joy"[3] rather than all of the above, plus a sizable portion of drudgery. Needless to say, many mothers, who have wiped puke since the beginning of time unsung (and continue to wipe most of it), are royally irritated by these rhapsodies to the Men Who Diaper and the Babies Who Love Them. If fatherhood is so rewarding, they want to know, how come men didn't invent it centuries ago?

But this propaganda is nothing compared to its effect on the men in black robes who have the power to shape women's and children's lives. When fatherhood moved off the style page and into the divorce courts, a potential boon to overworked mothers became a terrifying threat. There, the myth (or ideal) of equal parenthood and a feminist-inspired principle of juridical gender neutrality effaced all memory of the reality of individual families or the world at large, where most men live at arm's length from their children.

As we saw in The Abandoner, the "no-fault" principle of divorce has had an ambiguous effect on women. Reflecting a welcome moral neutrality in the matter of marital dissolution, divorce law no longer forces spouses to prove some sort of "wrongdoing" in order to separate—it largely takes the stigma out of divorce, at least legally. But at the same time it fails to acknowledge the myriad sexist attitudes and practices that put divorced women at a decided disadvantage to their ex-husbands both socially and economically. And, where custom and religion used to determine a woman's fate if her marriage ended, today her interests are in the hands of other forces, over which she often has little influence.

> The man who wants to end his marriage now simply files a petition alleging that it is irretrievably broken; there is no defense against such an allegation. The wife seeking alimony, property division, or child support has no leverage to demand such compensation as the price of her husband's "freedom," but must rely instead on the substantive law governing these issues. Thus, the laws of alimony and property [and I would add, custody—JL] now count in a way neither did before.[4]

Whether one endorses the concept of "fault" or not, the fact is that the more codified the law, the less room a woman has to maneuver. And while women have gained considerable influence in the justice system, the law is still prejudiced against them; its practitioners, particularly in the higher echelons, are still mostly men. In custody decisions, judges are increasingly demonstrating what Nancy Polikoff of the Women's Legal Defense Fund calls a "paternal preference." Ninety percent of fathers do not contest custody awards to mothers, but in cases where men do contest, 68 percent win, according to Lenore Weitzman.[5] "There has not been a revolution in childrearing, and mothers still bear most of the responsibility," says Polikoff. The data "suggest the possibility that men who have not been the primary child-care providers are prevailing over women who have been."[6]

The "fathers' rights" movement portrays men as loving, willing, and capable parents who have been excluded from their kids' lives during marriage by the "reverse sexism" of their breadwinning role and after divorces by their vengeful wives. Most crudely, the movement demands a kind of economic-emotional "fair" deal. If a man is going to pay to keep a roof over the kids' heads, he should be allowed in the door to visit them; if he's forking over for tuition, he should have some say about where the kid goes to school. These demands, which are the basis of many custody arrangements, are reasonable in themselves. But the formula itself tends to overshadow, and discount (as the culture has always done), the quotidian care that mothers usually give, and which, many women believe, affords mothers superior knowledge and entitles them to superior decision-making power. Besides, mothers fear interference in all kinds of everyday affairs from ex-husbands less concerned about Junior's welfare than eager to harass Mom.

Fathers' rights alone would not carry sufficient legal or emotional weight to tilt a custody decision, however. The child's "best interests" still is the divorce judge's primary legal concern. Now these two interests are dovetailing. As it becomes a psychological commonplace that children need fathers to grow up healthy and happy, fathering, once regarded as the kids' meal ticket, is considered an emotional staple as well. If this argument along with fathers' "rights" were not enough to tip the scales in Dad's favor, unspoken social prejudices against mothers diminish her claim, and his is suddenly the weightier.

It's easy to see that mothers' and fathers' nurturing skills are held to entirely unequal standards—and the professional child advocate, now a fixture in divorce proceedings, applies the ruler as differentially as anyone. A mother, always compared to the ideal of Motherhood, can hardly help but fall short. If she works outside the home, she's negligent; if she doesn't, she's overinvolved in her kids' lives. Fathers, on the other hand, look cute and sweet—and extraordinary —just picking up a teddy bear; they get extra points almost no matter what they do. Indeed, argues Canadian lawyer Susan B. Boyd, simply *wanting* custody works in a father's favor, while it may subtly handicap a mother's case. Because she is *expected* to be self-sacrificing and always put her children first, Boyd says, her personal desire to have them with her (read: "selfishly deny them a father") is regarded as antagonistic to their interests. Meanwhile, any contribution a father makes to his children's well-being is celebrated as a bonus; that he wants to be with them marks him as special—so his needs and desires are compatible with theirs.[7] Add to these ideological factors men's superior earning (and lawyer-retaining) power and men's greater likelihood to remarry, thus forming another "normal" family unit, and the litigious dad is way ahead.

Divorcing mothers have another reason to be fearful, and suspicious: there is an increasing body of anecdotal evidence that fathers' requests for sole physical or legal custody represent the cynical maneuvering of lawyers more than the genuine desires of fathers to live with their kids full-time. Robert H. Mnookin, a professor of law at Stanford University, and his associates suggest that when parents of either sex are represented by counsel, they are more likely to petition for more custody than they actually desire. Mothers, with a lawyer or not, almost always ask for what they want—physical custody. Among fathers in their survey, however, only a fifth of those without counsel requested physical custody, whereas four fifths of those with lawyers did so.[8] They conjecture that the request may be a bargaining chip, and other lawyers and experts on divorce concur that the practice is common.

Here's how it works: Father threatens to sue for custody. He counts on Mother's desire to spare the children the trauma of undergoing a custody battle, her relative inability to pay for it (in New York, costs can be upward of thirty thousand dollars) and her fear that she might lose. Usually, the gamble pays off. She makes a counteroffer: she'll agree to less alimony or child support if he "gives" her the kids. *Business Week* quotes West Virginia state judge Richard Neely saying he's not proud of the tactic he claims to have invented, but "it is repeated across the nation every day."[9]

When gender-neutral legal language obscures sexist reality, twentieth-century fathers' rights, it is true, begin to look suspiciously like nineteenth-century patriarchal privilege. Mothers, once again, are left in a painful dilemma. Married and divorced, they have acknowledged a desire and a need for men to share the work of parenting. But they are bitter when all the rewards and few of the costs seem to accrue to men who do it, even if they do it just a little. Should women willingly cede their only, already compromised, power over children for the promise of male commitment, and endorse laws that embody that promise? Men's prior record and current behavior make the odds of fulfillment look slim. (Why, for instance, don't men use their power at the workplace to push for parent-friendly flextime and nongendered leave policies?) The wager seems foolhardy—in feminist theorist Ann Snitow's lovely metaphor, like Jack trading his mule for a handful of beans.

Still, how else will equal parenting evolve? Is it possible to insist that men take on equal obligations to children and at the same time argue that motherhood confers on women a superior claim to parenthood? Women may have to relinquish the privileged status of childbearer in return for equal status as child carer.

Every vision of a different future requires a large measure of hope and an open eye to incremental change in the present. In reifying male deficiency (no matter how real), the stereotypes presume stasis. In obliterating men's faces with all-of-a-kind masks—the clown face of the Bumbler, the leering ball mask of the Seducer, the black sash across the Abductor's eyes—women blind themselves too: they can't see a friend behind the false villain's countenance.

In feminism, images of the Bad Father are inseparable from, and secondary to, images of the Good Mother—or more accurately, the intrinsic goodness of motherhood. In fact, to earliest second-wave feminists fathers were almost invisible. These women were most concerned with removing the links between biology and destiny. Motherhood had been the means of and the justification for keeping women down. In the late 1960s, abortion was illegal and contraception unsafe, pregnancy was treated as an illness rather than a life event, and forced sterilization, particularly of women of color, was practiced rampantly. Almost all doctors were men. Feminists were young too: it made sense that they'd put more energy into preventing motherhood than glorifying it.

In the first edition of their ground-breaking manual of women's self-help, *Our Bodies, Ourselves* (1969), the Boston Women's Health Collective displayed a marked revulsion toward motherhood, which they saw as women's primary oppression, an odious condition with a few salvageable graces, a consummation devoutly to be prevented. The text surrounds the discussions of anatomy, contraception, abortion, and sexuality with glee and excitement, yet the approach to pregnancy and childbirth is gingerly; the writers tiptoe in, holding their noses. Pregnancy is damned with faint praise as "a life crisis with tremendous growth potential." Then comes "prepared childbirth," in which the doctor is cast as a maniacally controlling technocrat, and the postpartum period as beginning with an almost inevitable depression ("a mental disorder").

The physical changes occurring in the post-partum period are enormous. Although they are considered "natural" they closely resemble pathology.[10]

There's a bit on nursing and nipples and some other clinical aspects of physical mothering, but not a word on motherhood itself. Subsequent editions of the book softened this tone, but as the first major work on women's self-help, *Our Bodies, Ourselves* can't be ignored for its pronounced antinatalism. Contemporaneous books of feminist political theory were as hostile to motherhood as they were oblivious to fatherhood. In *The Female Eunuch* (1970) Germaine Greer, who would later become a near-fanatic booster of motherhood, describes the family as a sickly organism, of which "Mother is the dead heart."[11] The next year Shulamith Firestone declared pregnancy "barbaric"[12] and espoused a feminist revolution whose "first demand" would be "the freeing of women from the tyranny of their reproductive biology by every means available," including making babies in laboratories.[13]

This period, and the production of what Snitow calls the "demon texts" against motherhood, was fleeting. Soon another stripe of feminism, which would practically beatify motherhood, was clashing with the early "radical" feminism that saw the way to women's equality in minimizing, or eliminating, gender differences. "Cultural feminists" felt that women's bodies and "women's ways" had been put down too long, and valorized those qualities designated as feminine. Violence or child neglect, competitiveness, or selfishness in women were swept under the rug, along with the already evident differences among women of different races, ethnicities, and classes. An undifferentiated femaleness characterized by nurturance, emotional openness, associativeness, and nonviolence was celebrated, and a "women's culture" was created, holding itself separate from and opposed to the competitive, aggressive, and greedy, dominant "men's culture." Some historians have seen in cultural feminism a wish for female unity that transcends the thorny conflicts of race and class, as well as a retreat from the daunting project set out by the radical feminists. "It was easier," says historian Alice Echols, "to rehabilitate femininity than to abolish gender."

As cultural feminism elevated femininity and denigrated masculinity, motherhood, both potential and real, became its magnetic center. In August of 1973, *Ms.* magazine published a lengthy missive from Jane Alpert, then a fugitive from the FBI, convicted of conspiracy to bomb war-related buildings in New York. Entitled "Mother Right: A New Feminist Theory," it became a blueprint of cultural feminism, and of feminist essentialism. Female biology, specifically "the capacity to bear and nurture children," is "the basis of women's powers," Alpert argued. "Biology," she said, "is hence the source and not the enemy of feminist revolution."

> *It is conceivable that the intrinsic biological connection between mother and embryo or mother and infant gives rise to those psychological qualities which have always been linked with women . . . Motherhood must be understood here as a potential which is imprinted in the genes of every women; as such it makes no difference to this analysis of femaleness whether a woman ever has borne, or ever will bear, a child.[14]*

In an ideal—that is, matriarchal—society, "the paradigm for all social relationships is the relationship of a healthy and secure mother to her child." Alpert's goal: "to reshape the family," and all of society, "according to the perceptions of women." Men are all but deleted from this program; they're mentioned in passing, as workers, alongside older children, in mother-controlled child-care centers.

Calling for an "uprising . . . based on more than opposition to the oppression and the definition of Woman as Other,"[15] Alpert would replicate, in reverse, the men-on-top/women-on-bottom hierarchy that had so injured women. Patriarchal history had defined Woman not by what she was but by what she was not. "The female is a female by virtue of a certain *lack* of qualities," Aristotle said, and twenty-two centuries down that line of thought, Freud located the "lack" in the body—specifically, the genitals. The little girl recognizes her "deficiency," he said, which explains her incomplete experience of the world and her limited ability to affect its, and her own, fate. When Alpert located women's "power" in the capacity to mother—that is, literally, in her uterus and ovaries—she was defining one gender as that which has, and therefore *is* (and is better) and the other as that which has, and is, not. Mother Right, like the reproductive and family politics of the 1980s that would succeed it, made Woman the One and Man the Other.

In the late 1980s, after more than a decade of debate and cross-fertilizations between the feminists who would maximize and those who would minimize biological difference, "Mother Right" is again on the offensive—or one might say, the defensive.

Among those leading the charge is the writer and psychotherapist Phyllis Chesler, whose indefatigable activism, prolific output, and hortatory style helped rescue a number of her causes from the backwaters of the women's pages. Infusing Chesler's writing on women, men, motherhood, and divorce are the assumptions shared by Mother Rightists: mothers bond prenatally to their children; in a contest, natural mothers deserve custody of children either by dint of labor and love invested, or—drawing on a tautology of "common sense"—simply because they are their mothers. Only a demonstrably depraved or grossly negligent mother ought ever to lose custody of a child.

On the other side, a father's connection with a child can never approach the depth of a mother's; most fathers have little enough to do with their children to render them useless. And fathers who seek custody must be doing so because they want to punish their ex-wives, not because they love their kids.

Chesler's *Mothers on Trial: The Battle for Children and Custody* inaugurated this position on the trend of divorced fathers winning custody battles. From the first, the reader understands that Chesler finds nothing commendable in this development: in her view, it is a form of legally sanctioned kidnapping, yet another victimization of women. Like much of her work, *Mothers on Trial* is characterized by a moral outrage and personal pain that hums off the page, bursting through in capital-letter-studded pronunciamentos (*"Question: What Is Going on?* Answer: Patriarchal Law Is Going On") and pages-long mythological exegeses, which end in heartrending Messages. In one section, just in case the reader doesn't find harrowing enough the accounts of women denied custody because they fed their children health food or didn't have a basketball hoop, Chesler intercuts them with descriptions of the torture of suspected witches during the Inquisition.

Such hyperbole is a common, covert strategy of stereotyping: who does these hideous things? it asks silently. *Men.* Ex-husbands, male lawyers, male judges: accusers, inquisitors, hangmen. Women are innocent and downtrodden, men imperious, monstrous. Chesler's most consistent tactic is to splice empirical evidence with polemics so skillfully that it's hard to separate the two. Her survey questions are value-laden, her attributions finessed so that the reader can't tell which are her subjects' statements and which her interpretations. The same method is used in reporting on other researchers' data.

A good way to demonstrate these tactics is by comparing Chesler's book with another that treats similar questions, *Mothers Without Custody*, by Geoffrey L. Greif and Mary S. Pabst. Both books are based on the authors' own surveys and interviews with noncustodial mothers. Neither blames the women or considers them "unfit"; both note men's advantages in custody disputes and the male threats that make women's "voluntary" relinquishment of custody not an altogether free choice.

But where Greif and Pabst ask mothers and fathers separately why the men sought custody and divide their answers into two sections, *On Trial* melds the two. Regarding "The Eight Major Reasons Sixty North American Fathers Battled for Child Custody (1960–1981)," Chesler later informs us that "the information I have about these fathers is based on my interviews with their ex-wives." Interviews with fifty-five fathers, only five of whom were the same men discussed by the women above, "confirmed most of my findings."[16]

Not only do the authors' statistics vary monumentally (Greif and Pabst find 16 percent of fathers out for revenge;[17] Chesler sees as many as 62 percent bent on punishment,)[18] their underlying assumptions are like night and day. Where Pabst and Greif refer to "competent" fathers and name paternal love and concern as the main motivation for seeking custody, good fathers seem barely to exist for Chesler. She terms the rare loving father "maternal," as if fathering were nothing but mothering in drag. And in describing their parenting styles, Chesler calls 100 percent of her women "traditional" parents, while the men are either "traditional patriarchs," "peer-buddies," or "smother-fathers."

In Chesler's world, a father who wants custody must be a tyrant, a big baby who needs his child as a friend, or an overbearing competitor with the child's mother. To win their love and loyalty he must brainwash, bribe, or physically intimidate his kids. After all, what child would freely choose to live with such a man—a stranger in a car, loitering outside the schoolyard and proffering drugged lollipops, a white slaver driven by narcissism: a kidnapper.

• • •

While battles rage in the divorce courts, on another front another Abductor is sneaking up on unsuspecting women and, allegedly, snatching their children. In the new businesses of technologically aided reproduction and surrogate motherhood, say groups like FINNRAGE (Feminist International Network of Resistance to Reproductive and Genetic Engineering), mad scientists and arrogant sperm donors are taking yet-to-be-born children hostage and holding a scalpel to the fetuses' necks, extorting women to comply with men's demands.

Like the women who are fighting male custody awards, women's suspicion about the reproductive technologies and the people (mainly men) who profit from inflated claims of their efficacy are often justified. Women, after all, have struggled for years to seize childbirth from the medical experts and return it to mothers. After all, infertility, the disease requiring all these medical remedies, is often the iatrogenic result of other "salutary" medical technologies like intrauterine devices and DES, or of botched gynecologic surgery.

Yet thousands of infertile women (even feminists!) have put their bodies and souls in the hands of the practitioners Barbara Katz Rothman calls the "technodocs." Their feelings about in vitro fertilization, embryo implants, and hormone treatments are bound to be ambivalent—fearful and hopeful, angry and grateful all at once. "Women want other things from reproductive technology than merely to get off our backs," says anthropologist Rayna Rapp.[19]

Still, FINNRAGE and its enraged sisters speak unconditionally for women. "We did not ask for these technologies. We do not need them. They are produced at our expense," said a German women at one of the group's conferences. Constructing a world chillingly similar to the fictional Republic of Gilead in Margaret Atwood's *The Handmaid's Tale,* they attribute to men little innocent interest in childbearing and child rearing. Rather, they see men as sadistic torturers in white coats, binding women by tubes and straps to their hospital beds, feeding them propaganda intravenously, and releasing them only when they've fulfilled their function as barefoot, pregnant slaves.

"In reality we live in a world dominated by men and the interests of men," says sociologist Jalna Hammer.

Every aspect of women's reproduction is controlled in a very collective way in the interest of their continuing power domination over women . . . [We] need to explore the interpenetration [interesting word—JL] of professional and scientific groups with state, political, and financial support. We need to know how dominant ideology is used to further scientific and medical control over women. We need to understand how women are silenced, our complicity and collusion assured, and how our challenges are undercut.[20]

Anthropologists and philosophers have theorized that patrilinearity and patriarchal marriage (with its function of policing women's sexual lives) evolved out of men's envy of female fertility and their need to establish ownership of the offspring whose paternity they otherwise couldn't be sure of. But that envy, say others, runs deeper still. Mary O'Brien, in *The Politics of Reproduction*, argues that for women reproduction is a continuous experience from sex through birth and beyond, whereas for men it is discontinuous: ejaculation is separated from birth by nine months and then rewarded only by that profound uncertainty. Maternity is an experience, paternity an abstraction. Women are the perpetuators of the cycles of human natural life, and compared to such a bond, the law and custom that connect men to those cycles are filaments. Generations move through women's bodies; they travel under men's names, lightly.[21]

Elaborating on O'Brien's theory, journalist Gena Corea argues that man has developed obstetrics, gynecology, and the new reproductive sciences to mitigate his alienation, to assuage an "unbearable" sense of his "nullity as a parent."[22] Like Jane Alpert, Corea designates woman the gender with, man the one without; again, man is the Aristotelian female.

Technology offers a man a sense of genetic continuity over time in several ways, Corea says: by freezing his sperm in a sperm bank he can presumably "father" children even after death; by practicing sex determination ("[e]nsuring the birth of a son, a man assures himself a form of immortality"); and, someday, by cloning an "exact replica" of himself. Already, contends Corea, technology is creating a male-controlled "dismembered motherhood."

Women's claim to maternity is being loosened; man's claim to paternity strengthened. Moreover, these techniques are creat-

*ing for women the same kind of discontinuous reproductive
experience men now have . . .*
    *As paternity always has been, maternity is becoming an
act of intellect—for example, making a causal connection between the extraction of an egg and the birth of a child to another woman nine months later. Meanwhile, those men who
extract eggs, culture them, transfer embryos, surgically birth
babies, or control the dials on the artificial womb will have a
more continuous reproductive experience than men have ever
before had.*

These men would "bring forth life through 'art' rather than
nature [which I would also put in quotes], and enable a man to be
not only the father, but also the mother of his child."[23] In Corea's
dystopia, Phyllis Chesler's "maternal" father would become an actual mother. Beyond kidnapping his already born-and-raised children, the Abductor would steal motherhood itself.

Along with the anonymous technicians in hidden laboratories, the
Prenatal Abductors count among their numbers those identifiable
men who have utilized the technologies and new social arrangements of childbearing to their advantage. In recent years, the most
newsworthy of these men has been William Stern, who with his
wife, Dr. Elizabeth Stern, hired Mary Beth Whitehead to be artificially inseminated, carry, and give birth to his biological child. When
Whitehead gave birth, she waffled on her decision to give up the
baby (whom she called Sara and the Sterns called Melissa); when the
Sterns pressured her, she and her family became fugitives, the Sterns
got a warrant that allowed the police to enter the Whiteheads' home
and seize the baby, and a hugely publicized custody battle began—
which Mary Beth Whitehead lost.
    The battle, conducted in Bergen County, New Jersey, in the
first half of 1987, focused attention on a tangle of legal, moral, and
political issues, and forced people to reexamine profoundly felt an-
cient beliefs about the sanctity of childbearing, the nature of parenthood, and the sources and possibilities of love and duty between
generations.
    Many feminists, ethicists, and legal scholars were asking them-
selves the same questions: Where, if anywhere, did Mary Beth

Whitehead's claim to the baby lie? Is pregnancy a relationship? Is there such a thing as prenatal bonding? If so—and there is—should the gestation of a fetus and the birthing of a child, absent a further connection, privilege the woman's claim to parenthood?

And what about Bill Stern's? Can sperm donation be considered the social equivalent of pregnancy even if it is not the biological or emotional equivalent? A man who masturbates into a bottle and anonymously donates his sperm for money may fairly be denied paternity rights. But how about the man who deliberately artificially inseminates a woman, then expectantly waits for his baby to be born? When the baby is born, does he already have a relationship with it too? As in the debates around divorce, uncertain tradeoffs were being considered: women's claim to parental rights for men's assumption of parental obligations, the privileged status conferred by biology for an equal status socially negotiated.

The Baby M case muddled the issues of surrogate motherhood almost beyond recognition. The real people, eminently unstereotypeable, kept getting in the way of the abstractions. Whitehead was not pure enough to make a good heroine, and her plight was too tragic for a villain's. Stern was too nice to be the bad guy, but his righteousness and genetic hubris disqualified him as a hero. Personally, I wondered what kind of man would want so badly to have his "own" child as to involve a woman he didn't know in carrying out, for only ten thousand dollars, a life-endangering project and then hound her when she decided she'd made a grave mistake. On the other hand, he seemed to have fallen in love with the baby as hard as Mary Beth had. Frequently seen shuttling the chubby, snowsuited infant back and forth (Betsy was rarely in evidence), he was obviously willing to go to enormous pain and expense to keep her.

The Mother Rightists, in a group called the Committee for Mary Beth Whitehead (which included Corea and Chesler, along with playwright Karen Malpede, novelist Lois Gould, and prominent Canadian lawyer and antipornography activist Kathleen Lahey), nevertheless managed to make Stern the emblem of all contractual fathers—by implication, all fathers—and Whitehead of all mothers.

Their leaflets and press releases, the amicus curiae brief they submitted along with Jeremy Rifkin's Foundation on Economic Trends, and Chesler's book, *The Sacred Bond: The Legacy of Baby M*, mounted a major assault on the Abductor by striving to re-cement maternity to motherhood and undermine the developing faith in the connection between paternity and fatherhood. "The paramount importance of the mother's claim grows out of the bonding and attachment arising through the gestation period and after birth, relationships of critical importance to the wellbeing of mother and child that can be experienced only by the biological mother, not the father," states the brief.

Chesler proclaimed a "sacred bond" of mother and child surpassing any other, from conception unto death. In a fulmination against adoption, alarming not least for its anachronism, she asked:

> Is the need to return to the birth mother a biological drive, an instinctive or evolutionary force? Is it possible, "all other things being equal," that most human beings need their birth mothers, that a surrogate will not do as well?
> . . . Is it possible that a child's own birth mother is meant for that child; that premature physical separation from that mother—even by the child's genetic father—will cause trauma and injury?[24]

If a reader wonders under what star this mother-and-child union, or reunion, is ordained, the answer is not far behind. For, when not appealing to a pious sentimentality for Dear Old Mom, these Mother Rightists allude, perhaps unconsciously, to God. Here, they tread almost in lockstep with the fundamentalist Christians whom they claim to oppose. Both groups evoke a "natural" and eternal order of mothering and fathering. When challenged as to its origin, both must fall back on preordination. In the committee's propaganda, as in *The Sacred Bond* (whose title could easily caption a Sunday school text illustration) the themes of religious sacrifice and maternal sanctity recur, over and over.

> Let us give up something until Mary Beth and her daughter Sara are reunited. [Are we being asked to fast? Renounce meat or sex?]

> Let us give up our feeling of powerlessness [shift, via buzzword, to feminist sentiment].
> Let us each write to express our feelings on this case.

*Let us each send $1.00 plus our letter to The Friends of Mary
Beth Whitehead.*[25]

The fund appeal is almost funny: change the specifics and you could be reading an appeal from Jim and Tammy Bakker. But the homiletic cadence (unmistakably Chesler's) is an artful strategy. Strictly secular, it appeals subliminally to God—and so also to Nature —both of which imply loftier causes, higher moralities. Religious sentiment reinforces the secular political aims.

Religious allusions are not always even as subtle as this. "Who will cast the first stone?" reads one press release. In it, Mary Beth suddenly becomes "Mary," a name she is not usually called: "Mary is not a murderer. She has not abused or abandoned her children. She is our 'Mary,' the mother of a child who happens to have no genetic relationship to her legal husband."[26] An intriguing mixture of allusions—the first, "casting the first stone," to Mary Magdalene, the second to the Virgin. Whitehead is either a good whore, selflessly donating her body, or she is a Madonna, giving birth to a child chastely conceived—something of a miracle, if only a run-of-the-mill medical miracle. The tacit equation of Stern to Joseph is interesting too, calling up the paradigmatic Christian tale of paternal irrelevance.

"A child can be used as a symbolic credential, a sentimental object, a badge of self-righteousness," wrote Adrienne Rich. Here, the Mother Rightists superimpose the sweet face of Mary, chaste and self-sacrificing, over the gritty but saintly Mary Magdalene, over the not-so-saintly Mary Beth Whitehead. By the virtues of victimhood and motherhood, she becomes pious and humble, the deliverer of a message to humankind. And Bill Stern is petty and petulant, a jealous cipher, like Joseph.

Whitehead and her supporters took to referring to Stern as "the sperm donor," synecdoche for all mere "biological" fathers, whether they jerk off into a jar or directly into a woman's vagina. Sometimes they called him "Bill Sperm," reducing the person to a spurt of jism.

What could such a man—Man—do, fallen from mighty patriarch to humiliated "nullity," consigned to biological Otherhood? What could he be, his organ defined by Mother Rightists as nearly vestigial to the real survival of the species? What else but invader, desperado, every-other-Sunday father, kidnapper: Abductor?

3

The Beast

Nothing is more material, physical, corporeal than the exercise of power.

Michel Foucault, Power/Knowledge[1]

The Brute

SEDUCTION AND ABANDONMENT ARE A KIND of negotiation, wildly anarchic yet circumscribed by the protocols of money, morality, and law. Promises, prizes, alliances, betrayals, and revenges are traded on a rickety bridge, near to but not in the bloodiest theater of battle between the sexes. The Betrayers are volatile, wily, and conniving diplomats of masculinity. They employ politics and brinkmanship; rape is their deterrent, their Big One. Women, who have their own diplomatic dossiers and ready arsenals, threaten to withhold, to torture sexually, ultimately to castrate. Still, most of the negotiations of seduction are pleasurable and heady, and in them these threats are abstract; fear is a memory or an apprehension, a fantasy, even, as we've seen, a joke.

The Brute is the ogre under that bridge, and his weapon is real: rape. Representing predatory, rapacious, implacable, and misogynistic male sexuality, the Brute embodies what every man *could* do to every woman, and crucial to his efficacy as a terrorist is his penchant for disguise. The rapist could be the elevator man, a distant uncle, the flower-bearing friend of a friend. (As many as 75 percent of rapes are committed by someone the woman knows.) He's a Big Man on Campus, the all-American boy next door: sports stars and fraternity boys, say campus rape counselors, are responsible for more than their share of sexual assaults.[1] In fact, he's even closer to home than that. According to *Ms.* magazine, one in seven married women is raped by her husband.[2]

Clinicians have been remarkably unsuccessful in defining, and thus confining, the sexual offender as deviant. Personality profiles, family histories, genetic testing, the usual indicators of pathology, have not reliably predicted a syndrome of sex offense. Psychologist Judith Lewis Herman, a respected authority on violence against women, says that even the popular "cycle of abuse" theory—that a battered or molested child becomes a battering or raping adult—isn't a totally reliable standard. The rapist *is* distinguished by his notably sexist attitudes (but then too are many nonraping judges, clergymen, and Congressmen). In almost all ways he is notably "normal." One therapist who treats offenders told Dr. Herman:

> *I look at the case file and then I look at the offender and the two don't connect. The offenders are often bright, attractive, they take care of themselves, they have lots of social skills, and they can appear very competent or they can appear pathetic and hurt. My first reaction on meeting a new offender is always "there must be some mistake. He couldn't have done what his record says he did."[3]*

"They're not all mad dogs," said William Pithers, the director of the Vermont Center for the Prevention and Treatment of Sexual Abuse, when interviewed by *Newsweek*. "Rape is a sick act committed by sane people."[4]

Sane, that is, within a cultural context that views male aggression as sane.

> *Cross-cultural studies have shown that a high prevalence of rape is associated with male dominance. Rape is common in cultures where only a male creator/deity (rather than a couple or a female creator/deity) is worshipped, where warfare is glorified, where women hold little political or economic power, where the sexes are highly segregated, and where care of children is an inferior occupation.[5]*

A cultural context like the United States, in other words, which ranks first for rape among record-keeping countries. Government statistics estimate that an American woman's chances of being sexually assaulted in her lifetime range from one in twelve to one in four. Of the subjects in Diana E. H. Russell's study for the National Institute of Mental Health, 44 percent have been the victims of rape or attempted rape.[6]

Other studies have found that American men widely regard forced sex as okay—strategically advisable and arousing. A significant minority say they'd commit rape if they knew they wouldn't get caught. Recently, of 1,700 Providence, Rhode Island, sixth-to-ninth-graders, a quarter said it was all right for a man to force a woman to have sex if he had spent a lot of money on her. Half said a woman who walks alone at night and dresses seductively is asking to be raped.[7] Rape, to Americans, is evidently entertaining: at the time of this writing, one in eight current Hollywood movies had a rape theme.[8]

Both well known and incomprehensible, the rapist is a prime candidate for stereotyping. As the Brute, the inscrutable rapist becomes knowable; at the same time the too-familiar is distanced, removed to foreignness. Rape, after all, is the confounding of two opposite female expectations. A little girl learns to fear men, from the Big Bad Wolf to the child pornographer, from the boys on the playground to the gangs of teenagers waiting for unsuspecting walkers in the park. Yet she is also indoctrinated to conflate sex with love (boys learn to separate the two). Love's body deployed as weapon makes for the profoundest of cognitive dissonance. Rape is a mind-fuck too.

Sick/normal, foreign/familiar, enemy/friend: women's descriptions of the Brute erupt in oppositions, for which the word *ambivalence* is not quite apt. Andrea Dworkin, preeminent biographer of the Brute, calls normal intercourse rape: the lover is a hater. "The normal fuck by a normal male is taken to be an act of invasion and ownership undertaken in a mode of predation: colonizing, forceful (manly) or nearly violent; the sexual act that by its nature makes her his.[9] Elsewhere she says, "Violence is male. The male is the penis; violence is the penis or the sperm ejaculated from it. What the penis can do it must do forcibly for a man to be a man."[10]

Susan Brownmiller, documenting the staggering universality and perpetuity of male sexual violence against women, gives us sexual violence as a sort of "peacekeeper," in the same sense as Ronald Reagan used the expression to describe his favorite missile.

> We cannot work around the fact that in terms of human anatomy the possibility of forcible intercourse incontrovertibly exists. This single factor may have been sufficient to have caused the creation of a male ideology of rape. When men discovered they could rape, they proceeded to do it.
> . . . Man's discovery that his genitalia could serve as a weapon to generate fear must rank as one of the most important discoveries of prehistoric times, along with the use of fire

and the first crude stone axe. From prehistoric times to the present, I believe, rape has played a critical function. It is nothing more or less than a conscious process of intimidation by which all men keep all women in a state of fear.[11]

These arguments reduce themselves to a bleak tautology: men rape because they are men. And as long as they can, they will.

In cultures where women are the most sexually vulnerable and restricted, male bestiality is correspondingly more accepted as a given. Yet where sex is veiled, his power is that much more magical, strange. Mexican women and Texan Chicanas, for instance, tell the tales of what anthropologist Rosán A. Jordan calls "the vaginal serpent"—the *chirrioneras,* snakes, water dogs (or axolotls), lizards, or salamander larvae that make their way into a woman and impregnate her.

> . . . *And there was this girl that was real young, and some kind of animal got inside of her, and so she got pregnant; and she was like she was pregnant. She had morning sickness and she started getting fat, so her parents thought that she had been running around with a boy, you know, that somebody had gotten her pregnant. They used to beat her up and try to get her to tell who the boy was that was responsible for her condition . . .*
>
> *So this went on for some time, a few months, and so one day they went out to town or someplace and they locked her in the house, and when they came back—they were gone I guess a couple of days or so—and when they came back they found it, that she had given birth to a whole bunch of little animals, and they were eating her up, and she was dead.*[12]

In the Ozarks, Jordan heard of a woman who had swallowed some "balls" her husband found in a creek and gave birth to a water moccasin six feet long and almost ten inches thick. She was "never again the same in the head."[13]

This lore reflects anxiety and fear, sadness and anger, at the male abuses of women, and surely despair: "[The women in the stories] suffer, are humiliated, and are vindicated only in dying," says Jordan. "The narratives . . . reveal a certain degree of self-hatred in women and a distrust of their own sexuality," she adds. "Women's sexual nature, they seem to say, is instrumental in bringing about her suffering."[14]

To me, the tales resound just as loudly with feelings about *men's* sexual nature—that man is a threatening and sneaky beast, his penis a slimy thing which forcibly plants a seed of suffering, presaging even more horrors, more oppression. Sex will drive a woman crazy, if not kill her. Given the alternatives, she is safer chaste.

Storytelling about a magical Brute is not confined to remote parts of the world; it is a regular feature of those repositories of modern folklore, the tabloids. Almost weekly, the tabs' headlines announce, "My Baby Was a Snake/Dog/Monster/Alien." The *Weekly World News* recently reported the birth, to sixteen-year-old Zairian Miki Jack, of a half-human, half-baboon infant. Jack "now admits" she was attacked by the baboon outside her village. However, she says she was "almost sure" the baby she was carrying was her boyfriend, Komani Lumumba's, adding a hint of racism to this allegory of male bestiality: could the simian baby be the black man's child?

Like other gender stereotypes, the Brute is endowed with the attributes of "inferior" classes and races, compounding his alienness and fearfulness. Stablemen, gamekeepers, circus-animal trainers, and cowboys in literature high and low are the bestial objects of forbidden desire, and the sources of terror. Living with the animals (or, in the case of chauffeurs, with their mechanized equivalents), these men presumably develop eating, sleeping, sanitary, and sexual arrangements like the bulls' and stallions'—instinctual, impulsive, volatile, and potentially violent.

The story of slavery (which literally used humans as beasts) and white racist terrorism in American is vividly illustrated with images of the black Brute, who had to be chained by his master lest he defile chaste white womanhood. When in 1892 the great black antilynching crusader Ida B. Wells published her first documentation of the hundreds of black men mob-murdered for allegedly raping white women, rumors of freed slaves marauding across the land were rampant. These men "found something strangely alluring and seductive in the appearance of White women," wrote Philip A. Bruce, a leading "expert" at the time. According to historian Paula Giddings, similar rhetoric was published so widely and in such reputable journals and magazines that the likes of the reformer and lynching opponent Jane Addams, and even some African-Americans themselves, began to wonder whether black men really did have a penchant for rape.[15] In the same period, turmoil among suffragists over the Fifteenth Amendment, which gave the vote to black men but not to women of any race, stirred the same racist suspicions. Invoking the story of an African-American man lynched in Tennessee for allegedly raping a white woman, the white suffragist Elizabeth Cady Stanton fulminated that the vote would make black men more uppity and more violent: "The Republican cry of 'Manhood Suffrage' creates an antagonism between black men and all women that will culminate in fearful outrages on womanhood"—in other words, rape.

A century later, prominent male thinkers of the 1960s black power movement, like poet Imamu Amiri Baraka (LeRoi Jones), psychologist Frantz Fanon, and sociologist Calvin Hearnton, raised the specter of the black Brute themselves, when they variously described rape of white women as a psychologically understandable or politically legitimate act. Eldridge Cleaver, after "practicing" on the African-American women in his neighborhood, enacted this revolutionary appropriation of the white man's property, pontificating at length on its correctness in *Soul on Ice.*

Surely many black women were outraged by these men's pronouncements, but few came out and said so. When Michele Wallace did, in *Black Macho and the Myth of Superwoman,* the book was roundly panned for its "anti-male" attitudes and the author accused of betraying her race. A decade later, the feature film of Alice Walker's *The Color Purple,* which tells of black-on-black sexual abuse, garnered similar criticism. Walker, like Wallace, was accused of airing the community's dirty linen—violence against women being one of the filthier items, as it is in all communities—to an already racist white public, and of conspiring with a white women's movement against her own brothers.

Of the film, the charge of appealing to white racism may have been partly true—but directed against the wrong person. In filmmaker Steven Spielberg's telling, Mister is a Brute from start to finish. In Walker's, he undergoes a transformation as near-miraculous as

Celie's: as she grows into a powerful articulate woman, he becomes humble, tender, and nonviolent.

But male critics who worried that African-American women were conspiring with white feminists could not have been farther from the mark. Deep differences had divided black and white women activists throughout American history, and, as I will discuss further in "Sisterhood and the Patriarch," the second wave of feminism was no exception.[16] When the white women's movement did set out to fight sexual violence—which afflicts women of all races and classes equally—some black women discerned racism in its analyses.

Susan Brownmiller's ambiguous treatment of black-on-white rape could not have laid black women's misgivings to rest. While admitting that the crime is a statistical unlikelihood (almost eight of ten white rape victims are raped by white men), she nonetheless dealt with it as a significant phenomenon—and not only for its role in the white imagination. Appropriately outraged by the story of Emmett Till, a fourteen-year-old black boy who was lynched in 1968 for whistling at a white woman in Money, Mississippi (his murderers were acquitted by an all-male, all-white jury, although everyone in town knew they did it), her conjectures about what was going on in the teenager's mind were bound to raise eyebrows:

> *We are rightly aghast that a whistle could be cause for murder but we must also accept that Emmett Till and J. W. Millam [one of the lynchers] shared something in common.* They both understood that *the whistle was no small tweet of hubba-hubba or melodious approval for a well-turned ankle . . . [I]t was a deliberate insult* just short of physical assault, *a last reminder to Carolyn Bryant that this black boy,* Till, had in mind to possess her [emphases mine].[17]

Is Brownmiller's analysis racist? In one way, no: she imputes violent fantasies and motivations to men throughout the book, men of all races. Yet inasmuch as she represents a particular white-feminist tendency of the early 1970s—to place sexism above racism in a "hierarchy of oppression"—she is as racist as any of her sisters at the time.

For the white antiviolence movement, this subtly racist theoretical stance had its manifestations in practice. While women of color were being served as clients in rape crisis centers, when it came to employment and decision-making in organizations and service agencies, the ranks were white. There were exceptions, such as the Rape Crisis Center in Washington, D.C., one of the country's first. Loretta Ross, a longtime activist in African-American and feminist politics who directed the center in the early eighties, explains how the chain reaction of segregation was interrupted.

> *The center had such a precious history. It had been founded almost entirely by white women . . . They saw that 90 percent of the clients were black women, because this was Washington, D.C. So they made a commitment to give up their staff positions and they codified in the bylaws that the staff of the center would have to reflect the population that it serves . . .*
>
> *Our particular history forced us to find [black] women in other movements and then convert them to feminism. If you constantly only look for feminists, you constantly only get white women . . . They had to go find me in the housing movement and convert me to feminism. The woman who was the director before me, she was the defense captain in the Black Panther Party . . . Now she's a lifelong feminist like I am. But without that special effort, it wouldn't have happened.*

The antiviolence movement, which has become a network of shelters, crisis centers, and advocacy groups, is far more integrated than it once was; in addition, groups like Women Against Violence Everywhere (WAVE) in New York, and the National Black Women's Health Project, with branches in several cities, are organizing on a grass-roots level in communities of color.

Still, the rift between those who charge sexism and those who charge racism has not by any means been bridged. This fact was painfully evident during the much-publicized 1990 "Central Park jogger" case in New York. When a group of African-American teenage boys were accused of the vicious gang rape of a promising white stockbroker and marathon runner, the mainstream press played on the image of barbaric black youth out of control—picking up the dubiously accurate coinage *wilding* to describe the rampage of robbery and terror the boys were said to have carried out that night. The "woman's angle" was played down; this was a racial issue, according to the press and large segments of the public.

Including, apparently, many African-American New Yorkers.

Their suspicion raised by the paucity of forensic proof and their ire roused by the racially prejudiced attention the case was receiving (a black rape victim was thrown off a roof by her attackers the same week and the story hardly made the papers), some blacks denied that the attack even happened. Outside the courtroom, supporters of the defendants chanted, "[Her] boyfriend did it, [her] boyfriend did it." The self-appointed leaders of this support group, lawyer Alton Maddox and the Reverend Al Sharpton, grandstanded the same claim. In an interview on the black-owned radio station WLIB, Maddox said, "I have not seen any evidence of this woman being assaulted or attacked at all . . . What are we going to do, accept some white person's word that she's over there [at the hospital]? . . . This whole thing could be an outright hoax."[18] The *Amersterdam News,* New York's major African-American newspaper, frequently referred to the "alleged" rape.

If whites were going to conjure black youths as Brutes, the boys' defenders would counterattack with representations of white women (and, one can fairly infer, all rape victims) as liars. The failure of women to join together in challenging these propagandistic outrages speaks as much of shared sexual intimidation by men as of mutual racial alienation among women, not least those organized in their own defense.

Assigning wildness to people of color is as old as all lore, as is the association of wildness (Nature) with irrationality and evil. The "savage" Caliban is untamed, wicked Nature to Prospero's art, culture, and decency; "civilizing" the natives is the ideological justification for the outright theft that is colonialism.

Classically, Woman is categorized along with the "darker" races as untamable Nature. She is a Force that floats, blows, or flows. She is the moon, whirlpools, and weather systems (hurricanes have only belatedly been given men's names, an odd sop to feminism). She's a creature, stupidly bovine, flightily birdlike, and feline—sly and sexually treacherous.

The Brute, like so many other misandric stereotypes, turns that phenomenology on its head. Large, furry, muscular, rodentine, scaly, slimy, or insectlike, ravenous and panting, Man becomes the uncivilized Other; to Woman's culture, *he* is Nature.

If men are Brutes bent on harm, in order to be safe women must get them out of the way or stay out of their way—cage them, hunt them down and shoot them, exile or confine them to preserves.

Historically, one faction of feminists and moral reformers have taken the first tack. Constructing practically every form of male sexual expression from seduction to pornography as a violation of women, they've striven through religion and politics, law and civil disobedience, to protect women from it. Unable to imagine a social transformation of masculinity and femininity and daunted by the conditions that promote sexual exploitation, these women have rejected the ideal of sexual egalitarianism through equal opportunity. To them, men are oversexed; women, rather than repressed, are sexually overtaxed, and deserving of legal protection.

Furthermore, as we saw in The Abandoner, unbridled sexuality is in this view male by definition. To resist male advances, then, is to defend not only women's freedom to move unmolested through the world, but also to defend one's very femaleness. Not to do so—for instance, by tolerating pornography and suggesting that women might even enjoy it—is, more than a traitorous act against women, an attempt to *be* male. Of her fellow antipornography activists, lawyer Catherine A. MacKinnon writes, "A concept of sex equality that opposes the intimate violation of women for the sexual pleasure of predators speaks to something real in these women's lives that the aspiration to live a male biography did not." She could have been talking about protectionist feminists down through the centuries.

The Female Moral Reform Society, founded in New York in 1834, had as its express goals closing the city's brothels and converting their denizens to evangelical Protestantism. At the same time it aimed to cleanse every American home of all forms of licentiousness—from lewd thoughts to adultery. From their "angry and emphatic insistence upon the lascivious and predatory nature of the American male" no man was excluded, writes the historian Carroll Smith-Rosenberg. Their newspaper, *The Advocate,* described women in glowing tones: they were "open-hearted, sincere, and affectionate," "unsuspecting lambs" gazing unsuspectingly into the jaws of the deceiving wolf. In their view Man, says Smith-Rosenberg, was "a creature controlled by base sexual drives which he neither could nor would control."[19] Presaging efforts in the 1980s to outlaw pornography as a form of "victimization of women," the society lobbied for a bill, passed in 1848, making seduction (by their lights indistinguishable from rape) a criminal offense.

The ladies of the Society, reciting from the Bible at the brothel door, looked the epitome of Victorian prudery, and in one sense they were: their thinking reinforced, and sought legally and educationally to enforce, a strict division of gender roles and a single moral standard for men and women—presumably, women's. Yet in another way they were radicals: in a time when sex was hardly discussed in private, these prefeminist reformers also advanced a courageously public critique of male sexual domination and the double standard.

This contradiction, between an implicit ratification of essential gender difference and a radical rejection of the inequality which is its consequence, would repeat itself over and over through history. "Men almost universally have a greater desire for sex than women do; they are less discriminating in terms of time, place and choice of object than women are," wrote Abby Rockefeller in an early 1970s tract with the nihilistic title "Sex: The Basis of Sexism." "It is this divergence of inclination which, moreover, constitutes the basis of the oppression of women by men."

For the Brute to exist, he must have a victim. If his crime is desire itself, this analysis implies, then she must be a creature without desire.

Like their nineteenth-century ancestors who indicted prostitution as the central agent of female exploitation whose eradication would free women from sexual danger, contemporary crusaders home in on pornography as "a condensed metaphor for female degradation," in the words of historian and journalist Lisa Duggan. Women Against Pornography and its allies argue that sexually explicit imagery is the *cause* of misogyny and violence against women —and indeed *is* violence against women—and not the other way around. In the 1980s their efforts to scour the cities of smut won enthusiastic support not only from fanatic Bible-thumpers but from conservative lawmakers as well, and at the height of the movement's legitimacy Andrea Dworkin and Catherine MacKinnon were employed by the cities of Minneapolis and Indianapolis to draft ordinances making pornography a form of sex discrimination and a civil offense.

Relying on a few controversial clinical findings, the drafters asserted that looking at dirty pictures makes men want to rape and predisposes them to child sex abuse and battery. Significantly, it is images of sex, and not unsexy violence, the reformers wanted outlawed. The Brute is allegedly incited by tits and cunts laid out passively like pork chops on a plate. Images of blood pouring from bodies mutilated by Uzis, kitchen knives, or chain saws are bad too, but they're worse if those bodies are female. Male (one assumes, heterosexual) sexuality, in other words, is inextricable from male violence.

The wording of the ordinances, which are a distillation of almost a decade's worth of theory and rhetoric, define porn broadly and vaguely—a long list includes images of "women in postures or positions of submission, servility, or display" (lying on a bed moaning "fuck me"?) and depictions of women as "whores by nature" (flirting with strangers in bars?). All participation in pornography, moreover, is by definition coerced, even if "the person knew that the purpose of the acts or events in question was to make pornography . . . showed no resistance or appeared to cooperate actively," made a verbal or written contract, or was paid.[20] In other words, a woman, totally compos mentis, cannot willingly consent to commercialized sex acts; the societally brainwashed female cannot make that decision rationally, based on economic need or—heaven forfend!—desire.

Interestingly, when the antiporn campaigns lost steam (the Minneapolis ordinance was passed by the city council and vetoed by the mayor; in Indianapolis the bill passed, was appealed, and was declared unconstitutional) WAP resurfaced, this time with no less august a backer than the United Nations. Its new crusade is against international "trafficking in women," which, on closer examination, turns out to be a scary name for prostitution in other countries. Just as the antiporners indiscriminately condemned all sexually explicit material from soft core to snuff films, this campaign targets all forms of commercial sex, from the indentured servitude of Filipina teenagers in Subic Bay to the weekend tricking of a London call girl working her way through art school. Also like their former incarnation, the antitrafficking groups see all women in the sex business as victims of men rapacious for profit as for sex, almost quaintly resembling their nineteenth-century forefathers, the white slavers.

Throughout the centuries, same "crime," same unwitting victims, same Brute.

There are many women (whether they countenance porn or not) who don't trust the cops and the courts to protect them from sexual violence. These women prefer to take the law into their own hands; to them, vigilantism is the answer. One antiporn leaflet identifies "Vulnerable Areas on Your Attacker's Body—and What You Can Do to deliver a body blow to the Pimp and Rapist-in-Chief." On it a photo of a naked man with *Penthouse* publisher Bob Guccione's face and a camera with a telephoto lens for a penis is surrounded by instructions such as "Snap knee into groin, or grab testicles, twist and pull," and "Tense your fingers and bend them slightly—jab straight into the eyes." The broadsheet is distributed by the "Outlaws for Social Responsibility."

Shame, an Australian film written by Deborah Lee, tells the story of a young woman gang-raped in a small town. She is beleaguered; even her family collaborates in hushing up the crime. Then, just when she is about to succumb to terminal distress, her rescuer zooms into town on a motorcycle. But this black-leathered biker turns out to be . . . a lawyer! The perfect man, tough but tenderhearted, except for this decidedly modern twist: he's a she. The film has a dark denouement—the victim is killed by the enraged men of the town—and a moral: don't look to men's law for protection, for men protect only each other in a conspiracy of violence against women.

The action in *A Question of Silence,* made by the Dutch filmmaker Marleen Gorris and released in the United States in 1983, begins when three women shoppers are, independently of each other, irritated by the male shopkeeper. Not a word is exchanged among them, but they surround him and kill him. Scanter than their apparent motivation is their remorse. As the trial progresses, two testify that they'd reached the ends of their ropes; sexism made them do it. The other remains silent. Then, on the witness stand, she slowly begins to laugh. She laughs and laughs; soon she is cackling maniacally. The female spectators in the courtroom join her—and, in the theater where I saw the film, so did the women in the audience. As their laughter rose, the men beside them, like those on the screen, seemed to shrink into their seats. This laughter, not the murder, is the cathartic moment of shock and recognition in *A Question of Silence*. It is enraged, vengeful, barbaric, anarchic. It reflects the absurdity of the film's premise—that women would get together and spontaneously do violence to men (as men commonly do to women). But it is also hysterical, despairing. It is the mad giggling of a sex that finds itself, like visitors to a modern zoo which lets the beasts roam free and puts the people in moving cages, surrounded by violence yet entrapped, entrapped by its own "protection."

Women who sojourn in an all-female environment—a woman's conference or music festival—often comment on the relief, energy, and serenity they feel. It comes as a surprise—the sudden absence of fear. Women's fictional utopias understandably have often exiled the Brute to the outlands, establishing free zones where sex is egalitarian and lesbian, and sexual violence is unknown.

Some women's speculative fiction creates worlds in which gender assignments are reversed or nonexistent. In Egalia, the land imagined by the Norwegian writer Gerd Brantenberg, the "wim" are burly, surly, and warlike; they keep the "menwim" under their thumbs, forcing them to cook and clean and mind the babies, teaching them to be ashamed of their bodies, and, well, you know the rest. And the "wim" rape:

> *He felt the cold metal against his stomach. She cut the waistband, pulled off his peho and threw it to one of the others, who caught it. She tore the cloth and threw it away. One was on top of him now. She smelt of alcohol and sweat. She grabbed his penis and thrust her nipple into his mouth. He felt her wet crotch against his thigh . . . The grip on his penis tightened. She was breathing hard against his ear, bouncing violently up and down, forcing his thigh against her crotch, pumping and moaning. He looked up at the others in desperation. Were they just going to stand and watch without helping him?[21]*

The Gethenians of Winter, the glacial planet of Ursula K. Le Guin's *Left Hand of Darkness*, are androgynous—the result, a foreign investigator conjectures, of an experiment long ago. For about a fifth of each twenty-six-day cycle, the Gethenians' sexuality is dormant; during the other five days, when they go into "kemmer," they may assume either maleness or femaleness. Without gender, life is entirely different. "Consider," says the observer, a woman:

> There is no division of humanity into strong and weak halves, protective/protected, dominant/submissive, owner/chattel, active/passive. In fact, the whole tendency to dualism that pervades human thinking may be found to be lessened, or changed, on Winter.[22]

There is no division of labor, no rape, and no war. The observer wonders:

> Did the ancient Hainish postulate that continuous sexual capacity and organized social aggression, neither of which are attributes of any mammal but man, are cause and effect? Or, like Tumass Song Angot, did they consider war to be a purely masculine displacement-activity, a vast Rape, and therefore in their experiment eliminate the masculinity that rapes and the femininity that is raped? God knows.[23]

Both Brantenberg and Le Guin suggest that sexual violence is the product not of masculinity, but of gender itself.

Other writers, however, place the responsibility for violence in men's hands, communicating that as long as there are men in it, the world won't be free of rape and war. How can women reach this man-free peaceful state?

Some, writes Adrienne Harris, solve the dilemma—"the price of peace is the eradication of men"—by killing them off nonviolently.[24] The Hill Women of *The Wanderground* by Sally Miller Gearhart fled from the City after "there was one rape too many," leaving most of the men, without female nurture, to perish.

Others, not violent by nature, reluctantly fight fire with fire. The inhabitants of Charlotte Perkins Gilman's Herland (the book of the same title, written in 1915, described one of the earliest feminist utopias) descend from a race of virgins who murdered their male rulers. According to their legend, a huge volcanic eruption walled the country in, killing off most of the army and most of the male masters. The surviving male slaves slew the rest of the masters and set about to enslave the women.

> *But this succession of disasters was too much for those infuri-ated virgins. There were many of them, and but few of these would-be masters, so the young women, instead of submit-ting, rose in sheer desperation and slew their brutal conquer-ors.*[25]

Or the writer preserves one violent woman, a cautionary mem-ory of times past. Seja in *The Wanderground* is a former warrior, who is still driven into a bloodlusty frenzy by the memory of rape. In *The Female Man* Joanna Russ gives us the man-killer Jael of Womanland, a country perennially at war with Manland. She is the last avenger, murdering men with her stainless-steel fingernails. Like Seja, Jael "is a sacrifice to the future," writes Harris, "essential to change, but anachronistic and dangerous to the utopian culture she has been instrumental in bringing about."[26]

In these lands, heterosexuality even for the purpose of repro-duction is unimaginable, though lesbian sex goes beyond the bounds of outsiders' imaginations. Herland's babies are produced by parthe-nogenesis, a funny and original idea in Gilman's time. Russ's Janet Evason of Whileaway, who has appeared out of nowhere on Broad-way in New York City, circa now, is set upon by a TV crew and whisked away to a studio, where the host tries to extract information about sex among her countrywomen.

> MC: . . . *and we know that these marriages or tribes form very good institutions for the economic support of the children and for some sort of genetic mixing, though I confess you're way beyond us in the biological sciences. But, Miss Evason, I am not talking about economic institutions or even affectionate ones . . . there is more, much much more—I am talking about sexual love.*
> JE (enlightened): *Oh! You mean copulation!*
> MC: *Yes.*
> JE: *How foolish of you. Of course we do.*
> MC: *Ah? (He wants to say, "Don't tell me.")*
> JE: *With each other. Allow me to explain.*
> *She was cut off instantly by a commercial poetically describing the joys of unsliced bread.*[27]

In Gearhart's tale, the women are not so amused (or amusing). There, the only men with whom women can ally (though cautiously) are the Gentles, who have foresworn all sex. These men realize, along with the Hill women, that "women and men cannot yet, may not ever, love one another without violence; they are no longer of the same species."[28]

Cordoning off the land and keeping the Brute under armed guard is a fantasy not confined to speculative fiction. In "Being Safe," a 1990 *New York Times Magazine* "Hers" column, Patricia Volk recounts the self-defense advice she receives from various men—a karate expert at a kosher resort in the Catskills; her husband, who says, "Stick a finger in the person's eye"; her father, who vows to teach her to use a stun gun. Wielding no weapon but intuition she takes her daughter to the park to sharpen her self-protective instinct of fear. But Volk's ultimate fantasy is of a safety achieved by removing the danger: men. "I think how safe I would feel if women got, say, Manhattan and the Bronx and men got Brooklyn and Queens and people happily married 20 years or more took Staten Island. Women wouldn't have to be afraid any more."[29]

Volk would keep the Brute in a wildlife preserve, separated from civilization by bridges and tunnels. Only domesticated, housebroken animals (pedigreed by marriage) would be trusted to cohabit with women.

The Pet

IF THE BRUTE CAN BE MANAGED AT ALL, it's through religion, medicine, law enforcement, or a violence matching his own. Karate, the Mace can, the shotgun: against the Brute, woman uses the stick, not the carrot.

But Dorothy, the suburban housewife in Rachel Ingalls' *Mrs. Caliban,* employs the opposite tactic. To soothe the savage beast, she proffers carrot, or to be more precise, celery.

> *. . . His eyes were huge and dark, seemingly much larger than the eyes of a human being, and extremely deep. His head was quite like the head of a frog, but rounder, and the mouth was smaller and more centered in the face, like a human mouth . . . The hands and feet were webbed, but not far up . . . and as for the rest of the body, he was exactly like a man—a well-built large man—except that he was dark spotted green-brown in colour and had no hair anywhere . . .*
>
> *She stretched way out across the table, took her eyes off his for an instant and picked up the long stalk of celery next to the knife. The growling stopped. She took a step forward slowly, and held out the celery in front of her . . .*
>
> *"Thank you," he said.*[1]

The vicious Brute who inspires terror and revulsion, militancy or retreat, is only one species of Beast. Another is the Pet, hot-breathed too, perpetually aroused, but never in need of manacling. Like the monster Dorothy calls Larry, the Pet comes humble and hungry to the kitchen door. He's got a raging hard-on, and he'd be much obliged, ma'am, if she'd pay attention to it. A creature of heart as well as hormones, the Pet would be predatory if he weren't so dependent, and so, well, *nice.* "You have to treat men like pets," a woman artist said, condescendingly, but without malice. Feed them, stroke them, scold them when they mess on the carpet, and let them out to run. "Treat them like pets and they won't give you any trouble."

Larry has killed his scientist-torturers in order to break out of the institute that captured him, but he's nonviolent by nature. Dorothy responds to his scrupulous politeness and the soft, firm, warm feel of his green skin. Soon they become lovers. He is tender and straightforward.

> He asked, "Are you frightened?"
> "Of course."
> "I'm not. I feel good. But it's very strange."
> A lot more than strange, she thought. And then: no, it's just the same. They rolled back on the bed.
> "Wait. Not like that," she said.
> "Show me."
> "I'm a bit embarrassed."
> "What does that mean?"
> She didn't really know. What the hell could it mean in such an encounter?[2]

But it's not the same. It's better, "perfect." The Pet wants and he takes, but he'd never cynically seduce or rashly abandon. He has one basic goal, which he'd be happy to go on attaining forever. Judy Straul, a comedienne, talks about dogs. "If they see it, they sniff it. If they like it, they lick it. If they love it, they pee on it," she says affectionately. "Why does that remind me of men?" This is bestiality within measure, the dream of perfect passion: ravenous yet accommodating, endlessly captivated yet requiring no capture.

A Pet may be exotic—a centaur or satyr, dolphin, silky, bear, or android—but his good nature makes him safe. He approaches familiarity, but he is not family. Dorothy hides Larry in the guest room (her husband is not home much; he's having an affair too), feeds him avocado salads, buys him sandals, and modifies a pair of sunglasses to fit his odd head. The two listen to Mozart, watch TV, discuss customs in their respective worlds, and swim together in the ocean at night. They make love, wherever and whenever they can.

Even a couch-potato Pet is not a same-time-next-week lover, however; Larry will eventually swim back to his deep-sea home.

The Pet is Ida Cox's Georgia Hound, who runs around all night, not always bothering to come home. He's Joni Mitchell's "wild thing, running free." He is never, needless to say, a husband.

The Brute's sexual savagery requires women's asexual purity as a foil. Born and raised a wolf, he breaks into the spaniel's kennel and mounts her, running off with his musk lingering in her cage. The Pet's lineage extends back to that marriage of wild dog and lapdog, but as he has become tamer, his bitch has gotten commensurately wilder, discovering her own randy spirits. Theirs is a post-sexual-revolutionary relationship. He arrives at the kennel, hot from a night out with the pack, and she, unperturbed, takes him in and offers him a drink (in a bowl, of course).

The Brute and his mistress have a lot more to negotiate before they can get cozy. The fairy-tale princess, for instance, marries her beast-suitor out of loyalty or obedience to Father, or in honor of a promise of her own. She's not happy about it, privately, but she loves the creature altruistically, in spite of his dirty coat and gamy smell. In the warmth of her pure love, he can shed his frog skin, donkey ears, or bear's fur and reveal the handsome human prince inside (even if, as in "Beauty and the Beast," he is not literally handsome, he has inner spiritual beauty). The woman's purity enables the man to divest himself of his carnality. The princess and the beast consummate their marriage, but it is not exactly a meeting of spirit and body: he attains humanity only in renunciation of animality.

But the Pet affects a woman in the opposite way: he affirms her carnality, so she can revel in it too. The process hasn't reversed itself completely: she's still morally superior, smarter, more rational, more in control, and more psychologically astute. She tolerates him lovingly, but as she would a high-spirited puppy. He's an unruly guest in the woman's civilized sphere. But the welcome mat is out, and he's not required to wipe his paws when he crosses the threshold.

Bear, by the Canadian novelist Marian Engel, is the tale of an archivist who goes to catalog a private library in an old house on a remote island. There, she discovers a pet bear living in the yard. The woman, Lou, is not the sort to be alarmed. She stays in the house, gardens, reads, cooks in the rudimentary kitchen, and grows to love the bear. Their relationship is simple: she feeds him, scratches his fur, and takes him swimming. He lumbers into the house and licks her to orgasm.

But unlike the bears in fairy tales, even unlike Larry, who learns to dance and to vacuum, this bear is undomesticated. He "makes love" to her out of ursine instinct. He does not adjust to her world, she accommodates to his: "As long as she made her stool beside him in the morning, he was ready whenever she spread her legs to him."[3] Lou begins to smell like the bear, and to consider him among the other males she has known.

After their first encounter, she wakes up shaken.

> [H]er sensation of narrow escape was not helped by the fact that it reminded her of a time when, in a fit of lonely desperation, she had picked up a man in the street. She still shied away from the memory of how he had turned out not to be a good man. Surely the bear . . . no: it was fright that linked them, fright and flight.[4]

In fact, she decides, the bear is superior to her previous lovers. "[R]ough and tender, assiduous, patient, infinitely, it seemed to her, kind"[5] he is, unlike many men, equal to her lust, and behaves as if she is equal to his. "[W]hat she disliked in men was not their eroticism, but their assumption that women had none."[6] Having sex with the bear, she doesn't feel debased, but elevated. "She tested herself, pinching her conscience here and there to see if she felt evil. She felt love."[7]

Lou's bear gives her what she most requires, as Blake said, the lineaments of a gratified desire. And that, being so much more than she had ever expected, is sufficiency itself.

> Bear, I cannot command you to love me, but I think you love me. What I want is for you to continue to be, and to be something to me. No more. Bear.[8]

The bear does not continue indefinitely to be something to Lou, however. The winter nears and he readies himself for hibernation. Seeing his erection for the first time, she positions herself for him to mount her. But when he reaches across her back, he claws her, cutting her deeply. Fearing he'll wound her further, she runs to her room and locks the door. The next day, he is "something else: lover, God or friend. Dog too, for when she put her hand out he licked and nuzzled it . . . Something was gone between them, though: the high whistling communion that had bound them during the summer."[9]

It is over, time to return to the city. But their "love" has produced an erotic by-product: a happy, easy assignation with her neighbor, Homer, whom she had at first rejected in deference to the rules of fidelity—his to his wife and hers to the bear. The bear, trusted and unchained, has given her the gift of her own unfettered sexuality.

The bear's bloody swipe at Lou, preventing a final consummation, suggests the limits of dangerous pleasure, and hints at the incompatibility of a thoroughly "animal" sex with civilized communion. Where male erotic art has played with these boundaries—for instance, Rubens' *Leda and the Swan* or Hokusai's woman ravished by an octopus—mostly it depicts rape, to which the victim is usually responding favorably. Female renderings of lovemaking between women and animals are marked by a blend of danger and pleasure, violence and safety. Gail Schneider's paintings, for instance, are soft-colored yet crude and spiky—ghostly animals mounting women, paws on breasts; a crude yellow dog with red tongue licking a brown woman—dream-images, sweet and scary at once.

Art like this edges toward a further-out boundary, the fantasies of sadomasochist bestiality. In Angela Carter's *The Company of Wolves* or the pornography of A. N. Roquelaure (a pseudonym of Anne Rice) wolves, little cats with irresistible tongues, naked male sex slaves harnessed and driven as ponies, are the agents of erotic pleasure, as well as humiliation, degradation, and lascivious pain. In these stories the woman is not only victim of the Beast's bestiality, she is drawn down to her own bestiality.

"I AM THE MOTHER OF BIGFOOT'S BABY," announces the tabloid *The Sun* in a story about the twenty-nine-year-old Annie Porcheza, who is now "torn between aborting her beastly child or allowing its ungodly birth in the name of scientific research." While Annie was on a canoe trip in northwest British Columbia, her boat allegedly capsized and "she found herself tossed into swirling river waters

. . . A warm, rather comfortable feeling came over" her, and eighteen hours later she awakened, lying naked in a cave with a "large hairy creature." After three weeks of captivity, during which the monster was kind to her, she "knew [she] had to escape," and finally did.

The story—so typical of the genre it's practically parodic—not only reveals feelings of revulsion toward male bestiality, but suggests its attraction too. Passionate and caressing erotic language (the swirling waters, the long sleep) alternates with that of capture and terror. Beneath Annie's conflict about whether to keep the baby is her ambivalence about "owning" that attraction to male bestiality— keeping a reminder of her animal love affair or casting it away, returning to safety.[10]

The forbidden ministrations of these creatures are desired—in fact desired *because* forbidden. Like the horses, donkeys, and dogs in the sexual fantasies women confided to Nancy Friday, they act without morality—that is the essence of bestial sexuality—so they allow the women who conjure them to push the limits of sexual permissibility too. Biting, nipping, licking, and impaling their partners on gigantic purple cocks, these Pets belong to the women they pleasure. They do what they're told, or, happily, more; even Bigfoot is a gentle giant. They are trained to pleasure, but take their own pleasure too. They are the bestial appropriated.

Indomitable yet tame, ever exciting yet habituated, foreign yet familiar, the Pet is an impossible contradiction. As a stereotype he embodies women's wish for passion that coexists with commitment, an integration of the sexual and spiritual, the amoral and the ethical, the new and the quotidian, both in women and in men.

And since he's a fantasy, the Pet may be made to order. In fact, no rule says he must be mammalian, reptilian, or for that matter a creature of the natural world at all. Ulysses, in Susan Seidelman's *Making Mr. Right* is just such a Pet. Played by a goofy John Malkovich, he is an android, a man-made astronaut who becomes, under the tutelage of Frankie (Ann Magnuson), a woman-made man.

Cloned from his own creator, the scientist Jeff, Ulysses has had his emotional needs reduced to enable him to withstand months of solitude, and his memory cells increased to consume zillions of bytes of space data. He's also been endowed with superhuman genitals, not intended for use, according to his asexual and (wishfully) vain creator. Of course Frankie discovers the android's equipment—and his innate facility, sans user's manual, to employ it masterfully. (The Pet always has a natural talent for sex and a humble eagerness to learn more.) The story leaks out and the robot becomes a celebrity. "EX-CLUSIVE: ULYSSES RIVALS MEN. 10 SINGLE WOMEN SHARE THEIR SECRETS," the headlines shout. "PRINCESS DI TO BEAR ANDROID'S CHILD."

But as soon as Frankie starts to expose her robotic Pet to the enticements of the human world, he can no longer stand the confines of his sterile laboratory home. He escapes, wreaking havoc on a shopping mall before he can be safely returned. (Similarly, Larry, once he has felt and smelled the park at night, sneaks out in the car and gets into deep trouble.) When Frankie teaches Ulysses to love, he "breaks out" completely: he becomes unfit for solitary space travel. "How's he supposed to survive out there now, when all he thinks about is you?" Jeff demands hysterically as Frankie grins in satisfaction—and anticipation of future satisfaction.[11]

Seidelman has brought the sexy Pet full circle: she has invested him with humanity without diminishing his natural (or in this case, computer-animated) passion. Ulysses yearns for home and hearth; the Beast is in that sense domesticated. But while he wears a tuxedo, eats with a fork, speaks articulately from the heart and even cries real tears, this Pet has not lost his animal instincts. The denouement of *Making Mr. Right* is even happier ever after than the usual walk down the aisle. Frankie's robust robotic Beast, emotionally dependent at heart, remains, in body, forever wild.

The Prick

THE PRICK IS IMPERIOUS, self-centered and self-satisfied, puffed up and truculent. He marches around challenging everybody, knowing everything, posturing and picking fights—whipping it out at the drop of a hat. "To display the penis (or any of its surrogates)," wrote Freud, "is to say: 'I am not afraid of you. I defy you. I have a penis.' "[1]

The *displayed* penis is, of course, erect. It demands service, now. "I was thirty-five years old before I learned an erection was not an affliction I had to cure," said a woman in a self-help health class. The real penis, *exposed,* is another thing altogether: giddily excitable and dependent on kindness, among other embarrassing qualities. The proud Prick is also puny, imploring, silly, and sullen.

True prickishness, then, requires utter control of the prick by the Prick. His own PR person, he orchestrates its appearances: now he lets you see it, now he doesn't.

What hangs, so to speak, in the balance is the all-important difference between the symbolic penis, the phallus, and the real penis. The phallus stands for masculine authority, power, patriarchal law and language; it depends for its reputation on not being seen. The fleshly penis represents all too plainly the vulnerable sexuality of real men. It wants to come out, but it takes a risk doing so.

Even the Prick himself cannot flawlessly separate the ideal from the reality, for the penis itself—soft, or, paradoxically, erect—always casts a little shadow of doubt on the phallus' unimpeachability.

The prick, which as male organ might be expected to epitomize masculinity, lays bare its desire . . . The phallic role demands impassivity . . . The evidence of the pleasure undermines the rigid authority of the [masculine] position.[2]

This is why, although the phallus is everywhere—from the Washington Monument to the only-sometimes-innocent cigar— Western male culture is careful about how, when, and if it represents the biological penis. With few exceptions male artists, filmmakers, and advertisers have avoided the unadorned erect organ; they have concealed and emphasized it with drapery, or, if revealing it flaccid, alluded to its potential size and mastery by surrounding it with swords, clubs, or shotguns, tree trunks, cannons, or cars, vanquished animals or supine women.

U.S. broadcast codes prohibit the display of a hard-on. Arsenio Hall, hectored by his guest Dr. Ruth Westheimer, could hardly bring himself to say the word *penis* on the air. Republican Senator Jesse Helms tried to get the National Endowment for the Arts shut down when he discovered the agency had funded the making and showing of a few erection-related pictures (to which efforts the Gorilla Girls, an anonymous group of feminist artist-propagandists, responded, "Lick Helms in '90"). And in Britain, although breasts and buttocks abound in mass media, a set-to about the possibility of explicit male frontal nudity on the telly prompted a nervous spokesman to tell the press, "There shall never be an erection at the BBC!"

While the Prick is busy regulating his social life, women are contending with him—with the symbolic phallus and the real penis, and with their ambivalences toward both. As we have seen, each man, each physical person, embodies male power—linguistic, legal, familial, romantic, and sexual—and he may deploy it mercifully or violently. At the same time, the male body is the body of fear and vulnerability, of ambiguity in relation to the mother, reproduction, and sex. Women, along with the culture, inscribe the vast and various meanings of masculinity on the small territory of the male genitals; they reserve for sex the most intense expressions of love and hatred. The penis for them not only is invested with male sexual power and potency, it is testament to their own desire and desirability—facts which in themselves inspire both respect and resentment.

Women, particularly heterosexuals, face a dilemma: how to depose the Prick, phallic poseur, without bringing down that sympathetic friend, that source of pleasure and affirmation, the penis?

• • •

On the former order of business, as with all the man-hating stereotypes, the first step is to paint his portrait, take his picture, write his
autobiography, file his case history—represent him as you see him.
The represented penis, after all, is the phallus' nemesis.

But this act is not simply a matter of revealing that it ain't as big
as he says it is ("Looks like a penis, only smaller," a junior-high-
school girlfriend of mine used to say when men exposed themselves
to us in the park). The chapters in "Images of the Enemy" suggest
that to represent is to exercise a kind of power—the power of definition, interpretation, influence, and sometimes even coercion. In so
doing, the representer activates a relationship with the represented
person.

People in nonindustrialized societies often believe that a photograph steals the subject's soul, and this intuition about the power of
representation is at the heart of much contemporary theory of anthropology, film, and post-colonial relations. To observe, analyze,
and record, especially in a context outside the subject's own, is to
appropriate that subject, to make of her or him an object, *your* object. To look at and represent are in their ways to take, to own, to
have; to be looked at is to be taken, owned, had.

Men have always cornered the prerogative to look at and represent the female body, whereas women's role is traditionally to be
looked at. "Men *act* and women *appear*," wrote the art writer John
Berger in *Ways of Seeing*. The nude—a representation of the naked
body *to be looked at*—is in this sense female by definition. The Gorilla
Girls found that 95 percent of the nudes in the Metropolitan Mu-
seum of Art, and 5 percent of the artists, are female.

When film theorist Laura Mulvey analyzed film as an exercise
in male "scopophilia"—the psychological term for seeking eroticized pleasure in watching—she named looking a gendered, indeed a
sexual, act. When women "reverse the gaze," when they seize the
male role of spectatorship and become the "eye," the voyeur, they
begin to destabilize the assumption of male ownership of the body,
both men's own and women's.

Lizzie Borden, in *Working Girls*, her film about a New York
brothel, often trains the camera on the male customers' torsos from
neck to knees, not on their faces. Where mainstream film almost

universally glamorizes prostitution (e.g., *Pretty Woman*), Borden portrays it as commerce, not eroticism. More important, where film conventionally objectifies the sex worker herself (the films of Brian DePalma, such as *Body Double,* are a prime example), Borden's point of view is the working girl's own. She is a whole person, he is the generic john. Not only does her gaze depersonalize the man as the "girl" has always been depersonalized (interestingly, this is accomplished in part by clothing the penis, his erotic "personality," instead of showing it) but the camera altogether reinterprets the transaction between the two. Rather than representing an appropriation of a woman's body by a man, through his money and his penis—a phallic act—the filmmaker's (the sex worker's and the female viewer's) eye "takes" the male body, exposing the man's nervousness, the penis' insecurity. The film itself becomes a metaphoric reversal of prostitution—from buyer's to seller's market—and more generally, of the relationship between male and female bodies. Minus its phallic privilege, the penis is on the defensive, and it should be. Just looking, women take over a fundamental masculine posture; they subdue the man into passivity, "femininity"—symbolically, they castrate him.

The Medusa myth, said Freud, expresses both the fear of castration and men's reassurances that it won't happen. "The sight of Medusa's head makes the spectator stiff with terror, turns him to stone," he wrote. "Becoming stiff means an erection. Thus, in the original situation it offers consolation to the spectator: he is still in possession of a penis, and the stiffening reassures him of the fact."

"I defy you! I have a penis!" says Perseus to Medusa, standing with legs planted apart, groin provocatively pushed forward, meanwhile holding his shield before him, just in case.

Women, who have long been compliant in veiling the phallus, are beginning to call Perseus' bluff—to look at, and to state, the obvious: "The fear experienced by men of women's Medusa-like stare, which petrifies everything in sight, is in reality a fear that the female gaze will soften everything in its path," writes Suzanne Moore in an essay called "Here's Looking at You, Kid."[3]

When women paint or photograph a male nude, both sexes suspect a transgression of major proportion. Shown in public, woman-made nudes almost invariably unnerve their audiences. At a 1980 London Institute of Contemporary Arts show entitled "Women's Images of Men," penises were surely the most scandalous subjects. "An aura of sensationalism, of penises for penises' sake, undermines the savagery with which some of the exhibitors have entered the arena," wrote *Guardian* critic Waldemar Januszczak. A female critic saw "a forest of penises," although works that didn't feature the organ far outnumbered those that did.[4]

Among female image-makers who confront the Prick with what Januszczak might call "savagery," the political artist Sue Coe stands out. Her pictures, which are often reproduced in inexpensive books or prints, recall George Grosz in their brutal expressionism and Brecht for their didactic texts. Dealing with rape, sexual abuse, militarism, and political and religious hypocrisy, Coe makes unambiguous connections between male supremacy, male sexuality, and violence. In *President Raygun Takes a Hot Bath,* the President's penis is a missile. *The John Walker* (1986) shows four white men in suits (one with a priest's collar) in a line. Their faces are at their groins; each has a bright red tongue-penis grotesquely jamming through. A man in a window is hitting a woman on the back with a stick. "Be a REAL man / and give your girl a slam," its text begins.

Mira Shor and Judith Bernstein paint penile shapes of monstrous scale, taking up whole canvases. Lisa Tickner sees in Bernstein's hairy "screws" the "celebration but also the reappropriation for women of the heroic image and its re-sensualizing for their pleasure."[5] At the same time, these artists' images undermine phallic authority, interestingly, not by minimizing but by maximizing the image. At once monuments to phallic power and ludicrous advertisements for themselves, they simultaneously impress and amuse. Even a billboard-size penis, they suggest, is not as big as it's cracked up to be.

Big or small, idealized or humiliated, the exposed penis can hardly win. On the one hand, few men can hold their candles to Robert Mapplethorpe's Priapi or Judith Bernstein's behemoths. On the other, any representation of "normal" genitals comes up short. "That little piece of pendulous flesh, the symbol of masculine power and authority, cannot possibly sustain the phallic myth of superhuman virility. The exposed penis seems horribly vulnerable rather than resplendent with confidence and pride . . ."[6]

· · ·

Nor, however, can the observer win. Knowing the Prick to be an arrogant self-inflator, she finds gazing upon him almost painful. "When a woman begins to doubt men's superiority, their pretensions serve only to decrease her esteem for them," wrote Simone de Beauvoir. "In bed, at the time when man would like to be most savagely male, he seems puerile from the very fact that he pretends virility, and woman averts her eyes."[7]

It's enough to make a woman weep, or scream. Her alternatives are few. She can close her eyes and think of the king. She can kick the Prick out of bed and buy herself a dildo. Or she can look for a man who's neither "superior" nor "inferior" to her—the best idea so far, but, as we'll see, not as practicable as it sounds. For the fact is, she's as dedicated to that pretended virility as he is. She can't strip the cockiness from the cock without losing sexual interest in it. The Prick, sad to say, is a ladies' man—a successful one.

When all else fails, a woman can giggle—but later, with her women friends, for the Prick is not known for his ability to laugh at himself. He's touchy, this bundle of nerves, and unteasable—at least by women. "The penis," a friend commented, "does not appreciate sarcasm."

Humor is the great deflator. It punctures the vigilance of power, catches the guard off guard. Wives often even the marital scores by gentle ribbing. In fact, a common setup in female humor is the thick-headed butt of a joke who doesn't know he's being made fun of; he thinks he's being "humored," as in this early Nicole Hollander cartoon:

> Husband: *I've been impotent lately because of "ring around the collar."*
> Wife (doing dishes): *Oh, I'm so embarrassed. I've tried rubbing harder but it doesn't do any good.*[8]

Mimi Pond indulges two male diners curious to know what their dates do in the "powder room." Pond eavesdrops:

> *"So tell me, is Ralph hung?"*
> *"Hung? Like a horse, I'm telling you . . . With all that equipment, you'd think he'd know how to use it. But no-o-o-o . . ."*

The conversation continues, getting more and more explicit. Back at the table, the men look stricken. "Aren't you sorry you asked?" reads the caption.[9]

Not all female fun-poking is in unimpeachably good fun, in other words, and some just barely scrapes over the line. A cartoon in the new-comix magazine RAW shows a mother and a daughter at table. Whines Daughter, screwing up her face at the vile thing on her plate, "Oh Ma, not dick again!" Women I've shown this picture howl with laughter and demand photocopies. Men clear their throats, or fix the page—or me—with horrified stares.

The drawing stirs the real terror behind men's discomfort at any female reference to their penises. If men harbor a suspicion that women are walking around with knives in their purses (see! A Freudian slip! purse = vagina!) any reference to castration from a woman's mouth, particularly in jest, can hardly make a man feel cozy.

The writer Andrea Dworkin has considered these questions at monumental length, and she doesn't think they're a laughing matter either. By her own description "a feminist, not the fun kind," this militant crusader against pornography and heterosexual intercourse has come to personify male nightmares of the feminist man-hater-castrator. Her iconography makes of the penis a brutal invader, colonist, torturer—but one terrified by the vagina, that enticing lair without escape.

[H]e (his penis) is buried inside another human being; and his penis is surrounded by strong muscles that contract like a fist shutting tight and releas[ing] with a force that pushes hard on the tender thing, always so vulnerable no matter how hard . . . [H]is penis is gone—disappeared inside someone else, enveloped, smothered in the muscled lining of flesh that he never sees, only feels, gripping, releasing, gripping, tighter, harder, firmer, then pushing out: and can he get out alive? . . . [H]e is terrified of never getting his cock back because she has it engulfed inside her, and it is small compared with the vagina around it pulling it in and pushing it out; clenching it, choking it, increasing the friction and the frisson as he tries to pull out . . . he rolls over dead and useless afterwards, shrunk into oblivion . . .[10]

Help! Dworkin isn't called a man-hater for nothing. It's difficult to read empathy in these words or to miss the lascivious enthusiasm of her tone, the curiously prurient, almost sadistic, glee.

We tend to accept the fear of castration as understandable, and as a
given. But there is no concomitant fear in women. Freud explained
this by telling us that women, having discovered their natural castration in toddlerhood, have long since learned to live with it. They
have penis envy, but envy is not terror.

There's a more social explanation, however: women have
nothing comparable to phallic authority to protect, nothing like it to
lose. Castration fear lays bare the Prick in every man, the potentate
quaking over the theft of his potency.

On the public, cultural level, every penis has got to be hard
because its owner has got to be hard. Not only is the only real penis
a hard penis, the only real man is a man with a hard penis. Oliver
Stone's film *Born on the Fourth of July,* about the paraplegic Vietnam
vet Ron Kovic, could be viewed as a movie about a man's loss of his
balls masquerading as a movie about the Vietnam War. Kovic said it
in his autobiography: "I gave my dead dick for John Wayne."[11]

In a sense (an oversimplified one, admittedly) the story of
Kovic's dick and the story of the war are inextricable. One subtext of
the ideology of the Vietnam War (like the ideology behind other
interventionist foreign policy) is the First-World macho "defense"
against effeminate "Others" like the Vietcong and Sandinista leader
Daniel Ortega (whom George Bush derided as "a little man") or
threateningly macho contenders like Manuel Noriega or Saddam
Hussein. Bush was from the start of his presidency called on to
defend his masculinity, to mitigate the "wimp factor." But the Pan-
ama invasion didn't quite do it. A month later, attacking the Administration's caution around events in Eastern Europe, George Will
accused the President and his men of "intellectual and moral flaccid-
ity."[12] Lucky for him, the President got another chance in the Persian Gulf.

Women, moreover, have nothing *sexually* comparable to lose.
For penile potency means more than effectuality: the penis is the
emblem of men's very subjectivity. Psychotherapist Leonore Tiefer,
who works in a urologist's office where the ever-more-prevalent

penile implant is performed, sees men avid to undergo painful and unpredictable surgical procedures to "cure" erectile changes that may simply be the by-product of aging. These men are desperate. For whereas sexual "dysfunction," menopause, or hysterectomy may be troubling to women, these usually do not translate into feelings of absolute anomie. Sexual problems may represent an emotional or erotic crisis, but an inorgasmic woman can still feel like a woman, and a competent person. An impotent man, on the other hand, is more than just depressed. He feels he is not a man. He loses *himself*.

The threat of sexual humiliation by a woman, the possibility that she may cause or reveal him to be "inadequate" in genital size or stamina, has an analogous (if not equivalent) function to the threat of rape to women. It represents a seizure of one's whole person by an "enemy": absolute defeat. Castration is more than the loss of a part, a function, a talent, a pleasure—even more than the loss of power. Castration is no less than the total loss of control, of authority, of subjectivity.

Of course, heterosexual woman are no happier about impotence than men are. Jokes about soft penises serve as much to assuage women's own anxieties as to express irritation or anger at the big deal men make about their cocks. "What does it mean about me? What will it mean for our relationship?" are only two questions among many that plague the impotent man's partner.

Indeed, the triumvirate of equations—man = hard penis; hard penis = sex; sex = intimacy—affects women as it does men, suffocating new forms of friendship and sexual love. For men, "sex" means erection and intercourse, and the equation of erection with eroticism is almost as deeply embedded in the female unconscious. Women who've tried to create an erotic male image that circumvents the conventions of phallic sexuality—quite apart from the question of sexual dysfunction—have made little headway. Look, for instance, at Sylvia Sleigh's *Philip Golub Reclining,* a sloe-eyed, long-haired young man in the posture of Manet's Olympia, on a couch in lush surroundings. Critic Sarah Kent feels that the model's direct, challenging gaze, like Olympia's, "shames the viewer into guilty self-consciousness of her voyeurism."[13] Yet to me, the picture itself assuages that discomfort. The artist gives us little to be titillated by, to feel ashamed of looking at. The subject's penis is flaccid, his face womanly. The artist caresses him in a safe, almost maternal, sensuality. Reflected in the mirror, Sleigh appears at her easel, hard at work, businesslike. The viewer identifies with her: yes, we objectify the model, but no, we do not sexualize him as would a lover, or an intruder, in the boudoir. The Prick is subdued: he is, literally, softened. And soft just isn't sexy.

The photographer Carol Latimer romanticizes the male nude, posing her models in an empty candlelit studio, relaxed, "alert yet passive, awaiting [the female viewer's] pleasure." But that pleasure isn't forthcoming. "In her attempt to humanize and soften the male —to destroy aggressive phallocentrism in favour of a more diffuse sensuality," Latimer "weakens sexual tension. These men seem docile and submissive . . . [S]he has not only neutralised their phallic power, but has castrated them altogether."[14]

Away from art, in brute commerce, female producers of pornography are working a similar territory with a narrower aim. Whether they are doing a creditable job is a matter of taste. Believing (accurately? I'm not sure) that women respond to images of all-body sensuality rather than an intercourse-centered sexuality, and to romantic stories rather than sex out of context, these pornographers produce videos replete with ambience (wineglasses, pillows, fields of flowers—you get the picture), plot, and dialogue that goes beyond grunting. When the players finally get around to doing it (which, for some viewers, is an interminably long fast-forward later) there's a lot of kissing, oral sex, talk, foreplay, and afterplay. Gone is the giant cock, the pneumatic Tab A-in-Slot B scene, and the formerly obligatory cum shot.

In switching from these conventions to a supposedly more humane, egalitarian sex and more "feminine" sexual styles, producers like Femme Productions say they are not trying to exclude men but to invite them into expanded realms of enjoyment. The tapes are marketed in the "couples" categories, a code that usually connotes a somewhat softer-core content, i.e., minus shots that could be used in Gynecology—or Urology—101.

In one sense, deleting the full-screen body part implies that women aren't interested in cocks and cunts for their own sakes. That's unfortunate; porn is liberating for women precisely because it allows them to fantasize sex plain, without the permission-givers of love and romance. In another sense, the editing is sexually revolutionary. If they succeed in creating a nonphallic yet arousing heterosexual erotica, these videomakers are on their way to overturning one of the most firmly entrenched institutions of sexual culture.

Even if they don't, simply by deemphasizing the big hard penis these mavericks are putting the Prick in his place. Friendly as their intentions may be, they are defying a fundament of male power: they are representing not only the female body, but also the male body as they want to see it, deploying it erotically as they choose. Pornography reveals, but its revelation is rehearsed, timed, prepared for—until now, by men. In women's control, revelation becomes disclosure. Female pornographers strip the Prick of defense and pretense, catch the exhibitionist with his pants down.

The Killer

THE SCENE IS AN ANTIWAR RALLY in Washington, a week after the Persian Gulf War has begun. A small woman holds a large poster over her head—a crude drawing of two men, one light, the other dark and mustachioed, facing each other. Between them, huge and red, half as tall as the men themselves and practically touching head to head, are their erect penises. Above, the legend reads: THIS IS WAR.

Whatever role the price of oil or the territorial rights of Kuwait played in the Gulf War, a primary intent of the Bush administration was to reinstate the United States as a tough guy, the toughest—and to do so militarily, since it is losing the title economically. Saddam Hussein, at the same time, was trying to set himself up as the strongest of his region's considerable strongmen.

From the start, both leaders seemed to be spoiling for a fight, drawing lines in the sand closer and closer to an arbitrary deadline. Bush sent Secretary of State James Baker to meet with his Iraqi counterpart, Tariq Aziz, in Geneva carrying not a negotiating proposal but an ultimatum. Hussein, who might have saved face at that point by withdrawing, vowed to suffer death before dishonor. Man to man, macho to macho—it was almost immaterial who threw the first punch. At the front, the beefy, bullet-headed Norman Schwartzkopf and the reputedly bloody-fanged Republican Guard had already lost their patience. A struggle to the death was inevitable.

The United States "won," and although a year later the region is arguably more troubled than before, George Bush has not had to relinquish the title of world champion. As commander in chief, the President laid to rest doubts about what he himself called the "the manhood thing." Forty-four billion dollars[1] and an estimated

200,000 deaths[2] later, the cartoonist Pat Oliphant stopped drawing Bush with a purse.

While the President was reclaiming his balls, the United States government was showcasing a gore-free exercise fought in the sky, on television—in a sense, nowhere. Instead of the bodies of dead and wounded Iraqis, Americans spectators saw video-game images of the "surgical" excision of "military targets." Over and over, they witnessed Patriot missiles elegantly taking out Scuds in midair, a "smart" bomb lasciviously slipping down an Iraqi chimney. The government's persona was equally sleek: the Pentagon spoke through the impassive Pete Williams, a man who'd be impossible to pick out in a lineup. President Bush, appearing only a little piqued, refused to "screech" his golf schedule "to a halt" just because he was carrying on the largest bombing campaign in history.

At the intersection of these two representations of war—the contest of phallic gladiators, and the technological-nuclear distancing and euphemizing of death—stands the modern man-hating image of masculine militarism: the Killer, bureaucrat of destruction. The Killer sits in the Pentagon, looking adult and dignified, passionlessly eliminating portions of the map, reducing populations, coolly redistributing power. But beneath the mahogany table his hand works fervently: war as a grand-scale circle jerk, the ritual of what Robin Morgan calls "ejaculatory politics."

Driven by sexuality and infantile desire, the Killer is utterly terrified of his passions. His pen—the state, law, language, and institutional "morality"—is his only sword, and mighty as it is, it's pathetic, such a little phallus. This man who picks up the touch-tone phone to inform the private in the silo to push the button (Bleep, you're dead) would faint at the sight of blood. Skulking behind his Stealth bomber, he's Perseus trembling behind his shield. He's Henry Kissinger, bespectacled ideologue of war, not the brave Henry V, charging into the breach with his men.

The warrior is valor, energy, idealism, masculinity at its zenith. He's fearsome and venerable, hot-blooded and gorgeous in his hardness, tragically erotic in his wounded languor. He is master of his fate, as close to godliness as a person can be. Staring existential truth in the face, knowing everyone must die, he chooses his own reason why.[3] But the Killer, removed from *agon,* stripped of valor, doesn't even die: somebody else does it for him! This modern-day techno-Killer, Brute in a pin-striped suit, is bestiality castrated. If there is something unidimensional about him—he's less a man than the hologram of a man—that is his own doing. For he invests every ounce of energy in disconnecting intellect from feeling, mind from body.

But by covering up the body of war, disembodying the warrior, the Killer strips himself of eros. Without it, he becomes hateful, deeply, unequivocally so.

> Mariette: *Those are the people who have power over us and the whole world—white male Americans, and they're the most pathetic people on earth. I was in a discussion about the [Vietnam] war with a Protestant churchman last week; he said he's never more than 51% sure of anything, including his opinion on the war, because he doesn't let his "random feelings" interfere with his rational judgements. He's the epitome of the WASP male who runs this country.*
> Joanne: *And the most pathetic of them all is Nixon himself . . . He's a power-hungry, mighty, terrible man. But deep down, he's a little schmuck, and I want to step on him . . . Earth Onion [a women's theater troupe] should do a skit: we should make him this little schmuck, with a huge penis, and have it shrink. We'll do it in front of the White House every day.[4]*

These words passed between two feminists during the Vietnam War and were recorded in a women's newspaper of the time. They describe the Killer in all his despicable contradiction: his power and his pathos, his might and his littleness. They express women's desire to "shrink" the Killer, to puncture his stern and stolid authority. While these two would deflate his big prick, other women employ a metaphoric strategy we've seen before: they reduce the Killer to an Infant, a man who simply has not grown up enough, or well enough, to handle the subtle nuances of compromise and diplomacy.

For the Killer-as-Infant, weapons, ever bigger and more sophisticated, replace model trains and planes as the playthings of male obsession. "Take the toys from the boys" is a common women's antiwar slogan. A cartoon from the Women's Pentagon Action shows three men gleefully playing ball with the globe. A tabloid tells the story, "WIFE DUMPS HUBBY OVER LOVE FOR A TANK!" Like a child so absorbed in play that he doesn't notice if it's raining or supper is on the table, this hubby is oblivious to the demise of his marriage. "The only thing that makes me cry is my tank," he says, referring to the thirty-two-ton World War II Sherman he keeps in the yard. "I weep every time I see it. It's so beautiful!"

Calling men babies—as we saw with the Babbler and the Bumbler—can serve symbolically to redress power imbalances in family and sex, to reward women for usually unrewarded talents, and gently to take men to task for fleeing romantic or household obligations. But viewing the Killer as a rambunctious schoolyard bully may have the opposite effect: rather than reveal, it obscures the dead seriousness of his game. A boy with a toy pistol is a chillingly insufficient metaphor when the weapon he's wielding is in reality a nuclear bomb. When the wild child is a man, or a superpower, belittling the infantility of his "play" masks his grown-up intent, and its potential consequences.

Anthropologist Carol Cohn, who spent a year among defense intellectuals, notes that male strategists and generals themselves employ such metaphors—or euphemisms—with similar, grave effects. One cozy phrase they use is "patting the missile," which means getting up real close to one of the Big Ones. The metaphor is affectionately sexual, says Cohn, but that is not its only connotation.

Patting is not only an act of sexual intimacy. It is also what one does to babies, small children, the pet dog. One pats that which is small, cute, and harmless—not terrifyingly destructive. Pat it, and its lethality disappears . . . The imagery can be construed as a deadly serious display of the connections between masculine sexuality and the arms race. At the same time, it can also be heard as a way of minimizing the seriousness of militarist endeavors, of denying their deadly consequences. A former Pentagon target analyst, in telling me why he thought plans for "limited nuclear war" were ridiculous, said, "Look, you gotta understand that it's a pissing contest— you gotta expect them to use everything they've got." What does this image say? Most obviously, that this is all about competition for manhood, and thus there is tremendous danger. But at the same time, the image diminishes the contest and its outcomes, by representing it as an act of boyish mischief.[5]

The naughty boy might skulk away chastened after being scolded by Mommy, but the Killer isn't so easily corrected. Judging from the impunity with which he razes cities and looks the other way while his men rape enemy women, this smudgy-faced lad appears to have little respect for his own mother, and a great deal less for other people's.

In fact, say some women, he is doing everything he can to defy Mommy. He is terrified of all that is feminine—the all-devouring mother of infancy—and exorcises it through war. Making a history and a future of war, says Andrea Dworkin in *Pornography,* the Killer obliterates the feminine in men, generation after generation.

> *Older men create wars. Older men kill boys by generating and financing wars. Boys fight wars. Boys die in wars. Older men hate boys because boys still have the smell of women on them. War purifies, washes off the female stink. The blood of death, so hallowed, so celebrated, overcomes the blood of life, so abhorred, so defamed. The ones who survive the bloodbath will never again risk the empathy with women they experienced as children for fear of being found out and punished for good: killed this time by the male gangs, found in all spheres of life, they enforce the male code. The child is dead. The boy has become a man.*[6]

Exorcising the feminine, war also casts out the infantile—the powerlessness of infancy. The boy becomes a man, and the man becomes a Beast.

How is he to become a true Killer, insulated from the dangers of his manliness and unsullied by the consequences of his Beastly actions?

The "toys" of war connect the Killer with his childhood, but like the model bombers and armies of tiny soldiers a child moves across the carpet, they also afford him a sense of omnipotence and invulnerability. The language he uses mitigates personal risk and responsibility even more, says Cohn, by abstracting the realities of warfare.

By talking about the destruction of weapons and not of people ("soft targets" and "collateral damage"), the nuclear technostrategist feels like "the planner, the user, the actor" and not the victim of nuclear weapons; as well, he distances himself from the vast suffering such weapons inflict. Sexual, romantic, and homey imagery "that domesticates [and] humanizes insentient weapons"—silos, "marrying up" systems, and BAMBI (Ballistic Missile Boost Intercept)—may also make it "possible to spend one's time thinking about scenarios for the use of destructive technology and to have human bodies remain invisible in that technological world precisely because that world itself now *includes* the domestic, the human, the warm, the playful . . ."[7]

Another result of anthropomorphizing weaponry, it seems to me, is that as eros drains from the cold and emotionally defended Killer, it takes up residence in the nuke itself. The bomb is Victor Frankenstein's monster, constructed of human parts and human drives, threatening the mortal world as it embodies the scientist's hubristic desire for immortality. But the amoral beast rampaging across the countryside in pain and rage is also entirely separate from its maker.* As the literary critic Kate Ellis has written, Mary Shelley's monster represents feeling outside the safe confines of the bourgeois family, all that is wild and terrifying, including untamed sexuality.[8] Similarly, if nuclear technology is the Killer's uncontrollable, disembodied penis, the Killer himself is disconnected from ethical and erotic sensation. He derives no pleasure from the technomonster's rape and pillage, but neither is he responsible for it.

The thinking man with clean hands, who "doesn't let his random feelings interfere with his rational judgments" is a true son of the West, of Aristotle, Descartes, and all the other Great Men who installed Reason on a pedestal from which he could survey Truth and govern the unruly, feminine rabble of the passions. Reason is still assumed to be opposite and superior to emotion, and is still equated with stability and masculinity, where volatility is linked to feeling and resides in the realm of the feminine.

Like most stereotypes, representations of the male Killer and his counterpart, the female Lifegiver, Nurturer, and Peacemaker, do not challenge this gendered dichotomy; they merely reverse its implicit hierarchy of value, derogating "male" values and elevating "female" ones.

---

* The Killer sometimes expresses a wish to control this out-of-control Thing, as when Ronald Reagan announced that once launched, missiles could be turned around in midflight and made to return, obediently trotting home like a lost pet.

The imagery of women's resistance to war has emphasized female marginality to war-making and celebrated a low-tech, homespun, "women's world" of domesticity and motherhood. In 1961, Women's Strike for Peace organized around the slogan "Pure Milk, Not Poison," drawing attention to the dangers of nuclear bomb tests that would release the radioactive element strontium 90 into the soil, where it would make its way through cows into milk—and into children. The Argentine Mothers of the Plaza de Mayo march in their housedresses and aprons, silently displaying photographs of their relatives "disappeared" in the 1970s by the junta's "dirty war." At the Greenham Common Women's Peace Camp, a tent city of resistance built around a U.S. base in Britain, women weave the gates shut with yarn; one protester disabled a transport vehicle by sticking a potato in its exhaust pipe.

Conservative organizer Dee Jepsen, addressing the General Federated Women's Clubs in Maine in 1982, subtly insulted women's rationality, alluding to a kind of math anxiety, in order to exalt their humaneness and point up their unique qualifications for restoring the world to peace: "We don't see numbers and statistics. We see the lives behind them. Women bring a quality to life that men cannot duplicate."[9] Women, Jepsen said elsewhere, "can be God's peace-makers, rather than simply settling for being power-seekers."[10]

Beyond hinting that the rational isn't all it's cracked up to be, and that a dose of womanly emotion might bring some needed balance to the workings of the world, women have also challenged the Killer by calling into question the nature of his rationality itself. Unpacking the subjective biases behind his "objective" numbers and statistics, disclosing the political interests in the supposedly disinterested *technos* of war, they strike blows against the very foundations of all rationales for war—law, justice, patriotism, and the maintenance of national boundaries.

The equation of masculinity with morality, and morality with fealty to abstract principles represented in laws or religious dogma, was perhaps best articulated in modern times by Freud. Men's superego, or conscience, is forged in the boy's early resolution of the Oedipus complex, when he breaks from his mother, Freud said. But because a girl does not thoroughly sever that bond, her ethical development is stunted, compromised. Her morality is never "so inexorable, so impersonal, so independent of its emotional origins as we require it to be in men." Women, Freud said, "show less sense of justice than men . . . they are more often influenced in their judgements by feelings of affection or hostility."[11]

Observing the ways that boys and girls made moral judgments, psychologist Carol Gilligan objects to Freud's postulation and replaces it with one of her own. Girls' (and women's) morality is not lesser, but different, from boys' and men's, Gilligan says. Yes, girls let affection and hostility affect their judgments—but this is not bad. Because of female socialization toward relating and nurturing, their morality resides always within a web of relationships and responsibilities; these, not abstract rules or laws, affect girls' ethical perceptions.

Gilligan's research found, for instance, that a girl is more likely to believe stealing is all right if it is done to save someone's life, and to think the robbed person will understand and work out a solution with the robber. Boys, on the other hand, will pronounce the act wrong—it is against the law—and expect the perpetrator to be punished.[12]

Law, we know, does not exist outside of value judgments; rather it is a rational codification of certain values that a society takes to be shared. These, Gilligan's work suggests, are not necessarily everyone's values, however; they are men's—or more generally, those of the people in power. Catherine MacKinnon discusses how the very supposition of legal objectivity upholds male domination.

> [The] imposition [of objectivity is] the paradigm of power in the male form . . . [T]he state appears most relentless in imposing the male point of view when it comes closest to achieving its highest formal criterion of distanced aperspectivity. When it is most ruthlessly neutral, it is most male; when it is most sex blind, it is most blind to the sex of the standard being applied. When it most closely conforms to precedents, to "facts," to legislative intent, it most closely enforces socially male norms and most thoroughly precludes questioning their content as having a point of view at all.[13]

MacKinnon is talking about rape and marital law chiefly, but a similar analysis can be applied to international law and the politics of war and peace. Military strategists decide policy within the confines of one particular worldview, erected on the cornerstones of "threat" and "deterrence," which are presumed by all inside their logical edifice to be objective facts. The system is one of airtight "rationality," defended by language and implicitly masculinized (though I would argue that gender is not its only parameter). To speak in visceral, passionate language about death and human suffering is to natter on like Xanthippe among the philosophers, crazed and womanish. No one listens.

One attack against this fortress is to expose the "rational" codes that justify war as *irrational*. To call war madness is an old pacifist tactic, and was particularly popular from the turn of the century to the First World War. Before 1914, 194 treaties were signed including provisions for arbitration; there were 425 peace organizations worldwide; myriad international peace congresses were convened. People set diligently to work studying the causes of war and proposing international laws; for this purpose the $10 million Carnegie Endowment for International Peace was founded in 1910.[14] Women were at the forefront of all these efforts, trumpeting their role as civilizers among the barbarians of both "friendly" and "enemy" camps.

The Killer, modern female peace-reasoners say, looks sane, but he's really a Dr. Strangelove, delirious with war fever. His ethical affliction, moreover, is a sex-linked genetic anomaly. "[W]e do not want that dominance which is exploitative and murderous in international relations, and so dangerous to women and children at home," says the Unity Statement of the Women's Pentagon Action. "We do not want that sickness transferred by the violent society through the fathers and sons."

These salvos against the Killer are compromised actions. While they question (and sometimes help to defeat) his logic and the actions taken under its camouflage, the insistence that he and his values are male and his detractors are female is to unwittingly aid in his defense and grease the gears of the war machine. For as long as women cede rationality to the masculine, they have given up a major weapon against war.

"It certainly is not antimilitarist to reject men's 'reason' in the name of femininity," writes the philosopher Sara Ruddick.

> *It is militarists who benefit from the equation of women with the emotional, physical, and subjective, who then call Cassandra mad and defense intellectuals people of reason. The struggle to be "rational"—to see what is real in all its complexity and ambiguity—is a peacemaker's struggle.*[15]

Some female peace activists are trying to undo not *rationality,* but this gendered *rationalism,* the worldview that not only opposes thinking to feeling but assigns them each a gender as well, and to replace it with what Audre Lorde called "a choice of ways and combinations." While recognizing complexity and ambiguity within gender, they want also to consider it alongside other systems of difference—race, ideology, nationality, wealth and poverty, to name a few—which are also at the roots of war. (To paraphrase a Jewish mother, sexism should be our only problem!)

To place a generic Woman outside of "male" militarism altogether and end the story there is to exclude women from a whole category of ideologically committed expression—like, for instance, the women who left home and hearth in order to serve in the Persian Gulf, who put their concerns about the larger world above those for their own families, and honored an abstract ideal above their personal relationships. (That they were prepared to do so with violence further explodes the image of woman as peacemaker.) It is to gloss over the differences between just and unjust wars, between liberation struggles of the powerless and the colonial wars waged by powerful empires. It is also to discount the different parts played in wars and civil uprisings by whites and by people of color and of the racial and class loyalties and conflicts felt by women in those various groups. In so doing, a largely white women's peace movement has often unintentionally excluded women of color from its ranks.

Kimiko Hahn, a Japanese-American born in 1955, explores these conflicts of loyalty and blame in "The Bath," a poem written in the voice of a woman in Hiroshima, whose husband is killed and her own flesh ripped by the "enormous blossom of fire." The survivor is tempted to name male evil her enemy.

> *. . . and it would be easy,*
> *satisfying somehow*
> *to write it off as history*
> *those men are there*

each time I close
my one good eye
each time *or lay blame*
on men or militarists . . .

Yet she can't forget the neuter economics of war and of race.

But it isn't air raids
simply
that we survive
but gold worth its weight
in blood the coal,
oil, uranium we mine
and drill
yet cannot call our own.
And it would be gratifying
to be called a survivor . . .
if I didn't feel
the same oppressive August heat
auto parts in South Africa,
Mexico, Alabama . . .[16]

In the rubble-strewn terrain this woman surveys, symmetries of masculine and feminine, violent and peaceful, cannot be discerned; maybe they don't exist.

"This fiction of opposites actually denies difference," says psychoanalyst and peace activist Adrienne Harris.

The stakes are not just peace but reality. If we accept the op-
position of peacemaker/woman and warrior/actor/man, we ac-
cept a perverse universe, where difference, heterogeneity, and
respected Otherness are impossible.[17]

The Babbler and the Bumbler, the Seducer and the Abandoner, the Prick, the Brute, and the Killer (along with their feminine counterparts, the Earth Mother, Bimbo, Madonna, Whore, or Harridan) are defending a crumbling stability, like nervous guards in a prison where discipline is already strained and all hell is just about to break loose. They stand between us and our fear of chaos, police our imaginations as they herd us, dumbly, toward a kind of safety. In inventing and nourishing them, we fortify the prison.

Inside, the population is segregated by gender, shackled by sexism, guarded by patriarchy. But if we are more content inside than out, we forfeit along with freedom the dream of equality. While we gain a temporary lull in hostilities, ultimately we destine ourselves, women and men, to enmity.

By making stereotypes of men, women, paradoxically, shore up the system of oppression and foreclose the possibility of real peace. A stereotype cannot sit down at the table and negotiate an armistice in the battle of the sexes; only whole people can.

PART II

Private Love, Public Hatred

4

Daughters and Fathers

Gender is . . . deeply embedded in the politics of family relations . . . Gender premises, like other passionately held beliefs, create relationship binds and paradoxes across the generations which are then internalized within the psyche, creating
for each generation a legacy of insoluble contradictions.[1]

You left me—Sire—two Legacies—
A Legacy of Love—
A Heavenly Father would suffice—
Had He the offer of

You left me Boundaries of Pain—
Capacious as the Sea—
Between Eternity and Time—
Your Consciousness—and Me—

Emily Dickinson[2]

HOW ARE THE LEGACIES OF GENDER passed down? How are its rewards apportioned, its injuries inflicted? How do girls and women become "less than" boys and men, and what becomes of the rage, longing, and hurt that afflict the daughter as a result? In Part I we explored some of the evidence that these feelings reside in women's hearts; we saw how the inequities of gender in adult relationships can emerge in man-hating. Now let us look further back, at the family's role in starting a female child down the path to man-hating, at the same time waylaying her in ambivalence.

Emily Dickinson addresses her father. Ambivalence, she says, is a daughter's *patrimony.* This is striking, for twentieth-century psychology accustoms us to searching the mother's legacy—indeed, to blaming the mother—for whatever becomes of us as adults. From compulsive eating to serial murder, all psychological problems may be attributed to too much, not enough, or the wrong kind of mother love. Father, long into adulthood, is exempt from scrutiny or open criticism; he is, Letty Cottin Pogrebin has written, the Teflon parent.

Yet even if, as Dorothy Dinnerstein argues, the intense relationship of mother and child is the birthplace of misogyny—a male defense against the omnipotent female—it is the attenuated relationship of *father* and child that births misandry. *Man-hating is born in the predominant quality of modern Western fatherhood: absence.* Father is gone, either literally or emotionally, from both boys and girls. For girls, compelled toward yet cordoned off from their fathers by gender difference, that absence is arguably more painful and distinctly more consequential.

As we've seen, man-hating and the ambivalence it breeds originate both in that amorphous thing we call the culture and in one of its most powerful institutions, the family. In this chapter, I will explore the role the family plays as the forge of gender, and the ways paternal absence ignites man-hating as it pacifies rage. The patriarchy's idealization of the father, and men generally; the girl's exclusion from the spoils of masculinity, its privilege, authority, and agency; her hunger for the father himself, a figure who becomes ever more desirable as he recedes into the distance; the mother's simultaneous propping up and tearing down of the mythic all-powerful, perfect father—these social facts and personal feelings are arrayed around man-hating and ambivalence not in dot-to-dot lines of causality, but in a cluster of concurrences and contradictions. They form a constellation like the Pleiades, floating sisters, not like Orion, with his arrow aimed straight for its target.

Where's Poppa?

The potential for abandonment is built into the very nature of paternity: it is a conditional connection, "a matter of opinion," said Gaius, compared with the "fact" of maternity. Unlike most animals, men have through much of history stuck by the females they impregnate and the young those females bear. This, Margaret Mead said, is one of the "social inventions" that make human families uniquely human. But the success, so far, of civilized people in cementing the bond between fathers and their offspring does not guarantee that they'll do it again, Mead cautioned.[3]

Committed fatherhood, or for that matter any given family form, is less a "natural" or inevitable human attachment than a contract which may be breached, outmoded, or superseded by migrations and resettlements, conquests and slavery, booms and recessions, technology, religion, politics, and shifts in the social winds. "Fathering," still an ill-defined activity, is learned anew by each generation, but it is always handicapped from the start by the deep cultural expectation of abandonment.

Recently, fatherly participation—or at least its social cachet—has increased in our culture. Dad is a superstar in the media, from Bill Cosby to the sexy models in Italian suits kitchy-kooing infants in their birthday suits. But for every New Father there are thousands of the old kind, men who are only minimally acquainted with their offspring. One recent study found the average father of an infant puts in less than thirty-eight seconds a day with the child.[4] Another study followed three-hundred seventh-and eighth-graders over a two-week stretch, and clocked an average of seven and a half minutes per week spent alone with their dads.[5]

The good news is that fathers are spending an increasing amount of time with their children. Time studies comparing data from 1975 and 1981 showed an increase of 26 percent in fathers' intense interaction with their kids—that is, time spent actually playing with or talking to the child, not just being in the same room. But that still represents only a quarter to a third of the time their wives spend. And almost none of these fathers have *any* responsibility for planning, scheduling, and overseeing a child's needs—knowing when a dentist visit is needed, making the appointment, and seeing that the child gets there.[6]

Even if men would like to be with their kids more (they all say they would), many don't seem to have enough hours in a day. In one recent Gallup survey, 37 percent of men with children under the age of six worked more than fifty hours a week, and of those a third worked more than sixty—obviously, leaving just about no time to be playing checkers with Junior. Fewer than 8 percent of moms with young children worked that many hours.[7]

Michael Lamb, an expert on fathering, has suggested that "quality time" can compensate for some lack in quantity time,[8] but, it appears, a lot of kids haven't grasped the fine distinction. In *Growing Up Free,* Pogrebin cites a survey in which half of preschoolers questioned said they prefer the television to their fathers, and another in which a tenth of the children said the person they fear most is their father.[9]

And these are the children who live with two parents. What about the kids who live with only their mothers—at any given time, a full fifth of American kids, twice as many as in 1970?[10] As we saw with the Abandoner and the Abductor, most of them receive such pitiful financial support from their dads that they could fairly be called fatherless. And postdivorce paternal neglect is not just economic. In 1988, sociologists Frank Furstenberg and Kathleen Mullan Harris studied the National Survey of Children and found that only 13 percent of noncustodial fathers saw their children at least once a week, and more than half of divorced children had not seen their fathers at all in the previous year. Furstenberg and Harris concur with other researchers that after divorce, paternal contact and commitment only wanes over time.[11]

A small mountain of data on paternal participation has been amassed in the past two decades, instigated by feminists and inspired by a growing faith in the saliency of fathering.* Before that, although psychologists and sociologists, perhaps moved by the casualties of the two World Wars, exhibited a minor obsession with the problem they called "father absence," there was scant research on the effects of father presence. A review of the academic psychological literature on families from 1929 to 1956 found only 11 articles about the father-child relationship, compared with 160 about mothers and children.[12]

Popular media from the twenties through the sixties did perennially treat the issue of what fathers should do and be, and the advice through the decades was remarkably consistent: be loving but firm, a masculine role model for boys, and for girls a manly mirror, an affirmation of their femininity. Underlying this advice was an equally consistent anxiety—that without two "proper" parents, children would miss out on forming the "appropriate" gender identifications. In fact, father absence was subtly abetted by popular advice: an "overly" involved father was considered "motherly." A certain distance from the nitty-gritty of kids' lives positively reinforced that all-important paternal authority—a dynamic whose desirability was assumed until the advent of feminism.

In one sense it may be argued that adults born in mid-century (the generations this book chiefly concerns) had *more* access to their dads than children currently do. While they were growing up, low rates of out-of-wedlock birth, divorce, and death made for a historically unprecedented family stability. Three out of four children born between 1930 and 1960 spent their whole childhoods with both parents.[13] And just because recent empirical data show an upward trend in actual time fathers spend with their children, we can't necessarily extrapolate backward and assume that they spent less time before those data were collected. History just doesn't work that way:

---

* Work on the father-daughter relationship is still paltry, however. In a recent Chicago Psychoanalytic Index, for instance, there are five pages of articles about fathers and sons and only a few entries on fathers and daughters. The popular literature doesn't do much better: you can count on one hand the number of books on the subject.

marriage statistics of all sorts have fluctuated significantly throughout the century.

And yet all anecdotal, literary, and nonquantitative psychological evidence corroborates the impression that even if Father's body entered the front door at five-thirty sharp every evening, he was, in a vast majority of families, an emotional phantom. "Dad was around, but vaguely," one woman described it. Said another: "He was, you know, the typical father: seen and not heard." In *Cat's Eye* Margaret Atwood evokes the shadowiness of the 1950s father.

> *Fathers and their ways are enigmatic. I know without being told, for instance, that Mr. Smeath lives a secret life of trains and escapes in his head. Cordelia's father is charming to us on the rare occasions when he is seen, he makes wry jokes, his smile is like a billboard, but why is she afraid of him? Because she is. All fathers except mine are invisible in daytime.[14]*

The girls in Atwood's book, one imagines, grew up reading the stories that instilled an expectation of paternal negligence and abandonment. They knew it was the wicked stepmother who beat and starved innocent children—but they learned too, more subtly, of the father who married her, a man so weak or preoccupied with his own interests that he failed to protect his children from her evil doings. Hansel and Gretel's papa, instructed by his second wife, obediently led the hapless children off into the woods to be victimized by yet another female witch. Cinderella's father allowed his daughter to fall into the hands of the cruel stepsisters. And where was Snow White's dad when her vain and jealous stepmother ordered a servant to take her away to the ominous wide wood?

Children in the 1950s and 1960s watched Jim Anderson on "Father Knows Best" abdicate to his wife when his wholesome kids started acting even the slightest bit strange. They laughed at Uncle Bentley on "Bachelor Father," a lawyer striving futilely to be the man of the house, but constantly losing ground to his high-spirited niece and Japanese houseboy, by racial and class implication the surrogate "woman" of the house. These men were different in style but not in substance from the ineffectual and infantile pop-culture dads of today, the sensitive, psychobabbling Michael Steadman of "thirtysomething," who chats with friends, works late, or whines while his stay-at-home (but putatively professional) wife Hope feeds, dresses, bathes, and amuses their two children, or his friend Elliot, a man who is only physically more grown up than the son he calls "Pal."

Women rightly complain that fathers have to do precious little to earn the honorific "New," while mothers knock themselves out just to make it to "good enough." Yet this paucity of qualifications is itself ironic comment on the expectations we have, and have had, of dads: very, very low.

"Father absence," far from a social aberration or an individual pathology, is virtually a foregone conclusion, "normal" American family life. "If paternal neglect is a problem," write Judith Lewis Herman and Lisa Hirschman in *Father-Daughter Incest,* "then most children suffer from it."[15]

No Girls Allowed

If most children suffer from paternal neglect, girls suffer most of all. If fathers are only intermittently there for their sons, they are there even less for their daughters. And because of the vital role fathers play in the gendered family in helping a child become a separate, competent individual in the world, girls are crippled, permanently and in the most fundamental ways. This injury is inflicted by twin bludgeons: the inferiority of a father's attention to his daughter, and the meanings of masculinity and femininity that the child observes as she grows up.

We rarely question parents' identification with their same-sex children and their desire to raise a child who is "like them" in gender-appropriate ways. But when examined, it turns out this desire is far stronger in fathers than it is in mothers. Pregnant women often say they want a boy ("I just knew life would be a lot smoother for him than for a girl," one woman confided to me. "Boys are easier," said another, voicing a popular maternal sentiment), but they show equal delight in learning the sex of a newborn girl. And contrary to widely held beliefs, many behavioral studies suggest that mothers tend not to correct a young child when its play strays from sex-role norms and in general treat boys and girls similarly pretty much throughout their lives. Fathers, on the other hand, view and treat their different-sex children differently; they simply do not treat girls as well.[16]

From before the child is born, fathers favor boys. A number of studies show that expectant American fathers "overwhelmingly desire male rather than female offspring, with a degree of preference far exceeding that of their wives."[17] I know a carpenter in Colorado, for instance, who has spent an extraordinary amount of time with his little boy since the child's infancy, teaching him to hammer and measure, read and think, but was miffed by the news of a girl baby on the way. "I don't know what I'll *do* with her," he said, and was amused and dismissive when I suggested he do what he'd done with his son.

Girls get the message that just by being female they've let their fathers down, and it's not always communicated gently. "I adored my father, but I was a disappointment—I was supposed to be a boy," says Dottie Bernstein, a forty-nine-year-old Chicago homemaker. "When the boy came, my father said I was worth thousands, but he was worth millions."

One of the facts now being trotted out to prove New Fatherly zeal is the increase of fathers present at their babies' births. A baby evidently holds a man's attention, but if she's female that attention is likely to wane precipitously once she's blown out the candles on her second birthday cake. Starting at that age, fathers spend on average twice as much time with their sons as with their daughters. As years go by, a father can be expected to spend less time with and know less about his daughter, to have fewer expectations of her and a less clear idea of her needs or the right way to raise her.[18]

This paternal withdrawal from daughters probably could not begin at a worse time than when it does. For age two is about when an infant starts to toddle further outward, exploring more, turning back less to the safety of mother. Mother has been the source of all sensual gratification, food, and comfort, the person on whom the baby has been entirely dependent, for whom it has had the most intense desires, and in whose power it has suffered the deepest frustrations and disappointments. Separation from such a person is, needless to say, traumatic. Yet separate the child must, and wants to do.

For the infant gingerly moving away, the father, a relatively unknown, idealized figure, is seen as a haven from the mother and a bridge to the bigger world. "The father image comes towards the child . . . from outer space as it were," says child psychologist Margaret Mahler, "as something gloriously new and exciting, just at the time when the toddler is experiencing a feverish quest for expansion."[19]

Not every child has a father, or father image, who appears in its orbit, of course, Recognition of cultural differences and changing family configurations makes it more and more problematic to posit his presence as a requisite for healthy development. African-American psychologists and scholars, for instance, have taken issue with the still inordinately influential thesis advanced in 1965 by Daniel Patrick Moynihan that the "pathology" of black America can be traced to a prevalent matriarchal family (other blacks object as well to the term *matriarchy,* pointing out that African-American mothers don't have the power that word implies). In spite of a perennial concern about the need of young black boys for strong male role models (black director John Singleton's *Boyz 'n the Hood* is a popularization of this longing), many black single mothers object to the assumption that their kids are going to grow up impaired if they have no father. Pam Brady, a young lesbian clerical worker whom we will meet in Part III, has raised her two bright and friendly children, a boy and a girl, alone.

> *Where I come from it doesn't seem that unusual. There are plenty of boys out there who were raised by their mothers, their grandmothers, and households of women. I feel like Kufi gets a large variety of women who have different personalities, who bring different things to his life. It would probably be good to maybe try to find some guy who could balance that out, so he could see things in a different perspective. But I would have to really do some searching. Because I don't know any men here.*

Sonia Prada, thirty-four, who moved to California from Peru when she was six, also grew up with few men around. She's been married for seven years, and hers sounds like an interesting and sexy relationship that's also fraught with conflict—in other words, a mature, struggling marriage. She and her husband have two children.

But asked whether as a child she expected to get married, Sonia laughs.

> *No. No! . . . Even if I did, I'd probably end up a single parent anyway. Because all my mother's friends—every single one of her closest friends—was a single parent. All these Latinas, alone with their kids. So I just said, "Shoo, that's what's going to happen with me, for sure . . ." And it was funny, I remember being in high school [a mostly white Catholic school] and one time I looked around and I thought, "Every single person here comes from an unbroken home"—you know, mother-father. It was, wow, it was something I didn't even know! Not in my life, not in any of the people around me. So I didn't expect it.*

Regardless of a growing acceptance of matrilinearity, however, "Father" and "Mother" are entrenched symbols in all human societies, and in ours the family's triangular configuration is driven deep into the unconscious. Kufi, Pam Brady says, is elated on the rare occasions his father shows up to visit—although, according to her, he's a cold and inattentive man. Even the father a child has never met is present in that child's wishes, desires, and fears. A businesswoman whose daughter was conceived by anonymous sperm donation was not surprised when the two-year-old announced unprompted, "I have a daddy." The absent father is a father too.

In fact, when there is no father to be found, a child is likely to manufacture one. Sally Wilkerson, a writer who is an apartment-building neighbor to three-year-old Lily and her lesbian single mother, describes herself as the little girl's "father"—a somewhat removed, though familiar, exciting figure, seen daily but only during special times. "When Anne brings Lily home from day-care, the first thing Lily wants is to 'go see Sally,'" she says. If the three are together in a roomful of people in the evening, "Lily will maneuver us and herself so that she is lying between us, rocking herself to sleep, like a little bird in a nest between the mommy bird and the daddy bird."

Theoretically, an adult of either sex can be the first caregiver, and either can provide a haven from this omnipotent figure. Moreover, as child psychologist Ernest Abelin has pointed out, the father and mother are not necessarily the only important figures in an infant's life. The baby also forms intense relationships with siblings, grandparents, and babysitters, and feels desire, rejection, and rivalry in those relationships too. As well, these people might stand in as the "escape hatch" from the primary infantile attachment. Cross-cultural studies and modern life show that biology can be relegated to playing a minimal role in parenting. And increasingly, the hegemony of the two-parent, split-role family is being challenged by sexually egalitarian parenting, single mothers and fathers, lesbians and gays raising children, and even an emergent minority view among social workers that stable, long-term institutional group care may be preferable to a series of foster families or restoration of children to very troubled biological families. What may be most interesting to observe as these kids grow up is how, and if, they divide the parental roles if their parents don't, how they shed infantile dependency if it is not decisively embodied in one primary caregiver and independence not represented by a more distant, other parent.

But these are almost idle musings. For the fact remains: the mother-father family is still normative in Western culture, and profoundly so. That family is defined by gender difference, into which it inducts the infant from day one. The child's first foray outward is a major milestone of gender acquisition, its first understanding of the mutual exclusivity of masculinity and femininity. In this, gender is ultimately *the* delimiter of psychological, erotic, and worldly possibility. Yet, as psychoanalyst Jessica Benjamin explains, in the gendered family, gender itself assuages the nearly unbearable terror of the child's first leave-taking. Idealization of the father makes separation possible.

> *Paternal recognition . . . has a defensive aspect; with it the child denies dependency and dissociates himself from his previous maternal tie. The father's entry is a kind of* deus ex machina *that solves the insoluble conflict of rapprochement, the conflict between the desire to hold onto mother, and the desire to fly away. The child wants to solve this problem by becoming independent without the experience of loss. And the "solution" to this dilemma is to split—to assign the contradictory strivings to different parents. Schematically, the mother can become the object of desire, the father the subject of desire in whom one recognizes oneself. Separation-individuation*

thus becomes a gender issue, and recognition and indepen-
dence are now organized within the frame of gender.[20]

For a boy, the journey is rough in one way. He must sever
himself forever from his first love object. But there's comfort: he is
following the road signs to the Promised Land—"This Way to Manhood." Because the culture allows a father to neglect a boy as he
does a girl, the son may have to make do with what Nancy
Chodorow calls "positional" identification with his father—emulation of the masculine role he assumes his father plays—rather than a
close-up personal identification with the ways and values of the man
himself. In either case, the boy takes on the mantle of masculinity.
He will make a mark on the world as an independent actor, desirer,
subject. Eventually, he will have the opportunity to seek as an erotic
object a woman, like his mother.*

The girl is stopped at the crossroads and, finding no father to
greet her and guide her down the road to independence, turns back,
back to mother and to femininity. Even if she does meet her father
on the road and he does take her hand, he probably won't lead her
to his world. As I've said before, the gender system is bigger than any
individual father or daughter; they can sidestep it only to a minimal
extent, and the child will grow up in a masculine-feminine world no
matter what her father does. Research shows that well-intentioned
fathers who spend time with daughters teaching them to swing a
tennis racket or use a power drill tend to reinforce a daughter's
femininity even as they involve her in "masculine" activities. They
show approval if the girl has fun and responds warmly, not if she
does the thing itself well. In fact, fathers are generally observed—by
researchers, by their wives, their daughters, and by themselves—to
discourage girls from competence and independent achievement.[21]
As Lissa Santini, a thirty-nine-year-old New York artist recalls, these
are reserved for boys.

My Dad and my brothers were this team, and I wasn't picked.
They went out and did things. They took trips, they played
baseball, they built stuff in the basement. And I stayed with my

---

* Needless to say, not every boy grows up to be heterosexual. I am laying out here a paradigm of
gender as the family creates it, intending in no way to present the normative as "normal," or the
myriad variations of gender as pathological.

mother. He loved me—we hugged and kissed a lot—but he sort of didn't know what to do with me. It was a warm relationship, but in some way . . . I don't know . . . empty.

The gendering of parental attention has enormous consequences, and for girls, grave ones. "The little boy's identificatory love for his father is the psychological foundation of the idealization of male power and autonomous individuality," writes Benjamin.[22] The father's rejection of the girl's identificatory love, meanwhile, is at the heart of her abiding envy of masculine independence and agency—what penis envy is the metaphor of. And the girl's love for her mother, the love of infancy from which she never completely breaks, forms the basis of the lifelong feminine skills of caring and intimacy. It is also the psychological foundation of the devaluation of those skills and the marginalization of the vital nurturing work that women do.

As more and more mothers work, femaleness opens to girls a richer spectrum of possibility, including both nurture and achievement. If women's struggles in the workplace and politics bear fruit, masculinity will be forced to relinquish its exclusive claim to autonomy and power. But women annexed this turf only in inches, and only very recently. To "stay with mother," as Lissa did, is, as it has been, to become feminine. And part of becoming feminine is a schooling in female deference.

Deference is not necessarily the equivalent of degradation. While they've always been underpaid and undernoticed, the feminine caretaking roles have also been romantically exalted. Domesticity and motherhood have been raised to an art, in some eras practically to a religion. Besides, whatever the current ideology may be, caring has deep personal rewards, serving has its compensations. Arlene Sharp, fifty-one, a voluble Atlanta lab technician, insists that her mother, a woman with a full-time job and four children, enjoyed her near-slavish wifely duties. Here, Arlene links love with uncomplaining servitude:

My daddy most certainly wore the pants. My mama? She loved it. I don't think she had a problem with it. Not really, not my mama, 'cause she loved my daddy and whatever he wanted. Let me give you some examples: My daddy was the type of person, he was real finicky. He did carpenter work. On several

*occasions his car was not working, so he'd go on the streetcar.
And she'd take his lunch to his carpentry job. It was in a brown
bag, of course. But if it was something greasy, she had to wrap
it up real careful . . . 'cause he didn't want to see the bag
greasy [and] he didn't want to take the bag on the streetcar
with him.*

From the earliest age, little Arlene was enlisted in her daddy's
care, which constituted a large part of her interaction with him.

*There was not very much of the time that he didn't work . . .
He worked at the Norris Candy Company a lot after he'd done
the carpentry work, like on weekends, and he'd always bring
us candy home . . . We had a Dynaflow Buick and he used to
have it stacked up in the back. And he'd come home and let
me sit in his lap and comb his hair and I'd braid it. He had
pretty dark long hair, and I'd curl it or whatever. He'd be
asleep. He didn't do anything like playing ball with you. But the
time he did spend with you was quality time; there wasn't a
whole bunch of it. It was very well merited.*

In the glow of memory, Arlene's father is like a storybook
figure—a sort of black Santa in a Dynaflow Buick piled high with
gifts. But her description of him also reveals a strict taskmaster who
expected perfect obedience and prohibited his daughter from dating
boys or even spending the night at a relative's house. He felt no
compulsion to indulge his children's wishes. He "didn't do anything
like playing ball with you"; in fact, he was asleep much of the time
Arlene saw him! Still, to her it was all "quality time."

Here is a prime example of the idealization of the absent father
—a precious commodity, an exciting visitor, who died when Arlene
was fifteen—and the particularly feminine way Arlene experienced
it. In the Sharp family, it seems, the gendered trade-off was affectionate and, on its own terms, respectful. Daddy was a man who
worked hard for his family and expected full service in return, but
(in Arlene's view) he received that service graciously. Taking pride
in the female role of caretaker, Arlene's mother made the most of
her autocratic husband's appreciation. And so did Arlene, through
service seeking to slake her thirst for a father she got too little of.

Other fathers are not so gracious. They exploit their male privilege harshly, making good on the threat of violence that is every

man's to wield. The father of June Carter, a rail-thin, pale, and plainspoken Cleveland postal worker, made endless and impossible demands, shared the spoils with his sons, and enforced what he called his "rights" by beating and humiliating his wife and daughter. Today, June unapologetically says she hates her father. And she sees him through a sort of protofeminist lens: in her mind, the family hierarchy and her father's abuse of power are inextricable.

Indeed, minus that abuse, the Carter family arrangement is "traditional," common. Although the Carters are lower-middle-class white Midwestern Protestants, in a fundamental way their household resembles the working-poor Southern black Sharps, or the middle-class urban-Italian Santinis, in which, Lissa says, her mother did "at least 99 percent of the housework." June's summary of her family, sad and stark as it is, provides a perfect description of the patriarchal setup: "My brothers sat at the table with my father and ate and drank and talked. And I was raised to serve."

A daughter's regard for her father is tainted by the assumption of feminine submission. More than her brothers, who pretend to the throne, she "looks up" to him, from below. Equally important, her regard for herself is poisoned by his—and by extension, men's—assumption of her submission. Writes Simone de Beauvoir:

> *If the little girl were brought up from the first, with the same demands and rewards, the same severity and the same freedom, as her brothers . . . promised the same future, surrounded with women and men who seemed to her undoubted equals . . . were she emotionally attached to her father . . . her love for him would be tinged with a will to emulation and not a feeling of powerlessness.*[23]

Current psychological theory might amend Beauvoir's observation: the daughter's love for the father *is* tinged with the will to emulation, but his refusal to respond breaks her will. No matter how lovingly a daughter's femininity is entertained, it makes her someone who does not reach for power, does not presume to do but only to be—to be of use.

The process of a child's feminization is no less than an amputation of self, whose profound and lasting pain is at the root of man-hating. "The way in which a daughter experiences her father's authority is her exclusion from the realm of authority," psychologist

Karen Hopenwasser told me. "What I see in women is a sense of diffuseness—a feeling of not being able to say 'I desire, I want, I will do. *I am.*' This denial of is the real source of rage."

Compromised Love

> *I wanted my father to be my companion, to praise me for wit and intelligence as [Jane Austen's] Mr. Bennet praised Lizzy . . . I was impressed by Eliza Bennet's ability to criticize her father as well as love him, since I was too far away from mine to know him well . . .*
>
> *One summer, aged about fourteen, I accompanied my parents on a trip to the south of France . . . My father commented on the beauty of . . . the young French women, their slim bodies, their long dark hair . . . their dark eyes. I felt jealous and depressed: I was plump, with short curly hair and a tendency to spottiness. We halted in the main square to watch a group of North African men dancing . . . Suddenly I leapt into the middle of the group of men and began dancing with them. They were amused, clapping [for] me and calling out, "Come on, English miss." I danced for my father; he laughed and clapped too.*[24]

The relationship between the writer Michele Roberts and her father was not an emotional tundra devoid of warmth or event. What she felt from him was love—and that felt good.

But his love was not enough, and not the kind she craved. Seeking his recognition as an acting subject in the world, a person who desires in the broadest sense, Roberts wrested from him only affirmation in the narrowest sense: as the female object of sexual desire. Reaching for affirmation in identifying with him, she received, as if by default, sexualized approval.

Fathers love their daughters. But, just as a father's encouragement of a girl's mastery of the world is subtly feminized, so is his way of showing intimate love. In all ways his recognition of her is gendered. More than mothers, fathers reinforce feminine gender stereotypes in their daughters; they encourage even the littlest of girls to be flirty, pretty, well-dressed, warm, and pliant—in short, "sexy" —rather than competitive, competent, independent, or resilient.[25] Of course, mothers encourage femininity too, by decorating their little girls and instructing them in feminine wiles and the folkways of beauty. But Mom can only prepare a girl for seduction; Dad enacts it. Fathers reward girls for being desirable, and there is only one way to do that: by desiring.

As we will see, a father's desire is concealed, sometimes nearly invisible. Yet it is often palpable to the daughter, and this confuses her. Is it real or imaginary? The feelings are threatening, enticing— or mutual, which makes them all the more threatening. Further confounding to the girl is that seductive affection can be hard to separate from the other, more benign attention; daughters can't always position the two kinds of love, as Michele Roberts does, at opposite ends of a pole, a safe distance apart. Because the father-daughter relationship cannot be stripped of gender, even "neuter" interest—that Bennet-like companionship—is contaminated with the sweet intimations of desire. The daughter feels thrilled and guilty, fearful and wanting.

I was told about a woman who, as a child, took walks with her father and talked about books. He didn't touch her or speak suggestively, yet to her consternation she would become sexually aroused. Here was the rare father who did relate to his daughter as a "nonfeminine," thinking person, and she could experience him only as a man, herself only as a girl. She could not construe his interest in her, or hers in him, as devoid of desire.

For another woman, thirty-seven-year-old community organizer Viola Jackson (of whom we will learn more in Part III), a complex family system made desire and "secular" interest even harder to segregate. Viola's father periodically left her mother for other lovers, abandoning eight children to poverty. Yet Viola speaks of her father in unmitigatedly admiring tones. When asked whether she harbors any anger toward him, she says, "I haven't visited that." Viola was Daddy's Girl, she explains; therefore she is loyal to him rather than to her mother. In fact, it was to Viola that the usually reticent man confessed the reason for his infidelities.

> *There was a big crisis where one of his mistresses got hold of our phone number and called my mother and said all these really inappropriate things to her. My five brothers were ready to kick my father's ass . . . and he basically told them to kiss off.*

> *But later that day he asked me to go to the store with him and get some beer. And that was a pretty unusual request coming from a man who says about twelve words a year. I stepped into the car and on the way he tells me that it was in 1955 that he and my mother stopped having sex. This was 1980 that I'm hearing this story.*

How did you feel? I asked Viola. "I felt privileged." Was she confused? Quite the contrary: "I felt so much that had been confused was cleared up." But was it not just replaced by another kind of confusion, this one less conscious?

As her father's confidante, Viola, rather than her brothers, was anointed "one of the boys." Yet she was not a boy; she was at the time twenty-five, a mother, and in her words, a "very sexual" woman. Making her a voyeur to his sex life, forming an alliance with her on the side of sexual freedom and against her prudish mother, inviting her to keep an intimate secret with him, her father drew her into an almost inescapable dilemma. Was she his pal or his erotic partner in crime, or both? The identificatory affirmation—"You're like me"—was an oedipal come-on too.

The two kinds of love made a potent mix, hard to resist yet also hard to swallow. Add to them the preciousness, predicated on conditionality, of the father's presence—at any moment, he could leave. Together, these forces stymie Viola in coming to terms with her father as a real person. Today, her mother, with whom she had a lot more trouble as a child, is enraging and exasperating, yet beloved, warts and all. Dad remains idealized, distanced, in some sense untouchable, like the justified anger that she still approaches as a timid tourist.

Before a daughter reaches adolescence and becomes a patently sexual being, a father is usually able to pal around with her and keep errant desire in check. Asexual affirmation and seductive love, while not mutually exclusive, are nonetheless manageably distinguishable. But, many women feel, at puberty all that changes. Confronted by the girl's changing body or new sexual expressiveness, Dad may flee. "My earliest memories of him were really warm. Then, suddenly, when I was twelve or thirteen the kisses and hugs stopped. No more little presents and jokes just for me," says one woman. "It was as if all that had been a hallucination. He was gone." Said another woman, who wasn't so lucky in early intimacy, "This stranger got even stranger."

Other fathers seeing Daddy's Little Girl become a big girl have a similar, if apparently opposite, reaction. Overcome by a near-phobia of the child's sexuality, they become overly involved and jealous, punitively restrictive and violent when "betrayed."

"When I was small, I loved to walk with him," says Selma Wiseman, a forty-four-year-old scientist.

> *There's a picture of me with him at camp. I was a kind of miserable child, but what was striking about this picture was the absolute beatific smile as I am holding hands with my father . . . [But] he couldn't handle pubescent girls. He had such sexual hatred, he just wanted to deny [my sister and me]. He found out my sister was sleeping with her boyfriend and he went into one of his terrible rages. And he cried at the same time he was screaming at us. It was such a terrible thing to have slept with a boy! We had become sexual and he couldn't handle it.*

When Arlene Sharp's girlfriends began dating, she asked her daddy, "When am I going to be receiving company?"

> *He said, "Oh, when you get about forty." And I said, "Forty? When I get forty, I'll have grandbabies on your knee calling you grandpa!" He got so very angry. He said, "Don't ever say that to me again!"*

Paternal possessiveness is often expressed more covertly. A woman I know, now nearly forty, says her father invariably tells dirty jokes to her boyfriends, in her presence. She sees this as "an assertion of his sexual ownership of me," a sort of negotiation in what Claude Lévi-Strauss called the "traffic in women," the handing-over of females by males that structures societies.

Like King Lear or Polonius in *Hamlet,* like the fairy-tale fathers who lock their daughters in castles to keep them from the wild beasts of the forest or the TV dads who are thrown into homicidal frenzies by their daughters' first kisses, these fathers are both perfectly sane and suspiciously crazy. They're exercising (if a little too zealously) the normal paternal role of sexual protector. They're also inappropriately venting their own sexual needs and desires.

Where the father's and his daughter's sexualities are concerned, distinctions between sane and crazy are not always obvious. That's not only because a father's behavior may be shady and hard to pin down, but because the boundaries he crosses, between "legitimate" paternal solicitousness and "illegitimate" intrusion, are themselves protean. Where is the line between a paternal healthy affirmation of his daughter's sexuality and inappropriate seductiveness? A father need not behave pathologically or even "misbehave" subtly for his interactions with his daughter to be suffused with disturbing suggestions of seduction. The problem, in other words, goes beyond individual psychology; it is *structural*.

When an incestuous father tells his daughter he doesn't want some strange boy touching her, better she should be initiated into sex by the man who has her best interests at heart—Dad—we view his as a pathological breakdown of inhibitions. But he doesn't succumb to temptation in a cultural vacuum. This is not to absolve him of responsibility, but a man who loses his moorings in this way is afloat in the ambiguity intrinsic to the patriarchal system. In that system, where men's sexual ownership of women and a father's control of his family is assumed,* "inviolable" erotic taboos are riddled with loopholes.

The Daughter's Seduction

Early in his practice, Freud wrote that he had heard many stories from his patients of "childhood scenes in which they were sexually seduced by some grown-up person. With female patients the part of seducer was almost always assigned to the father. I believed these stories, and consequently supposed that I had discovered the roots of the subsequent neurosis in these experiences of sexual seduction in childhood."[26]

Freud began to have doubts about this idea, however, and in September of 1897 he wrote to his colleague Wilhelm Fliess:

---

* As I discussed in Part I, these patriarchal arrangements are being challenged. In the current decade, thanks largely to a political movement of survivors, criminal prosecutions for incest are increasing.

I no longer believe in my neurotica . . . there was the aston-
ishing thing that in every case . . . blame was laid on per-
verse acts by the father, and realization of the unexpected fre-
quency of hysteria, in every case of which the same thing
applied . . . [I]t was hardly credible that perverted acts
against children were so general.[27]

Rejecting the idea that stories of incest were factual recollections, Freud revised his analyses to see them as fantasies, born in
repressed desire for the parent.

This volte-face created one of the biggest controversies in all of
Freudian theory. It has been denounced by feminists and incest survivors as the cowardice of a bourgeois unable to face the unsettling
truth that all over Europe upright family men like himself were
fondling and raping their children. The Freudian "assault on truth,"
as psychologist Jeffrey Moussaieff Masson called it, has been indicated as no less than the cornerstone of psychoanalysis' oppression of
women: analysts, say its critics, simply do not believe that women
are victimized by men—by implication, they do not trust women to
tell the truth about their own experience.

Today, thanks to the revelations of millions of incest survivors
in a therapeutic and political milieu that takes their words at face
value, we know that perverted acts against children are indeed general. In five large studies of "normal" middle-to-upper-class women
conducted between 1940 and 1978, one fifth to one third reported
some sort of sexual encounter with an adult male in childhood. And
while only one in a hundred reported incest perpetrators is a father
rather than some other relative or close family friend, fathers vastly
outnumber mothers in parent-child incest, representing 97 percent
of those cases.[28] Moreover, widespread as overt incest is, say Herman and Hirschman, incestuous relationships are pandemic. "For
every family in which incest is consummated, there are undoubtedly
hundreds with essentially similar, if less extreme, psychological dynamics."[29]

In the logic of patriarchy and gender, these dynamics make a
perverse kind of sense. Looking at history, one sees that periods
characterized by extraordinarily rigid patriarchal ideology—like the
Victorian era in which Freud wrote—are characterized as well by
cruel child-rearing practices and increases in sexual assaults on chil-

dren.[30] Similarly, incestuous families have been found to be highly patriarchal in their organization and values. In them, the father is often notably macho: his ability to show affection is stunted and his tendency to anger overwrought. Typically despotic and restrictive of other family members, at the same time he presents himself as pathetic and sad, needy of coddling and mollifying.[31]

Although such families are at the extreme edge of male dominance and sexual acting-out, they do not reside in a separate pathological category. For incest, like rape, is a cultural, political institution, overtly taboo yet covertly sanctioned. As men have a right to the bodies of women, fathers have a right, "guaranteed by the explicit or tacit consent of all men,"[32] to the bodies of their families, in particular the female bodies and those feminized by smallness, youth, or physical or mental frailty. "The only sexual right in their children that fathers do not have in any society is that of personal use. But given all his other powers, a father may easily choose to extend his prerogatives to include the sexual initiation of his children."[33]

This power is enforced by the weapons all fathers wield over all wives and children. From the withdrawal of love or money to the inflicting of violence, the father's sexual prerogative is fortified by the threat of abandonment, implicit in all fatherhood.

The taboo against incest is a cover-up, says an important group of French feminists influenced by and critical of psychoanalysis, a cover-up of the father's desire for his daughter. The father, the patriarch, originator of language and symbols, determines what is licit and what illicit in all relationships. He lays down the Law, and obeys or breaks it at will. Freud, the "father" of psychoanalysis, acquitted the seductive father of guilt as he forbade the daughter's real desire, neutralizing both in a stroke: the whole thing is her fantasy.

Not that Freudians take fantasy lightly. For in detouring around the real facts of paternal abuse, Freud the faulty navigator stumbled onto a New World. That world was the unconscious, a dark and multilayered repository of dreams, wishes, fears, and memories where, he said, "one cannot distinguish between the truth and fiction" fraught with genuine emotion.[34] In that world and out, argue the French feminists, the sociological truth that men can and do coerce their daughters into sex coexists fitfully with another, psychological truth: *daughters also desire their fathers.*

"[I]t is neither simply true, nor indeed false, to claim that the little girl fantasizes being seduced by her father," writes Luce Irigaray,

> *since it is equally valid to assume that the father* seduces his daughter *but that, because (in most cases, though not in all) he refuses to recognize and live out his desire,* he lays down a law that prohibits him from doing so. *That said, it is his desire which, come what may, prescribes the force, the shape, the modes etc., of the law he lays down and passes on, a law that reduces to the state of "fantasy" the little girl's seduced and rejected desire—a desire still faltering, barely articulate, silent perhaps, or expressed in signs or body language.*[35]

If Irigaray's language resembles a Möbius strip, it is because the feelings and contradictions she is talking about tend to loop around upon themselves, endlessly.

The young woman walking with her father, talking about books and feeling turned on, Michele Roberts dancing for her father, and Viola Jackson, privy to her father's affairs, were not exactly suffering. A father's affirmation of a girl as feminine and sexy is not altogether unwelcome. In spite of the power inequality between them, the unspoken coercion of a man over a girl, the child's understanding of the potential cost of not responding, men do not "make" their girls flirt with them. The "daughter's seduction," as Jane Gallop called it with deliberate ambiguity, is a dance for two.

Janet Gold, a thirty-six-year-old New York lawyer, recounts a story that vividly illustrates the conundrumlike atmosphere of the father-daughter relationship. On a family shopping trip in the mid-sixties, when she was about thirteen, she recalls,

> *My father went to buy tires or something, and I went with my mother to get my first bra. It was a training bra. Remember those? You got them if you were flat-chested but already in the seventh grade . . . We came out and met my father and he looked at me—I mean he looked at all of me; it was sort of a double take. And he said, "You look very nice. Uh, very grown up."*
>
> *God! When we left the house that morning I didn't have*

breasts and my father more or less left me alone. I mean, he paid attention to me but, you know, as a kid. Now, suddenly, I had them, and he was looking at me, at them, in . . . in this way! I said, "Daaa-deeee" [she imitates that uniquely teenage-female whine], and my mother said [here she switches to a classic tone of wifely reproach], "Herb . . . ," and then we all quickly started talking about getting a hamburger.

I guess he was trying to be complimentary, but I was mortified . . . but I also think, maybe I must have been a little bit thrilled, too—which of course made everything even worse.

Janet's father does mean to be "complimentary." But he is also asserting (probably unconsciously) his sexual ownership of her, his male prerogative to comment on her body. His comment is not just a well-meaning faux pas, though: it changes Janet. Before, she was just one of the kids. Now she has become the Other, the object of his sexualized gaze.

Janet's feelings about this are many and contradictory. It is terrifying, but also thrilling. It makes her a woman: to be looked at is to be female. She too is asserting her sexuality. Not yet truly pubescent, she wants to acquire the emblem of womanliness, an adult woman's undergarment. She feels invaded by her father, but she has also invited the invasion. She has chosen (also, probably unconsciously) to buy the bra when her father might notice it and to make sure he does by wearing a thin shirt. She senses her own desire for the father she now describes as "young, sexy, and suave," but immediately understands that her desire is wrong—it "*of course* made everything even worse."

Janet's father is seductive. He calls her "grown up," that is, sexual; the comment invites her desire. She desires too, she is seductive too. Both desires are forbidden, with the important difference between them that he may initiate or cut off the interaction at will and she must obey, that he is an adult, presumably with adult impulse control, and she, though somewhat grown up, is a child. Acknowledged, their mutual desire is quickly swept away and another appetite, for food, takes its place.

A trivial comment, a perfectly normal family interaction, hardly pathological, far from abusive—this is the daughter's seduction, structural, inevitable. Momentarily glimpsed, the attraction must be shuttled back out of sight.

Revelations of real incest tear only a tiny slice in the garment that cloaks fatherly desire. The outspokenness of incest survivors and even the criminal prosecution of seducing fathers gives only puny voice to female rage and does little to convict fathers in the hearts of daughters. It is a sad irony, but understandable, that the more wronged a daughter, the more she seems to deny the crime against her and hold on to the fantasy of a longed-for, "right" love. A parent who dies early in a child's life is enshrined in fantasized perfection. Similarly, when a father "abandons" a child by becoming her lover, she may continue to idealize him and to want him, the ever-absent good father.

"I do not think I am deceived about him," wrote the poet Sharon Olds, who alludes to abuse. "I know about the drinking, I know he's a tease, / rigid, selfish, sentimental, / but I could look at my father all day / and not get enough . . ."[36]

Most daughters are not abused by their fathers. Yet their reasons for rage are on a continuum with those of their victimized sisters. In paternal absence, emotional inaccessibility or passivity, inappropriate seductiveness, or violence, there is abundant cause for female hatred of the father, says New York psychologist Virginia Goldner. But in her practice Goldner rarely hears such feelings expressed. It's not the hatred itself, but its male object that accounts for this ferocious repression; women, Goldner reports, commonly experience and freely speak hatred for their mothers.

The feelings that hate comprises—resentment, contempt, frustration, envy, rage—fester in the shadow that the absent father casts. There's evidence that these repressed feelings make their way into the daughter's adulthood. Psychologist Seymour Fisher found that good female relationships with men depend on the daughter's feeling that her father will not desert her.[37] The unreliability implicit in fatherhood—the deep, unconscious expectation of paternal abandonment—nourishes the man-hating directed at husbands and lovers. In that sense, paternal conditionality undermines trustworthy heterosexual relationships.

Still, the longing that clings to paternal absence and the desire that is the underside of sexual threat are like hardy creepers choking out the negative feelings. Longing and desire are fertilized in the rich loam of idealization—both the personal idealization of the fantasized perfect father and the cultural idealization of the symbolic perfect father, the patriarch. There is almost no room left for hatred. By all rights, says Goldner, daughters should feel some hatred for their fathers. But, she says, they almost *cannot:* "Idealization is a thick, thick defense."

Servile Sedition

The patriarchy makes of men seers and heroes, strong and irreproachable emperors, and it entrusts women with polishing those images as they protect the men themselves. The flaw in this system, however, is that in the intimate empire the female subjects know their ruler intimately. It is women who weave the emperor's invisible clothes and the same women who reveal his nakedness.

A female underground passes along its intelligence—some fact, some rumor, some slander—from mother to daughter. Alone in the kitchen, in the car on the way to school, late at night when Dad is reading in his armchair, mothers indoctrinate their daughters in a secret code of cynical wisdom—teaching that men are frail, that their confident stride through the world is enabled by the women scurrying noiselessly around them, clearing obstacles, sweeping up messes, cushioning falls, kissing bruises with cool lips that murmur "baby," double entendre intact. By the palpable fact of maternal omnipotence in the infant's world and the propaganda mothers later transmit, daughters learn the female dialect of patriarchal doublethink like a second tongue: Men are powerful/men are weak. Women are weak/women are powerful.

"My mother called my father the Lord of the Manor," says Gracie Miller, a fifty-nine-year-old flight attendant.

She would jump up and greet him and make a big fuss: he looked tired, he needed to eat. He called her Mommy and he was the favored child. He didn't talk to us kids at all. Never talked. He had very little to do with what went on in the house. He wasn't cruel, just out of it . . . He was a diabetic and he did take insulin, but he gave his illness to my mother to take care of.

Not only Mrs. Miller but also her children were their father's mommies, an arrangement Gracie resents now and remembers resenting as a child who had no option but to participate.

She would give us candy to give him if we went anywhere alone with him. If she ever left, he would invariably have a [diabetic] reaction. He didn't talk to us and the only other relationship we had was his reactions. We were terrified of him—he was kind of a monster, although he was really a little, weak man.

"We had to act like he was really something special," says Gracie in flat, sarcastic tones venting bitterness at the parents who are both dead. "But I wasn't really sure why."

In her behavior, the mother honors the idealized father. Yet the assumption behind that behavior—that he needs to be held up—cracks the ideal. "He had a godlike, yet childlike, standing in the family," said Virginia Woolf of her father, Leslie Stephen, a rigid, imperious, and self-satisfied patriarch.[38]

Apprehension of the father's artificially enhanced power is one thing, though, and access to the anger that precedes wanting to topple him is quite another. Actually to topple him, as we will see in the next chapter, takes more than the muscle of one daughter, or even, as in the Stephens' case, a family of them. Before the thick defense of idealization can crumble and the full force of female resentment can pour through, there is another, auxiliary wall, which may be even tougher psychologically to storm: Mother.

Mother stands between children and father, charged with buffering each against the other. But because of her own conflicting loyalties she is not always successful, and along with her children she is the one—not he—who may suffer the casualty. In incestuous families, for instance, when a mother denies knowledge of the father's abuse or neglects to intervene, the victim often blames her for betraying a presumed maternal trust, not the father, who is expected to be absent at best and violent at worst.

Children compete with their fathers for their mothers' love, and in families where he gets incontrovertible priority, the slighted kids don't always accede. "My mother made it very clear to us that men were the most important things in life," says forty-five-year-old historian Suzanne Barsky, whose mother was a lawyer and father was a doctor.

> *She said if the house was burning down, she'd save my father rather than us. He was always right. He was a genius. He was a saint. Even though she was much faster and much brighter [than he], she never realized that. And he is still the center of the universe. If I criticize him—like say he drinks too much— she denies it. She'll deny anything about him.*

Such self-sacrifice and denial exact a toll on mothers, although few straightforwardly tell their daughters about it. Many daughters identify with their mothers' pain. "You are the pocket that was going to open/and come up empty any friday," writes Lucille Clifton, in a poem in which she is both seeking retribution for her mother and "forgiving my father."[39] Not uncommonly they bear the brunt of it. "My mother's rage toward my father was always taken out on us." Suzanne recalls.

Thea Krantz, forty-six, who grew up in a "matriarchal extended family" of poor immigrant Jews in New York, describes a sort of trickle-down effect in which her mother's rage at her father, a truck driver who worked sixteen hours a day and slept with other women, was visited on the daughter. Her mother's fury was hotter still, because she identified Thea with the prodigal husband: she "lumped me together with him." A good student, politically and sexually active, Thea was yet another family member who was moving out into the world, away from the hearth and out of Mother's control.

When Mrs. Krantz thundered, Thea ran to her father. But he did not take her in unconditionally. He made impossible demands: "He could make me cry by saying he was disappointed in me," says Thea. The daughter was rationally aware of the power hierarchy in her family, and she remembers rage at her father. But the emotion was removed, "almost abstract," as if it belonged to a character in a book. Hand-to-hand combat was with Mother.

> *My mother tried to leave my father, but she couldn't. She was stuck. She was depressed. She hated being a housewife, but she was ideologically committed . . . I hated him for disappointing my mother and getting her on my back. I always*

*blamed him for leaving her with me. I had to deal with her.
When she was mad at him she took it out on me.*

A daughter may clearly observe the harm her father does to her mother, with whom she identifies. She may understand that her mother's abuses of her are a kick-the-dog displacement of anger at the man she is too afraid of, dependent on, or defeated by to confront. Yet the daughter experiences her father's absence as the overbearing presence of her mother, who may not only be literally oppressive but is also symbolically so—she stands for dependency, passivity, and restricted possibility.

Thea's father neglected her mother—that she could see—but he also neglected her. He was absent. Not only was he out of firing range, he looked better from a distance. "Bastard" that he was, she could not help but long for him.

Mother-blame and a cultural reverence for men insulate fathers from the messy hostility of their daughters. The idealization of men comes locked together with the denigration of women, and these can paralyze women in self-hatred instead of man-hatred, self-blame instead of anger at the father.

Yet the fortress is not impermeable. The mother's disillusionment gains entrance where the daughter's disappointment has already secured a foothold, and together they steel like terrorists to explode the ideal of the perfect father. The family enlists the daughter in a kind of servile sedition: where she is schooled to submit to men, she is also, paradoxically, incited to rebel.

Man-hating is born, like Athena, from the head of the father. In the mother's pain, it utters its first words, tentative, pinched, and qualified. The women's movement of the 1960s and 1970s gave the daughter a voice and trained it to become steady and articulate, remarkably loud, and far-reachingly influential. In feminism, a chorus of sisters began to find harmony with their mothers. Struggling to free themselves of the shackles of daughterhood, they became new women.

5

Sisterhood and the Patriarch

Sexism is not the fault of women—kill your fathers, not your mothers.

Robin Morgan, "Goodbye to All That" (1970)[1]

BY THE END OF THE SIXTH DECADE of the twentieth century, the idea that men should be wiped from the face of the earth had gained a certain legitimacy among a surprising number of American women.

> *This society being, at best, an utter bore and no aspect of society being at all relevant to women, there remains to civic-minded, responsible, thrill-seeking females only to overthrow the government, eliminate the money system, institute complete automation and eliminate the male sex,*

wrote Valerie Solanas, a mad evangelist of man-hating, in her 1967 SCUM Manifesto. "The male's . . . a half dead, unresponsive lump, incapable of either giving or receiving pleasure or happiness," she continued.

> *He's trapped in a twilight zone halfway between humans and apes, and is far worse off than the apes, because he's . . . capable of a large array of negative feelings the apes aren't—hate, jealousy, contempt, disgust, guilt, shame, disgrace, doubt . . . To call a man an animal's to flatter him; he's a machine, a walking dildo.*

The tactics of the Society for Cutting Up Men (of which Solanas seems to have been the sole member) were as unconditional as her opinions: "SCUM'll kill all men not in the Men's Auxiliary of SCUM. Men in the Men's Auxiliary are those men who're working diligently to eliminate themselves, men who, regardless of their motives, do good, men who're playing ball with SCUM"—including, conveniently, "men who kill men." Nonmembers (potential victims) ranged from rapists, stockbrokers, and "Chairmen of Boards" to "lousy singers," "cheap pikers and welchers," and litterbugs.[2]

Needless to say, few women were ready to sign on with Valerie and drop a gender-sensitive neutron bomb on New York City, and most were horrified when she delivered on her promises and riddled Andy Warhol with a round of bullets. Yet declarations so preposterously hateful, jokes so thrillingly savage as SCUM's, had a kind of cathartic effect. As happens whenever history demands the profoundest rethinking—and for women the late 1960s was such a moment—a kind of lunatic nihilism helped burn over the old assumptions, clearing space for constructive revolutionary ideas. Compared with the likes of SCUM, a 1970 headline on the cover of the feminist tabloid *Everywoman,* asking "Are Men Human?" sounded moderate, a good topic for, say, the girls' high school debate club. Extremism made radicalism reasonable.

"The first time a woman said, 'Cut it off!' it was great," recalls the writer and early feminist Vivian Gornick. "You never dreamed for a minute she meant it. It was the announcing: we are no longer afraid to say the unsayable. At that moment a movement is born."

Early Stirrings

In reality, no movement is born in a moment, and this one had been gestating for a long time—as long as a century, and perhaps even longer. But the seeds of *modern* feminism, characterized by a unique blend of political and personal, were fertilized in the civil rights movement. There, would-be feminists were inspired by strong women and angered by sexist men. Later, when civil rights metamorphosed into black power and expelled white activists from the ranks, white women started to think about the desirability of an autonomous movement based around what is now called "identity politics." Although stung for a time by rejection, white feminists would ultimately take black nationalism as their model.

Women's relationship to the civil rights movement was always conflicted. Many of its first and most important leaders—Ella Baker, Rosa Parks, Fannie Lou Hamer, and Ruby Doris Smith, to name a few—were female, yet as early as 1964, when thousands of young people swarmed over the South to register black voters, women started to voice dissatisfactions with their roles in their organizations. One of the first public confrontations between women and men occurred within SNCC (Student Nonviolent Coordinating Committee), a linchpin organization of Freedom Summer. "On the front lines black women received their share of beatings and incarceration, but back at the headquarters—the 'freedom house'—they still . . . did the housework," writes Sara Evans, whose book *Personal Politics* traces the roots of women's liberation to the black movement and the New Left. "In the offices they typed, and when the media sought a public spokesperson they took a back seat. Gradually they began to refuse this relegation to traditional sex roles."[3]

Led by the very young, gifted organizer Smith, some women met to talk about their status in the group. "SNCC Position Paper: Women in the Movement" was in the end penned by three white women and presented anonymously at the Waveland, Mississippi, conference in November of 1964. As women, they were afraid of the reprisals they would suffer; "as white women," Evans notes, "they were in an increasingly ambiguous position in the black-led movement."[4]

White women, some African-Americans believe, may have compromised their own respect within the movement by what some saw as an aggressive campaign to bed as many black men as they could. Doubtless, sexism played a part in the opprobrium directed at these sexual adventuresses, but in any case their behavior piqued the black women's ire and did little to raise them in the eyes of their black male comrades, who, according to some sources, were on scoring sprees themselves.

For black women, the dynamics of sexism were not the same. African-American women had been aware, since early abolitionist movements, of their double oppression by race and sex; whites had used them not only as beasts of burden but as breeders and objects, willing or not, of the master's lust. But within the black community itself, women had historically maintained a measure of power. Slavery equalized the sexes in one way: all were workers. Yet women's dominance in the home endured, while men lost the status they'd traditionally held outside it. Perhaps for this reason, comments historian Paula Giddings, "In periods of Black radicalism, which always includes a self-conscious quest for manhood, Black men attempt to exercise their male prerogatives more vigorously."[5]

Of course, because racism does not mitigate the power of black men, as men, over women, black women are the ones on whom those "prerogatives" are exercised. Ella Baker, for instance, didn't push hard for the power she deserved in the Southern Christian Leadership Conference, of which she was a creator. "First," she explained, "I'm a woman. Also, I'm not a minister. And second . . . I knew that my penchant for speaking honestly . . . would not be well tolerated." As obstacles Baker cited "the basic attitude of men" and their "ego problems" with women who knew more than they.[6] Angela Davis, who left SNCC and later joined the Communist Party, wrote that she was "tired of men who measured their sexual height by women's intellectual genuflection."[7]

The SNCC position paper may have been the first document of feminism's second wave. Detailing women's subordination in both small and large ways, it declared that "women are the crucial factor that keeps the movement running on a day-to-day basis. Yet they are not given equal say-so when it comes to day-to-day decision-making."[8] The paper received little attention beyond ridicule, and National Chairman Stokely Carmichael's riposte lives on in the annals of misogyny: "The only position for women in SNCC is prone."

But no matter how disgruntled, most black women hung in with their movement. Few strode out into a movement of their own or white women's making. Like their mothers and grandmothers, these activists tended to place race above sex in their political loyalties. For one thing, an African-American man may mistreat a woman, but in the big picture he's not the Oppressor by a long shot; many black women simply do not view black men as the main enemy. Said Frances Beal, commenting on the women's movement in 1970, "It must be pointed out that at this time Black women are not resentful of the rise of the power of Black men. We welcome it."[9]

As we saw in the Brute, the pressure, both internal and from men, to present a politically united front, has straitened women's latitude in speaking out against male domination within the African-American community. This is not to say women haven't wanted to do so—or that they've been utterly silent. Linda C. Powell, in a review of Michele Wallace's *Black Macho and the Myth of Superwoman,* argued that the uproar around it and Shange's *for colored girls* . . . represented "the first stirrings of an understanding that Black male privilege *does* exist—no matter how limited, how circumscribed, or how specific"; they "show[ed] how much the Black community wants to talk about sexual politics," and pointed up the need for a black feminism that would inform women's grievances with analysis and address them with solutions.[10] Essayist bell hooks has for decades encouraged such a debate, and deplored the way it has been perverted and undermined by the white-dominated mass media, which perennially focus on whether black women are bad-mouthing their brothers.[11] Poet Audre Lorde suggests that solidarity itself may inhibit confrontation around sexual politics.

> *When a people share a common oppression, certain kinds of skills and joint defenses are developed. And if you survive you survive because those skills and defenses have worked. When you come into conflict over other existing differences, there is a vulnerability to each other which is desperate and very deep. And that is what happens between Black men and women because we have certain weapons we have perfected together that white women and men have not shared . . . certain additional weapons against each other because you've forged them in secret together against a common enemy.[12]*

Whatever obstacles African-American women have experienced in confronting sexism within their own communities, they have hardly been helped, and have sometimes been hindered, by white feminists. African-American women analyze white women's attitudes toward them in various ways. Some, like hooks, suggest that white women are titillated and terrified by a racist-stereotyped hypermasculine, violent black male; they therefore both "sympathize" with their black sisters' allegedly "worse" situation and condemn them for putting up with it. Hooks has concurred, to an extent, with African-American men's charges that white feminists' and their black allies' "focus on black male chauvinism is harsher and more brutal than critiques of patriarchy in general."[13] Wallace has written that white women practice a racism skewed in the other direction: they excuse black men, whom they view "not as men, but as fellow victims."

> *White women don't check out a white man's bank account or stock-holdings before they accuse him of being sexist—they*

confront white men with and without jobs, with and without membership in a male consciousness-raising group. Yet when it comes to the Black man, it's hands off.[14]

While individual white feminists exaggerated or underplayed African-American men's sexism, their movement from its inception did not address African-American women's issues and was unwilling to do so when those issues were brought to its attention. Poverty, poor health care and education, drugs, crime—these were often dismissed as not "women's issues." Meanwhile, Betty Friedan's "problem that has no name"—that sluggish ineffectuality afflicting middle-class housewives—was more than irrelevant to African-Americans, it approached the laughable. After all, the Victorian ethos that had put the white woman on a pedestal, at whose wobbly heights she was useless for work and out of reach for sex, knocked the black woman down as low as it elevated the white—but at least it left her competence and lust intact. African-American women didn't feel infantilized, they didn't feel weak. They felt tired! Cynthia Washington, a SNCC project director, observed in 1970, "It seemed to many of us . . . that white women were demanding a chance to be independent while we needed help and assistance which was not always forthcoming."[15]

Separatism was another serious impediment to black women's participation. Not only did it seem impractical and politically incomplete—a black woman couldn't split off her femaleness from her blackness—it resonated with ugly and painful associations. "We have a great deal of criticism and loathing for what men have been socialized to be in this society," wrote the Combahee River Collective, a Boston-based socialist-feminist group that formed in 1974, partly as a splitoff from the National Black Feminist Organization.

But we do not have the misguided notion that it is their maleness per se—i.e., their biological maleness—that makes them what they are. As Black women we find any kind of biological determinism a particularly dangerous and reactionary basis upon which to build a politic.[16]

To say that a tone of man-hating was the main thing that turned black women off white feminism is to oversimplify and even to misrepresent the truth. The other common explanation—that black women are cowed into silence by their men—doesn't get it right either. It is safe to say that African-American women found themselves at the beginning of the 1970s doubly oppressed, again, by the very movements allegedly founded to liberate them: black nationalism was gung ho to rejuvenate African-American masculinity at the expense of African-American women; white feminism denigrated and ignored black women in its own ways.

A fragile and far-flung black feminism did begin to germinate, eventually growing its own theory and scholarship, its own sexual liberation movements, its own activist and cultural institutions. What Alice Walker calls "womanism" also flourished, emphasizing a matrilinearity of strength and celebrating the lost arts and voices of African-American women. But the troubled relations between white feminism and black women would fester for decades; not until the middle 1980s would the white women's movement try seriously to exorcise the demons that marginalize women of color, including a kind of man-hating that made neither emotional nor strategic sense in an African-American context.

The "Boys' Movement"

White women would ultimately form an autonomous movement, as black nationalists had done. But before that, thousands signed on with the white student Left. If they harbored expectations of equal treatment there, those hopes were summarily dashed. In the ranks of what some feminists came to call the "male Left" (lesbian *Village Voice* columnist Jill Johnston referred to it as the "boys' movement"), women were quickly assigned to a sort of Ladies' Auxiliary, making the coffee, running the mimeo machines. The founding campaign of Students for a Democratic Society (SDS), in fact, was resistance to the Vietnam military draft. Strategically marginalized, SDS women were further insulted by their assumed role in the struggle. The slogan said it all: "Girls say yes to boys who say no." Women would be concubines to the revolutionaries, prizes for men's heroic acts.

New Leftists came out of the counterculture and preached militantly that politics were reflected in personal life. You were what you ate, wore, read, or bought (or more to the point, didn't buy);

your beliefs were mirrored in how, where, and with whom you paid the rent (communes shared everything from cooking duties to—in one of my houses—a cherry tree). Every word, act, and taste, down to a preference for the Beatles or the Rolling Stones, could be assessed for its political correctness.

Yet analysis of the sources of "false consciousness" (which might result in, say, liking the Beatles—or was it the Stones?—better) was more abstract. People talked about "white-skin privilege" but rarely admitted to fearing a black person on the subway. Similarly, a man could read Engels' *Origin of the Family, Private Property and the State* and parrot its thesis: women were the proletariat of the proletariat; he could discuss in his study group how the husband is the family's foreman and the wife its line worker—and still not think twice about running the meeting while she served the coffee.

An emergent feminist faction of the Left, however, was itchy to get down to cases. "I thought it was very important to see men as the enemy, to concretize men as the enemy," said New York historian Ros Baxandall. "The Left always had these vague things like social institutions. But this meant that men were in the positions of power and you could do something about it. It did mean *my* friends and *my* husband."

When women started making their complaints known, a few fair-minded men took their criticisms straight to heart and tried to mend their ways. But most men were self-righteously aggrieved, and in response to what they considered *ad hominem* attacks shot off a barrage of *ad feminem* attacks, including aspersions on women's looks, and the charge these chicks were man-hating crazies, nothing a good fuck couldn't cure. While black and Third World caucuses were vigorously encouraged (even though there were few black and Third World people to form them), men refused to put women's issues on the floor and when women tried to organize separate meetings obstructed these with accusations of "divisiveness."

Such hostility, some argue, left women no choice but to pack up their tents and go their own way. Virginia Blaisdell, a forty-eight-year-old lesbian photographer and art director, was married in the 1960s and active in New Haven. She believes "feminism needn't have been divisive, but [the men] made it that way by their responses."

We all started out calling ourselves socialist-feminists. We worked very hard to have our agenda included in the overall New Left agenda. After we had been meeting a couple of months, some of the women noted some flak from their husbands. So we did this whole presentation about why women are oppressed and why men should take it seriously. We dredged up every economic statistic we could. We talked about history, we talked about other countries. And all we got were hostile and stupid comments. They told us socialism would take care of everyone. Imagine if a black had gotten up and said, "Here's why you have to deal with this problem," the kind of sit-up-tall respect they would have gotten. With us, their first concern was, who's going to take care of the kids?

Male hostility came out in formal organizational as well as seemingly trivial ways. A woman editor at a left-wing magazine in New York (ironically, one of the first to run articles about women's liberation) recalls engaging a male coworker in a discussion of sexism at their office. As their talk progressed, they decided to tape it (like their President, they were afflicted with a compulsion to save every utterance for posterity), and when they finished, the man leaned back in his chair. "That was really great," he said, as after a good meal. "Why don't you transcribe it and run off some copies?" (She didn't.)

At another underground newspaper in New York, the female staff did more than refuse to type. In January of 1970, they took over the paper's offices, locked the men out, "liberated" the paper, and issued it as one of feminism's first publications.

The Rat was renowned for its uncensored copy ("Clit Flit Big Hit," on masturbation, was an article in the last issue before the liberation) and a classified section that served as recruiting ground for the grunts of the sexual revolution: a crudely lascivious photo captioned "WANNA SEE MY PUSSY?" ran next to "THREE CHICKS NEEDED FOR ORGY. 13 TO 15 . . . Ask for Arty after 9 P.M.," and so on. Working conditions for women reflected the words on the pages, and vice versa: *The Rat*'s masthead featured editorial comments beside the female staffers' names on their bodies and alleged sexual proclivities.

"We have met the enemy, and he's our friend. And dangerous," wrote Robin Morgan (later the editor of *Sisterhood Is Powerful* and now the editor of *Ms.)* in a lengthy battle cry called "Goodbye to All That," which dominated the flagship issue of the mutinous publication. Morgan and her coconspirators had had enough, she said. Enough of "the little jokes, the personal ads, the smile, the snarl. No more brothers . . . No more well-meaning ignorance, no more co-optation, no more assuming that this thing we're all fighting for is the same: one revolution under *man,* with liberty and justice for all. No more."

"Goodbye . . ." was subtitled "Women Inspired To Commit Herstory" (WITCH), and the *Rat* liberation did just that: it was a milestone not only in the formation of an autonomous women's movement, but of a faction that washed its hands of the Left altogether. "Let's run it down," Morgan began, and proceeded to name the names and list the crimes of the male leaders of both the old and New Left, from the pacifist, "sweet old Uncle Dave [Dellinger]" to "WeatherVain," the men of the Weather Underground, then called Weatherman. "In the light they are all the same," she concluded.

As this play on the old misogynist maxim indicates, the document was also a milestone for unrepentant man-hating.

> Let it all hang out. Let it seem bitchy, catty, dykey, frustrated, crazy, Solanisesque [sic], nutty, frigid, ridiculous, bitter, embarrassing, man-hating, libelous, pure, unfair, envious, intuitive, low-down, stupid, petty, liberating. We are the women that men have warned us about.[17]

Wavering

Other women were not so eager to repudiate the Left. Committed socialists, communists, and anarchists, they saw women's liberation as one part of the economically and racially just society they envisioned.* Besides, the Left was their life: it provided community, workplace, family, friends, and lovers. Politics was heady, sexy, and energizing, the barricades a fabulous mating ground. To erect new

---

* Recent events in Eastern Europe reveal how inconsistently socialist and communist countries have applied their principles of justice to women. Women's rights have consistently been sacrificed to the "greater good." In the Soviet Union, contraception is almost impossible to find and women resort to abortion as a regular means of birth control. In Rumania, brutal pronatalist policies forced women to have thousands of babies they couldn't afford to keep, and whom they ended up abandoning in hellish, AIDS-ridden orphanages.

barricades—with men on the other side—meant giving up a lot. "I grew up in the heterosexual holocaust, and wore miniskirts and flirted like mad," said Naomi Weisstein, a founder of the Chicago Women's Liberation Union and member of the New Haven Women's Rock Band. "I took off my makeup, wore pants, stopped flirting, and felt the enormous loss of male attention." Like Naomi, thousands of feminists in the Left would eventually take their placards and go home (and then back into the streets with the women). But few did it without regrets or a lot of vacillation along the way.

Today, when women have created separate spaces to do everything from pumping iron to drafting planks for the Republican Party platform, it is hard to conceive of the audacity of doing *anything* that specifically excluded men. Even in its smallest manifestation, the act was a major decision (which, like everything else in those days, required lengthy debate: *"How many feminists does it take to screw in a lightbulb?" "Five. One to do it and four to write the position papers"*).

"I remember once we were going to have a party in our women's group and someone said, 'Should we have men at the party?'" remembers Ros Baxandall.

> We had to decide: could we have a party on a Saturday night and not have men there? The question on the floor was: Would it be fun? We had a long, long discussion about whether it would be fun!

"People called us man-haters," she reflects, "but I thought of us as liking men too much."

Having a boring time wasn't the only risk, Ros implies. Girls had always to worry about their reputations, and feminists were, after all, still girls. If on Monday you distributed leaflets about sexism, on Wednesday you went to your women's consciousness-raising group, and then on Saturday night you had an all-women's party . . . what was the only logical conclusion? You were either a lesbian or you hated men (more or less interchangeable insults at the time). Some women were so sensitive to this charge that, like Washington, D.C., feminist Marilyn Webb, they tried to preempt it.

> *We have developed our own kind of femininity [she wrote in 1968] and enjoy being women who love men and do not see them as the enemy. We are not the cold, gray-suited women of the Twenties, nor the "masculinized" ones of the present. Staid suits have been replaced by the colorful dress of a turned-on generation of women who are asserting themselves as females as well as intellectuals.*[18]

Another symptom of the phobia of excluding men was the inordinate amount of ink spilled over the question, Will Women's Liberation Liberate Men Too? In a piece with the now improbable title "Are Men People?" Sylvia Hartman fulfills her female socialization to please men even as she tries to cast it off. After ruminating for a while on the main point—what will feminism do for men—she second-guesses her motivation for doing so. Is she "falling back into that typical 'feminine' way of getting what you want from men?" she wonders. Is she saying, in effect, "I'm only demanding equality and being a militant feminist for your sake, dear . . . It's your liberation that interests me." After interviewing a Few Good Men, Hartman comes to this I'm-okay-you're-okay conclusion:

> *So, MEN: I cannot, in fact I will not, promise you a rose garden. I care about your suffering. I care that you too are not free in this society. I want your liberation. But I want my own, too. And that's what I'm fighting for. That's where I must put my energies. At least for now. Women must fight for their own liberation and not cop out by saying it's all for you, for you men. If women's liberation does indeed lead to male liberation, that's beautiful. But, if not (to quote the late Fritz Perls), "it can't be helped." If, as men, you feel the need for male liberation in this society—then that's YOUR battle, not mine.*[19]

At two decades' distance Hartman appears a little schizy, capable of "are men people?" and "I care about your suffering" in the same three pages. But that schizophrenia was epidemic. The intimate enemy was sometimes impossible to live with, and women were keen to throw the bum out. On the other hand, they didn't want to get him too mad; he might be even harder to live without.

Such wavering was obscured by media images of hordes of saber-waving feminists heading straight in the direction of men's private parts. "Many of the new feminists are surprisingly violent in mood, and seem to be trying, in fact, to repel other women rather than attract them," opined *Time* magazine in 1969.

> *Hundreds of young girls [sic] are learning karate, tossing off furious statements about "male chauvinists," distributing threatening handouts ("Watch out! You may meet a real castrating female!"), even citing with approval the dictum of the late revolutionary Frantz Fanon: An oppressed individual cannot feel liberated until he kills one of the oppressors.*[20]

Accurate or inaccurate, such representations doubtlessly helped realize the alienation this writer was so concerned about. But even without the media's help, the movement had its own problems with some potential supporters. Many women who lived with, were married to, and had children with men felt that the exigencies of their lives were not being taken seriously by feminists whose youth, childlessness, and relative wealth made revolutionary talk easy and manhating a rash joke.

Although decent child care was a major feminist demand and most women's gatherings provided it, some mothers were threatened by an early (though short-lived, as we saw with the Abductor) feminist polemic that child rearing was nothing but drudgery and childbearing the prime cause of women's oppression. These mothers interpreted such theory as an aversion to children, and not always without reason—especially if the child happened to be male. One woman recalls taking her nine-year-old son into a women's bookstore in California and being asked to leave him outside. "After that," she said, "I never felt the same about the women's movement."

Women most dependent on men—working-class or poor women economically tied to husbands and the male-dominated workplace—could not readily walk out on bad marriages or quit their clerical jobs and join a women's printing collective. Although a strong working-class women's movement did later evolve (and groups like the Congress of Labor Union Women are among the few progressive women's organizations surviving in the 1990s) back then working-class women were likely to wonder if they had as much to lose as to win from women's liberation.

"We never called ourselves feminist publicly because we saw

that on a lot of the economic issues we were going to have to do things with men, like taking the city to court when they were paying janitors more than janitresses," says Judy Sayad, a thirty-five-year-old printer in Chicago. Sayad was drawn into the movement as a teenager when a youth worker set up a women's group in her working-class Chicago neighborhood of Cicero; she went on as a member of the socialist-feminist Chicago Women's Liberation Union to organize in other sections of the city, such as Albany Park. "We were always denounced for not being female-identified enough. I thought that was fine for nice middle-class communities to say," Sayad comments. "But people were coming to us who could not leave their husband even if he was berating them three nights out of four, because they'd be on the street if they left."

Some of these women, like the black activists I discussed above, felt that their husbands suffered alongside them.

> *I think one reason why our women did not become radical feminists was that they more clearly saw it had to do with the world more than with the individual man. They saw him as the carrier of the shit. You'd see in Evanston [a well-to-do Chicago suburb] the women had some charge, some ownership of the world. The husband had a secretary or ran a factory. None of us had any illusions about being in charge, or our men being in charge.*

Class solidarity did not "save" the destructive marriages of Albany Park. In fact, by creating institutions for women in need—battered women's shelters, day-care centers, and free clinics—and fighting for abortion and better pay and housing, feminism enabled women to leave unbearable situations. As well, Sayad says, a nascent lesbian-feminism provided Albany Park women with a kind of sanctuary, rickety though it was.

> *I think in practice a lot of them were in the closet and that was their way of getting out . . . Our intent in organizing Albany Park mothers was not to find lesbians. But we'd have these groups of mothers and within four meetings they'd be asking about the women's bars. Then they'd be involved in huge battles with their families and their husbands—having their car fucked with, getting thrown out, losing their kids. Burning all their bridges.*

Not only miserable and economically dependent women felt conflicts between feminism and married life. Happily married feminists felt a different, but also painful, tug. Bernadette Cray* was a member of a Cleveland women's collective in the 1960s; today, at forty-four, she has been married twenty-three years.

> I was always uncomfortable that my intimacy with women depended on seeing men as the Other. I didn't feel men were somehow different. For me it was things men did, but not that personalized sense of Us versus Men . . . I was in the civil rights movement and I had the experience of being the target of a lot of anger [from] blacks. And that always made me much more sympathetic to men's experience than a lot of women. I knew how unfair and angry that felt.

Bernadette respected her husband's opinions and sympathized with his pain.

> [After] every meeting, I'd go home and have to shuffle my married life with my feminist life . . . He'd say, "This isn't fair." He'd assert his point of view about some of the criticisms coming from the women's movement. More often than not I was persuaded it wasn't fair. So I was soft on men, and listening to men. People who didn't know him well saw him as a very traditional man—loud, bright, domineering. On the other hand, I knew the other side: he was terribly insecure, he would cry, he had a tiny self-esteem . . . When he would get criticized by women, it was very painful to him, he took it so hard. The women would get up enough courage to speak out against this big tough guy. He would feel so terrible. It was very hard. I knew the other picture.

A Cambridge, Massachusetts, anthropologist, Helen Whitney, was living with an older professor during the early women's movement. Although she broke up with him years ago, the issue of split loyalties is yet to be resolved.

> Increasingly, the relationship became quite difficult. Murray was supportive but he was the enemy—very much part and

---

* In this chapter, "Bernadette Cray," "Helen Whitney," and "Katherine Beasely" are not the speakers' real names. All the others are real.

parcel of the male Establishment, even though he was a leftist . . . It was a real problem in terms of taking stands. If you're going to take a political stand, how can you have an intimate relationship with someone against whom the battle lines were drawn? That has stayed with me, very much, since—that confusion about the contradictions of being a married feminist and trying to struggle against male power and privilege.

Needless to say, men also were unhappy about what was going on in their personal lives. The irony of their situation recalled whites' in the civil rights movement. These men were sexist, just as antiracist whites harbored racist feelings, but compared to most people they were reasonably supportive of feminism. Because they had the bad luck to be sharing bedrooms and kitchens with feminists, however, they caught the most shit.

Some of that support, I hasten to add, was lip service. For the fact was—and men sensed it—women's liberation would not just lead to men's "liberation." In one irreducible way women's liberation precluded men's: power is a limited commodity, and if women were to get some, men would have to lose some. The male fellow travelers who chimed in with the idea that sexism oppressed them too tended not to admit to having any power (the System made them do it). So how could they give it up? And among those men willing to endorse a feminist analysis in theory, few did much about it in practice. Among the men psychologist Carol Tavris interviewed for a 1971 study, "unliberated liberals," whose "attitudes are egalitarian but [whose] behavior is traditional," were in the majority. Seventy-three percent approved of equality in housekeeping and child care, for instance, but only 15 percent of the married men actually shared those responsibilities. "They agree that 'almost all men are unconscious sexists,' " she wrote, "but over half have been conscious sexists by deceiving a woman in order to have sex, and one in four does not think an intellectual peer is all that attractive anyway."[21]

With friends like these, feminists couldn't be accused of paranoia in seeing enemies under, and in, every bed. Man-hating was justifiable, and female apologists were getting harder to scare up. For women, man-hating was necessary, liberating, and productive—and, anyway, irrepressible; for their relationships, it was suffocating and counterproductive. Paula Webster and Lucy Gilbert wrote poignantly about the quandary many straight feminists found themselves in:

> Our rage, the very energy that has brought us to this point, alienates others . . . How can we expect men to give up their age-old privileges for us at the same moment we find everything they do selfish, rigid, tyrannical, soulless, and ruthless? What's in it for them?
>
> But if we try to suppress our anger . . . we're no better off. Expressing our anger leads to loss in the short run, and suppressing it leads to another kind of loss: a loss of the very self we have just started to discover, if only intellectually.[22]

Leavetaking

Like the demons in Pandora's box, that rage was out. Despite inner ambivalence, as the 1970s opened feminism was sounding brassier every day. The names of feminist publications and groups—*Battle Acts* in New York, *The Furies* in Washington State, *Rising Up Angry* in Chicago—cried defiance. *Bellyfull* in Toronto, *Goodbye to All That, Off Our Backs,* and *It Ain't Me, Babe* said women were fed up and weren't going to take any more. The slurs men hurled at women were caught and worn with smart humor: BITCH in Milwaukee, the magazine *Hysteria* in Cambridge, and in Chicago, *Killer Dyke.*

In the landmark essay "Man-Hating" (1970), Pamela Kearon donned as a laurel the crowning male insult: man-hater. "All arguments which tend to suppress the recognition of man-hating in our midst are reducible to this: *fear,*" wrote Kearon, a member of the radical group The Feminists, whose membership restricted the number of women who lived with men. "Man-hating is a subversive and therefore dangerous sentiment. Men, who control definition, have made of it a disgusting perversion."[23]

When someone oppresses someone else, she said, hatred, though regrettable, is inevitable. Usually, however, that hatred is directed at the victim, not the perpetrator, of oppression. "We have never given the idea of hating someone who has actually done something hateful to us a chance," she suggested helpfully. In the last paragraph of the short essay, she called for hatred of "a robust variety

. . . It is a difficult stance because it requires a fidelity to what is real in us and neither innocuous nor attractive to oppressors, to that part of you which turned you on to feminism in the first place. That part which is really human and cannot submit."[24]

Unapologetic, Kearon made man-hating more than understandable or excusable. Such hatred is the only position true to women's authentic humanity; it is, she implied, *necessary*. Eliding herself, "us," and "you," Kearon envisioned a female front united against men, stealing one of their ultimate weapons, the charge of unfemininity. She had, in both meanings of the day, "liberated" it. Appropriating man-hating, she disarmed, and empowered, it anew.

On its face, Kearon's article and the rhetoric that crackled around it represented an intensification of man-hating. But in another way, it indicated an opposite phenomenon: a relaxation of inhibitions against man-hating, and a cooling of passions negative or positive toward men, a new *indifference* to men. Kearon's piece was less a diatribe of man-hating than a reasoned theoretical treatise in its defense. She examined the subject rationally, because she had some distance on it.

Combing the literature of the time for attitudes about men, I was struck by a change around 1971 (I keep talking about gradual changes, but it's astounding, really, how fast everything was happening). Suddenly, discussion of men virtually disappeared. In *Up from Under,* a paper "For, By, and About Women," for example, the articles ranged from "How to Change a Tire" to "Vaginal Infections." There were pieces penned by welfare mothers, prisoners, waitresses, a piece called "Storybook Lives: Growing Up Middle Class," letters and articles by black women—but almost nothing on men. Until the mid-1980s, feminist journalism and women's studies were all but oblivious to men.

A woman in Minneapolis told me her husband had smirkingly asked her when she returned from a women's group meeting in the early 1970s, "So, what do you girls talk about? How good we are in bed?" She said it occurred to her that yes, their husbands' sexual prowess (and lack thereof) had been discussed in the early meetings, but that lately talk had turned to women friends, mothers, and feelings about work; men were hardly mentioned anymore. "He couldn't imagine a group of women talking about anything but men, and in a way, I couldn't either—until I sort of mentally checked down the list. Heavens! It wasn't men!"

Her realization was one of those small but grand moments of understanding that *Ms.* magazine calls a "click." Men, always the Most Important Issue even for feminists, had become minor players in a historical drama written, directed, and starred in by women. In every kitchen, feminists were downing pots of coffee, fueling themselves through nights of urgent, exhilarating, uproarious, wicked talk. In every burg women were kicking away in their karate schools, gobbling up the latest women's history in their bookstores, gazing at their cervices in self-help groups, writing and running off the latest issues of their newspapers, demonstrating in front of the bank, City Hall, and the courthouse. Out in Fresno, California, the housewives were calling a general strike. In Chicago, a collective called Jane was arranging safe illegal abortions for hundreds of women; within a matter of a few years, *Roe v. Wade* would stand as an achievement rivaling universal suffrage. Every other weekend, feminists were convening at some other campus to jabber and plot, dance, demonstrate, and dream.

Where were the men? Home taking care of the babies? (Unlikely.) Crying in their cups? (More likely.) Watching the football game? (Most likely.) Lots of women didn't know, and furthermore, they didn't care. They were busy with each other.

One of the early and lasting triumphs of feminism was to revalue the female friendships that had sustained women yet for so long been denied and denigrated; these newly acknowledged and honored liaisons promised vast wells of potential love and support. Women had only just begun to sip. The happy feeling of sisterhood began to eclipse the pain of separation, the onerous burden of hatred, or indeed strong feelings in either direction for men. "I don't remember a contempt for men as much as an enormous liberation," said Naomi Weisstein.

Before, I thought of myself as being in prison vis-à-vis women, who had always been my primary companions, and yet there had been this great reserve and this great ranking of relationships. It was okay to break a date with a woman if a man called you . . . I was incredibly lonely after graduate school. I was married. We went places as couples. When women talked to each other in couple situations, it was like making radio connections from Shanghai to New York.

My own feelings of sisterhood were that the reserve was gone, we could love each other, we could respect each other. There was no longer a ranking of ourselves as subordinates making the best of each other but as independent actors in history. People fully deserving of the respect we used to squander on undeserving men. For once I had a community in the best sense of the word.

Recalls Katherine Beaseley, a Chicago schoolteacher:

My marriage was falling apart but I didn't know it. I was very happy that I was out of the house all the time and working all the time, and my husband didn't make a fuss about my not being home.

When Katherine realized he was in a frenzy of infidelities—"even sleeping with the babysitters"—she was hurt and angry, but had no impulse to dispense her husband's own medicine. "I was so involved in the women's movement, I had no time for affairs. I wasn't interested in men at all."

Fatigued by and ideologically averse to appeasing men and perhaps encouraged by the antiguilt cant of the personal-growth movement then reaching an apex, women were hanging up their emotional nurse's caps and letting their ailing relationships languish. "By that time, I wasn't struggling with my husband to understand. In the beginning of the women's movement I did, but quickly it seemed impossible," said a New York poet. "I was so turned on by being with women, and our collectivity and our activity, that men quickly assumed a much smaller place in my psyche. So I didn't think of losing your man as such a terrible, threatening thing."

Sisterhood fortified women against the fear of male rejection. Within the female circle, it was hard to feel abandoned.

Sisterhood Is Complicated

At its most glorious, sisterhood is a brilliant amalgam of female friendship, trust, and righteous purpose. A magical infusion of the best of intimacy with the best of collectivity—the sense of being profoundly known and the thrill of immediate mutual recognition, the safety felt among loved ones and the courage in numbers, personal affirmation and group solidarity, self-esteem and mass power. "[W]hen we're exhausted from dredging up facts and arguments for the men whom we had previously thought advanced and intelligent, we make another simple discovery: Women understand," wrote Gloria Steinem. "We may share experiences, make jokes, paint pictures, and describe humiliations that mean little to men, but *women understand.*"

At its worst—or less pejoratively, its most misguided—sisterhood excludes rather than includes, homogenizes all women to a political, cultural, sexual One (like homogenized milk, she's white, of course), and denies racial, class, and cultural difference. "The odd thing about these deep and personal connections among women," continued Steinem, "is that they often leap barriers of age, economics, worldly experience, race, culture—all the barriers that, in male or mixed society, seem so impossible to cross."[25]

Often, yes, but not always. In reality, those barriers are difficult to cross, and more so if you are climbing from the "outside" in.

The dazzling idea of a universal Woman—who is by virtue of oppression the same as her sister whether she lives in a grass hut or a high-rise apartment building, is a monogamous Goddess-worshiping lesbian or the wife of a polygamous Muslim—catapulted second-wave Western feminism into being and mobilized it into action. Yet the very construction of the category "Woman" effaces the separate existences of a large number (maybe even most) of the lowercase-*w* women it presumes to comprise. Relegating them to Otherness, it negates feminism's promise: self-determination for all women.[26]

Western sisterhood is predicated on one kind of difference: gender. By definition, women are in, men are out. Sisterhood can be pluralistic—and is trying to become so—but for most of feminist history, its de facto racism, xenophobia, and, often, ideological parochialism have privileged gender as the paramount, indeed the only, form of difference.

In fact, at the movement's inception, sisterhood itself was unselfconsciously sexist. Lesbians would soon wield considerable political and personal force in the movement. But when they first came out in certain quarters, the walls went up. In 1970, for instance,

National Organization for Women President Betty Friedan excoriated the group's Radicalesbian caucus as a "lavender menace," pronounced the struggle for gay liberation exhibitionistic, irrelevant, and potentially harmful to the movement (it would turn off the so-called mainstream, she said), and tried to purge NOW's leadership of visible lesbians. Rita Mae Brown, who'd been pushing lesbian issues in the organization, was fired from her job as editor of the New York newsletter, and left the group furious.

Fortunately, Friedan and her supporters did not prevail, and NOW currently has a substantial lesbian membership. Yet in spite of the early, radical feminist demand for the unfettering of female sexual expression, homophobia and its less combative cousin heterosexism were still rampant in the movement. New York's Redstockings, for whom sexual freedom was always a bottom-line demand, nonetheless operated under what member and writer Ellen Willis called a "heterosexual presumption."

> *It was tacitly assumed, and sometimes explicitly argued, that men's need for sexual love from women was our biggest weapon in both individual and collective struggle—and that our own need for satisfying sexual love from men was our greatest incentive for maintaining the kind of personal confrontation that feminism required.[27]*

Sharing details of their sex lives—one of the delicious activities of early feminism—would presumably help women in that personal confrontation and make straight sex better, and it did. But it also had the effect of undermining the heterosexual presumption. A lesbian architect, who was a graduate student in Wisconsin and living with a boyfriend in 1970, recounts with humor and suspense a consciousness-raising group meeting that year, on the topic of orgasm.

> *The very first woman, I'll never forget—this woman was a clerk at the college, married with two kids, I think she was around thirty—she talked a little and then she said, in this teeny-tiny voice, "I never come when he's inside me."*
>
> *There was this sort of hush in the room. I mean, the same was true for me, and I'd been walking around forever with this deep dark secret of my sexual neurosis—I hadn't even told my shrink—and, you know, faking [orgasm], the whole bit. I felt like running outside and shouting, "It's not just me! I'm not sick!"*

> *. . . I swear, at least half the women said they'd never had a vaginal orgasm and a few said they'd never had an orgasm at all. Then the only out lesbian in the group, who had the role of, like, Tickler of the Conscience, said kind of slyly, "You know, there is another way." Whoa! [She laughs explosively.] That was definitely one of the big moments of my life.*

Masters and Johnson had earlier challenged the idea of intercourse as the goal of sex and the route to women's satisfaction. Yet heterosexuality itself remained untouched; intercourse was still popularly accepted as "the sex act." It took feminism to put question marks around all genital sex.

In her influential 1968 essay "The Myth of the Vaginal Orgasm," Anne Koedt deployed the researchers' findings on the role of the clitoris in female arousal to suggest that intercourse was *irrelevant* to women's pleasure, that the penis—and by extension, men—might be "sexually expendable." Koedt challenged the unassailable: the "natural" affinity of the vagina and the penis. Calling heterosexuality a social invention and not a biological given implied that it could be dispensed with. If it was an institution, it could be smashed.

As more uncloseted lesbians entered the discourse, not only sex, but heterosexual love, came under attack. In "Vaginal Orgasm as a Mass Hysterical Survival Response," the radical lesbian Ti-Grace Atkinson wrote:

> *A man's penis and a woman's vagina are obviously different. Male orgasm is analogous to clitoral orgasm. Where, then, does vaginal orgasm come from? People say it's learned . . . Why should [a woman] learn vaginal orgasm? Because that's what men want. How about a facial tic? What's the difference?*
>
> *And love. As long as we're on sacred cows, let's finish them. What is love but the pay-off for the consent to oppression? What is love but need? What is love but fear? In a just society would we need love?*[28]

Looking back at that era in their introduction to *Powers of Desire*, Ann Snitow, Christine Stansell, and Sharon Thompson point out how this polemic, which reduced sex with men to an occasionally interesting means of keeping the sheets warm, helped to constrain some women's freedom of sexual expression. Although other feminists like Germaine Greer and Betty Dodson interpreted the new research expansively, as one more evidence of women's vast sexual capacity, Koedt et al. had a powerful influence. "[A]fter the salvos of Koedt and Atkinson, virtually no grounds remained for desiring sexual intercourse . . . Certainly, it was very difficult for a feminist to admit that she found penetration pleasurable or orgasmic."[29]

Still, for women whose sex lives had meant silently enduring their husband's pulverizing pursuit of the vaginal orgasm ("Sometimes, you know, you'd almost rather be playing Ping-Pong," one woman mused during a consciousness-raising session),[30] or for those whose homosexual desires had been quashed by conventional heterosexual expectations, the possibilities were earth-shattering. Women would no longer have to strong-arm unwilling men into performing cunnilingus. Lesbianism, once considered the biologically or neurotically determined "condition" of the few, became a conscious option for anyone—and many women chose it, at least temporarily.

If women could fix their own cars and publish their own newspapers, if they'd soon be making babies in test tubes, as Shulamith Firestone proposed, and now, if they could give each other orgasms, how important *were* men after all? If, as the New York Radical Feminists put it, heterosexual love was "an emotional cement to justify the dominant-submissive relationship,"[31] the idea that women could be "woman-identified" in all spheres promised a solution to the myriad problems of sleeping with the enemy. Like Moses, lesbians would lead the female nation into the desert, where they could live and love without masters and unlearn the slave mentality.

For a while, lesbians gently tried to sell tickets to the exodus. "Jill Johnston was always coming up to me and saying, 'Still straight?' " recalls Vivian Gornick. But when straight women did not readily join the cause and many did not change their homophobic ways, gay women started migrating into separatism. It was an ironically painful time, with lesbians denouncing and rejecting longtime friends solely on the basis of their heterosexuality. And while lesbianism (and the practical and theoretical contributions of lesbians themselves) would continue to play an inestimable role in feminism, while gay and straight women would again work together, the doctrinaire separatism of the early seventies sent some feminists packing, never to return to the movement.

Separatism is an ideology and a strategy of both high manhating and its utter mitigation. Lesbianism, gay women frequently point out, is not hatred of men but love of women. And when need for men is out of the equation, hatred is suddenly uncompelling; dependency, as we've seen, is one of the root causes of enmity. At the same time, to withdraw from men altogether, to declare them useless—this can surely be seen and felt as an act of hatred. For men whose wives marched out of their bedrooms to take up with their female lovers (and lots did) there was no greater shock, no greater rejection.

Old Castles, New Households

The "wimmin's culture" that separatists built constitutes a large part of what remains of the movement. Compleat from its Goddess down to its candida-free dietary guidelines, it has devolved in large part to a big cozy Women's Chamber of Commerce, the feminist corollary of hippie capitalism: "What's left of the counterculture," a friend quipped, "is the counter."

This network of women's institutions, though vital to the happiness of many women and the survival of some, has had minimal impact on institutionalized patriarchy. A primary reason is that the ideology supporting it does not aim fundamentally to take down the foundation of patriarchy: gender. "Wimmin's culture" represents the ascendance of *cultural feminism* over *radical feminism*—that is, it accepts the mainstream culture's definitions of masculine and feminine and "aim[s] at reversing the cultural valuation of the male and the devaluation of the female" rather than eliminating the gender system itself.[32]

Still, feminism, radical and cultural, spread across the globe throughout the 1970s, and it has fundamentally changed the world. Not only has it achieved reforms in law, politics, medicine, and the media (even the *New York Times* uses the word *Ms.*—and now *gay* too), it has altered the thoughts and expectations of women from the likes of Geraldine Ferraro to the Saudi Arabian women fighting for the right to drive cars or the Tanzanian villagers setting up women's agricultural cooperatives. Feminism has revolutionized sex, rewritten history, remade language, and unsettled our very trust in the "truth" of what we perceive. Although women are still poor and disenfranchised and their bodies still the site of combat, feminism has struck great blows against the patriarchy. In America, it has rattled his castle, the family, to the timbers.

Man-hating, we have seen, helped set off the tremors of these upheavals. And like the formula for a powerful explosive, feminism's slogan, "the personal is political," encapsulates the ideological, tactical, and emotional energy that ignited the bomb. To personalize the political—to identify father, lover, husband, or boss as patriarch—was to enlighten intuition and feeling with analysis and to endow daily skirmishes with seriousness: feminism was a worldview, not a personal gripe; a struggle, not just a domestic spat. At the same time, to recognize the political in the personal was to ratify and empower women's traditional realm of authoritative speech, the so-called private. Journals took on the pedigree of literature; the personal story made its way into mainstream journalism; "social history," the history of everyday life, became central to understanding the past; and even gossip was legitimated as a kind of rhetoric.

The twin forms of new-feminist political discourse—the private publicity of consciousness-raising and the publicized privacy of speak-outs on rape, battery, and illegal abortion—reinforced each other. They instilled confidence in their participants as they stripped male-inflicted injuries of shame and self-blame; they elevated formerly "trivial" crimes to places of rightful importance as women carried out a massive auto-da-fé against their perpetrators. In living rooms and on podiums across the country, "outrage, the outness of rage," as Alix Kates Shulman put it, thoroughly obliterated the false divisions between the public and the private.

Identifying the patriarchy as a social-political structure, whose seats of power could be located everywhere from a shah's throne to the chair of the chairman of the board to Father's favorite recliner, enabled women in seemingly opposite ways to feel strong and act forcefully. It simultaneously brought sexism close enough to experience viscerally and removed it to a place of rational contemplation. Sexism could be touched and smelled, and thus fought hand-to-hand. But the intellectual distance of theoretical analysis provided a margin of safety—just enough so women could contend with the intimate threats of rebelling against men. When things got really scary, you could hate the Male Power Structure instead of Tom, Dick, or Dad.

On the way to smashing the Family, feminism constructed an oddly shaped "family" of its own. In this new family mothers and daughters did not engage in what Amy Kesselman called "accommodationist sniping"—resenting Papa while they bowed to his will, ridiculing his foibles while they stroked his ego and competed for his meager attentions, swallowing their rage at him while they vented the frustrations of his neglect on each other. The snipers moved out, and installed in their place was a full-scale politically conscious battalion of daughters.

The daughters put Father in the cellar and locked Brother and Hubby in the yard. Banding together as sisters, they paid the bills, ate at the table, and then did the dishes. Happily, they ran everything.

Where was Mother in this house of the rising daughter? In one way, she had displaced Father in the seat of honor. A vigorous search into lost women's literature and history was unearthing the foremothers and celebrating new heroines. Feminist anthropology was listening for female voices in other languages and gathering data to vanquish the false orthodoxy of universal female inferiority forever.

In the process, I think, women began to feel a kind of solidarity with their own personal mothers, followed—gingerly and not without anger—by compassion. Measuring the enormity of what former generations had been up against, young feminists started to pack away some of the old impatience and contempt for their mothers' conciliation and discover tolerance and even admiration for their resistance and resilience. A newly politicized understanding of gender socialization enabled women to repudiate the *roles* their mothers played, yet embrace the women themselves as fellow sufferers or even early rebels.

Consciously, then, Mother was becoming both human and heroic, a living link to the history of women's oppression and liberation. But unconsciously, she was still enormously powerful—all-giving and all-denying. She was still intruder and competitor, too good, never good enough. Endeared by her imperfection in conscious life, women were still wishing for the perfect mother. This infantile quest, say psychologists Nancy Chodorow and Susan Contratto, obstructs the feminist project of truly restructuring gender.

In their 1976 essay, "The Fantasy of the Perfect Mother," the two analyze feminist writings about motherhood and find in them a vacillation between fantasies of the perfect, or (if not for patriarchy) perfectible, mother on the one hand, and mother-blame on the other—both facets of the culture's ideology of the all-powerful mother. In these, they discern "a progressive logic . . . that moves a woman from an identification as daughter to an identification as mother . . . [which] is in its turn full of rage and fear." From this limbo of identification, in which mainstream ideology is swallowed whole, emerges a politics of unprocessed fantasy. The daughter-identity can't distinguish between infantile need and desire and is throwing a kind of politicized tantrum over Mother's "denial"; the mother-identity is so undone by "a sense that the conditions of patriarchy totally oppress" and isolate her[33] that she cannot integrate rational choice and responsibility into her analysis of family violence or maternal neglect.[34] Obsession with the mother-daughter dyad, moreover, limits women's ability to understand the role of the father in child development and in the reproduction of gender.

Discussing the women's peace movement, which tends to romanticize an "innate" female humanitarianism, psychoanalyst Adrienne Harris makes a related point. She suggests that in sisterhood feminists both cling to the fantasized comfort of that early relationship and defend themselves against the memory of maternal power and the discomfiting role it continues to play in adult women's lives.

> *The passion and idealization of woman-based political groups must indeed pull some of their appeal from an idealized longing for the fused symbiosis of mother and infant. But the idealization of woman-to-woman experience may also be a defense against the more tumultuous and conflict-laden experiences of separation, particularly for mother and daughter. In women's political groups, we may find remnants of the unconscious undertow of envy and guilt that seems a part of many women's move toward individuation.[35]*

Feminism is moving in the direction of balancing these two identities, I think, and at the very least it is deepening its understanding of motherhood (Sara Ruddick's *Maternal Thinking* is a good example). But as a group the early feminists felt and acted as daughters, still locked in wrestling with their fathers and mothers. Sisterhood protected women from the anger of the rejecting father and restored the self-esteem that a father-fostered femininity had chipped away at. It also insulated women from anxious and painful feelings about Mother.

Fear of separation—of saying, "I am not you. I am another person"—still contributes to the feminist denial of difference. Along with the obliteration of the uniquenesses of race, class, and culture (a process which derives as much from socially inculcated racism as from any individual family dynamic), the dogma of sisterhood imposes a censorship on many forms of psychological, behavioral, and political differences among women. Competition and ambition, the will to domination or submission, and myriad "unorthodox" sexual tastes have all at one time or another been renounced as "unsisterly." (Psychologist-anthropologist Muriel Dimen, writing an essay about competition between women, was stymied for months by the anxiety and guilt arising from simply putting the C-word on paper. Those feelings, she finally realized, were not *preventing* her from attacking the issue but were the issue itself.) Ideological debates and schisms like those around pornography, which might be viewed as the mark of a mature and complex movement, thus something to be proud of, are instead mourned as feminism's death, the political "heretics" accused as the movement's assassins.

Circling the wagons against intolerable difference has not, in the long run, been good for feminism. But a crude and (within its own parameters) unified sisterhood has served a vital political purpose. The realignment of family loyalty by gender, the embrace of Mother as symbol and ally, turned maternal omnipotence from a threat to a weapon. Feminists both vanquished and incorporated Mother's power. Without killing the lioness, they had eaten her heart.

And if sisterhood declared certain emotions verboten, it was also cemented by other emotions that threaten the mainstream culture—what the philosopher Alison Jagger calls "outlaw emotions." Feminists alarmed everyone when they didn't find sexist jokes funny, for instance, or yelled profanities instead of smiling demurely when male strangers "complimented" their bodies on the street. Sharing these feelings "normalized" and politicized them and made them a basis for action.

> *When unconventional emotional responses are experienced by isolated individuals, those concerned may be confused, unable to name their experience; they may even doubt their own sanity . . . When certain emotions are shared or validated by others, however, the basis exists for forming a subculture defined by perceptions, norms, and values that systematically oppose the prevailing perceptions, norms, and values. By constituting the basis for a subculture, outlaw emotions may be politically because epistemologically subversive.*[36]

Man-hating and its less obvious complement, mother tolerance, are such subversive emotions. In the historic political and economic tempests of the sixties, they were whipped into "a force of tremendous power," as Virginia Woolf described the nineteenth-century women's movement. The daughters became a primal horde rising up to overthrow the Father. To the second wave, as to the first, "the fathers, who had triumphed over the strongest emotions of strong men, had to yield."[37]

PART III

Living with Ambivalence

WHEN FEMINISM RECOGNIZED THE ENEMY in the beloved, when it gave a name and a voice to man-hating, it also gave birth to the dilemma of a generation. While loving men, women would now live in the shadowy consciousness of hatred as well. No longer would they be able neatly to divide public from private, good from evil, the men they loved—husbands, lovers, friends, fathers, brothers, or sons—from those they hated—the rapist, the mugger, or cop, the misogynist judge or politician. The most politicized man-hating would never again be distanced or depersonalized, and personal hatred would always feel so much bigger than just him and me.

Calling him by his institutional name, Patriarch, women momentarily depersonalized the father, and Man. They publicly demystified him, pulled back the cloak of his power, reduced him to humanness. Now they would begin truly to contend with him.

Part III is about contending. It is about twelve individual women and the strategies they employ in living with, or without, men. Writing this section, I had two choices. I could arrange the data into themes—what I call "strategies," such as "Withdrawal," "Battle," or "Attrition"—then gather examples, bits of lives, making each chapter a sort of medley of tunes whose first lines have the word *withdrawal* or *battle* in them. Or I could program a number of whole-woman symphonies, with fast and slow movements, dissonances and consonances, all of them unfinished. I chose the latter, mainly because as a reader I prefer to get to know a few people well rather than scan a crowd of like-seeming folk (disgruntled registered Democrats, antique-car enthusiasts, single teenage mothers . . .). But as I mentioned in the Prologue, by laying out individual strategies I don't mean to imply that people are able individually to undo the problems of man-hating and ambivalence or overcome the social forces in which they originate. If the first two parts of *My Enemy, My Love* privilege the general, this one attaches real faces to the idea of Difference and immerses us in all those "exceptions" that don't prove, but are, the rule.

During the last three years, I traveled around the country and interviewed about eighty American women.* We talked, sometimes once, sometimes more than once, in conversations that ranged from two hours to twelve, about their childhoods, friendships, loves, marriages, and divorces, about sex, children, work, politics, violence, and men in general. These women were frank, indeed magnanimous in their frankness; they labored, I think, to tell difficult truths to the best of their understanding, and to admit what they did not understand.

Demographically, my small sample roughly parallels that of the United States, except in one respect: age. Because my study begins around 1968, the dawn of postwar feminism, I talked primarily to women who were already conscious adults by that time. So my subjects range, like the focus groups for advertisers of Toyotas or Nutri-Grain and the majority of people who read and vote in this country, from around thirty to about seventy-eight, with the bulk in their mid-thirties to late forties. Curiosity, and some points of accuracy and comparison, impelled me to interview some younger women (and, as you've seen, listen to their music and their comedy and watch their films). But, while this book is relevant to them, it isn't always specifically about them. Who are the women of the Class of 1990, the "postfeminist" generation, and how do they feel about men? That is a needed, and, in fantasy, enticing, book—but not this one.

In other ways, I've tried to trace the shape of American womanhood. About three quarters of these women are white and of European ancestry; about 20 percent are African-American, and the rest are Latina and Asian. Except for a few who were born outside the United States and came here as children, all are at least first-generation American, and most are second- or third-generation, or

---

* Almost all spoke under the condition that I would change their names and certain identifying facts about them, which I did.

more: one African-American woman, an intake worker in a Cleveland birth-control clinic, counts six generations of her family in America. Her memory of her great-grandmother—her grandchildren's great-great-great-grandmother—may be part legend and part fact, but a delicious bite of living history in either case. Great-Grandma was a slave, brought over from Africa, and, says Marjorie, she was 115 when she died. Crooking a little finger, other hand to her waist, Marjorie says,

> *She had fingernails about this long. They didn't curve, they were straight—and she had hair about to here. She had two plaits; she wasn't bald, and she wasn't all white, just mixed gray. And she still could cook. She cooked on a fireplace, you know, put this pot on this wire hanging it from the fireplace and put the fire under there. And she was sitting in her rocking chair when she died.*

As to class, that jabberwock of American social relations, I had to make some assessments on my own, for the majority of my subjects termed themselves "middle-class." Judging from income, occupation, family of origin, and lifestyle, however, I'd place about 25 percent in the working class, and about 70 percent in the middle class. A handful of the women earned more than eighty thousand dollars a year, and one is a self-made millionaire. About an equal number are indisputably poor, working in menial or low-level clerical jobs, supporting children, and barely—or not quite—making ends meet, sometimes with some government assistance. The one woman I spoke to who was on welfare lives with her three kids in a large house in a well-to-do suburb of Atlanta. About a year and a half earlier she had left her husband, and he, with the self-canceling aims of reconciliation and revenge, had vowed to run her into bankruptcy. By the time I met her, he had just about succeeded.

The sample is a mixture of mothers and women without children; of wives, divorcées, lovers living with or apart from their partners, and single women; of lesbians—10 percent or so—and heterosexuals. Aside from the very permanent category of motherhood, I found a remarkable amount of fluidity. People's actual marital status changed over time, and their described status didn't always match what others might observe it to be. For instance, one woman who had been married once, for about seven years about fifteen years ago, started out saying she'd been "single forever." When she got around to telling me about the marriage, it was as if she were talking about some old-fashioned fictional character. Another woman, now over fifty, finalized her divorce nearly a quarter century ago, but still refers to herself in relation to that marriage, as "divorced." Her ex-husband is remarried with grown children by his second wife, but she calls him "my husband." She has not remarried.

Sexual identity, as I've said before, is similarly protean and subjective. I encountered only one "pure" lesbian—a thirty-seven-year-old woman who had never had sex with a man and didn't expect to —and for that matter fewer "pure" heterosexuals than might be expected. Most of the gay women had had male lovers, many had been married, and at least half of them were mothers. Of the straight women, some had had lesbian affairs and plenty of others had come close. Almost every interviewee named women as the people with whom she is most intimate. Social circumstance and sexual taste didn't always fit seamlessly together, either. Describing a fairly common situation, one New Yorker whose work, politics, and friendships circle around women, but who prefers sex with men, dubbed herself "a heterosexual lesbian."

I set out with one thesis: that man-hating exists, broadly in the culture and in individual hearts and households. It was not a *hypothesis*; I felt, and still feel, certain about it, although I was not averse to arguing the point. (Among the disputants was Leah Goldensohn, whose profile appears in the chapter "Withdrawal.") Beyond that, whatever hunches I may have harbored acquired qualifiers and counterexamples so fast that they were soon all but obliterated, like a printed page made illegible by a querulous reader's marginalia. Happily for me (otherwise I would have sunk into a slough of boredom) expected patterns didn't always bear out. "Logical" predictors of man-hating—feminist ideology, lesbianism, even traumatic experiences with men, including rape—didn't always predict man-hating. Indeed, feminists and lesbians were frequently among the least man-hating of all my subjects.

Each woman was insistently, quirkily herself. But that is not to say everyone was unpredictable—nor that certain feelings, values, and reactions couldn't be anticipated or understood in the light of forces outside individual circumstances. As cultural analysts and social historians have shown, and I've demonstrated throughout this book, there is no such thing as a strictly private life.

People in other eras generally acknowledged this fact. In the Middle Ages, say, even such currently private places as the nuptial bed were sites of communal involvement. Individuals did not separate themselves from the collective, and even kings conceived of their lives as moved by larger phenomena—Fate, God's will, Nature —as well as the accident of birth.

In contemporary America, privacy is a hallowed, if contradictory, concept. A person may legally shoot an intruder in her house, but the state may compel that same woman to give up her urine for drug analysis or undergo a cesarean section against her will. On a more diffuse level, the public is ever present in our private lives. People confess their marital problems to Oprah on network TV, and Johnny Carson shares tidbits about the financial and sexual lives of Robin Givens or Rob Lowe like a small-town farmer gossiping about his neighbors at a church supper. All of us breathe the culture's messages like carbon monoxide in the air—or more accurately, over the airwaves.

It is ironic (or maybe, a psychologist would say, a reaction formation) that in this highly public time we should share the illusion of an inviolable "self," over which each of us has a high degree of control. Cults like est and Scientology espouse a worldview in which the effects of material reality—say, poverty or gender—are dismissed and the ability to shape one's destiny made to seem limitless. The mass media now present our very bodies as infinitely "plastic," says the philosopher Susan Bordo, through exercise, surgery, or the insertion of colored contact lenses.

Unfortunately, bestowing people with an exaggerated sense of self-determination, absent correction for material or social reality, quickly slides into blaming them for their misfortunes, and women, we know, are very good at self-blame. So, as we saw in "The Invalid," the Western world is burdened with a veritable economic sectorful of popular psychology that holds women responsible not only for their own but also for their whole families' and their lovers' troubles as well. These books proffer self-help regimens for all manner of unhappiness, much of which a job with good benefits, a husband who did the vacuuming, and a week at a health spa might cure twice as efficiently.

Fortunately, at least eighty women in America have not been irretrievably brainwashed by the pop shrinks (although everybody, has read at least one of those books). I think a sociologist would be impressed, as I was, by the degree to which the people I interviewed perceived the environment—that is to say, the social world of politics, money, and ideology—to be a determinant of their lives. Where gender is concerned, even women who hold to the gospel that the sexes were created different would, somewhere in the conversation, insert a caveat like, "Well, of course, so much of this we learn growing up . . ." Formerly accepted collective female fantasies— the knight-in-shining-armor, for instance—are almost universally, though ruefully, confessed and just as widely critiqued. Logically consistent or not, American women seem to have internalized Simone de Beauvoir's dictum that a woman is not born but made.

A less extreme variant of the psycho-ideology of infinite self-determination, and one which I believe Americans share to an astounding degree, is the idea that each of us is an *individual* first and a social creature only secondarily, that we must figure out how to our own selves be true before we can happily take on anyone else. Freudian developmental psychology combined with personal-growth and New Age ideals of self-actualization give us what psychologists call separation-individuation, and not *inter*dependence, as the paragon of maturity.

Now, the idea that a person sets off alone to find himself is nothing new, and surely does not originate with Freud. Since the first flame-bearer brought the first fire, and the first storytellers sat around it to retell the traveler's tale, people have been embarking on such searches for identity. But from the Native American vision questers to Stephen Dedalus, the vast majority of these people have been men.

That women might take their own journeys to selfhood is a newer, though not totally new, idea. Mary Wollstonecraft wrote about it in 1792, and other rare females here and there at isolated moments throughout history have dared to imagine it for themselves. We read the records of those brilliant women and their brilliant times like astronomers observing stars that have long since burned out yet whose light continues to brighten our own sky.

• • •

Today our sky is ablaze with female independence, and even those pop-psych pundits who blame the female victim also exhort her to get rid of the victimizer and on with her "own" life. It may be better never to have loved at all than to have loved a Man Who Hates Women—for in so doing, a woman has lost . . . herself.

Feminists have popularized the concept that women are the protagonists of their own stories, and furthermore that *sexism* prevents them from fully living those stories out. The firm installation of these beliefs in the collective unconscious is a feminist triumph, a deep and wide and revolutionary feminist triumph. In my travels I met no woman, be she in the most abject of circumstances or in possession of the paltriest self-confidence, who did not believe that she had a right to *be*.

Popular psychological ideologies of unrealistic autonomy, culturally shared narratives of the quest for independence, and feminist ideas of female subjectivity and self-determination, then, cross and recross each other like a complicated rope of hemp and velvet, horsehair and grosgrain. They form a sort of conceptual ladder, on which, I found, women of all classes and races hang the events of their lives. I was struck by how many women told a story that followed the paradigm "I used to be dependent but now I'm independent," and how many gauged their progress against a series of idealized rungs in that narrative ladder. There were some who felt they'd arrived or were on the way to arriving at independence. Those who did not were often apologetic or regretful, feeling compromised or defeated; they hadn't "fulfilled their potentials," they had betrayed themselves. A number of older women felt they were climbing two ladders simultaneously, forever stumbling between them. Having set their sights on stability, they now expected themselves to keep altering their course, forever to "grow and change." Marital longevity and fidelity, which they'd pursued like an Olympic gold medal, had been reduced to the status of a lucky pick, a lottery win, or worse, a booby prize for laziness or cowardice.

The role of men in this female bildungsroman is another striking feature, and another hallmark of its modernity. Rather than being cast as the rescuer or the grail itself, men stand along the way as spectators, impediments, and adversaries. Like Dorothy in the Land of Oz, written not by Frank Baum but by, say, Fay Weldon or Angela Carter, our heroine is swept up in a tornado (adolescence?) and sets off to find the Perfect Man, who will spirit her home, ensconce her in a safe, infantile haven, free her from the bothers of the world.

Along the way, however, Dorothy becomes an adult. Volleyed between Good Mother and Bad, she takes charge of a baleful little bunch of men, each deficient in a crucial way: one lacks smarts, one heart, and the third gumption (which might be read as sexual potency)—all faculties with which she is abundantly endowed. When she finally arrives at the door of Mr. Right, the Perfect Father, she learns immediately that he cannot help her. The veil across his phallic reputation is pulled back, and behind the curtain the Wizard is revealed: a fussy, bumbling, narcissistic fraud, scarcely Dorothy's height, reluctant to look her in the eye, much less rescue her.

Her own real father mysteriously absent, her male intimates sweet but ineffectual, Dorothy beholds the man she has spent a compressed lifetime yearning for—and he is a nobody, busy making excuses for himself. There is nothing left for her but to save herself, to step into her Good Mother's shoes and make her wishes come true. Of course, the 1990s Dorothy wouldn't have to find happiness in her own backyard. She could dial Auntie Em's number on her cellular phone, rev up the ruby slippers and point them not back to Kansas, but toward New York or Hollywood, Harvard or the Himalayas. Even homeward bound, though, our Dorothy is not the same girl who was carried away by the twister. She has faced her desire for male rescue and found instead male inadequacy. She has turned to women for help and received it, and—most crucial—she has discovered her own power.

Lives, of course, aren't navigated like Yellow Brick Roads with their destinations set out from the start, even though in the telling people tend to make narrative sense of them, connecting unconnectable happenstance with logic, as they would in telling a dream. The temptation is almost irresistible. Writing the chapters in Part III, I longed to be a novelist, to hew a tale to shapeliness when it stubbornly, inconveniently presented me with contradiction after contradiction, with waylayings, digressions, and culs-de-sac.

Indeed, while I employ the word, and the concept, *strategy* to denote the ways women live with ambivalence, I am aware that it is not quite apposite. For one thing, a strategy is so overarching, so of a piece. In fact, although I kept a list of them, categorizing and subcategorizing ad absurdum and, it seemed, ad infinitum, finally no strategy could fully represent a given life and no life conform faithfully to one strategy. The word, moreover, implies intentionality and premeditation, more intentionality than most lives, particularly most female lives, contain.

And yet women do make decisions and live by them; however they've arrived at this point, the women I talked to are making do, or making way, in the world—choosing one option, discarding another, foreclosing another. When talked about and assessed in an interview, these decisions (and errors) start to take shape and make sense, form psychological patterns and have political meaning.

In the end, I have not treated exhaustively every strategy on that long list, but I wanted to mention a few I did not. There was what I called Demilitarization, which might also be dubbed Cautious Neutrality, personified by Mary Louise Finnegan, a working-class daughter of Chicago now employed in machine-parts sales. Two years ago, at thirty-one, Mary Louise had a baby on her own (his paternity was indeterminate and she left it that way) and bought a little house. In a desultory but good-humored way, she continues to search for the guy a friend calls "Mr. Quasi-Right."

I could have written at greater length about Muriel Levinsky, a sixty-nine-year-old shopkeeper who is thoroughly fed up with her husband of forty-five years yet figures she's stuck with him, so she shouldn't make waves. Along with daily communication and financial decisions, another area in which they've given up on compatibility is sex. "You know the old expression, 'Wham, bam, thank you ma'am'? That's him. That's men. They won't slow down . . . In fact I saw a bumper sticker on a car the other day that said, 'Dial 911. The police come fast,' " said Muriel, with a gallows laugh. I'd call the Levinskys' strategy Détente—a tacitly agreed-on cessation of open hostilities, enforced by mutual suspicion.

There were also several women who I would say were Regrouping, feeling their ways from one path to another. I had coffee in Oakland, California, with Carolyn Kiley, definitely a woman on the verge. Having just been left by a man fifteen years her junior, she felt she had moved from Capitulation—giving in to his needs and demands—to Battle—fighting for what she wanted, without any real response from him—to involuntary Withdrawal. "There's nothing I can do about it," she said in a disgusted voice.

> *I mean, I'm so dominant. I don't know if I can be with anybody now, you know, unless . . . I mean I don't want to be domi- nated and I don't want to be dominant, but that's my personal- ity . . . It's hard to be demure and feminine. I can't not be who I am.*
> *. . . It's just that I'm so self-sufficient. I don't know if I want to call it dominant, even. I'm just so self-sufficient. And you can't go back to not being that way. I don't think it's a good thing for relationships. On the other hand, I don't think it's a bad thing, because it allows me to survive. So it's a mixed bag. But it almost sets a precondition, for sure. And so I feel like I probably will be alone just because it's really hard to give over.*

Some early-conceived and obvious categories were discarded because they represented a moment more than a period of time, an act whose consequences might last a lifetime, but not a life strategy. For example, Revenge suggests itself immediately as a way of dealing with man-hating—from forming organizations that espouse the cas- tration of rapists to actually killing a battering husband to the most common (and usually ineffectual) form of female revenge, "taking him to the cleaners" in divorce court. Revenge is a theme of women's legend, song, and comedy. "So many men, so few bullets," reads a mass-market greeting card. But for most women, I think, it is a wicked conjecture, a fantasy never realized.

In narrowing my selection to just a dozen women, I forfeited scores of wonderful stories, delicious cadences of talk, fascinating incidents and insights. But as I wrote, the others gathered around me in an anarchic chorus, here assenting to a generality, there dissenting one by one—"Not me!" "I'm not like that!"—when they thought I'd be wiser to forgo generalizing. I hope I've understood their col- lective song and listened with care to every solo.

6

Battle

Helen Whitney Leinsdorp

H ELEN W HITNEY L EINSDORP USES HER MARRIED name sporadically, unsystematically—indecisively, it would seem. After an early, tempestuous, "bohemian" marriage, followed by a decade of sexually footloose and politically combative single life, Helen married again, "much to the amazement of my friends," this time to a politically liberal but otherwise conservative businessman.

Today Helen is listed in the phone book under her husband's name. She uses it to sign official documents and checks from their joint account. But her passport—as an anthropologist, she travels about a fourth of every year—is in her "maiden" name. In her office on the top floor of the pleasant house she owns near Harvard Square in Cambridge, she usually—not always—answers the phone, "Helen Whitney." That's what her friends, mostly women, call her too, casting off the encumbering European respectability of a middle-aged wife and stepmother for the fleet moniker of a childless career woman, "free spirit," and passionate feminist.

"I must have been going through some revisionism," she recalls about her decision to remarry, thirteen years ago.

> I got tenure, I was about to turn forty. I met Hans, who's more like my father. He's Swiss, comes from a very traditional large family. A widower, with three teenage boys and his own business . . . affectionate, relaxed. I wasn't looking to get married at all, but he grew on me . . . It was a ready-made family: I could have stepchildren who were the age my own children would have been.

As her oscillating name indicates, however, Helen is still not altogether comfortable with either her reasons for marrying or the marriage itself. Hans, whose expectations might have been unrealistic, is also dissatisfied.

Helen is a Battler, a lifer in the Battle of the Sexes, in which the combatants are reconciled over no issue except the permanence of irreconcilability. A Battler like Helen harbors little hope for the cessation of hostilities, short of divorce, between herself and her partner. And while she likes marriage and was fatigued by the singles scene, she intimates that the whole project borders on the anachronistic, the impossible.

Still, like many such warriors, Helen sees her marriage as "a fairly stable one"; her love for her husband, this once-promiscuous woman observes wryly, has evolved into something rather stodgily middle-aged and middle-class, a (problematically) chaste fondness, a comfort. She defends her husband's merits—his good nature, morality, intelligence, and loyalty—but she is also highly, vocally critical of him. This she admits with regret; he wants her to be more supportive, and she'd like to be, but finds she cannot. And it is largely her anger at him, in which is telescoped a rage about men and women in the world, that defines the tenor of their relationship: "one of the most tense I know."

The Whitney-Leinsdorp marriage embodies not only Helen's own personal conflicts, or those between the particular person that she is and the particular person that he is. Theirs, it might be said, is the personal-political problem of a generation. Born in 1937, Helen came of age in one historic era and was reborn in another; she is both the Prefeminist Woman and Feminist Woman. At fifty-three, she carries a history of learned gender roles and the desires they engender, along with a complement of equally strong, usually more conscious and readily acknowledged "modern" expectations and desires for freedom, equality, and independence. Like a train trying to run on two schedules simultaneously, Helen's generation is constantly speeding up and slowing down, prone to derailments and collisions both intrapsychic and interpersonal.

Helen looks back on her decision to marry Hans as a kind of capitulation—"very explicitly a denial of the standards I had upheld" —but she knows he is also a mirror of what she refers to as her "conventionality." His bewilderment and exasperation with her is a reflection of her own confusion and inner turmoil. In this light, it makes sense that the feminist free spirit of the sixties seeks out the conservative businessman—"the Old Man, not the New Man," as Helen describes him, "but the Old Man with a conscience"—digs her trenches, and hunkers down for a long war.

Helen is the older of two girls in a "New England Puritan, conventional WASP middle-class family." Her mother was a homemaker, her father an engineer. The messages Helen received from her mother about men were classically contradictory. On one hand, Mother accepted and upheld Father's dominance in the family. "She felt what the husband wanted to do was what the family did." On the other, she made it clear that men needed emotional help and caretaking. She told Helen "women have to be the interpreter of men. They have difficulties expressing things, they have hot tempers. You have to understand this, you don't confront this, you don't fight it, you work around it."

This kind of generous loving was evidently one-sided in Helen's family. While both spouses were reserved—the children almost never saw them touch one another—Dad was even more withholding. So little open affection trickled Helen's way from her father that a memory stands out from her early childhood: "He was holding my hand on the way to the dentist. He was trying his best to be sympathetic. It felt odd and unusual."

The Whitneys exemplified the typical 1950s trade-off: woman contributes love, man brings in the bacon. But the traditional bargain wasn't exactly traditional. Helen's mother had a small inheritance, which enabled the family to buy a house.

> *That made a strong impression on me: that it was important, absolutely, for women to have their own money. I came early to the conclusion that I didn't want to be totally economically dependent. She had some leverage in the relationship.*

Helen's parents let it be known that she would "do the socially correct thing: finish college, marry a boy from a good family, have children. As far as career—you should have skills in case you ever had to work." As if on cue, the teenage Helen set out to overturn those expectations, one by one. She married her high-school sweet-heart, a "rebellious, cynical, charming, handsome, guy [who] drank a lot" and hadn't finished high school, and started her academic career.

The marriage soon dissolved in alcohol and inertia. Helen wanted children and meaningful work; David seemed uninterested in, or incapable of doing anything about, either. When Helen left, she says, "in a sense, my conventionality won out." She had em-barked on adult life determined not to replicate her parents', and in the early sixties, the obvious way to do this was to marry a man without prospects. In this, she achieved a sort of financial indepen-dence by default: she won the bread for two.

What Helen regarded as bourgeois conventionality—her desire "to do something interesting and important"—was also a kind of *un*conventionality. Particularly for that time, her independence and drive made Helen an iconoclast of gender. Before the slogan existed, Helen wanted to be the man she was supposed to marry.

In another way, Helen's relationships would unwittingly mimic her mother and father's. She was drawn to stubborn, difficult men she'd have to take care of emotionally—men unlike her father only on the surface. "I guess I really liked these older, divorced, Jewish, romantic, depressed neurotics," Helen says, laughing. David fulfilled most of those qualifications stunningly, and Helen's next major lover, a professor named Murray, fit the description to a T. Yet each time, Helen would get fed up with the care and feeding of the needy men she'd chosen—a rejection of a prescribed gender role that may be more firmly at the heart of her battle with men than her ambi-tions are (except insofar as the roles vie for the same time and en-ergy).

With David, Helen had no sexual-political description of what was happening between them—feminism hadn't formulated it yet. But she moved in with Murray in 1969, during the opening salvos of the women's movement, and all of a sudden, nothing was personal and everything was political. Although Murray supported her femi-nism in concept, his demands of her were as old-fashioned, genderwise, as ever. Embroiled in a nasty divorce, undergoing "crisis upon crisis," voicing "vague physical complaints" and suffering "endless depressions," he expected Helen to hold his hand and take his side.

But she would have no part of it. He was bitter about paying alimony. She didn't feel it was unfair. He was involved in disputes with his department at the university. She often thought it was his fault. "There was lots of door-slamming. There was my not putting up with things, and his being hurt. I was able to articulate my impatience with that life, but he still wanted a lot of nurturing."

Leaving Murray was "the turning point in my life in terms of really confronting the contradictions between the personal and the political . . . I saw life wasn't going to be as easy anymore." In some ways single life *was* easy.

> *Having made a decision I really didn't want to get married again, the men I went with I could take more on their own terms as interesting people . . . I'd take the best and leave when things got bad, rather than going through a long educational process with each man.*

This avoidance of romantic entanglements, plus a small inheritance, freed Helen in a number of ways.

> *I was feeling very confident in my work . . . being very explicitly feminist in my academic work and in the emotions that this gave rise to in me, about the pervasiveness of male privilege and power and what that does to women in every part of the world.*

Righteous and sisterly with women, financially self-supporting, friendly and undemanding with men, Helen ticked along with energy and purpose . . . But did she? What was wrong with this picture?

The fact was, Helen could attain freedom and independence in her sex life only if she didn't try to reshuffle the deck as men had stacked it. Such restraint was a challenge because, as she says now, with an ironic chuckle, "I was going out with men who were totally sexist." Try as she might to keep things strictly carnal, Helen couldn't drop her politics at the bedroom door. "I was always arguing with them, trying to convince them of the error of their ways."

Helen muses on that too familiar dilemma: "This is one of the

problems we live with, isn't it? The nice guys versus the sexy guys
. . . Let's face it: a lot of sexiness emerges from their being comfortable with their privilege and power." Although Hans' style and
social standing are miles from those lovers', his attractiveness is essentially the same. Hans is conventionally masculine: the mantle of male
entitlement lies easily on his shoulders.

It's a problem that Helen, like so many other women, still
grapples with. She is attracted to men for some of the same reasons
she hates them.

Helen is an academic feminist, and by her own estimation "not
a very introspective person." She understands her disputes with Hans
mainly in political terms, and the language in which she describes
them includes lots of phrases like "male power and privilege,"
phrases he seizes on to claim she's unfairly blowing their problems
out of proportion.

> *I push and nag and get angry, and he gets resentful and with-*
> *drawn and accusatory, and says I hate men. That I've had bad*
> *experiences with men and am blaming him for things other*
> *men have done to me. He says I hold him responsible for what*
> *all men have done to all women . . . That's the only way he*
> *can interpret my hostility.*

In one sense, Hans' interpretation of Helen's anger—that she's
mad at him for what all men have done to all women—is accurate:
"It takes only a small incident," she says, "for me to flash on the
worldwide hierarchy."

> *If his coffee cup is empty he will sit there and say, "Is there*
> *more coffee?" and I will say, "Yes," and sit there. And Pia [the*
> *au pair] will get up and get more coffee. Then I will say, "Hans,*
> *you could have gotten your own coffee." What I see in that is*
> *an assumption that the woman's role is to serve the man—and*
> *that's the big picture I get, and I immediately flash real fury. He*
> *can't see this at all. We have a lot of battles over those very*
> *little things. In our household, the battles are not on the big*
> *picture but on the daily incidents.*

To Hans, the battle *is* on the big picture—too much so. The
daily incidents, in his view, are much too trivial to merit the magni-
tude of Helen's outbursts. Another battle royal took place when he

let Pia carry his bags at the airport. To Helen, his act "compounded the sexist thing and the age thing and the fact that she gets a small salary." Hans just "got very upset and bewildered at my rage."

On one level, the Whitney-Leinsdorp war is a clash of worldviews. For Helen, as for many women of her generation and milieu, "The Personal Is Political" is indelibly inscribed, like a billboard on the inside of her contact lenses. Part of Helen wishes she could, once in a while, wipe it from view—take the personal personally, period. But her reactions are irrepressible. "It's such an instantaneous flare-up, I don't think I could let the stuff go by."

To Hans, the political is political and the personal is always personal.

> *There's nothing that resonates in his own history or background that would help him understand. He comes from a working-class, traditional-gender-role European family. His first wife had a very strong temper, but it was more about other things. He sees that women get hysterical, but not something in male behavior that triggers it.*
>
> *I've tried and tried to educate this man for thirteen years, and he's become very educated about the big issues—women and poverty, women and divorce—but he has never made a linkage between that and his own behavior.*

Helen is exasperated by what she represents as Hans' constitutional inability to comprehend what she's telling him. "It doesn't sink in!" she cries. "It's like, I teach statistics and some students just never get it." An intellectual with a deep faith in rationality, she holds fervently to the belief—probably a fantasy—that if Hans, a decent and rational person, understood the world and his place in it as she does, he would change his behavior. Still, as a woman whose life's work is to analyze the world in terms of power, she knows a crude power struggle when she sees one. Around housework and family responsibilities, for instance, diplomacy has failed; the couple is deep into a shooting war.

> *This weekend I've been resentful about a very typical female thing. I realize that I've taken responsibility for paying all our bills, doing all the investments, initiating all the work outside the house, and all the inside work too. I kind of thought, "What is his role in all this?" He just gets defensive and says, "Well, I*

do a lot," because he'll occasionally make the bed or do the dishes. I think basically he thinks that's my role and I'm competent at it. That I'm on his back all the time and he wishes I would get off.

How do Hans and Helen deal with this kind of struggle? "Not very well," says Helen. They bicker, they snipe, they yell. No true compromise is reached, and, she says, a "low-level aggression" persists.

As Arlie Hochschild skillfully demonstrated, the struggle over housework is more than a straightforward practical problem. If it were, more couples would be able to resolve it equitably and to both people's satisfaction. Most, however, don't. Underlying Hans and Helen's fights about who takes out the garbage and who calls the plumber are deep schisms in their concepts of fairness, which themselves are underpinned by what Hochschild calls their disparate "gender ideologies," their ideas and feelings about who they are and ought to be as men or women.

Helen calls her marriage a stable one. Both partners are committed to staying together in spite of their difficulties, and each, she says, trusts the other. Yet inconsistencies within and between their gender ideologies, when translated into how each wants to love and be loved, make for a relationship that is prone to instability, miscommunication, feelings of betrayal and resentment—prone, in other words, to mistrust.

This is apparent in Helen's description of their overarching emotional problem. As she presents it, Hans has a sense of entitlement, anchored in masculine power, to the "personal services" of women. She acknowledges that his needs, desires, and expectations were forged in another time and place, and not likely to change much. Nevertheless, she wants him to relinquish that power, to stop feeling he deserves to be looked after. In the meantime, she refuses to comply.

Yet there are hints Hans does not feel powerful at all. His wife flies off the handle when asked to perform even the most (to him) reasonable wifely tasks; for heavens sake, she's perturbed if he asks the hired help to do them! At the very least, she could listen to him complain about his business, but even that is a burden, and politically incorrect on top of it—some kind of male chauvinistic piggish demand.

Like many couples, Helen and Hans entered their marriage in good faith, intending to tolerate and compromise. At the same time, each undoubtedly harbored some wishes that the other would change to fit more nearly their ideal of a partner. Helen must have looked at Hans, at his decency and sense of justice, and expected that it was only a short step to his "seeing the error of his ways," admitting his guilt as a man in a sexist society, and tempering his demands accordingly. He must have regarded her deep commitment to righting the world's wrongs and assumed that she would expend the same compassionate energy on his needs.

Unfortunately, these perceptions and wishes work at cross-purposes. Hans seems to feel that his individual integrity and generosity distinguish him from the male "oppressors," and that her insistence on placing him in a category of Men contaminates him. Meanwhile, this New Woman's sudden interest in marrying—marrying *him*— must have telegraphed some messages, among which might have been a covert desire to be more like *him*.

Helen chose a conventional man for a husband, but his conventionality constantly irritates her. She sees him as a classic Mama's Boy —needy and imperious, worldly and competent beyond the front door, babyish at home.

He chose an independent woman, but her independence threatens him.

> He'll sometimes say, "You don't really need me, do you?" That I'm not financially, or apparently emotionally, dependent on him. I'll say, "In the traditional sense, no, but I enjoy being with you. The woman will stay if she's getting something out of it."

Hans was drawn to her "energy and fighting spirit. What he didn't count on is how it would be turned on him." He was taken with her intelligence and drive, impressed by her accomplishments and intrigued by her work. Yet when she travels, he invariably feels bereft and neglected and gingerly challenges her "right" to leave him to fend for himself.

He tests it out. I told him before we married that this is part of our life. Of course, each time he gets all petulant and says, "What would you do if I told you you couldn't go?" The answer is, I would be astounded and I would certainly go.

Then, Helen feels, he punishes her for unwifely behavior. "It's pretty tense for a couple days when I get back. He pouts a little, and there's my resentment when I see the things that didn't get cared for in my absence—like the houseplants that died."

Their pattern is a fairly common one: Helen openly badgers Hans to change. Hans applies his own pressure, but more passively. She reads his behavior as both aggressive and halfheartedly wishful—"wistful"—a maddeningly slippery combination. For instance: One of the couple's "basic agreements" upon marrying was that once the boys left home, the two would move from the suburbs into the city. But when the time came, Hans had "one excuse after another." Helen set about looking for a house and trying to sell theirs; he simply did not participate. Finally, "he just said, 'I'm not moving.' "

Helen "took the bull by the horns" and threatened to spend the weekdays in her house in Cambridge. "It became clear that if he didn't move, I would," an arrangement both knew their marriage would not survive. They did move, "but it was a very bad year—a real crisis in the marriage—because I felt he was reneging on a deal that meant a lot to me."

Why was he so intransigent? A power struggle, for sure, but a strong wish too. "He thought I'd get used to his house in the suburbs and like living there. He thought I would just give up that idea."

Issues around money don't fit neatly into conventional Hans–unconventional Helen categories. Hans was pleased to meet a woman who had been financially self-reliant for so many years. Now, with his concurrence, Helen is quitting her university job to do research full time and complement their income with consulting. She anticipates contributing to all their expenses except their mortgage, but because she can support herself on consulting, she won't strictly be dependent on him.

Hans is somewhat piqued that she will be getting a "free ride,"

Helen says, and also feels a "status loss" of "My Wife the Professor." But she also thinks he's secretly happy about the new arrangement. She'll be losing her trump card in their controversies about what he sees as her profligacy. "When he objects to something I've spent money for, I just say, 'Okay, I'll write you a check.'" When Helen won't be able to write that check, will he bring the weight of his financial clout down on her in other ways? A little worried that he will, Helen also suspects he doesn't think he'll have to. "In one way, it makes him feel things are more 'natural,'" she says. "I think he's hoping it will change my behavior and I'll be nicer to him." Helen dismisses as delusion this dream of winning gratitude, and with it a cessation of hostilities: "I feel sort of sorry for him, poor guy."

No two ways about it, this Battler will not sign a truce with the beloved enemy she has married. But it isn't malice that keeps her on guard and on the offensive. At one level, Helen believes that their differences are structurally irreconcilable.

> I often feel women and men try to mate across species, which makes it impossible. I think of men as the aliens, of course. I see men as difficult, not sharing a similar worldview, having a very different perspective on personal, even political life, as having, in general, a lot of masculine energy, which attracts me. I get pulled into that world, and at the same time repelled by the difficulty of making real human contact across a kind of a void. It's a physical, emotional void that is very difficult for women to cross. Men think they cross it, women know they don't. And we don't.

Although she loves Hans, Helen feels he is no better equipped to cross that void than any other man. She has "no illusions that he's the exception . . . I think he's a standard male species," but, she says, she doesn't feel deprived or lonely because of the distance between them. He, on the other hand, longs to bridge the gap.

> He is quite explicit in telling me he is jealous of my relationships with my women friends. I have a better time with them—which is true. I treat them differently—which is true. He feels excluded from a large part of my life—which is true. With women I see . . . a natural empathy, an understanding, a lot of things that go without saying, a shared worldview that gets us halfway there toward an intimate relationship.

Helen's perception of the void is a common one; I heard it from many women living many kinds of lives. It is related, on a broad cultural level, to this disjuncture between men's and women's needs, between his expectations of a certain kind of feminine care-taking and her reluctance, indeed inability, to fulfill them. Helen isn't the only woman, nor Hans the only man, who is ambivalent, confused, and angry about who should give how much to whom.

On that level, Helen's largely political understanding of her situation is accurate. Her efforts to force Hans into a different division of emotional and practical labor are part of the storming of sexism's fortress, and her contempt and anger for him are part of what constitutes collective man-hating.

Yet the vigor with which she rejects Hans' needs belies the rationality of her stance as a political act. Unconscious factors rooted in childhood motivate everyone, Helen included. One clue: Helen came from a family where good behavior, good grades, and social successes were required, never rewarded. "I remember a lot of times being very disappointed when I brought home what I thought was good news, and they would say, 'Well, we would have expected that,'" she recalls. "No celebration, no joy, no hugging." It makes sense that this woman might be allergic to expectations.

After the crisis over moving, Hans and Helen made a stab at couples therapy. They both went in feeling "we had needs the other was not meeting," but it soon became clear that they were equally reluctant to delve into their own pasts for the deeper reasons of their unhappiness, mutual or individual. The treatment was aborted after about six sessions.

> *I think I have basically decided to let sleeping dogs lie. There was some undercurrent that if I really looked closely at my feelings I might not want to stay in the marriage, and I didn't want to take that risk.*

So the dogs sleep. Helen continues to be painfully aware of the global oppression of women; in that way her marriage is no haven. Yet she is glad to be off the sexual meat market in her mid-fifties (although she is sexually tired of Hans) and likes the companionship, the shared jokes, the daily life of marriage; despite her criticisms, she likes Hans, a lot. Now that her parents are both dead, moreover, she feels more attached to him, more like his family. She may not admit it, but she probably needs him a little more than before.

For this woman whose life has traversed the cusp of two eras and whose heart and mind reside in both, neither course—to stay married or leave her husband and be single again—is the obvious one. So Helen wears her marriage defiantly, a warm garment that nonetheless feels too tight, a politicized struggle, a hairshirt. Helen is resigned to, though hardly resolved about, this situation. She seems bemused, even embarrassed, and somewhat depressed about it.

> In one sense, I can't believe it's happening, that I'm having these struggles now. The next question is, what do I do about it? There's where the big compromise comes . . . I could leave the relationship, I could keep fighting, which I probably will do, and keep feeling a lot of tension and we'll both keep being unhappy. I could give up and say, "It's not worth the hassle, so why not just pull back and have a little more relaxed home life?" I am tempted in some ways in that direction.

If, in Helen's mind, to relax a little is to "give up"—to surrender—she may not ever find peace with honor.

7

Attrition

Deborah Markowitz

THE WOMAN WHO SUGGESTED I INTERVIEW Deborah Markowitz said she was "at a crossroads." When I mentioned this to Deborah on the phone, she laughed, somewhat doubtfully. No? I asked. She laughed again: "I'll have to think about that." She would be glad to talk with me anyway, she added quickly, and we made an appointment to have lunch after her morning shift as a part-time high school guidance counselor.

The restaurant, in downtown Cincinnati, was one of those that are stuffed with imitation Tiffany lamps, hanging plants, and knick-knacks and overseen by waiters who tell you their names and ask you every ten minutes whether everything is all right. After about the fourth query, I was ready to gag John-Your-Waiter-For-This-Afternoon with his smart little apron. But Deborah bore the interruptions with unruffled humor. Hers, she suggested modestly, is the endurance of a mother of three.

Petite, with an open and animated face, Deborah is self-contained and poised, yet chatty and unpretentious. Intelligent, introspective, and trained in psychology, she neither clutters her conversation with jargon nor obscures her feelings with over-intellectualization.

The facts of Deborah's life surely place her at a crossroads. She is thirty-nine, in her nineteenth year of marriage to Arthur Markowitz, a vice president at a large company. Her youngest child has entered the first grade, and she is rearranging her duties as a mother, thinking about going on for a higher degree, and looking for a full-time job. She is dealing with old marital wounds and expressing newfound anger, confronting her husband on issues of money and religion. As she describes it, the couple is not doing well working out their differences. Quite the contrary: their styles of solving problems feel to her increasingly incompatible. Deborah and Arthur seem to be striding fast in opposite directions—he toward a more traditionally gendered marriage, she toward a kind of independence that neither of them would have anticipated when they married almost two decades ago.

The weekend following our conversation provided a perfect metaphor for "the interesting direction our marriage is taking." Arthur had been exploring Orthodox Judaism, which prescribes a segregated and subordinate role for women, and with his all-male study group and his Orthodox rabbi he was off for a weekend retreat. Deborah, an observant conservative Jew (the denomination ordains women and includes them in all aspects of the service) was dropping the children at her mother's and driving to Cleveland for her first weekend alone since she'd been married—all of which Arthur vociferously opposed. What was Deborah doing in Cleveland? Attending a conference on the family at which the Jewish feminist Letty Cottin Pogrebin was to be the keynote speaker!

Still, as we talked, I began to understand Deborah's quizzical response to my question on the telephone. As she portrayed her life right then, it resembled not so much a crossroads as a path that had started out straight and well-paved and suddenly turned rough, steep, and hard to follow. What faced her was less a critical decision than a test of endurance.

Another woman in her position might have been considering separation, or at least some kind of ultimatum to her husband. But for Deborah divorce is not a reasonable option. She enjoys the comforts of marriage, has three young children and "a typical wife job—twelve thousand dollars, minimal benefits, and you couldn't live on it if you tried." Yet personal changes she's undergone have made her impatient for commensurate changes in Arthur. She has always longed for more closeness; now she wants more respect and equality too. But he is not about to offer these voluntarily. He's satisfied with the way things are, and like men in general, she avers, he has his limitations.

Living with him has taken a toll on this apparently chipper woman. As she speaks, submerged rage seeps through, profound hurt, frustration. She sees her husband, in many ways, as a Typical Man—which in her book is not a flattering characterization. Yes, she admits, every woman hates men. But this thought is not really helpful in her considerable marital struggle, which requires a more subtle balancing of feelings and opinions, strategies and tactics.

Deborah and Arthur are engaged in a war of attrition. Each perseveres toward his or her own goals, goals that largely cancel one another out. At our first meeting, in 1988, it seemed the two were about evenly armed. Deborah's good-natured fortitude had the potential either to serve or to undermine her efforts. She could send forth just enough kindness, as a sort of peace offering, to reassure her husband that her independence would not threaten his status or their children's security. At the same time, that patience enabled her "to keep putting up with things," as she'd done for most of her marriage, and continue to suppress the part of her that's powerfully fed up—the part that unmistakably *does* threaten his position as ruler of the roost.

Arthur had seventeen years of traditional marriage and a world of male privilege on his side. Accustomed to earning and controlling the family's money and in most important ways ordering their lives as he saw fit, he appeared to be banking on the sturdiness of the status quo to outlast her blows against it. He even had the luxury of being amused by their standoff. He chose, for instance, to represent his forays into fundamentalist Judaism as a curiosity, "a hobby," says Deborah, "like fishing or astrology." Yet he had invited the children to his *shul* on Saturday, instead of the conservative one they'd been attending all their lives. Deborah was vaguely worried that he was trying to restructure their religious practice, which in Orthodox Judaism means restructuring family life entirely, placing the father as its unconditional, unquestionable head. Perhaps taking the kids with him was a defensive move, though: was he shoring up a fortress that he felt was shaking, even if just a little?

Deborah grew up in the Midwest in a financially comfortable, observant Jewish family. Her father was a businessman; he was "in a word, absent." Raised strictly, with little permission to make her own decisions, she was an obedient child, and an adolescent with an uncertain sense of self.

My mother made a lot of decisions for me. She told me what clothes looked good on me, what was good, what was bad, what was my personality, and I followed that. I didn't trust my own judgment, so I relied on hers.

Mom (and presumably, Dad) wanted Deborah to marry a man who was "respectable, reliable, a good provider—all that kind of thing." Her parents liked Arthur, and she was not disposed to rebellion.

I did choose a man you could really depend on, who would always be there. I like that, but I think I miss some of the following my feelings. I missed letting myself find the kind of person that would have been more like me, more understanding. I feel like it cut me off from a lot of experiences, to find what was safe instead of what was satisfying.

Like other girls growing up in the 1950s, Deborah had a romantic image of marriage. She had little experience dating—only one relationship before Arthur.

I thought getting married would be like a long date. You'd wake up in the morning and you'd talk all the time and you'd go places and you'd share . . . And I found out real fast, at least in mine, that the sharing was not going to be there. As far as sharing duties—this was 1972—I thought, well, we both worked all day, we both would share jobs at home. Well, that sharing wasn't there much, either. Romantically, at the beginning, it was alive, but I definitely didn't get what I expected.

Deborah worked part time and got her master's degree in counseling. When the first child, a boy, was born, she stopped working. Another boy followed close behind. The third child, a girl, was born in 1982. Arthur advanced in his company, traveling more and more. Deborah ran their large suburban house and got involved in the PTA and the synagogue. When Mindy was in preschool, she went back to work, still part time. In spite of his being out of town a lot, Deborah is more than satisfied with Arthur's fathering.

He's very close with the kids, very good with the kids. He's a real, real involved father . . . Now, does he know when they need a dentist appointment or this or that? No. He needs to be told. He doesn't take the initiative. He's not intimately involved with who their friends are. But my daughter wakes up and he's

*in the shower. She walks in and says "Where's Daddy?" and
sits outside the bathroom and waits until he comes out.*

In fact, it was, in a sense, around parenthood that the Markowitz marriage underwent its first major crisis. Deborah got pregnant, had an abortion, and at the same time had her tubes tied. Although the decision was made more or less jointly, Deborah felt Arthur's style of facing problems made him unable to help her through the trauma. The episode opened a maw in their relationship that has not to this day closed. That distance between husband and wife represents to Deborah a built-in distance between most women and most men.

Telling the story, interestingly, Deborah started out by saying she felt sorry for men because they can't have children and usually aren't very involved in their children's lives.

*I liked being pregnant, I liked giving birth, I like being a mother.
I liked the option of staying home and enjoying it. I'm glad I
don't have to . . . work at a job I don't like. But I think men
don't understand how it is to be pregnant.*

She paused, started, stopped, then began to talk about the abortion. Although the event took place three years ago, she recounted the story circuitously and spoke haltingly, as if her doubts and regrets, her confusion, sadness, and anger, are still fresh.

*I still have rage about that. I felt I worked it through, but it
resurfaces and I don't know if it was my conflict or his, or
whatever. I think maybe I'm still angry at him. I knew when I got
pregnant—first of all I felt it was my fault that I got pregnant—
somehow I knew he didn't want any more kids. I'm not sure
how I felt about it. I think I wanted more kids . . . I think I felt
some rage that I knew he didn't want any more kids so I was
going to have to get rid of it, immediately. You do have to
share it—for seventeen years we'd been together—but I don't
think he understood the conflict that I felt.*

Arthur could not manage to listen to her, says Deborah, so he could not find out about the conflict she felt. She needed to talk about her ambivalence, but when she did, Arthur believed she was waffling and would launch into lecturing and trying to persuade her. She felt silenced and neglected, more and more alone.

I think he felt every time I brought up the issue I was question-ing and trying to decide. In reality, I had decided, but I still needed to keep talking about it. It was hard for me to reconcile . . . But again, that's his black-and-white thinking: "This can't happen. This doesn't fit in the plan." I never felt that he really understood the complexity. When I'd try to talk about the loss, he would say, "Oh, you want another baby? You don't really want a baby. The reality is, blah blah blah, my salary, the house, blah blah." Never really looking at the feelings.

Arthur's approach to the abortion was a typical one for him, Deborah says. "I don't think he's empathetic."

Arthur can't just listen to my feelings one way or another. He wants to solve the problem. He wants to make a decision, a very bottom-line thing, not just hash things around. He wants a deadline, he wants a timetable.

How does that affect her? "It shuts me down, and I shy away from bringing things to him before I resolve them."

Deborah sees this "black-and-white thinking" as "a male char-acteristic—or the males I know." Arthur is a Babbler: perfectly flu-ent in "rational" language, but when it comes to emotions, terrified and tongue-tied. As we saw in that chapter, Deborah's perception is corroborated by the psycholinguist Deborah Tannen. Made anxious by aimless "troubles talk" and socialized to think instrumentally, Tannen says, men feel compelled to find an immediate solution to a problem, while their women friends often see talking as the solution itself: it assuages sadness or clears up confusion. As in many other heterosexual couples, Arthur's unwillingness to just "hash things around" is one of Deborah's biggest disappointments, and the source of much anger, disapproval, and misunderstanding between them.

For Deborah, not being able to talk to Arthur leaves a serious deficit in her life, for she is only starting to consider herself a woman with a "woman's network." Three years ago, she was a "regular middle-class married lady"; she sought solace from her husband and advice from her obstetrician and her therapist, both men. Very recently, she has told some women about the abortion and they've shared similar stories with her; that, she says, is helping her put the turmoil to rest. But during her crisis, she turned to men, which only exacerbated her loneliness.

> God knows why I talked to a male therapist about it. I mean, yeah, he's a real sensitive person, and he listened real well, and he did empathize and help me look at both sides and pointed out what I was saying. But there was no way he could understand.

Deborah is aware that Arthur had feelings—mixed feelings, she suspects—about losing the baby and foreclosing their chances of having another. But she is still consumed with the difference between his experience and hers, with how hard it was for her and how relatively easy, she believes, for him. In our conversation she returned several times to the fact that she had to undergo major surgery to be sterilized, and a man wouldn't have to. "It was his idea" that she get sterilized, she says; when she suggested vasectomy, he categorically refused. "That wasn't something he would consider. The thought of someone touching his body or damaging his masculinity was threatening to him."

Deborah's first impulse is to be sympathetic: "I think he was sad it happened," she says. But within a few sentences her sympathy turns to resentment and her voice takes on an edge of hostility.

> He's never expressed any sadness or sense of loss. As a matter of fact, he was glad. And I guess that made me angry too. Now he's getting what he wants. He's getting me to get my tubes tied, he doesn't have to worry at all. Because the copper thing with the little string, the string hurt him. And the birth control pill—I was kvetching too much. And the diaphragm is yucky and condoms are yucky.

Unresolved feelings about the sterilization plague Deborah in other ways. Nervously laughing, she explains.

> Since I had my tubes tied, I felt, well, okay, this stage of my life is over, I can mourn that, it's okay. And I'll have this newfound freedom. But I became very depressed. I felt like a eunuch, like I was sexless. I said, "I think they took out the G-spot." I felt

totally unresponsive. I thought I'd feel totally free, but it was the opposite effect of what I thought would happen.

. . . So that's why I was thinking, maybe I was harboring resentment that I had to go through this because of him. Because he made me pregnant, because he didn't understand my feelings. He was wonderful. We went to the hospital, he was with me. He took care of me when we came back. He was sympathetic and warm during the experience. But I still felt alone and alienated. I had to go through it; I was getting the IV and being put under anesthesia. He didn't have to do that.

That was three years ago, I say, and ask, "Have you begun to feel sexual pleasure again?" She puts down her fork and says simply, "I think that the baby would have been going on three."

After a bit, I ask again. "Was that just a period you went through, being sexually unresponsive?"

Well, it was more pronounced. But I don't think it's ever been . . . I think the fear and the excitement of maybe thinking you can be pregnant is part of what sex was like, with my husband at least. So it's never been as good. I don't know if it's combined with the other things going on in my psychology.

Again she pauses and thinks, then straightens up and adds almost briskly, "I have trouble leaving things behind, anyway."

After the abortion and sterilization, Deborah began to leave another, cumbersome part of her marriage behind: acquiescence. Maybe the trauma of losing her fertility freed her. "What more do I have to lose?" she may have thought. Or, "I've given up this much. I don't want to give up more." In any case, the apparent irreparability of the rupture between herself and Arthur seemed to embolden her, make her—for Deborah Markowitz—rash. If her marriage was to endure, it would have to do so on a basis other than her molding herself around his desires and needs.

Arthur did not comply.

Money, typically, was a point of contention. Deborah inherited money from her mother and announced that she wanted to open her own bank account and buy a car. Arthur was against it. His is a traditional male means of maintaining control—protection—and her attempt to establish even a small measure of financial independence threatened that control, she says. He saw her desire as a breach of their pact: she didn't trust him to take care of "their" money, and by extension, her and the children. He felt he could get his way by convincing her that it was "inconvenient" to have a separate account. He believed the "practical" approach would mitigate all the messy feelings, Deborah says.

But neither did Deborah act or speak straightforwardly. In part, his opposition and his superior power of argument compelled her to act surreptitiously. She employed a kind of guerrilla warfare, throwing Arthur off kilter, unsure as to when or whether she would "attack." Of course, neither of these strategies contributed a jot to working out the problem.

> *He feels that I'm not open about what I want, that I'm trying to finagle it. I'm kind of passive-aggressive. I'll say, "Oh, I don't mind if I don't keep my money in my account. I'll just put it in the joint account," because he'll convince me with all these logical arguments that our account has more interest and he can get at it more easily because there's a checking account with it. And I'll say, "Oh, yeah, you're right." Which doesn't necessarily mean I'm going to do it. Then he gets irate, because he thinks I've agreed and we get into more arguments over have I agreed or have I not.*

Deborah "temporarily" deposited the money in the joint account, but the argument persisted. She did not have the gumption simply to take it out and open her own account (something she could also have done, incidentally, with any of her paychecks). The check for her new car was written on the joint account. Arthur had won the battle.

The last few years have seen a pattern of such showdowns, in which Deborah challenges family traditions and Arthur resists. Often, he uses the issue of the children's security—a surefire weapon—to counter her. On family car trips, for instance, Arthur customarily drives. Deborah ferries the kids around town, to Little League, birthday parties, doctor's appointments—the usual maternal trips. So recently, out with the family, she asked to drive on the highway.

Arthur flatly refused; he accused her of endangering the children's lives.

This year, Deborah is being offered a full-time job at school, which she is tempted to take. Predictably, Arthur is against it, arguing that the children will be deprived of her time and attention. Deborah, who has been working on these issues in therapy, is not totally inured to guilt. "I think I will make the decision based on what's good for me," she says, then adds, "The kids being older makes me more independent."

But the drawn-out war of attrition grinds on.

> He said, "Why would you want a full-time job? You don't need the money." His career has also advanced. I said I'd like the security. I still have that sense that I would like to know I could earn enough to live on. But he said that makes him think this marriage isn't secure.
>
> He said, "You're not going to put it in a separate account." I've given in on that. I try not to think of that as an issue. I think he's right. If I trusted him I shouldn't want to put it in a separate account. To defend my position, it would sound like I was thinking about divorce.

Deborah's is not the victorious tale of a woman reborn in feminism. On one side, she is resigning herself to what she calls the "trade-offs" of marriage: He is locked into working "fifty hours a week at a high-pressure job, and all the things that being a man involves" and she enjoys the leeway to work or stay home. "I love the work I do and I love the options that I have." On the other side, she feels trapped. She senses that this "leeway" is not freedom, and now, "I also want the freedom and power and independence." Winning freedom, independence, and power, however, means fighting her husband, possibly forever.

Nor is her story a case history to be written up in an assertiveness-training handbook. On her journey toward independence—if that indeed is where she's going—she strays and halts and backtracks. The two years between our interviews were tempestuous and often disappointing. "I turned out to be—looking back—very true to my traditional upbringing and the part of me that said 'Don't go too far.'"

I was turning thirty-nine in the fall. I guess what I did is decide the conflict was too great and for a while decided the only way to deal with it was to not deal with it and get depressed. I blamed myself and went into therapy in a major way.

I said, "I'm not powerful enough to make changes. If I learn to accept my lot and not challenge everything, this will work out. I can't throw away nineteen years and three kids and this whole lifestyle. Maybe it's my issues—I'm not happy in myself." That route has always been easier for me. I took antidepressants and had anxiety attacks. They say thirty-nine to forty-four is a time for women to get depressed. So I was right on time.

When I got to the end of the therapy I felt stronger within myself—about my childhood and my self-esteem. I don't regret it. We came up at the end in that I needed to see where the marriage was going to go—to look at that. The next step was to go into marital therapy.

Which they did, and "just graduated from." It yielded no momentous results.

I still don't think I have the strength to decide, Does this marriage have enough to give me? I decided I want the marriage and want it to be somewhat better. We learned to communicate better. I think we developed more mutual respect. Our next goal was to develop more closeness.

But, she says, "I couldn't stand being in therapy anymore," intimating that the closeness goal might be a bit overambitious anyway.

On the issue of respect, Deborah seems to be yielding her share of ground—maybe more than her share. "I'm more willing to compromise," she says, reciting the therapeutic creed like a Girl Scout. "Not to give up myself, but to realize that there are trade-offs, and some things I do have that are valuable."

The religion question still divides the Markowitzes but the conflict has not escalated to all-out confrontation. Arthur is still pursuing his Orthodox studies but has not insisted she or the children participate. Their older son is being bar mitzvahed next year, in the conservative synagogue.

And Deborah the humorous trooper carries on.

Right now, my goal in life is to survive this bar mitzvah alive and with the family intact . . . It means a lot to Seth, and to us all. Arthur and I are focusing on joint goals—stuff they tell you to do in McCall's. I can't say it feels wonderful.

8

Capitulation

Elizabeth Storey

THE INFAMOUS MAN SHORTAGE STUDY surprised Elizabeth Storey about as much as the ring of her alarm clock on a weekday morning. For a second, it was a bit of a shock, but it was hardly unexpected. Like many single women of her age and social class—she's white, forty-one years old, and earns over sixty-thousand dollars a year—Elizabeth has not exactly been overwhelmed with marriage proposals from eligible bachelors. But the study did not propel her into a mad reassessment of her entire life, as distressed women were allegedly doing in therapists' offices and over glasses of Blanc de blanc from coast to coast. Elizabeth didn't hustle to the nearest video-dating service, go on a diet, or consider relocating to Wyoming, where the demographics are better.

Elizabeth Storey has many friends, both women and men. Her professional life could not be more challenging, fascinating, and full ("Do you have any more questions?" she asked me near the end of our interview. "I have about seven more minutes"). She is ambitious and energetic, in fact "a little off the page" on both scores, she allows. A lawyer with a busy practice and an elected politician in the South (she required that I not name the state), Elizabeth got her formative legal experience in civil rights and poverty law in rural counties which, even in the 1970s, were still not friendly to integration. She has been highly visible wherever she's worked since.

"I was the only woman in every bar association I practiced in," says Elizabeth. "I was the only woman in all these courthouses, I was the only woman in a hundred lists of things." When she started out, many courthouses in the state didn't even have a woman's bathroom outside the jury room. Women used the bathrooms once relegated to blacks—in the basement, entered from outside, around the back.

Elizabeth's quick political climb and her firm stance on the issues that concern her—including women's right to abortion—have only increased her visibility, as well as her suspiciousness in the eyes of the Good Ol' Boys who largely control the state. Understanding the threat she represents, Elizabeth has worked out a strategy for getting what she wants done. It includes the conscientious adoption of a manner overly reliant on neither open combat nor feminine wiles.

> *These guys don't even have a concept of a professional woman beyond the teacher and the nurse. So knowing that, . . . I decided with very strong discipline that I was going to be affirmatively friendly with people. In litigation I'm affirmatively unfriendly, pleasant and professional but not friendly. I have a tendency to be stern and negative and snarl. And that's paid off. You've got to, in that environment. [In politics] I think I am such a totally different animal to them that it was important that I be friendly, and smile.*

Elizabeth's instrumental, goal-oriented, practical, and principled approach has been remarkably successful, almost astonishingly so for her gender. She has managed to gain the respect even of many of her staunchest opponents. And, sitting across from her at her large wooden desk in a light-filled downtown office decorated with whimsical gifts from supporters and newspaper photos of herself, one cannot help but share that respect. Tall and strikingly dressed, she is likable yet unflinching, a mover and a shaker, a true professional—all confidence, all power.

In the halls of power, that is. For when she's just Liz, in private, that confidence and capability seem to drain. There, her eyes-on-the-prize game plan simply does not yield results. "Fighting for what you want works a lot with me politically, in the public, in litigation, and in work," Elizabeth says, drawing the line that divides her life in incongruent halves. "Fighting for what I want personally has not been successful." It is a conclusion she gives the impression of having come to as methodically and empirically as her ideas about running a campaign or promoting a bill. "I'd say I have tried it," she says, "and failed absolutely."

Elizabeth does not blame herself for the sorry state of affairs between herself and men. She knows lots of great women in the same situation as she—having unsatisfactory relationships or none at all—and does not buy the pop-psych line that they love, work, or want too much. Rather, she states, men are the problem: they are in a sorry state themselves.

> *The women I know—close friends of mine—successful, make a lot of money, over fifty thousand dollars a year, over eighty thousand dollars, attractive, I mean really attractive, good people who extend themselves and do a lot of stuff very very positively—I know a number of those women who have totally failed personal lives vis-à-vis men. And the men who are their contemporaries, of the same do-dah, mid-thirties to mid-forties, simply don't have those qualities, those emotional giving, personal qualities. They're just—this sounds prejudiced now—in that age where there is just a sociopathic distance from shared responsibility for society or for the relationships they're in.*
>
> *They have no interest in the competition of women who are equal to them. They're intrigued by it—the ones that are real confident—and kind of enjoy it as an illusion, but they don't want it for day-to-day life at all. They don't have the energy to make that commitment or they don't know how.*
>
> *They just don't know how to act, really don't, in a way that's not really selfish.*
>
> *I am constantly perplexed by the total ineptitude of how to act with women. Total either ignoring or inability to recognize an emotional need. The constant metaphor, the constant example of "I will call you and we will do X," which is never followed through. The total lack of any kind of appreciation for what that causes . . . I don't know, I just find it bizarre how inept they are. And I have a lot of stories of women who are my age roughly, a lot of similar stories.*

With characteristic succinctness, Elizabeth sketches out those women's stories.

> *It's exactly the same thing: an enormously positive short term, very very interested, very want-to-be-here, enjoying this—then gone. Not a thank-you letter, not a call, how're you doing? Nothing . . . Just this kind of distance, this come-and-go mentality. No interest in sitting down, in sharing on any personal level.*

Elizabeth attained the vantage point from which she makes these observations by no extraordinary or convoluted path, no inordinate pain, no abuse or victimization, abandonment or pathology. Her family was eminently functional and her childhood sounds as normal as can be imagined. Mr. and Mrs. Storey, two shopkeepers, have been together in what Elizabeth considers a loving, accommodating, happy marriage for over fifty years, living simple, quiet lives. Although they did not push Elizabeth to be ambitious—they tended in fact to encourage her to relax—"they've sat around and watched, particularly what I've done in the last five years . . . with a kind of acceptance and bewilderment and interest and pride too, I'm sure."

The messages Elizabeth received about love, men, and marriage were

> *just so very traditional and very predictable, given when I came along: It doesn't matter who a man marries, because the family will assume the position and the comfort and the success of who the man is. But it matters a lot who a woman marries, in terms of those issues of comfort and wealth and prestige and community.*

The story of her love life is not unusual, either. During college and through her twenties, Elizabeth had a few serious boyfriends. In her first relationship, she began to realize she didn't have to do everything she was programmed to do.

> *I had this traditional kind of Southern college romance from lavaliere to pin to engagement ring and then decided not to marry that guy. I see that as pivotal, because you're supposed to marry the guy you're pinned to.*

Although she assesses her ex-fiancé as a "pathological kind of controlling case," and in that way atypical, their struggles were pretty typical sexual power struggles for that milieu and time: "I wanted to do things that he didn't think I had any business doing. Like being involved in some mild political activities, and this newspaper work I was real active in [and] really enjoyed doing."

In another relationship, conflicts between her worldly interests and ambitions—litigating rural civil rights cases—clashed with her boyfriend's tastes and personality. In a sense, she outgrew him.

I'd say those three years after law school were a really enormously expanding time for me. Big issues, big people, big players. Big-win, big-loss kinda thing. And he was the most unsocial person. His total social activity was sports, which I love and which we got along fine in. But he was just absolutely uninterested in so many things, particularly social-public issues, so . . .

Elizabeth has never been married—"in the last ten years, not even close"—and as she's risen in influence and power, her romantic prospects have diminished in direct proportion. She's gloomy, but humorous about it.

My friend who was a prosecutor and is now a judge, I said to her recently, "Which would be worse for some guy to pull out of the bag as who he has to go out with Saturday night: a sitting judge or a politician?" She said, "He's not going to be thrilled with either one. It's sort of a dead heat."

She has not, in theory at least, given up on men. Yes, she'd like to be in a committed relationship or a marriage, but she has an unvarnished view of that institution too.

Yeah, I'd like to be married, but I don't see it happening. There's a level of injury and suffering and damage by not having that . . . but I do a lot of divorce work and I know that there's a level of injury and suffering and damage by having that. So I want it, but I don't see it happening.

I feel pretty powerless about it. I don't feel like I can create that for myself. I have not been able to create that for myself. And I don't see other women that do either. And those that do are buying problems a large, large extent of the time. I mean, I see them making compromises and sacrifices for men who devalue rather than value their lives. There's just a lot of that I see. So I'm pretty negative and pretty cynical about it.

Men, Elizabeth says, are unlikely to change.

Can they change? People my age? No. Do they want to? No. Do they see any benefit? No. Why should they? What's in it for them? They've always got a new load of twenty-five-to-thirty-year-olds. A hundred new ones a week.

It is this estimation of a pervasively, intractably bad situation between men and women that defines Elizabeth's personal life. In the small world of individual men and women, men are unapologetic Babblers and Betrayers, and women can't make a dent in their power. This savvy power-manipulator in big-world politics feels impotent to shape her own relationships in even the slightest way. She does not identify with women's liberation outside of big issues like reproductive rights or job discrimination; her love life, she says, is not a feminist project: "I'm not changing the world in these personal relationships."

In one way, Elizabeth has given up on men: they're jerks and they aim to stay that way. In another, she hasn't: she still wants them in her life, for "fun, sexual satisfaction, doing something different, spending time with people you like and care about and respect to a certain extent." So she capitulates to their demands as they are, operates within the power structure as she finds it.

For a number of years Elizabeth has carried on two long-distance, on-again-off-again, exceedingly casual sexual relationships, one with a married man, one with a single man. Both Bob and Wendel seem to consider her a friend and an occasional good time—and that's all.

> *These two men that I feel in a way closest to, that are highest on my agenda of major figures in terms of emotion, you know, are not the kind of people who can sit there and explain to me what's going on with them. It's very frustrating, very distancing. It feels very unsuccessful, not being able to achieve an articulate sharing of what's going on between us.*

But Elizabeth has long since given up trying to share with these two. The liaisons, which afford her sex and a certain amount of fun without financial, emotional, or sexual dependency, are only apparently in her control. In real ways, they represent major defeats: Elizabeth would *like* to depend on someone emotionally. She'd *like* to be sexually beholden.

> *I don't think they consider me a woman in their life. I don't think they are men in my life! They're sort of historical neurotic emotional attachments with men that I see.*

So Bob and Wendel don't feel possessive, I said, noticing the elephant at the dinner table. "That's definitely not the issue," she answered with a tough laugh. "The level of inattention to my emotional package is pretty extreme, I think."

And what does Elizabeth do about this state of affairs? She does not—as a radical feminist would advise—try to change the men. She does not—as a couples therapist might counsel—try to change the patterns in the relationships. She does—although she claims never to have cracked a pop-psych book in her life—follow the tactic many "postfeminist" (and most prefeminist) pundits recommend to women: accept men's limitations and change yourself accordingly.

> *I try to discipline myself to the point where you just don't expect men to take any responsibility for their relationships, on an analysis that men are simply not as far along the evolutionary ladder as women.*

And what about anger? "Anger's a big issue. You've gotta deal with anger. You know, anger turns to depression, or something." So, just as in public life, where she has learned that a negative "enemies-list politics" does not achieve the desired results, she tries to prevent her resentments from completely blotting out all positive feelings toward her men friends. This "technique," at which she admits to being "not too successful," she calls "anger management."

Does she see this as a conciliation?

"Sure," she says, "but I think conciliation and compromise and acceptance is a management technique."

And would success in this "management" make her happier? She laughs again.

> *To be more accepting, to be more forgiving? To be less judgmental? Yeah, I think that would make me happier. So I think that's a goal. But, uh, it's not an achievable goal every day. I get pissed off a lot of times in trying.*

Again, that goal is hers, not theirs. Acceptance and accommodation are unilateral. Bob and Wendel decide on the shape of the table (one with lots of distance between the conversants), draw up a limited list of issues on the agenda, and Elizabeth sits down and honors the protocol.

I don't feel like I've got the right to cross-examine these guys on why they did X, Y, and Z to me. Or did not do A, B, or C. I don't feel like that's a good plan. To the extent I've kind of tinkered with that, I haven't done well. And to the extent I feel like I know them over a period of time, I don't think I push these guys a lot in terms of what I say. I may push them a lot in terms of what I represent to them. But I don't think I push them a lot in our personal interactions.

It sounds like you're getting a portion of satisfaction, I say, which appears to be better than nothing.

Yeah. But I don't think asking for that satisfaction is in the cards. I don't think that's a reasonable thing that's gonna work.

A buzz on the phone interrupts us as our conversation is drawing to a close. Excusing herself, Storey pulls out her calendar and searches through the densely covered pages to find room for yet another appointment. She addresses her assistant in a familiar yet respectful manner and graciously begs my patience while she takes a second call. By her tone I can tell it is a friend, a dinner engagement, male or female I do not know. Elizabeth laughs heartily at something her friend says, expresses her eagerness to see him or her, and hangs up the receiver, turning back to me her honest, intelligent face—a face that in a different world would be welcomed over many a marital breakfast table.

Is she being too pessimistic in thinking it will never see that breakfast table? Has she given personal politics, and herself, too short shrift? Perhaps hers is just hard-headed realism, her tactics realpolitik. Anything else, she feels, is utopianism.

By way of winding up our conversation, the senator says she hopes she has been of help—she doesn't usually give much thought to these things, and least of all to her own situation. "I think the issues I have are boringly typical," she concludes.

Are they personal, are they political? I don't know. I think they're boringly typical . . . I don't have a lot of background in theoretical constructs. If I saw a book with—what is your title?—it would depress me. It would just put in a structural framework all the personal frustrations I feel. And I've gotta use my energy in other ways.

9

Separate Peace

I've got a disposition and a way of my own
When my man starts to kicking I let him find a new home.
I get full of good liquor, walk the street all night.
Go home and put my man out if he don't act right.
Wild women don't worry.
Wild women don't have the blues.

Ida Cox

Cyd Harpur and Viola Jackson

SOME PEOPLE MIGHT CALL THEM WILD, these women who've reached a separate peace with men. They describe themselves as iconoclasts—and, as near-middle-aged heterosexual women who eschew both marriage and celibacy, they are.

Like all roads, theirs are paved with an uneven mix of stones, among them those they did not lay themselves. Yet these women have traveled the roads not taken, so more than others', their lives are determined by conscious choices—choices *not to*, as well as choices *to*. Perhaps because they have been compelled to make internal sense of their unconventional and "abnormal" desires in order to justify them to families, suitors, friends, or employers, these women tend to have rather articulate personal ideologies and well-wrought narratives about how they came to be where they are.

Many Separate Peacemakers were, or believed themselves to be, nonconformists even as children. "I was a rebel child," said Viola Jackson, who came from a family of ten. "If a black person can be a black sheep, I was it." In telling their stories they focus heavily on decision-making and play down happenstance; they trumpet courage and rashness and soft-pedal fear, anxiety, or neurosis. Perhaps defensively, they often present their own ways as politically, spiritually, or psychologically preferable to the mainstream and sum up their tales with a moral, a lesson. This self-exoneration is entirely understandable: as women who have transgressed rules that are deeply ingrained and strictly enforced, they have enjoyed few social supports and suffered social sanctions.

Do Separate Peacemakers, who relegate men to a secondary place in their lives, hate men (as they've certainly been accused)? Or are they, like lesbians, simply less negative toward men because they are less dependent on them? Perhaps a little of both. Cyd Harpur and

Viola Jackson learned in childhood to mistrust men; both also developed strong senses of self and powerful passions outside of love. As adults they keep to a minimum the frustrations, betrayals, financial and emotional dependencies, and power struggles that are the volatile ingredients of sexual enmity. With men at a distance, they can covertly express man-hating (consigning men to sideline amusements surely implies some contempt, or at least indifferences) and stave off overtly feeling it. They have experienced men as Seducers, Brutes, and Abandoners, but have decided not to be their victims. They could probably make men Slaves, but don't want to "lower" themselves to play that game, either.

Cyd Harpur

Cyd Harpur has been, at various times, a folklorist, a waitress, a writer, a filmmaker, and a teacher. Always a free spirit, now forty-three, she has more or less settled down in her own little house in Missoula, a university town in northwestern Montana. She's a little mistrustful of the comfort she's found in Missoula. "My self-image is of struggle," says Cyd. "When things are easy, I can't believe it."

Around the issue of men, however, Cyd seems to be glad to have finished struggling. Turning forty had something to do with giving up the fight. "When I was younger I thought of myself in relation to men, and now I don't anymore. My sense of being, my goals, my self-worth [are] no longer reflected off of men." Sex and love are still of paramount importance to her, but she says, she has no illusions about what they will provide.

> Society touts the sexual relationship as the end-all be-all thing in life, and children too. So you pick a relationship and you think it will fill other needs you have that you're not addressing. For many women, if there are other things in her psyche, it won't work.

Among the things in Cyd's psyche are an intense curiosity, which has taken her across Europe and Asia and as far north as the North Pole, a broad-ranging creativity, and a restlessness that makes

302 / SEPARATE PEACE

a nine-to-five job feel like "death on wheels." That restlessness precludes married domesticity too. She knows: she's tried.

> I would get into a stable relationship—living with a guy—and I would get these horrible feelings that Middletown was encroaching on me. I could see my life playing out like all the sad women I had seen. I would be stuck. I wanted to get on the road again.

Although she has long-term lovers, Cyd no longer attempts to live with them.

> When you live with someone on a daily basis there is a lot of compromising. It's not a lifestyle I covet. I love to have men in my life, but on the sideline, not constantly.

There are hints in Cyd's childhood as to the sources of her firm —some might call it phobic—preference for sexually passionate yet emotionally undemanding friendships with men. Her mother, as Cyd describes her, is an angry, intrusive, possessive, "vengeful and destructive" woman. Her biological father, divorced from her mother when Cyd was a baby, was to her an unimpressive stranger.

> As a kid, my mother described my father in contemptuous ways . . . When you hear anger from a person directed at someone else, the other person seems dynamic. When I finally saw him, he was a butcher in tacky clothes; he was kind of pitiful.

Mrs. Harpur married a number of times, "in quick succession . . . within a ten- or twelve-year period. Then she was finished with men." The only one among the Husbands (as Cyd refers to them) who was anything like a stepfather was Herbert. But in Cyd's memory, he too was unexceptional, "a Milquetoasty guy" like her own father.

> I saw him, when I was a child, hide from [my mother] and stay in the shadows. So as I grew up I didn't expect anything from him. If you got him away from all threats, he was a sweet, passive guy.

After Mrs. Harpur divorced Herbert, Cyd tried to keep up the relationship, seeing him on and off until she was eighteen. At that point, in a paroxysm of jealousy, her mother accused her of sleeping with Herbert and forbade her to see him again. Yet, it seems, Cyd had unconsciously prepared herself for such an eventuality: "I missed him, but I wasn't staking too much on it." Herbert lives on in Cyd's heart not so much as a person in his own right but as "a real sore spot in my relationship to my mother."

Cyd's intense, conflicted feelings throughout childhood were obviously for her mother. Whatever anger she might have felt toward the series of absent fathers who migrated through her childhood she seems to have repressed. In any case, she got proficient early at not forming attachments to men: fathers and families were something other people had.

> *I didn't conceptualize what father meant. Herbert was my buddy . . . I'm sure I had friends that had regular families. But I can't say I was pining for a conventional family.*

Through observing her mother, Cyd learned that men are impressionable and malleable. In spite of the child's hostility to the woman, the lessons stuck.

> *My mother was extremely attractive in her heyday. I saw from her that she was marketing herself with men. She looked like a hag until she'd meet somebody. Then she would look beautiful. I thought men bought superficial packaging. That men are easily duped. I still do.*

Cyd, like many Separate Peacemakers, is also extremely attractive. For a woman to take and leave lovers at will, it helps to possess enough sexual capital to command her bidding. (Actual capital helps too. The image of the gorgeous gold digger, à la Marilyn Monroe or Rosalind Russell, is a myth; economic dependence and sexual independence are largely incompatible.) Whereas her mother was "traumatized by her forties," Cyd seems to be acquiring new confidence as she moves further into hers. Her figure is relaxing out of youthful tautness to slim sensuality, her hair is sexily disheveled, her laugh deep and easy. Cyd dresses in jeans and T-shirts. Not quite a woman *d'un certain âge,* she appears still to be on the way to the peak of her beauty. (Maybe, in these youthful times, her fifties will traumatize her.)

Cyd insists she doesn't use her beauty manipulatively, claiming to possess none of the feminine wiles that were her mother's other weapon. Such machinations are among the bottom-line requirements of marriage or full-time heterosexual relationships, Cyd believes, and because she won't or can't manage the moves, she has to stay out of the game.

> *I got from my mother that men are less wily than women. Women are operating at a disadvantage in the world, so you always have to be very wily with men. I must add that I don't consider myself wily at all. I am very forthright, and the only way I can be this way is to be alone.*

It would be a disservice to Cyd Harpur to diagnose her as a hurt and neglected kid running from the risks of commitment. She struck me as quite together—happy, productive, strong, smart, unsentimental, and self-knowing. Independence serves her: it allows her to pursue her myriad passions and pursue her wild quests. Coming from a family in which mutual respect was scant, moreover, she places a high value on it and shapes her relationships accordingly. She not only demands respect and equality from men, she avoids liaisons with men she doesn't hold in esteem. Earlier, Cyd used to try to instill that regard through personal "education": "I'd train each one to how I want to be treated." In hindsight, she considers the effort counterproductive.

> *Occasionally, a man says he appreciated it. I like to hear that. If I can stand back, I think, "nice." In the long run, though, it's damaging to the relationship. It's that constant tension all the time.*
> *Underneath, there's recognition that everything I demand, really, why should he [comply], unless he really likes me? Because there will be some little chick who'll be just how he likes.*
> *. . . It wears down after a while. You work and work and still have the same problems, just in different guises.*

In her late twenties, weary of that work, Cyd started becoming less involved with men and more involved with women, though not sexually. As her need for male stimulation lessened, so did her desire for male approval, and along with it the need and desire to approve of, and "correct," men. She discovered that a quotient of control and comfort could be gained by changing the *forms* of her commitments to men, not necessarily the men themselves. These liaisons would be nondomestic, not necessarily monogamous. Eschewing romantic cohabitation means relinquishing the struggles to mesh in myriad ways, from how much you want to talk before breakfast to how promptly you pay your bills.

Unconcerned about having children or even being in a couple (there was no family pressure to do so), Cyd was able to form satisfying alliances with formerly "inappropriate" men, much older and much younger men, men of other cultures and other races, men with other primary relationships. This has given her more maneuvering room for creating the egalitarian relationship she has so vigorously, and often so futilely, sought in the past.

> *I think I have one right now, but it's a rather aberrant relationship. I have a friend who's seventy-five. He's an old communist. He's a delightful person and we have sex. By no means would I want this person in my life on a twenty-four-hour basis. He brightens up my life when I see him.*
>
> *The difference in age is why it's egalitarian. The powers he has as a male I have with my youth. He's lost footage as a male in our culture because he's old. It could be because I'm young in this culture, at last male and female is almost equal, in ways that are important. More than that, he's an old soldier from all these social battles, so there's a commonality of language. I respect him.*

Cyd has become more aware too of what is most important to her in a heterosexual relationship. When the passion has dissipated, keeping an affair going is painful and, she feels, useless. Many marriages, she believes, survive on emotional and sexual artificial-life-support systems.

> *When the physicality between men and women is gone, what is left? You sever what connects you. Even if you have to force it a little, you have to need that person for physical comfort. I fear that most in relationships. I fear that not so much for the sexuality, I fear what that means. When that happens, the com-*

fort I would have gotten from this man, I would get from a woman.

My greatest needs are physical affection and touching. I fear that will go if the sexuality goes. You leave before that happens.

With changed needs and expectations, and changed relational forms in which to satisfy them, Cyd's sources of anxiety and hostility have dried up considerably. She looks back differently on the men she once felt intense anger, and hatred, toward.

The feeling I have now for men is that I have never had a brutal man that was just trying to damage me. Some women really feel damage. I think the sparring I've been in was two personalities, his and mine, trying to get self-respect.

Like a true Separate Peacemaker, Cyd formulates a lesson from her trials and failures. And she feels she's found the path she was meant to be on all along.

When I was a kid, boys had this aura of mystery and power. I bought the package that they would make the difference in my life, they would give me happiness. For years, I bought my mother's package that I would find someone who was more intelligent, had a better job and higher pay than I could ever make. Whenever I did find this person there was all this anger. In my heart of hearts I don't think I was gravitating toward that.

We seem to be drifting toward our own private direction in life. As I get older I feel that, strange as this course is, it's the one I was destined for.

Viola Jackson

Viola Jackson was her daddy's girl, not her mother's. Her father, a career soldier, was "the strong silent let-the-woman-raise-the-kids type . . . the kind of guy who said twelve words a year, and I was the special child who got eight of them." He lived on and off with the family, gone sometimes because he was stationed far away from San Antonio, sometimes because he was estranged from his wife. Although the family's fortunes fluctuated wildly with her father's whims—"There were times we were living in solidly middle-class black neighborhoods and times when we were receiving our daily food from Catholic charities"—Viola has nothing but sympathy for her dad. She feels she's "symbiotically related" to him, and, partly because of that closeness, alienated from her mother (she has recently moved toward reconciliation with her mother, and has begun to understand more compassionately the trials of her mother's life).

Mother was a strict Southern Baptist, "practically phobic" about sex and the body, says Viola. In the Jackson household, "there was no such thing as running a quick trip to the bathroom in your pajamas to take a leak before you got dressed." Once her mother caught her masturbating, and "Honey, that was the worst beating I ever got."

When Viola was twenty-five, her father confided that her mother had stopped having sex with him in 1955, after her eighth child was born. Mother "literally equated sex with having children," says Viola, and, of course, with marriage. As Viola sees it, her father had three options: live a celibate life within marriage; leave the family altogether; or have affairs on the side. He took the third, and although his girlfriends caused strife in the family—her six brothers, loyal to her mother, still despise him—Viola ratifies his choice.

Through circumstance and intention, Viola has never been one to hew to conventional morality or lifestyle. She was raped by a soldier at eleven and started having sex "voluntarily on my own" at fourteen, with the twenty-seven-year-old third cousin who was appointed her chaperon. She got pregnant within the year but told no one until it was too late; anyway, the only available abortion would have been "a Mexican butchery job." Viola was sequestered in a home for unwed mothers, expelled from the school honor society, and, at the behest of the school guidance counselor, had her scholarship to Radcliffe rescinded. Against her family's wishes, she kept the baby, an act she now regards almost as ordained by Fate: not too long after, she was sterilized by using a Dalkon Shield. As a second-best solution, her mother exhorted her to marry the cousin, but Viola would have no part of him; to this day, she hasn't contacted him.

Often at odds with her mother and sometimes under severe economic hardship, Viola raised her son alone. Not only a single mother by choice, Viola is also polygamous, a bisexual, an atheist, a feminist, and an active African-American liberationist. She has worked in women's and black organizations her whole adult life; today, at thirty-seven, she lives in Washington, D.C., and directs a literacy project for inner-city families.

Large and sensuous with dramatically defined features, dressed in African garb and draped in African jewelry, her hair in beaded dreadlocks, Viola is an arrestingly handsome woman. Having had men when she did not want them—after her rape at eleven, she was gang-raped by some fraternity boys during her freshman year at college—having had no control over her father's comings and goings, she now has men on demand, and precisely according to her specifications. Men are pals, lovers, or comrades; none has ever been a husband. She has enjoyed and loved them, hated them too, but she has never considered them central to her life.

At Howard University, which she entered at sixteen, Viola discovered the passion that shapes her life today: politics. There too her sexual ways were established. Those ways have changed in the decades since, but only in quantity ("Oh god! In my college years I think I might have slept with a hundred men!"), not in quality. At college, Viola slept with her sports buddies, card partners, and fellow partygoers. But she kept her twin passions, sex and politics, separate; in that way, she could manage the sexism of her comrades. In fact, the only time she broke her rule was to have a relationship with a woman.

> One of the things that was so flagrant in the black movement in those days were men who were sleeping around with five or six women who were in the movement. I mean, setting up things like polygamous marriages, babies littering the scenes . . . We were actually being told to throw away our birth control pills and have a baby for the revolution. Well, hell, I wasn't into monogamy, but that was disgusting to me. I'd already had a baby . . . I'd had an abortion, and I'd had a miscarriage. I was not interested in having any babies for a so-called cause . . .
>
> Most of my political comrades were of that type, the sleep-around type. And so real early I had made a decision I wasn't going to sleep with men in the movement, and all my political career thereafter, I'm real proud of the fact that I have not . . .
>
> It stood me in such good stead. I can grab the leadership

and power without having the compromising lingering relation-
ship standing in the way, and I can be very critical of these
dishonest men who were playing pussy politics, because I was
not one of the pussies.

Out of college, but still in the movement, Viola continued to
raise her son and steer clear of entangling relationships.

Being very protective of my own psyche, being very indepen-
dent. Actually getting angry at men who would, like, offer to
pay my rent, because I saw that as a way of control. Never ever
allowing them to develop any closeness with my son because I
didn't want him to get confused as to who was his father,
because I wanted him fatherless. Alvin [Viola's only live-in
lover] was the one guy who ever I allowed to get close to my
son. So much so that my son still does see him as the father.

If the relationship with Alvin crossed into something resembling family, it did not threaten to muddy the line between passion
and palship—because it was never passionate. Alvin and Viola were
best buddies, who "hung out together forty out of fifty-two weekends in a year," even slept together in the same bed but never made
love. Theirs was something like a marriage of convenience.

The first time we made love I told him I didn't like it because it
felt like incest . . . We kinda like forced ourselves to do it with
each other so that we could now say that we're dating. It was
not fun, it was like, why are you bothering with this? We
worked on it and it got better, but he was quite frigid really
. . . very uninformed sexually, very uninformed.

The lack of enveloping passion, Viola suggests, allowed her to
trust Alvin as she had not trusted any of her lovers; the two are still
friends. But if Viola was sexually unsatisfied, Alvin felt something
was missing emotionally. "One of his frustrations was that he never
really got me to open up to him, and he would say this."

A point of contention was that Viola did not want to get married. She understood her aversion to the prospect as a combination
of liking independence and fearing abandonment.

At one point me and Alvin were going to get married and all my antennae came up and a whole lot of fears I had around that. Also for him and me there was a problem in that I was sterile by that time, and he wanted kids. And so that created a lot of reservations in me, because I had a vision of being in a marriage with a guy that was sleeping with other women to have kids, ya know? We had an open relationship in that we did deal with other people, openly throughout our whole relationship, and I thought that was one of the most wonderful aspects of it. But I was terrified, not because we would stop loving each other or stop being close to each other, but because I knew how passionately he wanted his own children, and I was really scared that I would get beat out by someone who simply was more fertile.

Viola, a risk-taker in other ways, says time proved her caution wise.

He kept saying, "It's not that, it's not that. That could never happen." But actually my worst fears came true. We broke up in '85, and by '87 he had a son—by a very inappropriate woman, I must say. And so it was there. It was there.

This self-protection, combined with a taste for sexual variety, a desire to insulate her son from transient attachments, and a refusal to make compromises with behavior she considers sexist, has shaped Viola's social life. Having tried to make an exception for Alvin, which failed, she returned to a sedulous division between "buddies" and lovers.

What I found was that I never could sleep with a friend because then it would totally change my perception of them. It's like the closeness that we had before I slept with them would be lost, because then I started bringing to the relationship all my fears, all my anxieties, all the untrustworthiness-type stuff. Where I had no problem trusting them with my last dime and my son or whatever up until we became sexual, when we became sexual . . . I would literally shut down on them.

Viola's love life is not entirely limned by fear or avoidance, however. In fact, the friend-lover divide may be more conceptual than real. Actually, she has maintained a number of long-term, committed, sexual relationships over decades of time and miles of distance, and she considers these men dear friends. Since Viola has a rule against sleeping with married men (although she is polygamous), the sex, but not the friendship, comes to a halt when a man gets married. If he gets divorced, often sex picks up again. At present, none of her lovers lives in her city, but because her job pays decently, "when I get horny I get on a plane and fly to Atlanta or New York."

Viola is anything but indiscriminate in her choice of lovers. On her list of inviolable criteria is complete and open honesty with her own lovers and her lovers' lovers.

> *I don't shadow-dance with other women. You know, she needs to know what she's into and I need to know what I'm into. And if you can deceive her, I really feel that it's only a matter of time before you start deceiving me.*

Jealousy and possessive suspicion are not tolerated from men.

> *I met a guy one time over at Bobby's [a platonic friend's] house, and so we dated. The second date he asked me, "Who is Bobby and what is he to you?" "He's a friend." "I know Bobby. He don't have women just as friends." "You obviously don't know him as well as you think you do." I thought that was a bit strange.*
>
> *Well, boom, next date he asked me basically the same question because obviously the answer I'd given him before didn't satisfy him. Well, honey, there was no third date. Because that's like a basic test. If you can't pass the basic test and accept what I'm telling you, I am not interested.*

Most important, a history of nonviolence within her home, sliced through by rape, has made Viola unable to abide even a hint of physical threat in her love relationships.

> *It was enough for a man to raise his voice to me for the relationship to be totally discontinued. I would never stay in it long enough to see if they could get violent beyond that.*

She notes that her policy is somewhat self-defeating.

I mean, that small pool of available men got real small when you disqualified men who raised their voices! And that's not normal. I've raised my voice for years and I've never struck a person in anger in my life. But I couldn't trust men who raised their voices.

When Viola began to work in a rape crisis center, her tolerance for violence diminished even further. The work forced her to confront feelings about her own rapes—rage, terror, and a sense of abandonment—that she'd never grappled with. Coworkers, whether victims of assault or not, could not help but be changed by the day-to-day involvement with sexual brutality.

Women's relationships with men never stayed the same once they started working at the center. The brothers used to accuse us of turning their women into lesbians.

Actually, none of the African-American women on the staff had slept with women—except Viola. But because of what she perceived as serious homophobia in the black community, she kept that fact under wraps (she was then living with Alvin). Besides, she laughingly recalls, she was feeling inexplicably voracious for men, "in spite of themselves."

I was addicted to dick! If I could get it any other way I probably would. I was even of the crowd that bought dildos and tried to substitute—it just didn't get it. Something about having hair attached to the scrotum, I don't know.

Whatever combination of psychological factors caused Viola, a bisexual, to choose heterosexuality just at that moment, I won't venture to untangle. At any rate, rather than intensifying incipient man-hating, the work tended to mollify—or more accurately, complicate—feelings of anger, contempt, and alienation in regard to men. One project in particular profoundly affected this process. Some convicted rapists in a nearby prison had formed a group called Prisoners Against Rape and approached the center to come to the prison and work with them "to grow their consciousnesses" about women and women's issues.

*We took twenty of us because we were scared. We're con-
fronting rapists? We're talking about working with rapists? It
really felt like embracing the enemy.*

The center agreed to work with PAR, which expanded into a
sort of socialist-feminist study group. Eventually there were similar
groups in other prisons around the country.

*So I had the input of working with men who were rapists, com-
bined with working with the women who were victims of rape.
And I liked it because that kind of kept me balanced. Of
course, you can't teach a guy for a period of three years without getting to know him quite well. And no longer seeing him
as the dick that goes out and fucks women over. It's kind of
hard to continue to see someone in that light.*

At the same time Viola was beginning to see rapists as regular
guys, she was recognizing that plenty of the regular guys she knew—
including men high up in the movement—were privately committing acts of sexual violence against women.

*I'll never forget the official representative from [a major black
nationalist organization] who was a very good friend of mine
who actually raped two women I was doing work with. Now he
would not define them as rape. He would define them as aggressive sex. They kept saying no and he kept saying yes. He
had just spent X number of dollars on her for dinner and blah
blah blah . . . and "why do they throw themselves in my face,
then when it comes time to give it up they all say no. And I'm
gonna take it!"*

Viola says her varied experience with men at that time helped
her "not to tilt too hard in one or the other direction"—too trusting
or too suspicious. A close friend, whose father, uncle, and husband
had abused her, and who then came to work at the rape crisis center,
developed "an open phobia around men."

*She's not a lesbian, mind you. She has openly aggressive hos-
tility towards men, but wants them. In a way it was part of my
education to be a good friend of hers because it kind of maybe
helped me from going that way . . . She was the extreme that
allowed me to be the moderate.*

Not that Viola lets men off easy about violence. She contends that heterosexuality is rife with male violence, that "men are conditioned to hit out and strike out at that which makes them unhappy." As "one of the guys" watching football and playing poker, she's often privy to uncensored corroboration of this impression.

> I knew a lot of men who were good friends of mine but who also talked about how they kicked their woman's ass. I never had any threat of violence from them because I wasn't in a relationship with them like that. But I would privately tell them, I would never be in a relationship with you, sucker . . .
>
> I would be the one that would call them on things around women, and sometimes they hated me for it, they'd avoid me for it.

This male volatility makes Viola especially averse to paternalism.

> The word that pisses me off most is, I want to protect the black woman. It keeps you subservient to the man. Some men protect you, some beat you up, but always you need men to survive . . . Far as I can tell, the one I might need protection from the most might be you! I'm not impressed, so let's try this another way.

Having committed her adult life to finding that other way, Viola believes men can change. She blames a rigid cultural ideal of masculinity—not biology—for men's offenses against women.

> I mean, we've got a definition of manhood in this country that says you have to be sexually virile, you have to be able to provide for your family, you have to be able to tolerate any amount of pain psychic, mental, or physical without crying, without showing how much it's really hurting you . . . And you have to win most competitions with other men. I know no men that can meet those four requirements. And they'll overcompensate in one area because they're fucking up in the other three. And that's what I keep experiencing—men who are extremely financially successful who have hang-ups around sex; men who are very, very sexually active who cannot play the economic ball game and win; men who work themselves to death and still do not make enough money to provide for their families or men who stop trying to work because they

know they will never make enough money to provide for their families.

So I feel real sympathy for the men black and white who have to have that as a working definition of men. At least we women have had a movement that's redefined who we're supposed to be. So that we no longer feel guilty because we're not Suzy Homemaker.

Viola is sympathetic to men, but she does not completely trust them. She likes and loves some, but she doesn't "fall in love." Around the edges, she allows, there is hatred too. Viola enters relationships with men by choice, one day at a time, and maintains them at precisely the level she is comfortable with. These are neither established nor perpetuated by a marriage license, a checking account, or a raised and threatening hand.

In terms of trusting men now, that's basically where I am. I love male energy, so I seek to have it around me in a lot of ways. But I do not seek to become intimate with it. I'm still too uncertain about what I want with male intimacy in my life, and I'm comfortable with having to fly to California or New York to have a lay, and I'm privileged that I can afford to do that now.

All the pressures I had on me to have a man in my life around having a home and raising a kid, a son, by myself, not making enough money to pay the bills—all those reasons that drive us into relationships with men and keep us there, they're no longer pressures on my life. My son is in his third year of college. I'm not going to marry to make him happy at this point.

Viola Jackson makes no effort to conceal her ambivalences. Her Separate Peace, while it has provided serenity, pleasure, and the freedom of self-determination, is not an ideological stance; it's not even necessarily permanent. For now, she says, "This is what I can deal with." Of her love affairs, she says simply: "The criteria is wanting to be there."

10

Withdrawal

Pam Brady and Leah Goldensohn

WITHDRAWAL FROM RELATIONSHIPS WITH MEN is never total, and it is almost never totally voluntary. Not even lesbian separatists, who have excised men from their very dictionaries (i.e., *wimmin*), can avoid day-to-day contact with the butcher, the baker, or the male mail carrier; the devoutest separatists have brothers, fathers, sons, and ex-husbands. A single woman can have a baby by artificial insemination, but she has to get the sperm from someone, and only the hardest-hearted man-hater will give up her newborn because he happens to have a penis.

Ideologues who pontificate against intercourse sometimes turn out to live with men. (Andrea Dworkin has long cohabited with John Stoltenberg, who advocates "refusing to be a man," and does not acknowledge any sexual relationships with women. A friend of mine refers to this species of heterosexual as the "metaphysical lesbian.") And, alas, throughout history some of the most upstanding opponents of passion—a wonderful fictional example is George Gissing's "odd woman" Rhoda Nunn—have been disarmed by love.

Just as those who intend to avoid men aren't always able to, many live apart not by choice. I know personally and have interviewed many vigorous, mature, friendly, attractive women who find themselves subtly ushered from the heterosexual marketplace because they are "too fat," "too old," or otherwise devalued in an increasingly competitive and rigid system of female desirability. They feel debilitated by a sexual quest in which they begin to expect rejection, exhausted by the never-ending, never-sufficient effort to stay "young." In Barbara Raskin's *Hot Flashes,* a single woman in her forties plaintively wonders when she will be allowed to stop holding in her stomach.

So for long periods, or permanently, these women remove

themselves from a race they no longer want to suffer running in. A boot-camp-worthy standard of physical beauty perpetuated by the media is only the most obvious manifestation of the values of this contest. A more pernicious, pervasive social current blames the problems between the sexes on women's hard-won gains, scolding women for their uppityness and advising them to reconsider prefeminist roles and feelings. "Women's expectations of relationships have been exaggerated by the belief that they can have it all," say Drs. Connell Cowan and Melvyn Kinder in their bestseller, *Smart Women, Foolish Choices.*[1] The doctors are happy to report that some "smart women today want to reembrace many of the truly substantive traditional values without relinquishing the gains of recent years."[2] Aware of the perfectly oxymoronic nature of such a goal, some women have reached a point where, far from expecting to get it all, they doubt they'll wind up with any of it.

Withdrawers, the conscientious objectors of man-hating, refuse to put their own bodies on these hard lines. For them, trying to make the grade is not only painful, it's insulting; the whole project contrasts too starkly with the high degree of self-actualization and social reward they have attained in other areas of their lives. Many women, discovering that sexuality is more protean than they'd imagined, join the ranks of already self-identified lesbians and find happiness in intimacy with other women. Others, immutably straight, resign themselves to stretches of celibacy. Said a successful businesswoman I know, fifty-two, heterosexual, and divorced with two grown children: "I'd rather sleep alone with my integrity."

Sexual preference doesn't predict either a desire to withdraw or the degree of comfort found in doing so. A good example is Maria Rosario, a twenty-eight-year-old lesbian, a welder who works on all-male crews around Chicago. She told me:

> *I honestly think I hated men when I was married. But now I'm with women—this goes to show how strange life gets—two of my best friends are men, and once in a while I make love to a guy and it's nice. I like it. Men don't control my life, in no way, so I can let them into my life.*

Meanwhile, Gracie Miller, a fifty-nine-year-old retired flight attendant, is nominally heterosexual but has been celibate for the last fifteen years, having absented herself from a game she always felt unable to play. Aside from the husbands of friends, she rarely even has dinner with a man.

> It seemed to take so much energy to be with them. I had to laugh at everything they said and make sure they didn't get angry. Even if I didn't like them I had to make sure they liked me. I would be so submissive, so sweet, so good. It was such an effort, it was so hard.

Is it still?

"Now," she says flatly, "I don't try."

Then there are those women who might banish men from their lives if only they could. A friend overheard the following conversation between two older women on a ferry in Maine and wrote it in her journal:

> "Let's face it. We've put up with a lot of guff they wouldn't put up with anymore."
>
> "Damn right."
>
> "We still do."
>
> "Better than being alone, though."
>
> "That's the choice."
>
> "I don't know, though. Now they've got those senior citizens' organizations. They get together and have a ball. Don't even need a husband anymore."
>
> "Long as you can take care of yourself and live alone."
>
> "Long as you can afford it."

Just as sexual preference is not a predictor of withdrawal, I found, neither is a "dysfunctional" family, a bad marriage, sexual harassment, or rape. When she was nineteen, Kit Stern, a New York artist, was raped in a Boston train station, dragged down a flight of cement steps, and left for dead. She suffered brain damage that left her partially paralyzed and comatose. While Kit struggled to regain the ability to move and speak that a man had destroyed, she was intent on staying in the world of men, fearless and loving. She continued to sleep with men and consciously chose to live in a coed communal house. She is now bisexual, as she was before the attack, but for a long time sex with men was one of her last connections with her "old self."

• • •

Pam Brady and Leah Goldensohn are two Withdrawers from different sides of the tracks, socially, economically, and emotionally. Pam, a thirty-one-year-old African-American, is exclusively lesbian and has almost no men in her life. She doesn't like men much—considers them egotistic malingerers for the most part—yet feels no active animosity toward them. One of her two children (both conceived the old-fashioned way) is a six-year-old boy, but to men and issues around them she says she gives little thought.

Leah, a forty-eight-year-old first-generation American Jew, is celibate, childless, and unmarried (she had one short marriage in her early twenties). A feminist art historian, she has given an immense amount of thought to these issues. Ideologically, Leah is committed to a reconciliation between women and men on new, egalitarian terms, yet in her own life she seems to have closed the book on the possibility of such reconciliation. On political principle, she is optimistic. Yet her personal withdrawal and the way she describes it indicate deep pessimism and cynicism and a hostility based categorically in gender. Leah's way of dealing with those feelings, I think, is not exactly to deny them, but to *oppose* them as politically incorrect *ideas*. Whereas Pam is comfortable with the notion that man-hating exists—of course it does, she says, as if discussing the fact that the sun rises in the east—Leah argues eloquently that it does not. Or rather, that it should not. Or that she doesn't—or maybe, shouldn't—feel it.

Both Pam and Leah live in predominantly female worlds, Pam's in poor, black Detroit, Leah in the rarified circles of Los Angeles' feminist academe. Both find satisfaction, stimulation, support, and love there, with the obvious difference that Pam finds sexual love as well. Both acknowledge that the Battle of the Sexes is with us for the foreseeable future. Yet where this for Pam is a sort of disinterested observation, and her alliance with the women's "side" is as easy as it is noncombatant, Leah's understanding of the conflict between women and men as the legacy of history, economics, and millennia of culture, her feeling that a political struggle is imperative, combined with her heterosexuality, make her response much more troubled. For Pam lesbianism is a way of loving, not a political statement; her withdrawal from men is secondary to her closeness with women. For Leah, whose personal and political lives are one, withdrawal is a personal choice overlaid by political analysis. She employs ideology both as a defense against the ramifications of her choice and, in an attenuated and distant way, as a source of comfort and hope.

Pam Brady

It's no surprise that Pam Brady shies away from dogmatism. Since adolescence she's been evading the long arm of a powerful Deep-South Pentecostalism, in whose church her father was a minister. Her parents taught her that men were untrustworthy opportunists.

> *You know, all they wanted was to have sex with you, and once you're pregnant, they're gone . . . It was up to me to say no. And to always have my dime in my pocket so I wouldn't have to do what some man wanted me to do.*

Once married, however, men metamorphosed from footloose lechers to upstanding patriarchs, and women's attitude toward them was expected to alter correspondingly. Descendant of Adam, men directed the family according to their first-come, first-served order of creation. Their dominion was not to be questioned.

Living in a small town near Jackson, Mississippi, the Bradys had an exemplary Christian household. Father ruled and mother obeyed. As the oldest child and the only girl among six brothers, Pam's responsibilities far outweighed theirs. She cooked, served, and cleaned along with her mother. Yet she did not enjoy the privilege to come and go as her brothers did. By the age of thirteen, she'd already had enough of being kept in line by men.

> *"When I get married": We had very little conversations about that, because it was clear I wasn't going to do that. If we had them, it was "When are you going to get married?" I would say, "Never." Why? Because I don't believe in having somebody telling me what to do . . . just because. Nor do I believe in turning my money over . . . just because. We couldn't get past that.*

Still, there were air pockets in the claustrophobic ideology Pam was being taught. Adamant that she marry, Pam's father nevertheless wanted her to be able to divorce. He insisted she get an education and required her to take typing all through high school.

> *He would always say if you get married, I want to know that you can take care of yourself, and if this guy all of a sudden starts to act up, that you don't have to stay there, that you have your own money and you can leave.*

Of course, if one stays within the church, separation is only second-worst to a bad marriage. Divorced people are allowed to live apart, but one is married for life and forbidden to remarry unless she catches her spouse in the act of fornication.

> *And you have to see them with your own eyes, and it can't be hearsay. And even if you see an offspring of this relationship that looks exactly like your husband, uh-uh. So you can leave, but after that you're on your own, forever alone. That's heavy. That is truly heavy, mm-hmm.*

Pam's childhood—weekday evenings and weekends, social life, education, and creative outlets—were dominated by the church. Rebelliousness helped to loosen, but didn't altogether free her of, the stranglehold it held on her imagination, even into her twenties. Any sexual attraction to women Pam might have felt was immediately obliterated by terror.

> *It was something I knew about but for a long time I refused to acknowledge that. I just wouldn't even toy with it. I was still so much involved in traditional Christian thinking that I felt like if I could conceive that, my soul was going to be damned right then and there. And I wasn't so sure I wanted to be damned to hell so quickly. [She laughs] I didn't want to be thinking about this for the next forty years!*

Still Pam took steps, one after another, to break with her family. She had premarital sex, with men; in 1980 she conceived her daughter, Aqisha, but refused to marry the father, Lester; she dropped out of college after a year and joined the Marine Corps, "because it was my decision . . . It was the one thing in my life that I could say was mine."

In the Corps, although the women were extremely close, consorting sexually with a fellow female soldier was grounds for immediate dishonorable discharge. Lesbians stayed strictly in the closet, and out of Pam's purview.

During and after her tour of duty, Pam continued to see, though not to live with, Lester, and her son, Kufi, was born nine months after she came home. But she chafed in the relationship. Like other Withdrawers and many Separate Peacemakers, she felt a relationship with a man fundamentally compromised her integrity.

> We had a decent relationship. I just could not commit to it. I felt like too much was required of me. I had to be too much. A mother, a lover, a friend, and I couldn't see where I would have time for myself in the relationship. Even when he would come over to visit or if he stayed for periods of time in my home, it was like pulling teeth to get this man to help me do dinner— that kind of stuff.
>
> While my baby was in there needing attention and I felt like he would do what daddies do, go in and pick the baby up and kind of bounce her around, and then come in and say like, "Here, I think her diaper needs changing." And I would say, "Why the hell didn't you change her diaper?" And he'd get mad and go off into this other stuff.
>
> I had seen too much of that. I felt like I would die if I committed to that. It was just that strong . . . My vow to myself was so ingrained that I was never going to get married. I knew that I wanted a family but I could never see male-female-child. It was myself and child. I was thinking like that at like thirteen years old.

Lester moved from Jackson to Little Rock, Arkansas, which suited Pam. The relationship deteriorated. The issue was not that she was secretly a lesbian. Instead, theirs were the classic man-woman issues: rights versus obligation to the children; power and money.

> We had a long-distance relationship. It was easy to say okay to that because I didn't have to see the man. I liked him. I wanted that to work out, but it just didn't seem possible. A part of me had to die to make that work out. I wasn't willing to compromise.
>
> We had fights about, like, this man was away when Aqisha was born. He was overseas. So he came back when she was six months old and he automatically assumed that it was his place to discipline that child, and to come in and take over my

household. And I had worked very hard to get to that point to set up a house and to remain in the military with a child. I resented that. It invalidated everything that I had done to that point, where he could just come in and take over and not real- ize that I had a mind to think with.

I said, "You can't come in and change things. This is my home and just because you have a child here doesn't mean that you can move in." . . . Every time we came together it was like, "You have my child. Why can't I move in here? We say we're in love with each other. Why can't I move in here?"

He would give me support as long as I was acting "right." As long as I allowed him in my home and would be his woman. But the minute I'd say, "This relationship is not working for me" or "I don't want to see you tonight because I just don't want to see you tonight," it was like punishment of the child: "I'm not going to give you X amount of money or support or time . . ."

That's difficult to deal with. There's bargaining power there.

Pam and Lester broke up, but the power struggle didn't end. Years later, he sued her to change the children's last name to his (he won), and she took him to court to enforce child support (she won, and his paycheck is garnished every month). Now she's talking about trying to get the kids' names changed back.

That was the last heterosexual relationship and the last male intimate in Pam's life.

One day at the office, a coworker asked Pam what she did for fun.

I said, "I go home, I take myself to a movie, that kind of stuff."

"What about clubs? Don't you wanna date somebody?"

I said, "No. I got children to take care of and I don't have time to be dealin' with somebody else." And somebody asked me about men, and I made the statement: "You know, I think it would be a lot easier just for me to be with women." And the room got real quiet.

You know sometimes you say things because they've been there unconsciously for so long, and they come out and you don't even realize they're out. That's what happened . . . And out of that I started allowing myself to look at women.

Today Pam works as a file clerk in a large city hospital not far from her one-bedroom garden apartment. She has managed to make a life almost devoid of contact with males, save Kufi. Her coworkers are all women; so is her supervisor. Her friends are women, lesbians for the most part, black and white. She is in a steady relationship with a woman, and although her lover does not have children she helps Pam with Aqisha and Kufi. There are power struggles between the two women, Pam concedes, but nowhere near as intense as those between men and women.

> She too knows what it's like to be a woman. She's grown up in this world just like I have. Our experiences might be different but we're still women. And the women I deal with know that we don't want to relate to each other in a male way, not power-tripping or calling on any "rights" they might think they have over me.

Through Kufi's day-care center, Pam rubs shoulders with fathers, but she doesn't cultivate them as friends or involve them in her own children's lives. Pam says she would like to "break the cycle" of male domination in her family: she's trying to raise Kufi to be a different kind of man, and eventually a different kind of father, than his own father. She wants him to respect women and not to expect women and girls to take care of him. So far, it seems to be working. As Pam and I talked on a Saturday morning, Kufi ran in and out of the house with his friends, made himself snacks, and occasionally crept into the living room to drape himself over his mother's shoulder and shyly talk into my tape recorder.

> He does have responsibility for what he puts out in the world . . . Karma comes back to you. That's what I'm teaching him. Your actions affect more than just you.
> . . . [I want him to] realize that his sister is just as important as he is. I think in families the boys are taught that they are important . . . It's not said necessarily, but when your brother gets this huge plate of food or you can't get the biggest piece of chicken because that's your dad's or your brother's, you know, that's the little subtle stuff that we teach our daughters.

Pam has alternative models of lesbian motherhood. One friend from the day-care center is a black lesbian psychotherapist who comothers a daughter, Lisa, with another woman. The therapist also limits her own social and professional contact with men, yet she has found a man, picked for what she considers his unusual tenderness, to godfather Lisa. Like a child of divorce, Lisa spends one day a week and every other weekend with her godfather and his wife. Pam believes the minimal fathering her own children receive is sufficient, and—as I quoted her in "Daughters and Fathers"—typical of African-American families.

Meeting them briefly, I found Aqisha and Kufi to be happy, well-mannered, curious, and humorous children. They may have troubles, of course, but there are myriad possible reasons for these besides the lack of a committed father.

At any rate, Pam's insistence on the dispensability of fathering might be a little less certain than she lets on. Would she like more men in her life? I asked.

> *I have one gay male friend. We see each other periodically. I don't have any straight male friends. It's not a matter of not liking them, but what would we talk about? How would we relate to each other? How would I relate to a straight man who was having problems with my being a lesbian? . . . I don't think all of them would, but the question is, do I want to invest that much time? If I could find a nice balance, then yes, I would prefer that. I haven't thought about it a lot.*

Is this answer disingenuous? Pam says the lack of men around her is "just the way it happened." But would a woman who has made so many deliberate choices under such difficult circumstances, who seems to have thought a great deal about the best way to raise her children, leave such a matter to chance? She says she doesn't particularly like men, then shifts the dislike to them: what if a man "was having problems" with her lesbianism? Pam has made a distinct choice to insulate herself from male society and satisfies her social, economic, sexual, and family needs without men. Yet even her withdrawal may not be entirely unambivalent or without costs— ostracism, perhaps, or poverty for her children. Perhaps the blind spot in this otherwise careful observer's purview—"I haven't thought about it a lot"—is her way of dealing with that ambivalence, of not dealing with the social consequences of Withdrawal.

Leah Goldensohn

A looker and a thinker by profession, Leah Goldensohn has thought about "it" a lot, and for a long time. But it was not until the late 1960s, when she encountered feminism, that thoughts about the relations between the sexes were suddenly clarified in the light of a new worldview.

> *My first flash of insight was visionary, total. It was like religious conversion or the discovery of Marxism. You saw the world differently and would never see it the same again. I saw that, as Simone de Beauvoir said, I had been made a woman . . . that I was a creation of culture. It was astonishing. These were large, crude, insights. Sophisticated in a certain way, but not psychologically refined.*

Leah is continually struggling to find a balance among intellectual sophistication, political vision, and psychological honesty, and as we discussed man-hating that struggle emerged. The intellectual finds man-hating too "large" and "crude" a concept; the visionary finds it pessimistic, fatalistic, and politically counterproductive. And it seems to me, the emotional being, the woman, doesn't quite know what to find it. Leah has surely withdrawn from men, but she is still heterosexual. If man-hating resides in her, it occupies a painful place —a place she would prefer to protect, or, with her dazzling intelligence, cover up.

Like many women of her time—she was born in 1940—Leah married young. She was a beatnik, and she and her husband were going to have a bohemian marriage. They both contributed to the kitty, but true to beatnik custom, she worked more steadily than he did. As far as other sex roles were concerned, her marriage differed little from the "straight" postwar marriages all around her. He was depressed; she cheered him. He blew up; she placated him. He was hungry; she cooked. He went to "their" studio and had writer's block. She, a budding artist, worried about him as she cleaned the house.

They divorced after a few years, but Leah's expectations for some yet unnamed ideal lingered. She was disappointed, over and over.

> I was twenty-three years old when we all read [Doris Lessing's] The Golden Notebook. We were all those weary women. That book is drenched in disappointment in men. None of them deliver, none can be the thing that she deserves. That is the big character fault of the book, but its truth too.

As we saw in "Sisterhood and the Patriarch," at the dawn of modern feminism, when women started naming those disappointments, many flew into a fury. Leah insists she did not react as many of her sisters did.

> How I felt was elated. I wasn't enraged. I was so absorbed and amazed by seeing my own history. When I saw, oh god, I married this guy because . . . I was amazed by the politics. I wasn't enraged at my husband.

Her political superego was more powerful than any visceral resentment; she did not feel rage because she felt a movement of rage would not succeed.

> This woman got up at a meeting and was very angry. My first instinctive response to this first instance of open man-hating was, You've got it all wrong. We will reduce them to a prescription and to a litany and the narrow view of life that we ourselves are suffering from. It will not help us free ourselves. The next sentence in my head—which remains—was from Chekhov: Others have made me a slave but only I can squeeze the slave out of me drop by drop. That has sustained me through all the years of feminism. Whenever I felt despair. Even now. I must do the work on myself. I believe the slave mentality is in us. Men can't undo it.

Even then, Leah could afford to be an ideological integrationist and espouse friendly male-female alliances. She was free as well to cast aspersions on men, if that's what she felt like. She was safe from the perils, and the rage, of bringing those alliances home, safe from the fear of endangering those alliances. For since her divorce, Leah had had many male lovers, but her affairs remained at minimal levels of intimacy.

> We were two kinds of girls, the stars and the groupies. The groupies who played the ordinary feminine role and married UC professors. The others were like me, belligerent. We were all involved in men who were intellectually inferior to us, what I called "apes in human dress."
>
> When women were talking about their bad sex lives, I was shocked. They were rehearsing the hundreds of little ways they felt humiliated, hamstrung. I didn't know from that. I was going out with guys who didn't have the imagination to be tyrannical or impotent. I didn't experience what it was to be set up with a man who provided.
>
> I was thirty. I was unmarried—free to think, free to fill the rooms with my presence. I wasn't living out the dailiness of living with a man. My house, my life, my world, were my own. Men came and went erratically, but I was struggling through alone.

In the early stages of Withdrawal, Leah had already drawn a bottom line: "The only way I could be independent," she says, "was to be alone." Yet in spite of her de facto avoidance of heterosexual love, she says she didn't feel alienated from men. Again the political strategist, the visionary, the hopeful heterosexual, seized the "floor" of her consciousness: "I knew we had to do it together. I was heterosexual and had to go on loving men."

As time passed, Leah had a few longish relationships with men, but each came to an impasse. As on an overland journey toward each other, man and woman would reach a wide chasm across which they could not connect.

> What did not exist was anything remotely like equality of feeling, of directness of apprehension, the equality that comes when people are not making a deal but are simply allies in a struggle against life.

Leah says she didn't blame this on individual men—although she experienced plenty of day-to-day anger at those partners. Describing her feelings at that time, her determination to reject the *politics* of hatred melds with a denial of any personal *feeling* of hatred: she "should not" hate, and therefore she "did not." Feeling and thinking are in this sense conflated—or, rather, the former is at the service of the latter. In our conversation, it seemed to me, often her ideas mediated anxiety-provoking feelings.

Here Leah contrasts "maleness" with "men as such," proclaims she does not have a feeling she doesn't like someone having about her, and disowns emotion that impedes clear thought. Working to distinguish between politically constructive analysis and destructive, untheorized emotion is a worthwhile endeavor, I agree, and the distinctions are real and fair. Psychologically, however, the dividing lines are murkier.

> *When you describe the feeling [a combination of rage, contempt, impatience, alienation, envy, fear], yes, I would say I felt hatred. My feelings were a part of the complex of feelings that shaped early feminism. But I never said men are evil, stupid oppressors in their very being . . .*
>
> *When I feel the maleness of a sentence or a position, I do hate that. Hating men as such is appalling to me. I'm so appalled by having been hated as a woman that I really shrink from it.*
>
> *I grew up in primitive circumstances [in a communist family]: hate the boss, hate the landlord. That was empowering. When I got older it wasn't the part that was moving, interesting, enriching. To have feelings of tender sorrow made you think better.*

Describing that sorrow for the state of things between the sexes, Leah begins to admit to man-hating, then pulls the punch.

> *I believe [men and women] are not friends, we do not feel for each other. Any woman in the world can tap in me a generic strain of sympathy for the idiom of her life that practically no man can . . .*
>
> *The truth, of course, is that the relations between the sexes are so deeply corrupt, there is no way for us not to hate each other. And I don't hate men. In fact, they have become fellow sufferers to me since I became a feminist.*

Together, says Leah, women and men are suffering under the burden of a stifling gendered emotional heritage.

> *All relations are laden with this extra immense load of the cultural expectation inside of what it is to be a man and what it is to be a woman. You must constantly struggle to separate the fantasy from the reality.*
>
> *. . . It is the corrupt nature of the whole deal: You do this and I'll do that. You be this and I'll be that. That has to end. As long as love is a deal, enmity and inequality are inevitable.*

But if men suffer, Leah is quick to acknowledge, they also benefit from the way things are. Saying this, a little pain and rage seep out.

> *Deep within [even] the good men I have known, in their not-so-secret selves, is the half-decent recognition of the necessity of us being equals and the half-love of mastery and submission.*
>
> *You can get to hate it. With all the good intentions in the world there isn't a man I have ever met who does not have a natural assumption of his centrality in his life that places me as a peripheral place. After years, that can make you kill.*

Like an environmental activist whose body can no longer abide environmental contaminants and sickens to a scent of gasoline or chemicals, Leah more than ideologically opposes the institutions of heterosexuality, such as legal marriage; she is emotionally allergic to them. She no longer strikes the male-female "deal" and because she has the power of her own life in her own hands, says she doesn't suffer from impossible expectations or tragic defeats: "No man can be a disappointment to me anymore. No man has the power to drag me into his destiny." She believes her independence keeps her on an even keel morally: "When you still want things from them," she states, "it makes you dishonest."

In throwing out the harmful, hurtful fantasies, has Leah forsaken the realistic expectations, the attainable fantasies? "A Prison gets to be a friend," wrote Emily Dickinson. Has Leah settled for "the slow exchange of Hope—for something passiver—Content"?

In the collective, public struggle that is feminism—a women's world of friendships, trust, and intellectual excitement, of parties, meetings, demonstrations, and long juicy conversations—Leah is as hopeful as any. Trained in childhood as a soldier for the cause, she understands that the battle against sexism is "a long, long haul . . . It doesn't end in a generation."

For that political haul Leah has all the stamina anyone could wish for. Yet personally, the long march seems to have fatigued her beyond revival.

It took me years to understand the depth of the corrosiveness of our relationships. It took me time to start concentrating on how penetrating is this profound antagonism. Misogyny and man-hating are literally the same. They are the deracinating, psychopathic ends in both cases of this corrupt and antagonistic relationship we all have.

I can see now in the slightest exchange with any man I have loved a battle of wills that makes me more and more dug in as time goes on. I struggle not to act out on that resentment. But I can't give on it. Because the years have passed . . .

When I hear a woman with this deep, settled, cold, unnegotiable sound say, "I can't do it anymore," I never argue with it. It's been twenty hard years of sobering realization. I understand perfectly.

Maybe the decision to stop the fight on the home front gives Leah the energy to keep it up at the barricades. In this sense, she doesn't quite qualify as a total Withdrawer. She flashes two messages alternately: her deeply felt convictions advertise hope, while her own relationship to love between the sexes signifies surrender. The battler against injustice, the diplomat of sexual goodwill, crows:

Now women have a different view of ourselves. We separate the men from the creeps. Men struggle when you present them with this stuff. They can't stop and we can't stop.

And the defeated prisoner of sex says:

I was ready to live alone. I thought, "This I can't do." I am not going to live in the daily presence of feeling my spirit and my mind and my life truncated and cut in half. I am not willing or able to make a liaison in which I do not feel myself absolutely real. I don't sleep with men I hold in contempt, and I don't sleep with many men at all.

Leah's life is far from dreary. "There are plenty of times I feel the relief and the exhilaration of living without men," she says. But her choice to withdraw appears less like an option taken victoriously than an indomitable imperative. "I can no longer make the accommodations of love," she says. "If I have to live alone the rest of my life, it's a deformed condition, a sad thing. But I can do it."

11

Infiltration

I've had major battles establishing respect within this organization. Major battles. And there's a lot of people in this organization that are very chauvinistic, and they'll make remarks and I just stare them down. I just ignore them when I have to . . . I can't find the fire within me to fight every little thing. I have to pick my fights, because I can't have this energy always fighting.

Zulma Cruz, thirty, union organizer

I think a lot of times men's careers fall prey to their need for either ego gratification or sexual dominance. I've seen a lot of men losing control of companies or not being as successful as they could have been because they felt a need for . . . individual personal visibility and control, where in fact the better path to success . . . would be not to take that personal heroic act. It's hard in general for them to be supportive, good team workers, particularly when there are women around.

Kat White, thirty-four, president of a $25 million business

Zulma Cruz and Kat White

MAN-HATING AT WORK IS A PURER STRAIN of the resistant virus that at home is kept under control with doses of love. Personnel disputes aren't quite the same as personal disputes. The prize—whether it's a promotion, a smoother-running department, or the cessation of sexual harassment—is not the adversary's love but his respect, and failing that, his acquiescence.

At the workplace a lot may depend on fine-tuning personal interactions. Kat White saw a company practically go under when this couldn't be achieved. But if getting along is a necessary tactic at work, it is not, as it is in a marriage or relationship, the primary objective. "I just have to sell soap with this guy, I don't have to raise kids with him," said an advertising executive, who resolved a long-standing problem with a coworker by divvying up most of their formerly cooperative tasks. Except at the beginning and the end of a project, the two barely talk to each other—an unrealistic strategy for husband and wife.

Not only practical considerations but desire and need soften women's derogations of the men who are closest to them. But those same women, without the ambivalences of intimacy, can tear savagely into the guys they work with. The Bumbler, the Slave, the Prick, and the Mama's Boy parade undisguised, and unprotected, in the office corridors and on the factory floor. Secretaries laugh contemptuously at their bosses' bad spelling, social clumsiness, and professional disorganization: "We've saved their asses more than a *couple* of times," one executive secretary told me, narrowing her eyes and glancing around her office like a potential blackmailer. Tradeswomen stoically put up with their crewmates' machismo; nurses and female physicians decry male doctors' neglect of elementary compassion ("The heart is a muscle to him, nothing more").

Work not being the primary focus of this book, my interviews did not focus on it at length. But whenever they touched on the subject, I heard undiluted contempt: men are needy, headstrong, cowardly, incompetent, psychologically blind, and incurably sexist.

Of course, there are exceptions to the rule of thumb that women will negatively stereotype men when discussing work and not when discussing life at home. For instance, there's the classic critical-wife, tolerant-secretary scenario, in which the love affair is ignited by the words "My wife doesn't understand me." Besides, nobody leaves her psyche at the factory gate or in the office-building lobby each morning. Bosses stand in for withholding fathers, coworkers for sadistic lovers, subordinates for pesky little brothers. The workplace is a family, a love affair, a club, a community, and a therapy group, and all share a spectrum of feelings and behaviors—acceptance, rejection, scapegoating, idealization, competition, and jealousy, to name a few.

But affection or sympathy for a male coworker does little to prettify the ugly causes of so much enmity at work. Whether he's clever or dull, charming or boorish, a man is likely to make more money than a woman, to have a bigger office and better access to the boss's ear. Women make 69 percent of men's wages overall, an increase of only 4 percentage points since 1955. And in spite of gains in some sectors of the economy, occupational stratification and segregation are still largely in force. The vast majority of women work in fields that are at least 80 percent female, and these tend to be low-paid, low-status, and low-mobility occupations, often lacking job security, benefits, or union representation.

So whereas women in 1988 represented almost 15 percent of architects, compared with 4.3 percent in 1975, and almost a fifth of lawyers and judges compared with just 7.1 percent in 1975, more than 99 percent of secretaries are still women and in the last twenty-five years the percentage of female dental assistants has dropped from 100 percent to a mere 98.7 percent. Even gross gains in a field may disguise lingering inequities. In law firms, for instance, a quarter of all associates are women, yet only 6 percent of partners are. For women of color, racism compounds sexism to deposit them at the very bottom of the work hierarchy in every respect.[1]

At the rate we're going, women won't achieve full job integration until nearly the twenty-second century, and without cryogenic preservation, today's secretaries, dental assistants, and lawyers will be hard put to wait.

What all this translates into, aside from a vast and increasing stratum of impoverished women and women working two and three jobs to make ends meet, is an on-the-job power struggle that starts out with men at a substantial advantage. If women know they won't gain pay equity or decision-making power on their jobs, they may consciously adjust their goals. "I know I'm not that significant to the guys on top," Zulma Cruz says. "I don't want any position. I just want respect. I want to be left alone to do my work."

Commonly, women adjust by picking their battles. They may swallow a comment on how their legs look in that skirt, but will fight to the finish if they find out their salary is lower than that of a man hired after them. "You have to let them know what your limits are," says a factory worker. "You confront it as it's useful to you. The greatest skill you develop is discretion."

The 1970s and 1980s produced some of the most ambitious women American history has ever seen, and postfeminism has not sent these women back to the kitchen. Kat White was without doubt one of the three or four hardest-driven people I've ever met, and despite her disclaimer, Zulma Cruz isn't gathering any moss either. Notwithstanding concessions like the Mommy Track, which relegates "less committed" women (read, mothers) to part-time or nonadvancing status in law firms, brokerages, and the like, women continue to fight for better, more egalitarian working conditions. Some of the most vigorous union organizing this decade has been undertaken among female clerical workers; the only real increases in union membership during that time have been in the public sector, which relies heavily on women workers.

Traditionally male jobs, like skilled factory work, are in sharp decline, while female-dominated sectors, such as service and clerical work, are holding their own. But women are moving into every corner of the marketplace, according to Susan Shank at the Bureau of Labor Statistics, and working more and more in "male" patterns —as many hours per week and as many weeks per year as men. In the trades, the media, and some of the professions, many workers feel, the sexes are scrapping more fiercely for the same jobs. But even if this is not literally true, most women I spoke with said they sense a male backlash at work. If women are trying to steal their space, men are redoubling their efforts to defend it.

"They are colder, more defensive, and more rebellious against women," said a business manager at a hospital in Chicago, where women are moving into the top administrative and medical ranks. A road worker in Cleveland said she always has work, because the law requires a certain percentage of female hires on any government-funded project. But, she said, getting the job is only half the battle. "You have to carry twice as much, work twice as fast, take half as many breaks, and stay twice as cheerful while they just happen to get in your way when you're hoisting the bucket or swinging the shovel."

Zulma Cruz

A quick-minded, quick-tongued working-class Puerto Rican New Yorker and the divorced mother of three, Zulma is an Infiltrator par excellence. She has elbowed her way into the regional leadership of a major labor union. In an organization whose rank and file is largely female, black, Latina, and Asian and whose officers are almost uniformly white and male, she's up against sexism—from the shop floor to the president's office—daily. Zulma does what is required to gain influence in the union, yet she still has little power. Whenever she gains some, she says, it's questioned, challenged, or undercut by men.

Zulma is a scrapper and the daughter of a scrapper. Her father was a merchant seaman, whose alcoholism, frequent absences, and violent temper made for a frightening and tempestuous early childhood. Zulma's mother did not take her husband's abuse lying down: "She'd yell, 'I'm not taking this anymore!' and then they'd come to blows." But she stayed married; the reason she gives was Zulma's attachment to her father. When sober, he was sweet, funny, and attentive, Zulma remembers. But he died when she was fourteen, and everything seemed to fall apart. "It was a very bad time for me. I didn't get my period for three months. I went into shock." Her mother, not so much bereaved as relieved, did not look for another husband. She was, and still is, a brilliant survivor.

As a garment worker, she worked in a certain type of operation that paid her very well, and plus she always took in work, so financially at that point in time, you know, she didn't need him to be the provider. And she's very financially savvy in terms of making ends meet.

Mom stood up for herself at work too. In 1970, she became active in her union and, now in her late fifties, she still is. Zulma has been inspired by her mother's conviction, spurred on by her victories, and angered to vengeance by her defeats, especially those that were at the hands of her putative union brothers, not the bosses.

There's a lot of anger in her too that I feel for her. Because she has a picture of her institute when she first became involved in the union in 1970 and all the men are now managers and vice presidents and the women are maybe assistant manager in that region over here, without much power, middle management over there, but never the top position.

I feel in the same way they train these guys and have the time to send them to leadership classes they could have done for the women. She is so intelligent, and she is such a fighter. She feels very hurt that this was not done in her generation. And she has gone to the president in a group of women, when he had the nerve to say in a New York Times *article, when they asked him, "Why are you not promoting women within the union?" "We don't have the leadership qualities in the women." They were livid. She was one of a group of ten women who went and challenged that article to tell him, "We feel that we were qualified. You chose not to [promote us]."*

I have lived through those battles with her.

For Zulma, the battles against a hidebound union bureaucracy are sometimes hard to distinguish from the general fight against men. She has a boyfriend and male friends in the union: "They're like brothers to me, and we protect each other fiercely. There's nothing I wouldn't do for them and they wouldn't do for me." But she resents it when these men are promoted over her and other qualified women, simply, she says, because they are men. The justification, as in all historically inegalitarian workplaces, is that the women don't have enough time and experience in responsible positions to take on more responsibility. Of course, the catch-22 is they can't get the experience because they never get the opportunity.

I see the resentment that some of these male VPs had when a younger woman was made a VP. The words out of the mouth of my ex-manager were like, "She didn't pay her dues." I mean, never mind the woman is brilliant and she can run circles around you. How long does she have to be here? Ninety-nine years before you decide to put her in a leadership position?

The male leadership perpetuates itself, fortifying its power and entrenching itself in views and methods that Zulma and other women feel belong to the last century.

In unions, where rewards do not come in the form of bonuses and stock options, and elected and appointed officers work side by side, considerable power is gained by being on the right boards and committees. Highers-up hand out kudos in the form of appointments to these committees, trust is demonstrated by inclusion on prestigious and visible projects, and favors are called in when election time comes around. In unions, as in business, academia, and the professions, women find that they are outside the circles of influence when these crucial trades are being made. "So he didn't want me involved, because he didn't feel like it," says Zulma of a coveted committee position.

. . . Meanwhile, there's this guy. He's in his middle forties, not active at all, never been active, and he was appointed to be on the national executive board, and it was only because they have something for him in his future . . . You know, nothing is fair . . . They're like an old boys' school. Like I'll rub your back and you rub my back.

Zulma has repeatedly been passed over for deserved appointments by her male superior. Recently, the two nearly came to blows when he treated her rudely before a roomful of people.

The department was planning a street festival. When Zulma's boss tried to get people to cook hot dogs, no one raised a hand.

No one was volunteering, because he has the personality of a frog—a frog has more personality. He's very gruff. He's the type that like beats you on the head to do something . . . So he screams at me, "Zulma, cook!" My mother got up mumbling and grumbling, and I said, "Leave, I'll deal with it."

I was fuming! And I was like, What am I going to say to this guy because he is never going to scream at me in front of these people again. Never!

. . . So I went into my room, kicked the garbage can, and then I was too upset to speak with him. So I thought about it. And I walked into his room the next day and I said to him, "Is there a problem with me?" He's like, "What are you talking about?" I say, "I didn't appreciate the way you spoke to me at this meeting." He says, "What way?"

The conversation went on like that, back and forth. Finally, says Zulma, he apologized. "But he made my life hell after that."

Finding her supervisor perpetually deaf—and hostile—to her complaints, Zulma finally turned to a higher authority. That move, she says, wounded her supervisor's "male ego" and got her nowhere.

I worked very hard in certain areas, especially in literacy, and I am—still am—very involved in this [AFL-CIO committee] and I'm the recording secretary, and I'm involved in conferences and programs, and as such I demand that respect. And he wasn't giving it to me.

We were battling one another. And he's like, "I'm the manager and I will tell you what you need to do and I know what's best for this local." And he threatened me because I had the people from the AFL write to the president of this union and tell them such and such. So when they pulled his coat, like, What's happening? he got very angry. And he said, "You tell your committee people to stop writing letters because it's going to be worse for you." And we had battles to the point where I almost left this union . . .

I felt I had to deal with someone smarter and who respected women. And he had no—I mean, no—respect for women.

In a long interview, Zulma rehearsed the intrigues, jealousies, coups, and reprisals within a power structure worthy of Eastern Europe. When she recounted incidents of sexism, some were the standard variety, behaviors that could be plugged like generic parts into any workplace: inappropriate touching, comments on her figure and her manner of dressing. (Zulma does not go to work looking like a harlot, but neither does she affect the no-nonsense, masculine style that some of her colleagues favor. When I met her she was wearing high heels, a skirt and blouse of gold and brown hues, with lots of gold jewelry and a wide belt that emphasized her figure.)

She feels women's agitation has forced some changes. The union president, she says, "sees the writing on the wall. There's been a major exodus of young progressive people lately." After much politicking, Zulma was transferred out of her former department, and away from the odious supervisor, to one where she can "do my job, finally." But she has not forgotten her former boss's customary response to her contributions in a group. It emblemizes not only his attitude, but the reality of men like him, using all instruments available, including the bluntest, to defend a turf they feel is being invaded.

> *His resentment towards me was manifested in so many ways. I'd get up and speak about my educational work, and he'd go, "I can't hear you." And the women in the room heard me loud and clear, and I just looked at him. And I'm like, "Is this loud enough?"*
>
> *"You're an officer of this union! You should be able to speak loudly!"*
>
> *And the women are looking at him like, "What's his problem?"*

His problem, Zulma suggests, is not only his, but millions of other men's in positions like his. Unfortunately it is her problem too —and that of millions of women pressing for equality at work.

Kat White

Kat White does not have the same problem, quite. She is among the smattering of women who have reached the rarified stratum of top corporate management.* Hers is a young, socially fluid industry, one in which a relatively large number of women have risen, although the infamous "glass ceiling" is built into this edifice too.

In an industry of talented, ambitious women, Kat is extraordi-

---

* It is so rarified that to protect her identity I agreed not to name the industry or even the state she lives in.

narily talented, perfectionistic, and unfazeable. By the age of thirty-two, she'd made her first million. At thirty-four, she manages 250 people and runs a $25 million company. She skis and drives competitively, hang-glides, rides horses, and windsurfs. She lives alone, and although she has a boyfriend, does not expect to marry.

Slim and fair, with a polished yet unaffected manner, Kat says she has struggled not so much with sexual discrimination as with the subtler manifestations of sexism, which she identifies both in her personal and her professional life. An early serious relationship verged on marriage, but she broke it off, troubled by the same kind of sexual politics that continues to trouble (though not to undo) her. Of that relationship, she says, "I felt in the end like I was a merger candidate rather than a lover," and an imperfect one at that.

> Many times men are caught in a narrow bandwidth of emotions. The range in which he could perceive another person was narrow. If you operated outside that narrow band acceptable for a woman, you created noise in the system and were surprising all the time. That was not a good or rewarding behavior. There was competition in that relationship—I do believe a lot like what there is in business.
>
> I don't think men have [changed] much from the cave days. Desire for sexual conquest is still alive and well in normal day-to-day office politics.

In her work, which she describes with the zeal of a mountain climber or a missionary, Kat says she encounters frequent roadblocks of masculine arrogance, egotism, and insecurity. When the stakes are as high and the business as competitive as hers is, slowing down to negotiate such obstacles can mean fortunes lost or gained.

The losses are not just financial. For a woman like Kat, who has devoted her life to her career, they are blows to the heart and the spirit as well. When a promising company foundered because of what she analyzes as the psychosexual hang-ups of its top man, the setback was as painful and disappointing to her as a stumble in the final yards of an Olympic race, or (I don't think this is an overdramatic comparison) a miscarriage in the eighth month of a pregnancy. Such losses, the casualties of male pride, have made an already unsentimental woman cynical about men.

I had one boss who was so tied up about my femininity that he'd have sexual dreams about me. It was a matter of personal sexual integrity that he had to be smarter, better, faster than me in every possible way. He worked terribly hard to get my support and affection, but it always had to be by being better . . . What he really wanted was for me to walk into his office and say, "Blank, you're the most incredible, talented, smart person I ever met in my life and I'm totally devoted to you in every way."

That was a sentiment Kat did not feel, and could not dissemble.

It finally became so painful for both of us that I ended up having to leave the company. Which was by all visible measures recognized as a great loss to the company . . .

At first I was a little irritated. At the end, I felt very sad and disappointed and in many ways very angry. Because I felt that something that was basically an issue of sexuality and emotional maturity was standing in the way of me and several million dollars, and the success of a company of 250 people.

. . . At the same time, I don't hate him. I attribute it to being very insecure and needing a lot of reinforcement for his powerfulness or whatever. If I had figured out a way to do it, short of sleeping with him, I would have. He's a very talented person, but he has an incredible need to always be right.

Insecurity and need for constant reinforcement; sexualization of successes and failures at work; egotism, which precludes working behind the scenes toward a better collective end; and a limited and limiting emotional receptivity, "a narrow bandwidth of emotions" —these Prickish and Babbler-like traits predominate in Kat's descriptions of men, especially the kind of men with whom she consorts at work and, though she tries to avoid it, in her social life.

Kat isn't a prude; sexual vibes in the office don't disturb her. Yet she is irritated by what she sees as men's need to establish their sexual dominance in a business hierarchy, with women, needless to say, at the bottom. Maybe she's oversensitive to this issue, she concedes. Maybe she ought to offer her bosses more strokes. But, as she described in the above example, she can't and she won't.

Men bring more sexuality to business than women do. There's a lot of sexual innuendos in the basic interchange among people in business. That's become sort of a natural part of business life. I don't find it offensive or intimidating or surprising.

Interestingly enough, I've never had trouble with a direct report being fixated on my being a woman . . . but I've had a lot of problems with my bosses. For whatever reason I've gotten the impression they've needed my support, they expect a certain level of affection from women. And I give that to my direct reports because I want their loyalty, and I hire people I like.

I don't pick my bosses because I like them . . . A boss I expect to be better at most things, and at least as good at his job, as I am at mine. I have very high standards. That may be a flaw, but I ain't going to change that.

As much as by the need for support, Kat is irked by men's inability to admit their vulnerability.

I can go to my direct reports and say, "How am I doing with you? What can I do to do a better job?" Men are not as comfortable saying that. In a superior relationship, they just can't ask for that.

Men "pay a big price for pride," Kat believes. It's sad, she says, that "most men view their careers as their potency, their animal-killing ability." But unlike most people, including women, who view this masculine "killer instinct" as a hindrance to emotional health but a boon to competitive success, Kat sees it as a handicap to both. Because of pride, "they're not as willing or able to take risks. They aren't willing to put aside their pubic image to achieve something."

Kat prefers a "consensus-oriented, behind-the-scenes" management style, which, coupled with men's sexist misapprehension of her abilities, often gives her the edge.

I am consistently underestimated, which has been one of my greatest strengths. You can often accomplish a lot in an organization before people wake up. Then they overestimate your success because they expect you to be a bimbo.

Surprise attacks like this hardly compensate for the lack of day-to-day egalitarian cooperation, however, and the demand to prop up men is exhausting, "a high-maintenance requirement." Ultimately, it leaves her disillusioned and alienated.

> *I end up losing respect for men. I wonder, why is their internal view of themselves so fragile that they find this constant need? I don't think it makes me angry. I kind of pity them. When I meet a woman, I expect to find a richer, more multifaceted person than when I meet a man.*

In Kat's personal life, not surprisingly, the issues of support, pride, and competition arise frequently. She does not like being underestimated and wants her independence respected.

> *A lot of men want me to want them to take care of me. I don't want that. I want to be appreciated and loved. I had one guy constantly telling me what a terrible day I had had. I would say, "I had the day and it was kind of normal." I don't need to be rescued.*

Men's needs impede the progress of both love and business, she feels, yet at home, she says, she is much more willing to slow down and fulfill those needs.

> *I think most men do want to be taken care of, but they don't ever ask for it. That comes back to that pride or ego. Interestingly enough, they will put their pride before their passion. When I'm in love, I am willing to take some fairly serious risks with my identity or ego. I'm willing to hang around and be devoted, and do what needs to be done to make the other person feel good. Pride in some sense comes out of having the other person care for me.*

She admits that her standards for love are pretty hard for a man to meet, and she's not great at compromising. Her brand of good man, she knows, is hard—if not impossible—to find.

> *I think I need to be around a very self-confident person, yet someone who's also tender. That's very rare. I've found a lot of self-confident sons of bitches, and a lot of tender insecure types.*

As much as the sensitive man of the nineties is the coming thing, I think the macho guy of the fifties is still lurking there beneath the surface, in both the women's and the men's perspective. I'm attracted to powerful, dominant men. If this wasn't an issue for me, I would go out with good-looking gas station attendants.

And right there is the conflict. They have to be real powerful not to once in a while run into a situation where I'm going to seem like I'm stepping on their toes.

Some of Kat's dates are discomfited by her stratospheric income. But she tends to hang around with men whose salaries also hover near the moon. This doesn't leave them wanting for ways to compete, though. She recounts an incident a few years back.

I was having a great time with somebody. We ended up getting into a situation by accident. We were stuck in a snowstorm trying to get to an airport after a weekend of skiing. The car broke down, and we both needed, I mean really needed, to get back. You could either panic and get frustrated or do something about it.

I remember being in a position which was, Do what he wanted to do: flail around. Or figure out how to drive the car to a garage, pay some money to stick it ahead in the queue, and get out of there. The fact that I did that ruined the relationship.

Kat's sexual relationships replicate in many ways her relationships at work, yet the two are in conflict in more essential ways. Much as she wants love in her life, she has, for now, made her priorities clear.

You do have to genuinely make choices between career and having a family. Those choices aren't obvious. I can't say the grass wouldn't be greener if I had gotten married and had a fifteen-year-old kid by now. I believe choices are black and white. I don't believe you can both be a great mother and wife, and a really successful businesswoman. I don't think Superwoman exists.

I can tell you, money doesn't overcome that problem. It's psychic energy, it's emotions. The emotion it takes to do either one leaves nothing left over for the other.

Kat is a maverick but she is not a reformer. As a manager, she does not stand on "the woman's side." She doesn't even really think there is one. Kat battles men daily, and she is exasperated and enraged by their attitudes and their behavior. Yet she does not look at the workplace as an arena for introducing "women's values" of nurturance or noncompetitiveness. That sort of charity, she believes, belongs at home. At work, work gets done. And if that means discriminating against other women in some way, so be it.

> *The truth of the matter is, if I honest-to-god look straight across the desk at the young guy with the supportive wife, who can give 110 percent seven days a week because she is going to run his social life and raise his kids, and rub his back when he gets home, versus the equally talented woman who can only work thirty hours a week, the light-bulb reality is . . . the person that can give the 110 percent, seven-day week is going to be the one that gets the job. It's the laws of Darwin. It's not a matter of fairness anymore.*

If Zulma Cruz met Kat White, she might not see her as a sister in arms, but as a collaborator with the Enemy. Both women identify certain unsavory characteristics as male—egotism, self-protection, underhandedness based in an inability to be direct about one's needs and wants. Yet Kat does not assign gender to those values certain feminists have called masculine—i.e., placing productivity and profit above the needs of nurturers and families. In fact, they're *her* values too. Where Zulma advocates a sisterly overthrow of the male power structure, Kat is more interested in joining than beating them. She just wants men to remove the monkey wrenches of their personal hang-ups, and let the works hum.

12

Declaration of Independence

Dottie Bernstein

I FIRST MET DOTTIE BERNSTEIN ON her wedding anniversary. She was fifty-nine years old, with an athletic stride and a warm smile, well coiffed and tastefully dressed for a brisk day, a bright-colored scarf tied dashingly around her neck. Dottie looked the thoroughly modern grandmother, a woman who still plays a respectable game of tennis, volunteers her time to a variety of community groups in suburban Chicago, and regularly takes off on a solo trip to New York or Florida.

"Today is my thirty-fifth anniversary and I am feeling perfectly full of love," Dottie announced, adding that she might not be a hundred percent honest about her husband, Hyman, that day—she was feeling "just a teeny bit of protection of the man and even of myself." But with the help of her three best friends (I interviewed the "Gang of Four," as they refer to themselves, together), a pot of coffee, and some excellent little butter cookies, the protective shield was quickly pierced. And so was the profession of perfect love and the impression of Dottie's long-standing self-confidence.

The Bernstein marriage is "a struggle"—always has been, always, Dottie predicts, will be. "My struggle with him is fighting for my independence. I use the word *fighting* because it *has* been a power struggle—for my own place, my own voice."

That voice is still not absolutely certain—Dottie is often at a loss for the right word, she admits, doesn't always finish her sentences, and tends to get flustered in an argument. By contrast, Hy, as she describes him, is highly critical, articulate, exacting, and competitive. "I really experience Hy as being stronger than me," she said that day—but other conversations cast doubt on that assertion too.

Over the years Dottie has progressed from a feeling of ditsy inferiority through unalloyed rage and man-hating to a hard-won and still vigilantly defended "independence and self-worth." She has transformed a highly conventional husband-dominated marriage into one in which the partners strive for emotional and practical (though not financial) equality, a dependent together-all-the-time coupling to a relationship in which "we almost lead two separate lives." In the beginning, Dottie had painstakingly to entice her husband into the struggle, and she still keeps at him to engage in their marital jousting. (Now, she says, "a lot of the time we're on the same side.") She has waged combat in the kitchen, the living room, the therapist's office, and even on the tennis court. Over the years, she's amassed an arsenal of traditional and up-to-date weapons: Jewish immigrant daughter's temper, middle-American feminism, popular psychology, New Age spiritualism, and the support of a few good women.

Dottie and Hy wed in 1953, and theirs was typical of a certain species of mid-century Jewish marriage. He was the intellectual, she was handsome and a good sportswoman. He was a big shot in the political organizations they belonged to, she was committed too—but "kept quiet and made the coffee." He was a great debater, and she "did the feeling work for both of us." He had a promising business, she would make a beautiful home for their family. Dottie had some slim ideals of a relationship different from what her mother had. "I came into the marriage feeling like a modern woman. For the first three years, we were equal." But that feeling (whether it was a fact is unclear) changed when the children were born—three, in quick succession. "Our belief systems hooked right back into the old system."

The Feminine Mystique could have been written about Dottie Bernstein, down to the last detail.

> Hy felt if we had a nice home and all of that, he would meet my needs. And in some ways I believed that too. It wasn't until I had a home and three kids and a husband and was still crying, like Betty Friedan says, that it hit me. I didn't know what was happening.

Dottie was in a rage, and the kids were around to catch it. She pushed her two-year-old son against a wall. "I felt I could kill. It so frightened me, I went into therapy. It took me a year to find out I was really angry at Hy." Over thirty-five years, she says, when that rage has resurfaced, she's put her faith in psychological insight to assuage it. "The worst times and the deepest anger is when I don't know what it is. There's an injustice but I don't know exactly what it is."

Along with psychotherapy, feminism has been Dottie's window into those inchoate feelings of injustice.

> *The women's movement absolutely changed my life because it changed my thinking. It was then I got more in touch with my anger, and really found that the person who put me down the most was Hy. When I felt bad, I kept track of that it was him, and it was the little criticisms—I was not doing this right and that right. I began to understand the power struggle, and how I had lost me.*
>
> *What the women's movement did for me was I stopped being a wife and mother. All that was left of me was the rage. There was a period when I was extremely angry at all men. Because I had gone from thinking men were more interesting than women, men knew everything. I did not like women. They were gossips, they were this, they were that. Then as I began to listen to men and how men interrupted, and things they said, and when I paid attention to their attitudes, I was enraged. I think I did hate men, but my personal struggle was with Hy.*

Like so many women of her generation, Dottie was infantilized by men, especially her husband.

> *There is a tone and a way, if I make a mistake, there's a sharpness and a correction. When I don't finish my sentences or get mixed up, when a man tells me, they make fun of me and I end up feeling bad. I end up feeling like a little girl, reprimanded.*

A homemaker who has worked outside the home only for a short period (and then for near-volunteer wages), Dottie has been financially dependent on her husband throughout the marriage. This, needless to say, was another means by which she was kept as a child. In some ways, the "trusting" young wife collaborated: she did not even look at the family's books. Slowly, though, "it became more and more important to know about the finances. I think I had

to work at it because I didn't have a job and a career." She also had
to work at it because Hy didn't see the point in her knowing. He did
accede (he has never been exactly an autocrat), but not with huge
enthusiasm. "He wouldn't do it for me," says Dottie, articulating a
sort of motto for her whole marital strategy, "if I don't do it for
me."

Dottie was not docile, but she was domitable, and Hy continued to make the major decisions about money. In the early 1960s,
this role was "normal," it made sense. He earned it, he should spend
it. Before feminism, housework was not considered "real" work
entitling a wife to a say in family affairs beyond which sneakers the
kids should wear and whether to buy a vacuum cleaner on sale. It
was not until the children's teenage years, when Dottie earned some
money outside the home, that she understood what it meant to
spend one's own money. Returning to homemaking, she had the
gumption to demand a change.

> *I decided for myself that half of the money was mine. Hy
> earned it, but I was at home doing half the work. When I
> stopped working, I wanted a salary—twice a month and an
> adequate salary. If it isn't adequate, I demand what I want, so I
> feel powerful.*

Recently, when Dottie won a malpractice settlement, she
opened her own savings account. The amount is less than a hundred
thousand dollars, but with it she has established "my own little foundation," out of which she gives to the political groups and charities
of her choosing—always, until now, a point of contention.

Dottie's salary and savings account are declarations of independence more symbolic than real. After all, most of "her" money still
comes from Hy (not to mention the mortgage, the credit card payments, and the children's tuitions); presumably, he could cut it off if
he wanted to. But the power that Dottie feels is real—not only
internally but, it seems, between the spouses. Her demand to control
her own money and her newfound ability to hold out for what she
wants when a financial decision is in dispute signify Dottie's mutually acknowledged growing power in the marriage.

In their combat, Hy wields what they both consider to be his
intellectual superiority.

I'm very sloppy with words and Hyman is very meticulous with words. And Hy lots of times was correcting me in public, which always shut me up. It makes me angry—angry, humiliated, and embarrassed.

Dottie is speaking up: "I finally confronted him. I told him unless I am really giving misinformation, then he's not to do that." But, she admits, he still corrects her and "I have to keep telling him." If intellectually Hy wins by intimidation, emotionally and in disputes over housework and chores, he gets his way with passive resistance. These two tactics work best on a beleaguered adversary, one who is timid or exhausted, and for the early years of their marriage, Dottie—home with three kids, without money of her own—was both. Once she stopped being scared and began working on her endurance, however, she was more than his match.

In the Bernstein marriage, the tables are turning in a number of ways and for a number of reasons. As in other couples, aging has worked against him and to her advantage. Hyman's accustomed sources of male importance and personal gratification are drying up. His memory for words is failing him (she forgets too, but since she didn't have pride in verbal fluency in the first place, she says it doesn't bother her). He is retiring soon, and is unprepared for what will come next. (She has hardly worked outside the home, so the change is insignificant.) "He said to me the other day, 'You're tough.' For years and years, I was the one who was vulnerable and he was the one who was tough," she says. "It sort of surprised me."

As Hy depends more and more on Dottie's help, she is launching herself into the self-help universe. She's reading books like *You Can Heal Your Life* and *Embracing Ourselves,* has joined a "wellness group," meditates, and keeps a journal. Dottie employs "positive affirmation" in her tennis game and has learned to "nurture the scared child within" when she's feeling blue. Hy, she feels, is way behind her in all this. When it comes to self-exploration, however, "he doesn't have the tools." And while she says she spent years preparing for her sixtieth birthday, thinking about her past and her goals, and ushered the decade in with a women's ritual in which every participant was asked "to bring a symbol of what women meant for them in their lives, and another of what they loved about themselves," she wonders whether he can ever acquire the personal skills to find similar happiness. You can't teach an old Babbler new tricks, she says. "I think it's too late."

Had her own therapy not been enough to give her the lead on matters introspective, the couple has been in and out of counseling together, for about ten years. The process seems to have aided their marriage; possibly, it's saved their relationship. In the 1970s, Dottie says, "we saw dozens and dozens of relationships end primarily because the man could not accede to the change." Hy, though in her view handicapped, was "willing to do that struggle." The spouses communicate better now than they ever have. They are "processing more" and when they feel stuck, they go in for a few sessions. On the whole, she believes, "we're having much longer periods of feeling loving and great."

But the introduction of therapy into their marriage, while it mitigates some of their balder power plays, also places a premium on emotional expressiveness and affords Dottie an advantage in their more covert struggles. When the competition centered around ideas and language, he was the critic and she was on the defensive; when it came to plain stubbornness, he'd win. Now he is often befuddled, feeling unjustly criticized and—as she used to be—infantilized.

As we saw in the Infant chapters, women may employ their better-developed emotional skills to feel superior, and win power, in relationships. In the Bernstein marriage, a combination of this process and the emotional processes of aging have overturned the hierarchy and installed the wife at the top. Dottie describes her therapeutic endeavors as rewarding her with "inner peace" and relieving her of overwhelming, blinding anger. She says these have improved her sense of partnership with her husband. Yet might some of her spiritual calm come, consciously or not, from the feeling that after all these years of put-downs, Hy's finally getting his comeuppance?

When asked to recount their power struggles, Dottie describes a series of what might be considered trivial spats—over a dinner party, a daughter's birthday celebration, or a tennis game. But if all politics is local, the living room is the "ward" of sexual politics; a sink of unwashed dishes is an unmended pothole and a conversation in company is a televised debate over taxes.

As Dottie tells it, the pattern of their disputes is predictable: She asks Hy to do something. He resists. She asks again, this time expressing her feelings about it. When she asserts her independence, he grudgingly complies. His action is rewarded; he feels good.

> *Carolyn [their daughter] wanted to go to this concert. He was sleeping, and he wouldn't wake up. He was resisting and we were going to be late. So she said, "We don't have to go." I said, "I just want you to know, I'm disappointed if we don't go." I had those feelings. Hy said, finally, "Okay, let's go." We had a wonderful time, and it was what she wanted.*

Another story, about a fancy dinner party Dottie prepared recently:

> *I asked him to get some red wine, and he said no. He was tired, he didn't have the energy. He thought the white was good enough. At that point, I decided this was not "our dinner," I decided it was my dinner. My old behavior was to be furious at Hy, and not say anything before or after. This time I said, I'm not going to let him spoil this meal. I was perfectly prepared to get it myself. I asked him again and he went and got a fine wine, and everybody made a fuss about the wine and it was a big hit.*

The story doesn't end there, however. A week after the concert,

> *I said, "What I wanted you to say was 'I'm glad you talked me into it.' " Some acknowledgment of what I had done. And well, that was very hard for him to hear.*

Or after the dinner party:

> *What I now am asking of him is like when he resists, like he did on this wine thing, and I have to push him to do something, for my sake what I want is an acknowledgment afterwards: "Gee I'm glad you made me do the right thing." I'm wanting that. That becomes hurtful—he sees that as a put-down.*

Dottie analyzes these interactions as incomplete redistributions of power. As she sees it, Hy wields power in passivity. In the past, she would have totally capitulated by giving him his own way. Now, in cajoling him, she gives over, but strategically, not totally: expressing her feelings protects her dignity and integrity.

> *[The evening of the concert] I almost gave up my power. Instead of saying, "Hy, you stay home, we're going," I gave up my power. What saved it was saying, "I'll be disappointed." He took the power and decided to go. And two out of three of us wanted to go. That's ridiculous, it's old behavior.*

In this instance, she got her way: he went. But to settle the scores finally, Dottie feels Hy should leap over the net to congratulate her. She shouldn't have even to say, "I told you so." He should, in effect, say it for her.

When he does acknowledge that she "knew better," however, it seems she still feels unsatisfied.

> *I asked him if he got the wine and he said, "I'm so glad you reminded me," and I said, "I wish I didn't have to remind you." He was thanking me and thought he was being nice and I come back at him with a criticism. He's been concerned about his memory, so that was like a dig. To me it was just another additional thing to be responsible for.*

The economics of gratitude are complex. Should she be thankful that he "helps" her, when what she really wants is for him to take equal responsibility for home and family in the first place? On the other hand, should he be grateful that she forces him to take responsibility? Is that courtesy or surrender?

Hy's admission that he had forgotten the wine triggered another response in Dottie. "Underneath I felt, 'Aha! He hasn't done it.'" How did that make her feel?

> *Disappointed. I asked him to do this one thing, and I called because I was afraid he hadn't done it, and then he hadn't done it. I wished he had taken that responsibility on his own.*

In her better, more conscious self, Dottie would have been gratified if Hy had done his share. But unconsciously, she may have experienced his lapse as a small victory, albeit a Pyrrhic one. Like every wife of a Bumbler, Dottie gleans evidence of her superiority when Hy lets her down.

Of course, Hyman has not just rolled over and bared his throat. An experienced battler, he knows when not to fight as well as when to. Many of their bouts simply fail to materialize, because one combatant—he—doesn't show up in the ring. "He hides," says Dottie. "He runs away from it." The tactic, or avoidance out of fear—whichever it is—is probably self-defeating, Dottie believes. His failure to engage in hashing out their differences keeps them adversaries, whereas a constructive fight might leave them in the same corner.

Lest it seem that Dottie wants one of those relationships completely taken up in meta-relating—working on the relationship that's *about* the relationship—she feels that much of what keeps them together are shared interests and values. Most disappointing to her, competition has historically gotten in the way of their having a good time together in these areas. Political work, for instance, turned out to be something they just couldn't manage cooperatively.

> He's so far ahead of me in that political world, it took me twenty years before I got out of a group that Hy's in and found my own.

Tennis, in which "he's a very good player and I'm a good player," tended to degenerate into a volley of insults and accusations. And the two are still keeping score during social engagements.

> If I talk more than a quarter, Hy experiences that I'm talking more than half. There's a way that he needs attention. He can dominate the evening, and he insists that he shares and lets people in, and I've said no. There are times I've been the focus, and he said I dominated. He consistently experiences it as me dominating.

To avoid the anxiety of such competition, not just with Hy but with other men as well, Dottie has "built a life for myself, around women" and shares a limited number of "safe" entertainments with her husband—dancing, TV, dining. She often travels alone—she went to New York and rented an apartment for a month and also joined a tour group to China. On that trip, she was pleased that she missed her husband, and felt a renewal of affection on her return.

Despite their problems, the couple is firmly committed to staying married and has never considered divorce. Yet today Dottie says that "if I had it to do over again, I would want separate apartments, really space alone."

Dottie's declaration of independence is an optimistic, self-affirming, and forward-looking statement of newfound subjectivity. It is also a practical way of compensating in a marriage that is not entirely fulfilling and is often riven by strife. Her moving-apart doesn't solve all the couple's problems. Their desires clash in fundamental ways: she is determined "to stop taking care of everyone else and start caring for me" and he would like to be cared for more tenderly, especially as he feels his own powers waning. Her immersion in the world of self-help, moreover, sends him a clear message: she doesn't need or want his help; she has given up on his meeting her needs. Going off for weeks in Florida to read and write about her goals and performing rituals of passage to which he is not invited are surely rejections of a sort. From some of the most meaningful and intimate events of her life he is excluded.

While a married woman's independence is partly about what Dottie would call self-actualization, often it involves a measure of self-defense as well. The destructive and hurtful dependencies long in place in the Bernstein marriage became intolerable to Dottie— and perhaps, in a less understood way, to Hyman too—yet they could manage to dismantle them only partially. As it stands, the couple's increasing periods of "feeling great" together seem to require periods of being apart, even day to day.

> *We do a lot of things together, but I love being alone. And what has happened for us, and why our relationship has continued to grow, is that we almost lead two separate lives. I have built a whole world of my own around women. Hy and I eat together and we sit together in our office and do our political work together, separately. Then we'll stop and watch TV or whatever.*
>
> *We're so different, so I have found a way of being comfortable.*

She smiles and pauses, then adds (wishfully?): "And so has he."

13

Truce

Alice Mae Parks

ALICE MAE PARKS, a thirty-eight-year-old domestic worker
and babysitter, has good reason to keep men at a safe distance. Her
childhood, from the age of five to when she left home as a young
teenager, was dominated by her violent and sexually abusive stepfather, Joe. Her mother gave her little reason to trust anyone. She
looked the other way, taking no steps to protect her children from
her brutal husband. Alice still does not go home to visit.

This tall, somewhat gawky woman (her extra-long limbs and
large hands are at once excessive and expressive) has some fairly
unshakable ideas about men—about the restlessness and greed of
their sexuality, about their infantility and irresponsibility. Grievances
about her own husband, Leroy Parks, a meat-processing worker and
part-time truck driver, run the gamut—and then some. For periods
during the twenty-odd years she's known him, the two have been
too much at loggerheads to live together.

And yet Alice Mae and Leroy Parks have reached a cease-fire, a
truce. For Alice, it took a mixture of resiliency and tolerance, plus
perhaps a measure of denial, to call a halt to the sexual hostility that
was her patrimony and to overlook a lot of "playin' " on Leroy's
part. At the same time she possesses a powerful instinct for self-
preservation (no doubt learned in childhood) and a hard-won self-
respect that prevents her from trading her integrity for a man's love.

For his part, Leroy has lately "made the change," in Alice's
words, from a man skittish about obligation to a partner whose grit
and generosity can be counted on in crisis, if not always at other
times. Alice relies on him when she has to—when she was sick with
pneumonia at the same time their second-youngest son was diag-
nosed with cancer, or when she was laid off during their daughter's
four-month hospitalization for blood poisoning and a colectomy.

Still, she is far from dependent. "I would love that me and my husband stay together till death do us part," she says. "But if it comes to the point where it can't be that way, then I can keep living."

On a late-autumn afternoon, Alice and I drove from the small house where she lives in tidy clutter with Leroy, three of her four children, and her seventeen-year-old daughter's baby to a little park nearby. Sitting on a bench in the bright, cool air, as teenagers rapped along with the radio and wiry boys performed feats of daring on their bicycles, she left this pleasant, mostly black neighborhood in Richmond, which has been her home for fifteen years, and traveled backward to a wooden house without plumbing in dirt-poor, segregated rural Virginia. Alice's smooth brown face and soft wide-set eyes look younger than her difficult life might have turned them. Her serene, open demeanor belies the burden of having lived with her recollections, hiding them from everyone, including her husband, from early childhood to this afternoon with a stranger more than twenty years later.

> *I had a real bad childhood life. I don't like to talk about it too much. I left home at the age of fifteen because of my stepfather—he was one of those stepfathers that, I won't say, molesting, but, I left home before that really got into it. But my mother didn't see it, and she thought more of him than she did me. Because I never will forget the day—one morning he, um, he was sick and I was at home. I think I was about twelve years old at the time. You know, you don't forget bad things that happen to you; I don't care how young you are, there are some things that can happen to you that you'll take it to your grave.*
>
> *So, my mother was outside and he was sick. And I was in the kitchen washing dishes. He was waiting on me, you know. What happen was, I seen his shadow, and that's what saved me. When I entered the room, I seen the shadow, 'cause he was hiding behind a chest of drawers, and by that time when I seen the shadow he reached at me and I ran. And I ran out the house and I didn't tell my mother and to this day she still doesn't know, as of my knowledge she doesn't know what kind of man he was.*

As in many stories of incest, some of Alice's details are inconsistent and unclear. Did she leave home at thirteen or fifteen? Did her stepfather start "making signs" to her when she was five or seven? And—most salient—did he actually molest her? Therapists say that abuse victims almost universally repress memories of the actual sex, often unable to exhume them without prolonged and intense therapy (which Alice may never get). In Alice Mae's story, there are strong hints that Joe did have sex with her. If, for instance, he had never actually laid a hand on her sexually, how did she know he was lying in wait behind the dresser? There are gradations of incestuous behavior, from inappropriate flirting to intercourse. Wherever Joe lurked on that continuum, his behavior was threatening enough to warrant constant vigilance in little Alice.

> *When I was at home I couldn't sleep very well, because you know I was always afraid even laying down at night that he would try to bother me. I never wanted to go nowhere with him. My mother insisted.*

What Alice does remember clearly are Joe's wild, drunken rages and the beatings he inflicted on her and her asthmatic younger brother. She remembers too her mother's inability—refusal, Alice feels—to leave.

> *My mother drink. My father drink. My stepfather used to drink and he was a violent man . . .*
> *So this particular night, my stepfather was drunk and he would always go get the gun whenever he got drunk, you know, threatening us. And that night it was pouring down rain, I mean it was raining like cats and dogs. We was all in the bed and he started raging, talking about he was gonna shoot us. My baby brother, he had on his shorts. I did manage to put my shoes on and my brother ran out the house with nothing on but his shorts. And he ran to my other aunt's house because my mother had a sister live right down the street. So he went to her house and my mother and I went to my cousin house. And the next day came right back home. I mean, this was over and over and over again.*

Alice Mae asked her mother one last time to break up with her husband. The sense of betrayal at her mother's "answer" still plagues the thirty-eight-year-old daughter.

*'Cause I told my mother, I said, "You know, both of us can't
live here." I told her, I said, "Mama, one of us got to go."
These were my words to her. And she never, she never answered. She never did. As if she was leaving it up to me to
decide—I'm thirteen years old, and she's leaving that up to me
to leave home. And which I did.*

Alice went to live with her other brother in Richmond. He
was a good deal older than she—he was out of the house already
when their mother married Joe. He took her in, fed and clothed and
looked after her. But Alice did not voluntarily enlighten him about
what had happened at home, and he did not probe. Alice was still
alone. In escaping her mother's house, she had not escaped fear.

*You know what? When I first came up here I was scared to
death. I had so much fear in me when I came up here . . . I
didn't trust any man. I was afraid of them all, I really was. I was
even afraid of my sister-in-law brothers . . . You know, I was
even afraid to ride in a cab. I mean, I didn't trust mens to be
alone with me at all. I got out of it, you know, but I guess I
might have been in the tenth, eleventh grade when I finally
started to loosen up as far as not being so afraid. And I never
did want to go back home.*

At eighteen, while dating other boys, Alice became friendly
with Leroy. He was a little older than she, but, she says, looking
back, "young for his age."

*He was one of them real wild mens, and it took him a long time
to make a change, and when we first got married, the wildness
was still there. I don't think he really was ready for marriage. I
wasn't married when my first child was born and I wasn't married when my second child was born either. We was living
together. I wasn't comfortable living like that, so we broke up,
so he went his way and I went mines, you know, to raise my
kids.*

What do you mean wild? I asked Alice.

"I know naturally he was dating other womens, you know,"
she said, laughing.

Dating? You mean sleeping with?

"Well," she said slyly. "I'll let you come to that term."

. . .

Alice and Leroy broke up a few times over the first ten years. But they stayed in touch. She had two of his children. Whether perceptive or deluded, Alice saw the good in Leroy.

Afterward, we got back together. Deep down inside of all the wildness and to me at times being irresponsible, and I think that age had a lot to do with it, still there was something there. I knew that if I didn't give up on him that it would come out— because I knew his background from where he was raised. He just, to me, he just was a young man that wasn't ready for responsibility.

Men, Alice believes, are prone to "wildness." Her recitation of their propensities and vulnerabilities evokes images of the Infant, the Slave, the Seducer, and the Abandoner.

I think mens have a ego that they have to keep up. Well, some of 'em are real doggish, you know, but I think some are just, just this inner thing that's in them, like they have to have more than one woman, or maybe more than two or three, whatever . . . I mean, I've heard mens say it: you know, they don't feel right.

Now, I ain't been able to understand that. Because I always thought when you have two and three, maybe four and five women, that you're not satisfied, you're still looking for something—looking for that one person to fulfill that need that you didn't get from the first woman, the second woman, the third woman.

. . . When you change partners, to me, it's just like starting all over again and you got to get used to something else. You left one thing but you got to get used to something else that may not fit you. But most mens don't think that way. They don't worry about that. When they start thinking about that, most of the time it's too late. Because they've already gotten involved.

. . . I used to tell my husband this too, 'cause he has a thing that a lot of time women trap men by having babies. I said, well, in the first place, you can't keep a woman from having a child if you're having sex with her. But most men don't think about that. They really don't.

That's another thing I can't figure out: why it doesn't bother them. But when it happens, then they blame you for it.

Maybe some womens do trap men like that, I don't know. But a man to me is supposed to be the strongest.

In hers and Leroy's relationship (as, Alice guesses, in most) the man is not the strongest. Men abuse the privileges of maleness, she says, but don't shoulder the responsibility. "They act as if being the strong man is just a title, that it doesn't have a meaning to it." It was she who supported their first two children almost single-handedly until Antoine was nine and Vonnette was four. Leroy threatened to desert the family if she carried her third (and for her, wanted) pregnancy to term. "That put a real damper on our relationship." But when the baby came, Leroy fell in love with him. He was named Leroy Jr., and is called Little Roy.

Leroy was working hard for the family, sometimes seven days a week, and things were looking up. But soon, just after he'd been laid off from a factory job, Alice "got caught" again, with Alfred, called Teddy. As with Little Roy, abortion was not an option for her; her religion prohibits it. This time, "I was real depressed about it, 'cause I couldn't figure out where that child's gonna sleep." She was already working two jobs. Vonnette was taking care of Little Roy in the evenings. Leroy was thrown for a loop, and withdrew into morose isolation. "Oh my god, things was rough," Alice says. "He went into this slump. He said, 'My life is ruined.' "

Alice felt she was married to a hard-working but emotionally immature man. He showed his devotion to the family by putting in long hours, but his schedule served him well in another way: he could avoid intimacy. Until Little Roy, he more or less ignored his children. Toward Alice Mae, he is still almost phobic about open affection, and that has been the source of an abiding sadness.

I mean, we talk. He's my friend too . . . But . . . with me not getting the affection that I needed as a child and not so much as a teenager, I think I look for it in him and it wasn't there. He was just, I guess, an ordinary man.

. . . We don't go out to dinner . . . If I kiss him because I feel like it in the street, he says, "I don't like all that mushy stuff."

Alice feels her oldest son, Antoine, takes after his dad. This saddens her.

I was really shocked and it took me a while to realize that that's what happened. Tony's not a violent person; my husband's not a violent person. But I don't think he has that compassion . . . no, he doesn't have it.

. . . I wonder, and I guess it has something to do about it. My husband not being a compassionate man, Tony never did see my husband bring me flowers, not really being loving, caring, as far as taking me out to dinner, coming in the house and just giving me a hug or whatever. By him not seeing that, then he had no values to grow up from.

Sex, Alice hastens to point out, is not the problem.

I mean, really, we have a good relationship as far as sexualwise. I mean, we're compatible. I guess that's why we stay together so long . . . I dated a lot of men, but I have not dated a man that was like my husband. Although he's not a compassionate man, he knows how to make me feel. And if it's something that I don't do right to him or he doesn't do right to me, he gone tell me and I'll tell him. The only part that I'm missing is that affectionate part.

For many years, Alice set out to change Leroy, but he did not take kindly to her suggestions.

In fact, that almost cost my marriage. He was real wild, and I wasn't getting the attention. He wasn't doing things as far as being responsible, you know, being home, sharing with the work, with the house. Even not being affectionate, to me, there are still certain responsibilities that men should do. And I caused a lot of problems with that because I kept trying to make him see it differently. To change him, to make him know after you reach a certain age there are some things you just don't do anymore. When he got home, I had to have the dinner on, the kids had to be fed, through with the homework. I mean, all he had to do was just lay down. That was real hard for me but that was another pill that I had to swallow. I wasn't getting anywhere.

He used to say, "Oooo! You just nag, nag, nag, nag, nag!" A lot of times I would be like talking to myself, or either he would just leave.

Alice resorted to guerrilla tactics.

I stopped nagging. And there have been times where I didn't cook and me and my kids went out. Some nights I would even go up to my brother house, spend the night, not let him know where I was. One time I went all the way home and I didn't tell anybody where I was. To me, that was things that I had to do to get across, even though it wasn't from my lips, my actions had to do something.

He saw that you could live without him, I suggested.

Oh yeah, definitely I could. 'Cause I had been on my own a long time. I was living by myself before we started living together. Plus, living with my brother I was thinking for myself then anyway . . . I love my husband, I really love my husband . . . but. I never would let myself think that I couldn't live without him.

In some ways, though, it seems Alice felt she couldn't live without him. The marriage was at a breaking point, yet she clung to it. There were, after all, four children and a meager income even between the two of them, as well as a powerful passionate attachment and a long shared history. Alice was stretched thin, emotionally and physically.

Seeking refuge, comfort, and answers, she went to church. A nominal Baptist, she became a devout and active one. Interestingly, the lessons that Alice learned under the guidance of her minister are similar to those other women glean from psychotherapy: Love yourself, change yourself, take care of yourself. Her narrative suggests that despite her determination not to be abused as an adult, with Leroy she had fallen into some of the victimized patterns of her childhood. Her religious meditations began to heal some of those wounds too, enabling her to move forward.

I didn't really get serious about religion until I was going through this with my husband . . . There was things that I had tried [with him] and I didn't get an answer. I was looking for this change to come into him, but really the change was supposed to come in me. Not for him but for me. I was the one that was unhappy. I mean, he was doing things to me, but he was doing 'em cause he wanted to do 'em. He was happy! So I was the one that got the tail end of the deal.

So I had to make the change for me. And when I did make

*it, I felt real good about myself because I wasn't waiting on him
anymore. I had my health, I had a job. It wasn't a good-paying
job but I made enough to survive from it.*

*. . . I went to a Bible class and this minister, his name
was Dr. Smith, showed me how to love and care for myself.
From that point I was no longer at a standstill and depending
upon my husband. And I wasn't ashamed. There are some
people who don't like themselves. And I think at that point
where I was, and my husband was doing me, I thought something was wrong with me. But it wasn't! It wasn't anything
wrong with me. I wasn't in touch with me. Once a person get in
touch with themselves and focus on that, then they life goes
on. But you have to be in touch.*

Alice draws a direct causal line between her ceasing to nag
Leroy and his "making the change"—accepting his responsibilities,
committing himself to the marriage and the family, paying more
attention to the children—and between her new devotion to religion and her increased tolerance for his flaws. But she also recognizes
that other turns in their life together shook Leroy from his youthful
frivolity and drew out the mature man. As he showed his strength in
a series of trials that dwarfed their longstanding struggles with poverty, she began to feel more security, more respect for and from him,
and a gratitude that enabled her to overlook some of the disappointment and anger that had darkened their love.

In 1983, Vonnette suffered a ruptured appendix which went
undiagnosed until she developed blood poisoning. That necessitated
a colectomy and four months in the hospital. Besides the emotional
trauma, Alice and Leroy, who had just bought their house, were
overwhelmed with "gigantic" medical bills. At the same time, after
fifteen years Alice was suddenly laid off from her small-factory job
and had to go to work as a full-time babysitter. If all that weren't
enough, shortly thereafter Alice herself was hospitalized with severe
pneumonia. While she was there, Little Roy, then five, was diag-
nosed with cancer. To Alice's astonishment, Leroy "came through."

*Sometimes you can't ever predict men. I thought about this—
I'd never say anything about it—I think, when all that stuff happened to me I wonder when he'd book up and leave me, with
all this pressure . . . Most men can't stand the pressure.*

They'll leave, but he didn't. He worked seven days a week, day and night. He really did.

It is perhaps Leroy's tender attention to Roy, in her opinion the sweetest of the three boys, that has endeared her husband most to her.

He dealt with Little Roy more than I did. Oh, he let him get by with murder. Even before the sickness got to Little Roy, I think Leroy just kept his heart. That change came upon him when he was born and maybe it's just something that was there that came out.

Leroy "showed compassion" to Alice when she was sick too, "but when I got well . . ." Her voice trails off. Even this disappointment Alice seems willing to forgive. In the face of his new-found steadfastness, lapses in affection seem little enough to overlook. "I think if I had a choice," she says, "I would rather have a responsible man and a caring man than a man that would take me out to dinner and bring me flowers and then when something happened I couldn't depend upon him."

Alice is even willing to rationalize away failings in Leroy that used to drive her crazy.

You know, I don't want my husband to go out to dinner with me that much because he's a real picky eater . . . and if I go out with someone and they get real picky about the food, I can't enjoy my food. So what's the use?

Returning to this theme several times in our conversation (obviously it's a little more important to her than she admits) she indicates that she's wisely conserving her energy for the big battles.

Yes, that man is a picky, picky eater. And I think it's because he had a lot of sisters that spoiled him rotten. But at his late date I wouldn't dare try to change him. I think it would drain me completely if I tried to change his eating habits.

Needless to say, Alice's truce with Leroy—or with men—is not flawless. Unresolved, possibly irresolvable, issues remain. In crucial ways, Alice still does not trust Leroy: she has never told him that she was abused in childhood.

> *You know, I look at movies of girls and ladies that have gotten raped and had changed their relationship with their mate, and I don't know would that have happened to me. But that has kind of like been in the back of my mind as far as, uh, my stepfather trying to molest me. And I don't know whether my husband could accept it.*

It may be that keeping silent about her childhood serves a purpose for Alice too: she doesn't have to confront it directly. She views her reticence as a kind of pride.

> *I think if Leroy knew what I really went through like when I first met him, [he] would have been more compassionate. But I didn't really want pity. If a man wanted me or loved me, I wanted him to do it not because of something that happened to me. I think I might of feared that he wanted to do for the simple reason that I needed him at that point because of the type of life that I've lived.*

Conflating compassion with pity and intimate confidences with entreaties to be taken care of, Alice seems to circle around her reluctance to need. For if there were any knights in shining armor in Alice's childhood fantasies, they were forever jousting with, and often vanquished by, the real dragons all around her. Her real father, whom she saw on and off after he and her mother split up, left town when she was eleven, never to be heard from again. Her stepfather preyed on her and her mother betrayed her. Of course, many neglected and abused children continue to long for the protection and care they were denied; Alice said she wished for that sort of love too. But many—particularly girls—also are magnetized to victimization in adulthood. When they encounter it, it doesn't seem abnormal.

Alice has steered clear of violence and has never visited it on her children. Yet her fear of depending on anyone helps explain her staying with a man she couldn't count on for so many years. Her ambivalence toward Leroy exists at the intersection of a stripped-down, conscious expectation of neglect and a richer, less acknowledged desire for care and commitment. He has provided both—

coldness and a kind of emotional cowardice on the one hand, and on the other, loyalty over the long haul, perseverance and comradeship that have withstood severe tests.

Still, it is axiomatic to Alice Mae that women should not depend on men. She managed to escape abuse, and whatever blend of desperation and bravery empowered her to do so seems also to have immunized her against the "contagion" of those who are less strong. She expresses little sympathy for women who allow themselves to be hurt.

> *There are some womens that think that couldn't live without that man. Abused women, I have never in my life been able to understand them. I never have. They say they are afraid of them. I haven't been able to understand, why couldn't they get away? This is a big world!*

Toward her own daughter, impregnated and abandoned by the baby's father at sixteen, Alice is similarly disapproving, a disapproval gentled by a mother's love and concern. Alice has apparently been trying to teach her daughter that in terms of power, a beautiful woman is no match for a smooth-talking man.

> *My daughter's an attractive young lady. She has a good head on her. But I think she needs [men's] attention. You know some womens because they have a beautiful body and a beautiful face, they think men won't use them. Now I could be wrong, but this is the picture I'm getting from my daughter. That they won't use her. She thinks it won't happen to her again, with another child . . . [But] I tell her all the time. Attractive women get used by men just like unattractive women get used by men.*
>
> *She's on my heart a lot, but I don't know, I'm not keying in to her. And . . . with the talent she has, I hate to see her go backwards. It would be a waste! I hope she go to college. I really would like for her to go to college. 'Cause I don't want her depending on no man. I really don't.*

Dependence even on a reliable man, Alice suggests, is a trap.

> *I've seen it happen too many times where women depend on men, and they get caught up with it. It's almost like the abused women. They can't pull themselves out of it . . . You go out there and look and think you're going to get something as far*

*as getting a man who brought you flowers and give you money
and pay your rent and your electric. It's not always good.
Sometime even when that happen to you, sometime you get in
a deeper hole.*

In spite of the satisfying erotic life she has with Leroy, Alice's
distrust of men's sexuality runs deep. Her experience with her stepfather is ever with her, and she is as a result suspicious of every man
with every child.

*Even at this point, my mind flashes back, and when I see little
girls with their father or their brother, that flashes back in my
mind . . . I wonder, how is he treating that child? Now, I feel
like I want to protect them all, all the little girls. I know there are
good fathers, fathers that wouldn't dare touch their baby. I
know there are good fathers, but I have a hard time trying to
see the difference. I can't point them out.*

Alice is a rational woman; she knows men are not all alike. But
deep down, she expects them to be: childish, timid, and unreliable at
best; violent, cruel, and predatory at worst. Leroy is decisively not
the latter, so by these standards, he at first looked like man at his
mediocre best. Soon he revealed himself to be a bit better than that
—an attentive and eager lover, a hard worker, an occasionally straying but basically faithful husband.

And long after Alice's hopes had disintegrated, when things
were worst, Leroy delivered his maturity like a king ceding half his
land to the queen of a warring kingdom. With this gift, the two
called a truce and went off to fight the fiercer enemies attacking both
of them. There has been little time for feasts and celebration—no
second, or even first, honeymoon; poverty too is the enemy of romance. Says Alice, "We never really took a vacation. It's always
been one thing after another, you know. One thing after another."

14

Negotiation

Molly Madsen

MOLLY MADSEN, BORN AND RAISED in northern Louisiana, has a Southern voice you could listen to until the Mississippi ran dry. She tells a tale in a leisurely way, from the middle to the beginning, then meanders around to the end, giving the details their due, finishing off the declaratory sentences with curlicues of interrogation. Yet Molly utters not a coy syllable. You get the feeling what she's telling you is honest to the bottom, with the sugar syrup of guile or self-deception strained out. She's listening too, with no homilies to offer.

That ability to say what she means and hear others say what they mean—qualities she says her husband shares—have made this, the second marriage for both of them, a solid, loving alliance of equals. But Molly and Carl didn't get here easily, and don't always find it easy to stay here. The commitment to remain together is strong: "I don't see ever living without the man," says Molly, who also feels confident that she can take care of herself. But perhaps even more important is their commitment to make their marriage an ongoing negotiation.

Looking at the relationship retrospectively, it appears that Molly started out making more concessions, then gradually made more demands of Carl. Yet there are many ways, she feels, in which he has been the instigator of changes toward egalitarianism. Both partners have an unromantic, pragmatic attitude toward relationships. They don't resent fighting things out: "There's a *lot* of struggle in this household," Molly told me the first time I spoke to her. They don't think there's something wrong with their marriage if it takes a lot of doing. Neither expects the way to be clear; they don't even expect always to be walking side by side.

I think giving up the idea that there is a Right Guy out there for every woman, and it's just a matter of finding him and marrying him and living happily ever after, happened for me over lots and lots of years. Understanding that this is not a truth in life occurred for me working within the relationship I have now. It's so evident to me what hard work it is to feel satisfied. What's most important to me is that we each get to grow and change in the ways we want to—and that doesn't mean that the relationship is always going to be nurtured.

Molly's and Carl's professional expertise and the values inherent in their jobs help a lot: he's a family therapist, she's a nurse studying for a social work/counseling degree. Their many shared interests—in science and nature, politics, and sports (they both run, swim, and play soccer)—make for plenty of play interspersed with the work. And Carl's avid involvement in their two daughters' lives (she has a third, grown child by a previous marriage) make their family unusual. (So does their height: both Molly and Carl are six feet tall, and their daughters don't look like they'll be far behind. Six-year-old Billie "already has the longest legs I've ever seen on a child," says Molly.)

Neither of the partners was brought up to have an egalitarian, negotiated marriage. Of the two, Carl's childhood may have prepared him better. His mother "is very proud of having been a housewife and a mother" and still "is interfering with her grown children's marriages as much as she can." She taught her daughter to be neat and orderly, and her sons to expect their "cave" to be tidied up by the females. But at the same time, Carl was the firstborn, and his father, a career naval officer, was away a lot. "Carl became a little coparent early," Molly says. "He was left with the injunction to take care of Mom. He learned young how to fix things around the house . . . While he was picked up after by his mother, he also was trained to be responsible and be a grown-up."

Molly had no such flexibility in her family. She was raised with "very basic Southern values . . . very Presbyterian Christian and God-fearing. The highest aspiration was for the men in the family to become church elders." The household was "very strict but also very disorganized." Gender roles in the family were also strict, although that combination of rigidity and confusion also extended to messages about her future as a woman.

Everything in the family centered around the male head of the household, all the way down to really little things. Like in our family, there were four children and two adults. If there was an extra dessert, my father always got it. I remember how important it was to each of us to get to sit next to Dad at the dinner table. He was so revered and so the most important person in the family. My brothers came next. My sister and I were groomed to be wives, and somewhat Cinderella.

There was a strong belief that girls were to be taken care of . . . [but also that] the woman was there to take care of the man's needs. Other than that the female roles were real vague . . . It was somewhat confusing.

Molly still considers herself a spiritual person, but doesn't participate in any organized religion. "I felt so stung by what I grew up with that it's real hard for me to imagine making the church a part of my life." But she responded to the family's rigidity "by acting out." Like her sister, she got pregnant at eighteen and married right out of high school. The marriage, to the only child of a wealthy family, was traditional.

I think I was really a maid, I wasn't a real person. Sort of the babymaker . . . I didn't know what I was doing. I didn't know anything—any basic facts about relationships, how to stand up for myself. I certainly didn't know how to say no . . . I guess I got out when I hurt so bad that I couldn't stay in anymore. I couldn't figure out how to stop hurting—my repertoire was very small.

To talk to this self-aware and self-possessed forty-five-year-old woman, it is hard to conjure up the young wife she describes.

I thought I was doing a good job, but I felt really awful doing it. If he complained about dinner, somehow it was my fault. I knew something was not true about that; all I knew was that I felt bad. I didn't conceptualize it at all. I was bound in these strict and undoable rules about life: Don't think for yourself. Don't ever say no. Always be in control. Other people always come first. At a more personal way, that came down to: Don't think, don't want, don't feel.

. . . As I look back on that young marriage, I never trusted what I felt. Although [now] I know that what I was feeling was a real normal response to what I was living, I had a lot of people

*telling me I was misperceiving. When I left I had no support
from my family. Nobody had ever gotten a divorce in the family
and it was the most awful thing that anybody had ever had to
endure.*

Molly and her ex–husband improvised a sort of clumsy joint
custody, "which didn't work very well, really." Her daughter's father has had an erratic marital life, and Kerry "acted out wildly" in
adolescence. Like her mom she married young and had three children right away.

Molly, meanwhile, moved to Boulder, Colorado, where she
still resides, worked as a secretary, dated a number of men, and
started discovering "there was a world outside my family and my
church." After some years she went into therapy.

*That was the first time I started figuring out what relationships
were about. In the University of Life it was like Relationships
101 . . . I stayed with the therapist long enough to learn
some basic things about contracts between people: I'll do this
and you do that; I want this and I'll give that.*

After a while, she started to have sessions with a woman,

*a very powerful therapist and a very powerful person. She was
the first woman I was with who . . . I felt was more of a real
pure being, and being female or male was somehow secondary to the way that I knew her . . . I started looking at empowering myself as a woman, or empowering myself as a person,
almost despite the fact that I'm a woman . . . She also was a
lesbian and helped me learn to love myself as a woman, and
learn I didn't have to do a man's bidding. I didn't have to be
sexual with a man in order to be loved and cared for.*

Molly met Carl in a therapy group—which has been both a
plus and a minus. "We knew a lot of details about each other,
including the horrors," says Molly, laughing. "In some ways it made
us more sensitive to each other, but in other ways, we could manipulate each other in more sophisticated ways."

The relationship was put to the test early, when Molly got
pregnant. They talked and talked about having a child, and, although
they both agreed an abortion was the best decision at the time,

neither felt it was the only, unconditional answer. The event was destabilizing for the couple, and has had lasting effects.

> *I was ambivalent, and he really wanted an abortion. He didn't see himself as a parent and at that time he didn't want to get married. It was hard for me to do, and hard for me not to do. It was a terrible decision, even though I'm pro-choice. There's not a best decision to be made, and that's that . . .*
>
> *I don't think I felt terribly pressured . . . I think [we both] felt it was the only thing to do. He was not detached from it at all. It was a terrible decision for him too, and he was in a great deal of pain, and still has some lingering wistfulness and pain about it.*

But the conflict over parenthood would revisit the couple after they did marry, a couple of years later. Carl was in graduate school and Molly was in college and working part time as a student assistant doing secretarial work. She was twenty-seven. It was at that time, over the issue of children, that Molly first understood that both of them would not be able simultaneously to have everything they wanted. That in itself was nothing new to Molly—it was the cardinal rule in her family and her first marriage. The fundamental difference is that then, Molly would have automatically put her father's or husband's needs before her own, without thinking, without any say —and with a great deal of inarticulate pain. Now she and Carl were talking and fighting and coming to mutual decisions. Such negotiations do not make things easier; in fact, they carry a high risk.

> *What happened was we decided together that what was real important to him was to get through graduate school at his own pace and in his own way. There was a time I was real disenchanted with school and stopped going for a while . . . I wanted to have children and he wanted to be through with his dissertation first.*
>
> *I made a conscious decision, and knew that by deciding to wait, that didn't necessarily mean that when he finished he would want to have kids. It was the first time I was willing to live with that anxiety. I remember feeling real grown up.*

Enabling Molly to live with that anxiety was a sense, even early on in the relationship, of trust and fairness—that the tables would constantly be turning. Now, for instance, Carl is supporting the whole family while Molly's in school full time. This does not mean, however, that he is excused from his fair share of child care. As always, he does at least half.

I spoke with Molly one Sunday evening, and she described how they'd divvied up the kids that weekend.

> *Yesterday, this is how we split things up. I got up and ran ten miles while he helped them with their breakfasts and straightened up the house. Then I took our ten-year-old to her dance class that lasts an hour and a half and took our six-year-old to my mother's house to do something with her. I picked the big one up and he took the little one to her soccer game and then the big one and I met him, and we all went swimming. Then he managed their bedtime while he was rubbing my feet, which were killing me. Today he took them from noon until six, while I went and played soccer and then went and had a beer with the girls.*
>
> *When I got home, he and my six-year-old had made a blueberry pie. Actually, she had done it and he had read the recipe to her and helped her with the measuring. He's great at empowering them that way. I wouldn't have baked a blueberry pie with her this afternoon! He does things like that all the time. He knows about science and the earth, and he's always got some project going. He's always bringing bugs in the house with the kids. When Haley's Comet came, he got up in the middle of the night and packed them up and drove them out away from the city to look at it.*
>
> *He usually takes the kids almost full time on the weekends. When he comes home during the week, four nights out of five he walks in the door and I walk out the door to go run. He doesn't complain about it. He's very, very invested in them. Always has been. Always. He's very loving, very available, very playful.*

Molly and Carl are extraordinary in the degree to which they share child care. It is not the model either spouse grew up with, not one most families have achieved, and yet it has always felt almost instinctually right to both of them.

About money, however, they had to squirm a bit before they fit the "liberated" mold they'd assumed they already were in.

> *We found out we actually had more traditional views than we thought we had. Our circumstances presented us with different things to deal with. Like he took a year off from school and we lived on our savings and my work. We would talk about money together and then he would make decisions. He would take the power and I would defer.*
>
> *He became much more egalitarian about money before I was. If I was having a baby or in school, like now, it is very clear that as far as he's concerned, the money he makes is the money available to me and to him and to our children, to this family right here. He considers the money he makes our money. I was the one who was a bit more reluctant to see it that way. We had a joint account, but there were times in the past when I would say, "Will you give me thirty dollars to buy a new pair of jeans?" And he would say, "I don't want you to ask me for money." . . . I don't do that anymore.*

Relinquishing control over finances is no trivial concession; few men truly do it—even, as Pepper Schwartz and Philip Blumstein report in *American Couples,* in families where the woman makes more.[1] So there is an element of noblesse oblige in men's "letting" women make financial decisions. Carl could feel not only liberated, but magnanimous too.

Participating in housework holds less reward. Here Molly was demanding that Carl do something he didn't want to do—tasks that are degraded and devalued, perpetually unfinished, almost by definition thankless. Moreover, about laundry and dishes Molly was not going to be a grateful recipient of his kindness. She was sick of doing these things herself, she wanted him to do them too, and she was furious that he wasn't cooperating.

For years, Carl was "great with special projects and not with cleaning things up day by day." This is a traditional sexual division of household labor, but not really an equal one: changing the oil in the car, painting the upstairs bedroom, and even mowing the lawn are chores that can be done when one wants to do them, and don't have to be done very often. Laundry and vacuuming, grocery shopping, cooking, and dishwashing have to be done not only regularly, but on time and on demand. The dishes and dirty clothes can pile up only so high until you have nothing to eat off and nothing to wear. And you can't wait until Saturday to feed the kids.

Now Carl is better with both special projects and cleaning—

though their styles and standards aren't quite the same. She's a tortoise on an endless journey. "He doesn't pick up all the time like I do. I can't walk from the front of the house to the back of the house without carrying something." He's more like a hare running a sprint. "He'll come home from lunch, and dash around and make the beds or load the dishwasher . . . I feel like he's participating as actively as I do with the house."

This state of affairs was arduous in the creation.

> It started out with me complaining a lot. I was in nursing school. I said, "I don't have the time to do it myself and you don't have the time to do it yourself, so I'm going to have to do some and you're going to have to do some."

Arguing on principle did not work. In theory, after all, Carl agreed with Molly: he should do his share. But in practice, he didn't really think it needed to be done: he could live in a mess, and besides, he didn't feel like doing it. Making demands did not work. He dug his heels in. They were at a standstill.

> He would do passive-aggressive stuff where he just wouldn't do it, and we'd have these incredible fights . . . Sometimes I was so unhappy with the mess that I would do it. If I were living alone, I like things orderly. I like to go straight to where something is because I know it's there. I don't think I'm compulsive but I really do like things neat. I compensated some for him, and then we had this baby, and then we had another one. And there are three of them and they're all slobs, and then there's me. Within the negotiations I have lowered my standards some, and he's raised his some.

The way Molly and Carl finally reached a middle ground was the way they deal with most issues. She sensed that Carl would respond more to her as a person whom he was hurting than a partner not getting her contractual due.

> I decided to stop yelling and complaining and talk more about what it meant to me as a person. We had many talks where I said, "I don't want to live like this. It feels insulting to me." He used to throw things at the garbage can in the kitchen, and if it

> *didn't get in, he would leave it. There would be wads of paper towels all around the radiator.*
>
> *I couldn't stand it. I had asked him and asked him and asked him. I was just so frustrated, I just cried. I said, "I cannot stand this and I don't understand why you can't hear me."*

Tears were not a feminine manipulation, but rather a demonstration of the depth of Molly's feelings.

> *I said, "I believe if you knew how awful this is for me, you would hear this," and said, "Is there something that drives you crazy that I'm doing?"*

Offering, with that question, to concede on some other issue seemed to defuse the power struggle that was at the bottom of their housework wars:

> *Sometimes if I want to change something like cleaning the house or whatever, I think he's resistant . . . and looks at it with a wary eye, like, "Is she trying to control me?" I've wondered if it's my communication style, or whether he's just wary of control. It's probably a little of both.*

Rather than pretend power doesn't exist, Molly and Carl look for ways to share it and ways to negotiate around it when it cannot be shared. Holding together their highly flexible life system are some unbending, nonnegotiable personal "boundaries and limits," says Molly, which she defines as "knowing what you're willing to tolerate and what you're not willing to tolerate." Recognizing these in themselves and each other enables Molly and Carl to give without always worrying they will be forced to give up everything. They try not to overstep each other's boundaries, Molly says. "There's a lot of respect in this relationship, and that respect keeps the boat afloat."

Child care, housework, and money are the currencies of influence, value, and respect in a couple. Hoarding or distributing these coins can be a way of communicating love or withholding it. But sex is all of these and more. The sovereign of marital power, it stands for more than one person's love for the other. It comes to emblemize the health and happiness of the bigger institution, the marriage.

People marry to get their laundry done and have somebody to eat dinner with, to buy and own property, and to raise children, but at least in modern times, they are motivated by love and also passion. A sexless marriage—although they are probably more common than most think—doesn't feel like a marriage. Without lovemaking, why be husband and wife and not just coparents or roommates?

Molly and Carl have weathered infidelity; both partners have had heterosexual affairs, and Molly had also slept with women. But during those times, the couple's sex life did not suffer. In part for this reason, they were able to overlook or forgive side experiences in respect for each other's privacy. But when Molly's need to be true to herself meant celibacy, the marriage underwent one of its most perilous trials.

> *One of the things that frequently goes down the tubes for me when I'm studying and working and writing papers and all that is my sex drive, and that has at times been a real sticky issue. At first there is a lot of anger. He was very angry at me, and I was sort of befuddled and confused and didn't know why I wasn't interested, other than I was really tired a lot.*

How did they work it out?

In essence, they didn't—or rather, they tried, but could not come to terms satisfactory to both of them.

> *The way we worked it out was, I kept saying, "If I placate you, I know I'm going to do myself in. I think it's only going to continue a spiral downhill. This is my body, and I'm the one who gets to call the shots about it." We fought a lot and he was angry a lot. Basically, that's how we worked it out. It wasn't cut and dried for me. I felt, god, vulnerable, and I wasn't sure I was doing the right thing.*
> *. . . I stood my ground and sometimes felt real shaky, and he was real angry. His face would get red and he would kick things around—anything that was in his way, a toy or a chair—or he'd leave, and then come back and talk. The issue of splitting up never came up.*

Unable to force Molly to have sex against her will, Carl did keep trying to persuade her, against his better judgment, and the situation did spiral downhill.

> *What happened over the years is that I felt like he was pulling on me so much all the time, then I got real stubborn. I couldn't figure out when I wanted to be sexual and when I didn't, because I was so determined not to fall into "I have to have sex because I haven't for five days." I'd say, "If you just leave me alone and let me come to you . . . ," and he couldn't do that.*

Carl resorted to the cold shower: he swam, ran, and worked out an inordinate amount. But sex did not become a dead issue. As with most other things, said Molly, "We kept talking about it and kept talking about it."

Both of them were aware that this was a power issue as well as a "purely" sexual issue of individual energy or preference—if within a marriage such a thing even exists.

> *I thought probably we were redefining the power relationship, from having a real active sex life to not having very much of a sex life, and doing that largely based on what was happening with me . . .*

The lines got starker, the situation bleaker.

> *Eventually it got down to the basics of "This is what I want to do and I enjoy this and you're denying me pleasure." And I said, "Yeah, I am." We had a pretty sexless marriage for several years.*

Molly isn't exactly sure what changed in her—the pressure didn't significantly let up at school—but something did. One thing was a serendipitous arrival at a new understanding of what sex means to Carl.

> *I'm pretty clear that my husband and I are real different in terms of the role sex plays in our lives. For me, it's just having a good time, or sometimes it's real spiritual. For him, a certain amount of it is to relieve anxiety, a way to cool his jets. When I*

first became aware of that, I felt like some kind of machine to him, and I felt real resentful.

Then I had an interesting discussion with a woman that I'm close with. We're the same age, had similar families, both got married real young, have kids—our lives have a lot of parallels . . . She's very, very sexually active with a number of men and talks about sex a lot. And not only with men, but she masturbates frequently.

I said, "Why do you have sex so much?" and she said, "Because it heals me." I asked her, "Does it relieve anxiety?" and she said, yes, that's what she meant by it.

This secondhand explanation, from a woman Molly identifies with and admires, broke through a moral judgment of Carl's desires she realized she had been operating under. Some of the tension was defused, but she still wasn't ready to have sex. The unfair fact remained: on this one, Molly was in control, and short of becoming a Brute and forcing her into it, there was nothing Carl could do about it.

In other areas, their lives went along much as before. They fought, worked things out, had fun, pursued their separate interests and friends, and loved their kids together.

About not quite a year ago, I said to him, "You know, I always thought people were weird who had sex every Wednesday and every Saturday. But we've got this kid who dances three times a week, I've got class three days a week, another kid who has soccer once a week, you go to meetings twice a week . . . Let's decide let's have sex every Wednesday and Saturday." And he looked at me like, "God, where did this come from?"

I thought maybe I could just put it on the books. It seemed like that was the appropriate thing to try. I did it and it worked. We both enjoyed that. Between school quarters we would call that off. But it has worked very nicely.

With this agreement, they have stopped wheedling, feeling humiliated or humiliating each other, or jockeying for power.

Somehow doing that relieved his anxiety of "Am I ever going to be sexually intimate with this woman again?" And it was real helpful to me. I knew he wasn't always going to be pulling on me every day to have sex with him. It gave us both the chance to get what we wanted and not have to give up important pieces of ourselves.

Not having to give up important pieces of themselves: the principle of individual integrity reigns highest in Molly and Carl's marriage. The principle is not justified by the collective good; it supersedes it. Built into such a principle is a certain amount of conflict. Each integral whole cannot always adjust itself to make room for the other; as Molly says, the relationship is not always going to be nurtured. The question of control—wrestling over who's got it and who doesn't—plays a large part in their disputes. Carl is extremely irritated, for instance, if Molly phrases a suggestion "We need to do such and such . . ."

I think he thinks he has to jump up and down and do something. That's not at all what I'm saying. I'm saying, this has occurred to me, and we do need to do something! [She laughs.] It's just I've become enlightened on this issue.

Accepting conflict with this balance between selfhood and togetherness gives Molly and Carl a way of giving without giving in.

I asked Molly how much of their discord and of their negotiations have to do with gender roles. And what about man-hating? Does it ever come up? She approached the question in a roundabout way.

I don't know very many men that I like very much anymore. Twenty years ago I had a lot of male friends and not very many female friends in my life, and now it's the opposite. There are not many men who interest me, and most of the men I talk to seem very dull . . .

Carl is very . . . he's very female emotionally with me, meaning his feelings are really accessible, he's real verbal, he doesn't retreat from how he feels. He talks to me a lot about my emotional and spiritual life. It's real different from most men I know. The men I'm most attracted to have more access to their emotional parts of themselves, and I don't know a hell of a lot who do.

Like other women I talked to who were seeking emotionally richer relationships with men, Molly had befriended a number of gay men. Finding Carl, she says, was something of a surprise, and a relief: "I never have felt I was doing the emotional work in the relationship."

Understanding the ways femininity constrained her from developing as a person was a major enlightenment for Molly in her first period of therapy, and it continues to shine for her. Finding her "whole self" has made her a real player in her marriage. As well, Carl and Molly are lucky that both are professionals, both have some degree of control over their schedules, both can make enough money to support themselves, and neither makes vastly more than the other. In other words, the worldly weight of gender inequity does not press in on the private egalitarian structure they have built together.

With all those unbalancing factors absent, and with child care not a big issue, other gendered divisions of labor seem inconsequential.

> *I'm not sure anymore what the limits are that are imposed by gender, other than some real physical ones . . . He takes care of the cars, but that's not to do with gender, even though it's a traditional role. I don't like to do it, and he's willing to do that for me. I can't think of any other things.*

In practical, sexual, and emotional ways, Molly and Carl continue to hammer out the inequities of gender that make women and men resent and hate each other. In order to do so, both have had to throw away stereotypes on both sides. For her part, Molly has refused to accept the immutability of a domestic Bumbler, has not feared the Abandoner or the Brute, and has sought a man who is not a Babbler.

> *Carl is in some ways an enigma to me. I've never known a man like him. In some ways, it wouldn't matter if he was a man or a woman, or if I was a man or a woman. There's a really deep, deep bond that goes deeper than those levels.*

In this marriage, as perhaps in the bigger world, it is an attempt to transcend the limits of gender that makes for real understanding, real partnership.

Epilogue

WHEN SHE WAS ABOUT THREE, a tiny New Woman in the making, I asked my niece Sara whether she wanted apple juice or orange juice. She considered as I held the two jars down to her eye level, then said: "I want the other one."

I have often thought of this reply—a combination of intelligent circumspection, ornery resistance, and catholic imagination—when surveying the options offered women: Mommy Track or childless careerism, sexual violence or paternalistic protection, job discrimination or exposure to hazardous conditions, "settling" or celibacy. In all of the above, I want none of the above—the other one.

Faced with a plethora of lesser evils, women have become less radical and more stoical—*realistic* is the word I hear most often. "We have got a handle on our possibilities," a feminist friend said, "but we have forfeited our dreams." When women do glimpse those dreams, shimmering faintly around a distant corner, this "realistic" slouching toward possibility feels that much more like compromise, and reawakens rage. "Our rage," she added, "is different after twenty years. It's about what has *not* happened." Man-hating—both as it has intensified and as it has been neutralized—is now about how men have not changed.

Yet, as we've seen, contemporary rage and 1990s-style man-hating are also about what *has* happened, and how men *have* changed, for better and for worse. Each desired change carries its attendant threat, and also, because not everything surrounding a given change progresses equally, its mitigating consequence. Women are angry that fathers don't take more care of their children. But, it seems, the minute Dad hoists Junior into the Snuggli, Mom starts to fear the loss of her own status and power as a mother. Happily, many couples manage to work this problem out to everybody's benefit, especially the kids', with only minor friction remaining. But outside these better-managed loving family units, female fears are being realized. In child custody determinations, as we've seen, where mothers once could count on a kind of victory by default, paternal claims are inciting a new, sometimes brutal, contest, increasingly ending in maternal defeat. And the achievement of female reproductive self-determination in *Roe v. Wade* just two decades ago so threatened the male-dominated family that the rights procured by that decision began to be whittled away almost immediately, and now women are in grave danger of losing them altogether.

Do relations between the sexes really exist on a battlefront, where a gain for men is a loss for women, and vice versa? Does every male step toward domesticity, parenthood, or emotional expressiveness mean a surrender of precious social territory by women? When women advance in political, economic, and intellectual power, are they annexing men's turf?

Are women destined to hate men whether men change or not? Will women be compelled to hate by misogyny, which persists in making a wicked joke of female freedom?

As the lines are currently drawn, the answer is yes. Where the ground is limited and there is no frontier, men and women can't help but take up each other's space every time they stretch.

There are but two countries—Masculinity, rich with oil wells and skyscrapers and expensive four-star restaurants; and Femininity, a poorer land, but like many poor nations greener and prettier. In our day, there is plenty of travel between the two. Women cross the border, like migrants, to work for low wages, while men sojourn briefly and cautiously on the female side and return to where their best interests lie. But those who attempt to put down roots in the other place do so at the cost of severe alienation and under constant threat of banishment. Gender allows a person citizenship in only one country.

The anthropologist Esther Newton has suggested that there are in practice as many "genders" as there are permutations of biological body, sexual preference, personal decoration, mannerism, social affiliation, and medical alteration. A person with a penis who wears a dress and makes love to other biological males is not a fake woman or a half-man, but a real gay transvestite, just as a "butch" woman is a real woman and an "effeminate" man is a real man. The woman who eschews motherhood is a real woman; the man who is afraid to fight in a war is a real man.

Yet by "law" we all reside on one side of the divide and gaze over the border, wary of venturing too far into foreign territory, adulating and resenting, mystifying and demonizing what the Other is, and what we are prohibited from being.

It is not men or women, but gender itself that breeds sexual envy, fear, and hatred—misogyny and misandry both.

"The quarrel will go on as long as men and women fail to recognize each other as peers; that is to say, as long as femininity is perpetuated as such," wrote Simone de Beauvoir.[1] And, I might add, as long as masculinity is perpetuated, with its power to define and dominate. For gender isn't simply a mutual recognition of difference, not even just a mutual *suspicion* of difference. It is hierarchical; inherent to the current gender system is a valuation of men and a devaluation of women. Gender is an enforcement of inequality and therefore of oppression. And "all oppression," said Beauvoir, "creates a state of war."[2]

Although the constraints of gender hurt men, the system benefits them; individual men help perpetuate the system because it bestows privilege on them. Women, in rising up against the injustice of male privilege, did not create the state of hostility between the sexes, but they declared the war. The modern feminist disclosure of man-hating, which also existed long before feminism and way beyond the reaches of its influence, is one more salvo in that war.

In the end, though, feminism is neither a battle plan nor even a blueprint for change. At its most visionary it is a way of looking at the world; it imagines a world without the One and the Other, a world of "the other one," a world in which sex—the body—is but one fact of difference and not the defining factor of existence.

Realization of this vision requires two simultaneous, though seemingly opposite, efforts. While we conjure ourselves genderless, we must remain vigilantly aware of the crimes of gender—that is, fight against inequality. In her brilliant essay "A Room of One's Own," Virginia Woolf asserts that to write fiction, to create, "[i]t is fatal to be a man or woman pure and simple; one must be woman-manly or man-womanly. It is fatal for a woman to lay the least stress on any grievance; to plead even with justice any cause; in any way to speak consciously as a woman."[3] Grieving unequivocally as a woman against the damages inflicted by gender on women, Woolf prescribes the remedy of a genderless imagination.

My Enemy, My Love surveys the resistance to imagining beyond masculinity and femininity, one measure of which is the docility, even enthusiasm, with which men and women accept the places they are assigned by sex. Gender, no matter how uncomfortable and constricting, is also a familiar, and therefore comfortable, discomfort. Far as we have come in naming inequality, it remains almost indiscernible—the taste of our very tongues, the light behind our eyelids, the gravity that keeps our feet planted on the earth. To cast it away would be to feel almost formless, skinless, afloat in ambiguity. Without that body of proved and approved opinion about the self and the other, we would be forced to tolerate a great deal of uncertainty—and consciously, almost deliberately, to embrace ambivalence.

Western culture, epistemologically grounded in duality (with masculine/feminine the paradigmatic duality), does not tolerate ambivalence well. Duality implies oppositeness, and opposites are assumed to cancel each other out, so ambivalence (a word that itself implies *two*-ness) is regarded as a dangerous lack of resolution. If temporary, ambivalence can be a step toward decision; if chronic, it is a problem.

Yet as we have seen, ambivalence (or, more descriptively, *multi*-valence) is intrinsic to many basic situations of life, including intimacy. A kind of "positive ambivalence," furthermore, is crucial to critical thinking and art: an argument that effaces contradiction becomes a crude, and false, polemic; a representation without complexity becomes a stereotype. Ambivalence may be intrinsic to perceiving difference: one may fear or disagree with another's way of looking at things, but even to try to comprehend it is to reconsider one's own. As a prerequisite to the tolerance of that difference, a tolerance which itself precedes equality, ambivalence is a necessity, even a social good.

Neither the tolerance of ambivalence nor even the achievement of gender equality guarantees an end to the quarrel between women and men. For as long as there is intimacy there are expectations and disappointments, terror and rage, and as long as there is sex there is power—which all add up to conflict. Indeed, unloading the freight of pre-measured expectations and power, putting the rabble of stereotypes on a bus and sending them off to some historical theme park, women and men would be forced to improvise social relations. Already messy, the interactions of work, parenthood, friendship, politics, and sexual intimacy might become messier.

Unfortunately, we are still in the mess we are in. The worst of the sexual Cold War may be over, but it is premature to rush past feminism to a "postfeminism" that, like its concurrent smile-button presidencies, exorts everybody to hold hands and pretend to be equal, instead of actually doing anything that enables them to become so. The beneficiaries of inequality are eager to forgive and forget. Forgiveness from a position of power is a kind of noblesse oblige, gentle on the giver; and the mutinies of women, the poor, or people of color—well, these the powerful would be just as happy to forget. The casualties of inequality, on the other hand, have a harder time kissing and making up. With injustices against them hardly redressed, they continue to feel compelled to give discredit where discredit is due.

As long as women suffer under the idiocies and atrocities of sexism, their unilateral disarmament is impossible. For now, women maintain an arsenal of misandry, and while they don't always deploy it judiciously, neither is it the pipe bomb of wild emotion stuffed inside ironclad dogma that it was twenty years ago. A general rise in psychological awareness intercepts flashes of raw anger, and the lessons of two decades of politics usually prevent hatred from hardening into ideology.

Feminism has made a monumental difference: enduring prejudices notwithstanding, people may now be more able than ever before to see each other one by one, in three dimensions. Our humor and humility and the subtlety of our perceptions, no less than our grievances, have ripened during these decades.

When, if, equality is achieved, we may look back on "postfeminism" as the benighted *pre*history of an era that finds feminism truly vestigal. When better-than and worse-than give way to different-from, and different-from ceases to be a signal for enmity, categorical hatreds—misogyny, man-hating, and racism—will lose their utility, and we will be disarmed.

Notes

PROLOGUE

1. See Muriel Dimen's *Surviving Sexual Contradictions* (New York: Macmillan, 1986) for a rich exploration of this territory.
2. Martin Symonds, "Psychodynamics of Aggression in Women," *American Journal of Psychoanalysis* 36 (1976), 195.
3. Philip Blumstein and Pepper Schwartz, *American Couples* (New York: Pocket Books, 1983), 53.
4. Carol Tavris, *Anger: The Misunderstood Emotion* (New York: Touchstone/Simon and Schuster, 1982), 198.
5. Rosalind C. Barnett and Grace K. Baruch, "Correlates of Fathers' Participation in Family Work," in *Fatherhood Today: Men's Changing Role in the Family,* ed. Phyllis Bronstein and Carolyn Pape Cowen (New York: John Wiley and Sons, 1988), 76.
6. *The American Woman 1990–91: A Status Report,* ed. Sara E. Rix (New York: W. W. Norton and Co., 1990), 354.
7. Michel Foucault, "Truth and Power," in *Power/Knowledge: Selected Interviews and Other Writings 1972–1977* (New York: Pantheon Books, 1972), 119.
8. Mary Wollstonecraft, *A Vindication of the Rights of Women,* quoted in Josephine Donovan, *Feminist Theory: The Intellectual Traditions of American Feminism* (New York: Frederick Unger Publishing Co., 1985), 8.
9. Dorothy Dinnerstein, *The Mermaid and the Minotaur* (New York: Harper Colophon Books, 1976), 28.
10. Ibid., 161.
11. Teresa Bernardez-Bonesatti, "Women and Anger: Conflicts with Aggression in Contemporary Women," *Journal of the American Women's Medical Association* (May 1978), 216.
12. Harriet Lerner, "Internal Prohibitions Against Female Anger," *American Journal of Psychoanalysis* 40 (1980), 138.
13. Bernardez-Bonesatti, 216.
14. Alice Echols, *Daring to Be Bad: Radical Feminism in America 1967–1975* (Minneapolis: University of Minnesota Press, 1989), 17.

PART ONE: IMAGES OF THE ENEMY
1. Mary Ellmann, *Thinking About Women* (New York: Harvest Books/Harcourt Brace Jovanovich, 1968), 59.
2. Adrienne Rich, "Women and Honor: Some Notes on Lying," in *On Lies, Secrets, and Silence: Selected Prose 1966–1978* (New York: W. W. Norton & Co., 1979), 193.
3. Craig Owens, "The Medusa Effect, or, The Spectacular Ruse," in *We Won't Play Nature to Your Culture,* ed. Barbara Kruger (London: Institute of Contemporary Art, 1983), 1–5.
4. Faye Levine, "Four Types of Men," *Feminist Revolution* (New Paltz, NY: Redstockings, 1975), 113.

CHAPTER 1: THE INFANT
1. Toni Grant, *Being a Woman: Fulfilling Your Femininity and Finding Love* (New York: Avon Books, 1988), 151.
2. Adrienne Rich, "Husband-Right and Father-Right," in *On Lies, Secrets, and Silence,* 221.

MAMA'S BOY
1. Gloria Naylor, *The Women of Brewster Place* (New York: Penguin Books, 1980), 43.
2. Dee Jepsen, *Women: Beyond Equal Rights* (Waco, TX: Word Press, 1984), 199.
3. Marabel Morgan, *The Total Woman* (New York: Spire/Pocket Books, 1973), 175.
4. Darien B. Cooper, *You Can Be the Wife of a Happy Husband* (Wheaton, IL: Victor Books, 1988), 31.
5. Ibid. 41.
6. Jane Lazarre, *On Loving Men* (New York: Dial Press, 1978), 150–51.
7. "Notes on Women's Liberation: We Speak in Many Voices" (Detroit: News & Letters, 1970).

THE BABBLER
1. Sarah Kent, "The Erotic Male Nude," in *Women's Images of Men,* eds. S. Kent and Jacqueline Morreau (London: Writers and Readers Publishing, 1985), 98.
2. Irma Kurtz, *Mantalk: Tough Talk from a Tender Woman* (New York: Beech Tree Books, 1986), 12.
3. Ibid., 14.
4. Adrienne Rich, *Diving into the Wreck* (New York: W. W. Norton and Co., 1973), 3.
5. Laura Shapiro, "Guns and Dolls," *Newsweek* (May 28, 1990), 61–62.

6. Laurie Hetherington et al., "Whither the Bias: The Female Client's 'Edge' in Psychotherapy?" *Psychotherapy* 23 (1986): 252–56.
7. Deborah Tannen, *You Just Don't Understand; Women and Men in Conversation* (New York: William Morrow and Co., 1990).
8. Mimi Pond, *Secrets of the Powder Room* (New York: Owl Books/ Holt, Rinehart and Winston, 1983).
9. Luise Eichenbaum and Susie Orbach, *What Do Women Want: Exploding the Myth of Dependency* (New York: Coward-McCann Inc., 1983), 91.

THE BUMBLER
1. "Mandela the Man" *Ms.* (July/August 1990), 15.
2. Phyllis McGinley, *Times Three* (New York: Viking Press, 1960), 260.
3. Pat Mainardi, "The Politics of Housework," in *Sisterhood Is Powerful,* ed. Robin Morgan (New York: Vintage Books, 1970), 449.
4. Shere Hite, *Women and Love* (New York, Alfred A. Knopf, 1987), 4.
5. Erma Bombeck, *Family—The Ties that Bind . . . and Gag* (New York: McGraw-Hill, 1987), 7–8.
6. Barbara Ehrenreich, *The Hearts of Men* (New York: Anchor Press/ Doubleday, 1983), 4.
7. Personal interview with Pepper Schwartz.
8. U.S. Bureau of Labor Statistics, March 1990.
9. Arlie Hochschild, *The Second Shift: Working Parents and Revolution at Home* (New York: Viking Books, 1989), 263.
10. Arlie Hochschild, "The Second Shift: Employed Women Are Putting in Another Day of Work at Home," *Utne Reader* (March 4, 1990), 66.
11. Hochschild, *Second Shift,* 215.
12. Barnett and Baruch, "Correlates of Fathers' Participation in Family Work," 72.
13. Louis Genevie and Eva Margolis, *The Motherhood Report: How Women Feel About Being Mothers* (New York: McGraw-Hill, 1988), 161.
14. Deborah L. Rhode, "Gender Equality and Employment Policy," *The American Woman 1990–91,* 176.
15. Rayna D. Green, "Magnolias Grow in Dirt: The Bawdy Lore of Southern Women," *Southern Exposure* 4 (1977), 29–33.
16. Lillian Breslow Rubin, *Worlds of Pain: Life in the Working-Class Family* (New York: Basic Books, 1976), 152.

THE INVALID

1. Roszika Parker, "Images of Men," in *Women's Images of Men,* 46.
2. Helen W. Papashvily, *All the Happy Endings* (Port Washington, NY: Kennikat Press, 1972), 91.
3. *Ibid.,* 151.
4. Sandra M. Gilbert and Susan Gubar, *No Man's Land: The Place of the Woman Writer in the Twentieth Century,* vol. 1 (New Haven: Yale University Press, 1987), 72.
5. Roszika Parker, 46.
6. Marilyn French, *The Women's Room* (New York: Jove Books, 1978), 49.
7. Erica Jong, *Fear of Flying* (New York: Signet/New American Library, 1973), 88–90.
8. Joyce Brothers, *What Every Woman Should Know About Men* (New York: Simon and Schuster, 1981), 23.
9. *Cosmopolitan,* July 1989.
10. Toni Grant, *Being a Woman,* 153.
11. Leanne Payne, *Crisis in Masculinity* (Westchester, IL: Crossway Books, 1985), 12.
12. See, for instance, Darien B. Cooper's *You Can Be the Wife of a Happy Husband.*
13. Melody Beattie, *Codependent No More* (San Francisco: Harper/Hazelden Books, 1987), 19.
14. Ibid., 37–45.
15. Anne Wilson Schaef, *Escape from Intimacy* (New York: Harper and Row, 1989).
16. Sonya Rhodes and Marlin S. Potash, *Cold Feet: Why Men Don't Commit* (New York: New American Library, 1988), xii.
17. Carol Botwin, *Men Who Can't Be Faithful* (New York: Warner Books, 1988), 9.
18. Ibid., 28.
19. Margaret Kent, *How to Marry the Man of Your Choice* (New York: Warner Books, 1984).
20. Rhodes and Potash, 162.
21. Botwin, 200.
22. Ibid., 198.
23. "Mating for Life? It's Not for the Birds or the Bees," *New York Times* (August 21, 1990), C1.
24. Erma Bombeck, *Giant Economy Size* (New York: Nelson Doubleday, 1965), 55.
25. Sue Kaufman, *Diary of a Mad Housewife* (New York: Random House, 1967), 187–88.
26. Marcelle Clements, "The Jewish American Prince," *New York Woman* (October 1987), 74–79.
27. Sara Lee Johann and Frank Osanka, *Representing . . . Battered*

Women Who Kill (Springfield, IL: Charles C. Thomas, 1989), 4–5.

CHAPTER TWO: THE BETRAYER
THE SEDUCER

1. Samuel Richardson, *Clarissa* (1748), ed. John Angus Burrell (New York: Modern Library/Random House, 1950), 276–77.
2. Lord Byron, 15:12 (vol. 3, p. 461) Jerome J. McGann, ed. Oxford University Press, 1986.
3. Elizabeth Hardwick, *Seduction and Betrayal: Women and Literature* (New York: Vintage Books, 1975), 185.
4. Susan Brownmiller, *Against Our Will: Men, Women and Rape* (New York: Simon and Schuster, 1975), 271.
5. Anne Bernays, *Professor Romeo* (New York: Weidenfeld and Nicolson, 1989), 36–37.
6. Bernays, 275.
7. For an excellent exploration of sadomasochism, see Jessica Benjamin's treatment of *The Story of O* in *The Bonds of Love: Psychoanalysis, Feminism, and the Problem of Domination* (New York: Pantheon Books, 1988).
8. Brownmiller, 324.
9. Tania Modleski, *Loving with a Vengeance: Mass-Produced Fantasies for Women* (New York: Methuen, 1982), 47–48.
10. Vanessa Grant, *Takeover Man* (Toronto: Harlequin Books, 1989), 44.
11. Grant, 46.
12. Coral Hoyle, *Midsummer Masque* (Toronto: Harlequin Books, 1989), 68.
13. Pamela Beck and Patti Massman, *Rich Men, Single Women* (New York: Delacorte Press, 1988), 87.
14. Judith Krantz, *'Til We Meet Again* (New York: Crown Publishers, 1988), 40.
15. Rosemary Rogers, *Love Play* (New York: Avon Books, 1981), 321.
16. Susan Elizabeth Phillips, *Glitter Baby* (New York: Dell, 1987), 211.
17. Barbara Ehrenreich et al., *Re-Making Love: The Feminization of Sex* (New York: Anchor Books, 1991).
18. "Study of Teen-Agers Hints Gain for Those Having Abortions," *New York Times* (January 25, 1990), A21.
19. Catherine A. MacKinnon, *Toward a Feminist Theory of the State* (Cambridge: Harvard University Press, 1989), 172–73.
20. All quotes from *Smooth Talk,* directed by Joyce Chopra (Nepenthe/American Playhouse/Goldcrest, 1985).
21. Joyce Carol Oates, "Where Are You Going, Where Have You

Been?" in *Two Hundred Years of Great American Short Stories,* ed. Martha Foley (New York: Houghton Mifflin Co., 1975), 922.

THE SLAVE
1. Shulamith Firestone, *The Dialectic of Sex: The Case for Feminist Revolution* (New York: Bantam Books, 1971), 127–28.
2. Steve Chapple and David Talbot, *Burning Desires: Sex in America, a Report from the Field* (New York: Doubleday, 1990), 66.
3. Zora Neale Hurston, "Spunk," in *Spunk: The Selected Stories of Zora Neale Hurston* (Berkeley, CA: Turtle Island Foundation, 1985), 3.
4. Ibid., 7.
5. Ibid., 8.
6. Beck and Massman, *Rich Men, Single Women,* 414.
7. Judith Rossner, *Looking for Mr. Goodbar* (New York: Simon and Schuster, 1975).
8. Moms Mabley at the U.N.
9. Jackie Collins, *The Bitch* (New York: Pocket Books, 1979), 57.
10. Jackie Collins, *The Love Killers* (New York: Pocket Books, 1974), 52.
11. Ibid., 44.
12. Ibid., 108.
13. Ibid., 142–143.
14. Ibid., 267.

THE ABANDONER
1. Linda Gordon, *Heroes of Their Own Lives: The Politics and History of Family Violence* (New York: Penguin Books, 1988), 108.
2. "Father's Vanishing Act Called Common Drama," *New York Times* (June 4, 1990), A18.
3. *The American Woman 1990–91,* 373.
4. Herbert Gutman in *The Black Family in Slavery and Freedom 1725–1925* (New York: Pantheon Books, 1976) and Eugene Genovese in *Roll, Jordan, Roll: The World the Slaves Made* (New York: Vintage Books, 1976) both substantially discredited former notions of a predominantly matriarchical black slave family. And John W. Blassingame suggests that slave*holders* themselves often encouraged slave-family integrity; see his *The Slave Community: Plantation Life in the Antebellum South* (New York: Oxford University Press, 1979).
5. John Lewis McAdoo, "Changing Perspectives on the Role of the Black Father," in *Fatherhood Today,* 81.
6. "Father's Vanishing Act . . . ," A18.
7. Harriette Pipe Mcadoo, "A Portrait of African American Families in the United States," in *The American Woman 1990–91,* 82.

8. Mcadoo, 85.
9. Toni Morrison, *Beloved* (New York: Alfred A. Knopf, 1987), 23.
10. Ibid., 66.
11. Ibid., 128.
12. Ibid., 17.
13. Ntozake Shange, *for colored girls who have considered suicide/when the rainbow is enuf* (New York: Collier Books, 1975), 56.
14. Ibid., 60.
15. Mary Helen Washington, *Midnight Birds: Stories of Contemporary Black Women Writers* (New York: Anchor Books, 1980), xix.
16. Mona Simpson, *Anywhere but Here* (New York: Vintage Contemporaries, 1986), 163.
17. Alice Adams, "1940: Fall" in *After You're Gone* (New York: Alfred A. Knopf, 1989), 20–21.
18. Ibid., 16.
19. "Father's Vanishing Act Called Common Drama," *New York Times* (June 4, 1990), A18.
20. Weitzman, Lenore, *The Divorce Revolution* (New York: Free Press, 1985).
21. Stephen D. Sugarman, "Dividing Financial Interests on Divorce" in *Divorce Reform at the Crossroads,* eds. S. D. Sugarman and Herma Hill Kay (New Haven: Yale University Pres, 1990), 133.
22. "The Precious Rights ERA Will Take Away From Wives," *The Phyllis Schlafly Report* 7 (August 1973), 1.
23. Ehrenreich, *Hearts of Men,* 147.
24. Ibid.
25. Carson Daly, "The Feminist in the Family: The Femme Fatale?" *Fidelity* 2 (May 1983), 13.
26. Faye D. Ginsburg, *Contested Lives: The Abortion Debate in an American Community* (Berkeley: University of California Press, 1989), 215–16.
27. Rosemary Bottcher, "Feminism: Bewitched by Abortion," in *To the Rescue: The Pro-Life Movement in the 1980s,* ed. Dave Andrusko (Toronto: Life Cycle Books, 1983), 180–81.
28. Ibid., 181–82.
29. Ginsburg, 216–18.

THE ABDUCTOR

1. Sue Miller, *The Good Mother* (New York: Dell Publishing, 1986), 233.
2. Susan Crean, *In the Name of the Fathers: The Story Behind Child Custody* (Vancouver: Amanita Publishers, 1988), 139–40.
3. "Bringing Up Daddy," *Esquire* (November 1989), 117.
4. Herma Hill Kay, quoting Ira Ellman in "Beyond No-Fault: New Directions in Divorce Reform," *Divorce Reform at the Crossroads,* 15.

5. "Why More Dads Are Getting the Kids," *Business Week* (November 28, 1988), 118.
6. Nancy Polikoff, "Gender and Child-Custody Determinations: Exploding the Myths," in *Families, Politics, and Public Policy: A Feminist Debate on Women and the State,* ed. I. Diamond (New York: Longman, 1983), 139.
7. Susan B. Boyd, "From Gender Specificity to Gender Neutrality? Ideologies in Canadian Child Custody Law," in *Child Custody and the Politics of Gender,* ed. Carol Smart and Selma Sevenhuijsen (London: Routledge, 1989), 147.
8. Robert Mnookin et al., "Private Ordering Revisited," in *Divorce Reform at the Crossroads,* 65.
9. "Why More Dads . . . ," 122.
10. *Our Bodies, Ourselves* (Boston: Boston Women's Health Collective, 1969), 114.
11. Germaine Greer, *The Female Eunuch* (New York: Bantam Books, 1970), 237.
12. Firestone, 198.
13. Ibid., 238.
14. Jane Alpert, "Mother Right: A New Feminist Theory," *Ms,* August 1973, 91–92.
15. Ibid., 93.
16. Phyllis Chesler, *Mothers on Trial: The Battle for Children and Custody* (Seattle: Seal Press, 1986), 73.
17. Geoffrey L. Greif and Mary S. Pabst, *Mothers Without Custody* (San Diego: Lexington Books, 1988), 83–84.
18. Chesler, 77.
19. Rayna Rapp, "Feminists and Pharmacrats," *The Women's Review of Books* Vol. 2:10 (July, 1985).
20. Jalna Hammer, "A Womb of One's Own," in *Test-Tube Women,* ed. Rita Arditti, Renate Duelli Klein, and Shelley Minden (London: Pandora Press, 1985), 441.
21. Mary O'Brien, *The Politics of Reproduction* (London: Routledge and Kegan Paul, 1983).
22. Gena Corea, *The Mother Machine* (New York: Harper and Row, 1985), 288.
23. Ibid., 289–90.
24. Phyllis Chesler, *The Sacred Bond: The Legacy of Baby M* (New York: Times Books, 1988), 144.
25. Leaflet, February 18, 1987.
26. Leaflet, February 18, 1987.

CHAPTER THREE: THE BEAST
1. Michel Foucault, "Body/Power."

THE BRUTE

1. "Athletic Aggression and Sexual Assault," *New York Times* (June 3, 1990), 8:1.
2. "Special Report: Everyday Violence Against Women," *Ms.* (September/October 1990), 45.
3. Judith Lewis Herman, "Considering Sex Offenders: A Model of Addiction," *Signs* 13 (Summer 1988), 703.
4. "The Mind of the Rapist," *Newsweek* (July 23, 1990), 47.
5. Herman, 696–97.
6. Diana E. H. Russell, *Sexual Exploitation: Rape, Child Sexual Abuse, and Sexual Harassment* (Beverly Hills, Calif.: Sage, 1984).
7. "Date Rape Is OK, Grade Schoolers Say," *Philadelphia Inquirer,* May 3, 1988.
8. "The Mind Of the Rapist," 52.
9. Andrea Dworkin, *Intercourse* (New York: Free Press, 1987), 63.
10. Andrea Dworkin, *Pornography: Men Possessing Women* (New York: E. P. Dutton, 1989), 55.
11. Brownmiller, 14–15.
12. Rosán A. Jordan, "The Vaginal Serpent and Other Themes from Mexican-American Women's Lore," in *Women's Folklore, Women's Culture,* eds. R. A. Jordan and Susan J. Kalčik (Philadelphia: University of Pennsylvania Press, 1985), 27–28.
13. Ibid., 31.
14. Ibid., 35.
15. Paula Giddings, *When and Where I Enter: The Impact of Black Women on Race and Sex in America* (New York: Bantam Books, 1984), 26–30.
16. For discussions of this division, see Paula Giddings (op. cit.) and a number of Audre Lorde's essays, among them "An Interview: Audre Lorde and Adrienne Rich," in *Sister Outsider* (Freedom, Calif.: Crossing Press, 1984).
17. Brownmiller, 247.
18. *Amsterdam News,* May 6, 1989, 8.
19. Carroll Smith-Rosenberg, *Disorderly Conduct: Visions of Gender in Victorian America* (New York: Oxford University Press, 1985), 115–16.
20. Andrea Dworkin and Catherine MacKinnon, "Proposed Los Angeles County Anti-Pornography Civil Rights Law" (typescript; composed from versions of the Minneapolis and Indianapolis bills, 1985).
21. Gerd Brantenberg, *Egalia's Daughters: A Satire of the Sexes* (Seattle: Seal Press, 1977), 65.
22. Ursula K. Le Guin, *The Left Hand of Darkness* (New York: Ace Books, 1969), 94.
23. Ibid., 96.

24. Adrienne Harris, "Bringing Artemis to Life," in *Rocking the Ship of State: Toward a Feminist Peace Politics,* eds. A. Harris and Ynestra King (Boulder: Westview Press, 1989), 93.
25. Charlotte Perkins Gilman, *Herland* (1915; New York: Pantheon Books, 1979), 55.
26. Harris, 93.
27. Joanna Russ, *The Female Man* (Boston: Beacon Press, 1975), 11.
28. Sally Miller Gearhart, *The Wanderground* (Boston: Alyson Publishers, 1980), 115.
29. Patricia Volk, "Being Safe," "Hers," *New York Times Sunday Magazine* (January 11, 1990), 24.

THE PET
 1. Rachel Ingalis, *Mrs. Caliban* (Boston: Harvard Common Press), 26.
 2. Ibid., 34.
 3. Marian Engel, *Bear* (New York: Atheneum, 1976), 199.
 4. Ibid., 64.
 5. Ibid., 119.
 6. Ibid., 112.
 7. Ibid., 94.
 8. Ibid., 113.
 9. Ibid., 134.
10. "I Am the Mother of Bigfoot's Baby," *The Sun* (August 22, 1989).
11. All quotes from *Making Mr. Right,* directed by Susan Seidelman (Barry and Enright/Orion, 1987).

THE PRICK
 1. Sigmund Freud, "Medusa's Head" (1922), *Sexuality and the Psychology of Love* (New York: Collier Books, 1963), 213.
 2. Jane Gallop, *The Daughter's Seduction: Feminism and Psychoanalysis* (Ithaca: Cornell University Press, 1982), 37–38.
 3. Suzanne Moore, "Here's Looking at You, Kid," in *The Female Gaze: Women as Viewers of Popular Culture,* eds. Lorraine Gamman and Margaret Marshment (Seattle: Real Comet Press, 1989), 59.
 4. Jacqueline Morreau and Catherine Elwes, "Lighting a Candle," in *Women's Images of Men,* 18.
 5. Lisa Tickner, "The Body Politic: Female Sexuality and Women Artists," in *Framing Feminism: Art and the Women's Movement 1970–1985,* eds. Roszika Parker and Griselda Pollack (London: Pandora Press, 1987), 268.
 6. Sarah Kent, "The Erotic Male Nude," in *Women's Images of Men,* 91.

7. Simone de Beauvoir, *The Second Sex* (New York: Vintage Books, 1974), 769.
8. Nicole Hollander, *I'm in Training to be Tall and Blonde* (New York: St. Martin's Press, 1979).
9. Pond, *Secrets of the Powder Room.*
10. Andrea Dworkin, *Intercourse* (New York: Free Press, 1987), 64–65.
11. Ron Kovic, *Born on the Fourth of July* (New York: McGraw-Hill, 1976), 98.
12. "Good or Just Lucky?" *New York Times* (February 18, 1990), A14.
13. Kent, 96.
14. Ibid., 93.

THE KILLER

1. Estimated cost above regular Pentagon appropriations (Center for Defense Information, Washington, D.C.).
2. "Washington Whispers," *U.S. News and World Report* (April 1, 1991), 16.
3. Nancy C. M. Hartsock, "Masculinity, Heroism, and the Making of War," in *Rocking the Ship of State,* 139–40.
4. "The Antiwar Movement and the Women's Movement," *Off Our Backs,* June, 1972.
5. Carol Cohn, "Sex and Death in the Rational World of Defense Intellectuals," *Signs: Journal of Women in Culture and Society* 12 (1987), 696.
6. Andrea Dworkin, *Pornography,* 51.
7. Cohn, 699.
8. Kate Ellis, *The Contested Castle: Gothic Novels and the Subversion of Domestic Ideology* (Urbana: University of Illinois Press, 1989), 181–206.
9. Dee Jepsen, *Women: Beyond Equal Rights,* 32.
10. Ibid., 227.
11. Sigmund Freud, "Some Psychical Consequences of the Anatomical Distinction Between the Sexes" (1925) *Standard Edition of the Complete Psychological Works of Sigmund Freud* XIX, ed. James Strachey (Hogarth Press, 1961), 257–58.
12. Carol Gilligan, *In a Different Voice* (Cambridge: Harvard University Press, 1982).
13. MacKinnon, *Toward a Feminist Theory of the State,* 248.
14. Jeanne Bethke Elshtain, *Women and War* (New York: Basic Books, 1987), 231.
15. Sara Ruddick, *Maternal Thinking: Toward a Politics of Peace* (New York: Ballantine, 1989), 197.
16. Kimiko Hahn, "The Bath," in *Women on War,* ed. Daniela Gioseffi (New York: Touchstone Books, 1988), 207–8.

17. Adrienne Harris, "Bringing Artemis to Life," in *Rocking the Ship of State,* 104.

PART II: PRIVATE LOVE, PUBLIC HATRED
CHAPTER FOUR: DAUGHTERS AND FATHERS

1. Virginia Goldner, Peggy Penn, Marcia Sheinberg, and Gillian Walker, "Love and Violence: Gender Paradoxes in Volatile Attachments," *Family Process* 29 (December 1991), 343–64.
2. Emily Dickinson, *Complete Poems of Emily Dickinson,* ed. Thomas H. Johnson (Boston: Little Brown and Co., 1960), 319.
3. Margaret Mead, *Male and Female* (New York: William Morrow and Co., 1949), 192.
4. Letty Cottin Pogrebin, *Family Politics* (New York: McGraw-Hill, 1983), 83.
5. Perry Garfinkel, *In a Man's World: Father, Son, Brother, Friend and Other Roles Men Play* (New York: New American Library, 1986), 125.
6. Michael E. Lamb, "The Changing Role of Fathers" in *The Father's Role: Applied Perspectives,* ed. M. E. Lamb (New York: John Wiley and Sons, 1986), 9–11.
7. Anna Quindlan, "Men at Work," *New York Times* (Feb. 18, 1990), E19.
8. Michael Lamb, *The Role of Fathers* (Salt Lake City: University of Utah Press, 1981), 5.
9. Pogrebin, *Growing Up Free: Raising Your Child in the Eighties* (New York: McGraw-Hill, 1980), 142.
10. "Father's Vanishing Act . . ."
11. Frank F. Furstenberg, Jr., and Kathleen Mullan Harris, *The Disappearing American Father? Divorce and the Waning Significance of Biological Parenthood* (Philadelphia: University of Pennsylvania, 1990; typescript).
12. Greif & Pabst, *Mothers Without Custody,* 6.
13. Furstenberg and Harris, 3.
14. Margaret Atwood, *Cat's Eye* (Garden City, N.Y.: Doubleday, 1989), 175
15. Judith Lewis Herman and Lisa Hirschman, *Father-Daughter Incest* (Cambridge: Harvard University Press, 1981), 214.
16. Michael Lamb, Margaret Tresch Owen, and Lindsay Chase-Lansdale, "The Father-Daughter Relationship: Past, Present, and Future," in *Becoming Female: Perspective on Development,* ed. Claire B. Koff (New York: Plenum Press, 1979), 98.
17. Ibid., 95.
18. Miriam Johnson, "Fathers and 'Femininity' in Daughters: A Review of the Literature," *Sociology and Social Research* 67 (October 1982), 4–5.

19. Mahler quoted in Ernest Abelin, "Triangulation, the Role of the Father, and the Origins of Core Gender Identity During the Rapprochement Subphase," in *Rapprochement: The Critical Subphase of Separation-Individuation,* eds. R. F. Lax, S. Bach, and J. A. Burland (New York: Jason Aronson, 1980), 152.

20. Jessica Benjamin, *The Bonds of Love* (New York: Pantheon Books, 1988), 104.

21. Lora Heims Tessman, "A Note on the Father's Contribution to the Daughter's Ways of Loving and Working," in *Father and Child: Development and Clinical Perspectives,* eds. S. Cath, A. Gurwitt, and J. M. Ross (Boston: Little Brown, 1982), 210–30.

22. Benjamin, 107.

23. Beauvoir, *The Second Sex,* 807.

24. Michele Roberts, "Outside My Father's House," in *Fathers: Reflections by Daughters,* ed. Ursula Owen (New York: Pantheon, 1983), 90.

25. Henry B. Biller and Stephen D. Weiss, "The Father-Daughter Relationship and the Personality Development of the Female," *Journal of Genetic Psychology* 116 (1970), 79–93.

26. Sigmund Freud, "Autobiographical Study" (1925), quoted in Steven Marcus' 1977 introduction to *Sigmund Freud: The Origins of Psychoanalysis,* ed. Marie Bonaparte ed al. (New York: Basic Books, 1954), 28.

27. *Sigmund Freud: The Origins of Psychoanalysis,* 215–16.

28. Herman and Hirschman, *Father-Daughter Incest,* 12–14.

29. Herman and Hirschman, "Father-Daughter Incest," *Signs* 2:4 (Summer 1977), 754.

30. Louise A. DeSalvo, *Virginia Woolf: The Impact of Childhood Sexual Abuse on Her Life and Work* (Boston: Beacon Press, 1989), 8.

31. Herman and Hirschman, *Father-Daughter Incest,* 71–78.

32. Ibid., 56.

33. Ibid., 54.

34. Freud, *Standard Edition* 1, 260.

35. Luce Irigaray, *Speculum of the Other Woman* (Ithaca: Cornell University Press, 1985), 38.

36. Sharon Olds, "Looking at My Father," in *The Gold Cell* (New York: Alfred A. Knopf, 1988). 31.

37. Nancy Chodorow and Susan Contrato, "The Fantasy of the Perfect Mother," in N. Chodorow, *Feminism and Psychoanalytic Theory* (New Haven: Yale University Press, 1989), 81.

38. Virginia Woolf, *Moments of Being,* ed. Jeanne Schulkind (London: Hogarth Press, 1985), 111.

39. Lucille Clifton, "forgiving my father," *Memories of Kin: Stories About Family By Black Writers,* ed. Mary Helen Washington (New York: Anchor Books, 1991), 145.

CHAPTER FIVE: SISTERHOOD AND THE PATRIARCH

1. Robin Morgan, "Goodbye to All That," *The Rat* 2 (February 6–23, 1970).

2. Valerie Solanas, "SCUM Manifesto" (1967).

3. Sara Evans, *Personal Politics: The Roots of Women's Liberation in the Civil Rights Movement and the New Left* (New York: Vintage Books, 1980), 83.

4. Ibid., 85.

5. Paula Giddings, *When and Where I Enter,* 60.

6. Ibid., 312.

7. Ibid., 316.

8. Evans, 86.

9. Frances M. Beal, "Double Jeopardy: To Be Black and Female," in *Sisterhood Is Powerful,* ed. Robin Morgan (New York: Vintage Books, 1970), 386.

10. Linda C. Powell, "Black Macho and Black Feminism," in *Home Girls: A Black Feminist Anthology,* ed. Barbara Smith (New York: Kitchen Table: Women of Color Press, 1983), 290–91.

11. bell hooks, "Representations: Feminism and Black Masculinity," in *Yearning: Race, Gender, and Cultural Politics* (Boston: South End Press, 1990), 71–73.

12. Audre Lorde, *Sister Outsider: Essays and Speeches* (Trumansburg, NY: Crossing Press, 1984), 99.

13. hooks, 68.

14. Michelle Wallace, "A Black Feminist's Search for Sisterhood," *All the Women Are White, All the Blacks Are Men, But Some of Us Are Brave.* Gloria T. Hull, Patricia Bell Scott, and Barbara Smith, eds. (New York: Feminist Prss, 1982), 10.

15. Alice Echols, *Daring to be Bad,* 32.

16. Combahee River Collective, "A Black Feminist Statement," in *All the Women Are White . . . ,"* 17.

17. Morgan, "Goodbye to All That."

18. Marilyn Webb, "Women: We Have a Common Enemy," *New Left Notes 1968* 3 (June 10, 1968), 15.

19. Sylvia Hartman, "Are Men People?" *Everywoman* 1 (July 10, 1970), 11.

20. "The New Feminists: Revolt Against 'Sexism'," *Time* (Nov. 21, 1969), 53–54.

21. Carol Tavris, "Who Likes Women's Liberation—and Why: The Case of the Unliberated Liberals," *Journal of Social Issues* 29:4 (1973), 196.

22. Lucy Gilbert and Paula Webster, *Bound by Love: The Sweet Trap of Daughterhood* (Boston: Beacon Press, 1982), 163.

23. Pamela Kearon, "Man-Hating," *Notes From the Second Year* (Shulamith Firestone and Anne Koedt, 1970), 84.

24. Ibid., 86.
25. Gloria Steinem, "Sisterhood," in *Outrageous Acts and Everyday Rebellions* (New York: Signet/New American Library, 1986), 129.
26. For a good discussion of this problem, see Denise Riley, *Am I That Name? Feminism and the Category of Women in History* (Minneapolis: University of Minnesota Press, 1988).
27. Echols, 147.
28. Ti-Grace Atkinson, "Vaginal Orgasm as a Mass Hysterical Reaction," *Amazon Odyssey* (New York: Ti-Grace Atkinson, 1974), 7.
29. Ann Snitow et al., *Powers of Desire: The Politics of Sexuality* (New York: Monthly Review Press, 1983), 28.
30. "Women Rap about Sex," *Notes From the First Year* (New York: New York Radical Women, 1968).
31. New York Radical Feminists pamphlet (March 1975).
32. Echols, 6.
33. Nancy Chodorow and Susan Contratto, "The Fantasy of the Perfect Mother," 92.
34. Ibid., 96.
35. Harris, *Rocking the Ship of State,* 104.
36. Alison M. Jagger, "Love and Knowledge: Emotion in Feminist Epistemology," *Gender/Body/Knowledge: Feminist Reconstructions of Being and Knowing,* ed. Alison M. Jagger and Susan R. Bordo (New Brunswick: Rutgers University Press, 1989), 160.
37. Virginia Woolf, *Three Guineas* (New York: Harvest/HBJ Books, 1938), 138.

PART III: LIVING WITH AMBIVALENCE
CHAPTER TEN: WITHDRAWAL
1. Connell Cowan and Melvyn Kinder, *Smart Women, Foolish Choices* (New York: Clarkson N. Potter, 1985), 5.
2. Ibid., 12.

CHAPTER ELEVEN: INFILTRATION
1. U.S. Bureau of Labor Statistics. January 1976 and January 1989.

CHAPTER FOURTEEN: NEGOTIATION
1. Blumstein and Schwartz, 56.

EPILOGUE
1. Beauvoir, *The Second Sex,* 799.
2. Beauvoir, 797.
3. Virginia Woolf, *A Room of One's Own* (1929; New York: Harcourt Brace Jovanovich/Harvest Books), 108.

An Abbreviated Bibliography

LIKE MUCH NONFICTION, *My Enemy, My Love* required two kinds of research: primary research—the novels, poems, and advice books, movies, tabloids, advertisements, paintings, political tracts, legal transcripts, interviews, overheard conversations, jokes, and rumors from which I gathered evidences of man-hating; and secondary research—the books and essays I used to help me understand what I discovered.

Primary sources are catalogued in the footnotes, or in some cases attributed, journalism-style, within the text of the book. Secondary sources that I quote directly are also footnoted.

Rather than provide a long and undifferentiated bibliography of every word I read, I've chosen to highlight the books that have been most useful and influential to *My Enemy, My Love,* and which I also recommend. A number are anthologies; obviously, I did not use every contribution in every one of these, but they are the collections I returned to again and again.

So my list is incomplete; it includes only about a third of my sources and excludes many modern classics I referred to—the works of, say, Freud or Foucault or the major works of African-American history or postmodern theory. I suggest the reader consult the growing body of excellent bibliographies and curricula in these and other related disciplines, some of which are, in fact, published in the books acknowledged below. Also, since I am a voracious but penurious reader, most of the editions here are paperbacks.

For literary criticism, cultural theory, and philosophy, I used the following most:

BERGER, JOHN, *Ways of Seeing* (London: British Broadcasting Co. and Penguin Books, 1972).

BRAXTON, JOANNE M. and MCLAUGHLIN, ANDREE NICOLA, eds., *Wild Women in the Whirlwind: Afra-American Culture and the Contemporary Literary Renaissance* (New Brunswick, NJ: Rutgers University Press, 1990).

GAMMAN, LORRAINE and MARCHMENT, MARGARET, eds., *The Female Gaze: Women as Viewers of Popular Culture* (Seattle: Real Comet Press, 1989).

GILBERT, SANDRA M., and SUSAN GUBAR, *Madwoman in the Attic;* and *No Man's Land: The Place of the Woman Writer in the Twentieth Century,* vols. 1 and 2 (New Haven: Yale University Press, 1987).

JAGGER, ALISON M. and BORDO, SUSAN, eds., *Gender/Body/Knowledge: Feminist Reconstructions of Being and Knowing* (New Brunswick: Rutgers University Press, 1989).

KENT, SARAH and MORREAU, JACQUELINE, eds., *Women's Images of Men* (London: Writers and Readers Publishing, 1985).

MILLER, JANE, *Women Writing About Men* (New York: Pantheon Books, 1986).

MODLESKI, TANIA, *Loving With a Vengeance: Mass-produced Fantasies for Women* (New York, Methuen, 1982).

MULVEY, LAURA, "Visual Pleasure and Narrative Cinema," in *Women and the Cinema,* Karyn Kay and Gerald Peary, eds., (New York: E. P. Dutton, 1977).

OWENS, CRAIG, "The Medusa Effect, or, Spectacular Ruse," in Barbara Kruger's *We Won't Play Nature To Your Culture* (London: Institute of Contemporary Art, 1983).

RILEY, DENISE, *Am I That Name? Feminism and the Category of Women in History* (Minneapolis: University of Minnesota Press, 1988).

Two books that contribute enormously to the understanding of why women and men have such a hard time getting along are:
EHRENREICH, BARBARA, *The Hearts of Men* (New York: Anchor Press/ Doubleday, 1983).

TANNEN, DEBORAH, *You Just Don't Understand: Women and Men in Conversation* (New York: William Morrow and Co., 1990).

On the same score, psychologists and sociologists know that attitudes and behavior are often miles apart. These books offer not only good hard data but also smart and clear analysis:
BLUMSTEIN, PHILIP and SCHWARTZ, PEPPER, *American Couples* (New York: Pocket Books, 1983).

BRONSTEIN, PHYLLIS and COWEN, CAROLYN PAPE, eds., *Fatherhood Today: Men's Changing Role in the Family* (New York: John Wiley & Sons, 1988).

FURSTENBERG, FRANK F., JR. and HARRIS, KATHLEEN MULLAN, "The Disappearing American Father? Divorce and the Waning Significance of Biological Parenthood" (Philadelphia: University of Pennsylvania, 1990; typescript).

HOCHSCHILD, ARLIE, *The Second Shift* (New York: Viking Books, 1989).

LAMB, MICHAEL, ed., *The Father's Role: Applied Perspectives* (New York: John Wiley and Sons, 1986).
———, *The Role of Fathers* (Salt Lake City: University of Utah Press, 1981).

On divorce, and child custody:
SMART, CAROL and SEVENHUIJSEN, SELMA, eds., *Child Custody and the Politics of Gender* (London: Routledge, 1989).
SUGARMAN, STEPHEN D. and KAY, HERMA HILL, eds., *Divorce Reform at the Crossroads* (New Haven: Yale University Press, 1990).

On the politics of reproduction:
TAUB, NADINE and COHEN, SHERRILL, eds. for the Women's Rights Litigation Clinic, School of Law, *Reproductive Laws for the 1990s* (Newark: Rutgers University, 1988).

For excellent statistical information, with special attention paid to the issues of people of color:
The American Woman series, edited by Sara Rix for The Women's Research & Education Institute (New York: W. W. Norton & Co.); and also, those unsung but invaluable foot soldiers of data collection and analysis, the U.S. Bureau of Labor Statistics and the U.S. Census Bureau.

In the year-and-some I spent reading about fathers, mothers, daughters, and the acquisition of gender, I found myself most influenced by the feminist Freudians who are critical of Freud, and the psychologists of the object-relations school. Among these are:
BENJAMIN, JESSICA, *The Bonds of Love: Psychoanalysis, Feminism, and the Problem of Domination* (New York: Pantheon Books, 1988).
CHODOROW, NANCY J., *The Reproduction of Mothering: Psychoanalysis and the Sociology of Gender* (Berkeley: University of California Press, 1978).
———, *Feminism and Psychoanalytic Theory* (New Haven: Yale University Press, 1989).
GALLOP, JANE, *The Father's Seduction: Feminism and Psychoanalysis* (Ithaca: Cornell University Press, 1982).
IRIGARAY, LUCE, *Speculum of the Other Woman* (Ithaca: Cornell University Press, 1985).
JOHNSON, MIRIAM, *Strong Mothers, Weak Wives: The Search for Gender Equality* (Berkeley: University of California Press, 1988).

Two books that changed the ways we think about motherhood:
RICH, ADRIENNE, *Of Woman Born: Motherhood as Experience and Institution* (New York: Harper & Row, 1976).

RUDDICK, SARA, *Maternal Thinking: Toward a Politics of Peace* (New York: Ballantine, 1989).

There are thousands of books about sexuality and gender, many of them important, but the flagship, still sailing, of the new wave of feminist scholarship on the subject is:
SNITOW, ANN; STANSELL, CHRISTINE; and THOMPSON, SHARON, eds., *Powers of Desire* (New York: Monthly Review Press, 1983).

A similarly crucial book on sexism and racism is:
MORAGA, CHERRIE, and ANZALDUA, GLORIA, eds., *This Bridge Called My Back: Writings By Radical Women of Color* (New York: Kitchen Table: Women of Color Press, 1981).

For the history of feminism's second wave, I used mostly interviews and the ephemera in the Women's Herstory Archives and the Barnard Center for Research on Women. In addition, I relied heavily on a handful of books:
ECHOLS, ALICE, *Daring to Be Bad: Radical Feminism in America 1967–75* (Minneapolis: University of Minnesota Press, 1989).
EVANS, SARA, *Personal Politics: The Roots of Feminism in the Civil Rights Movement and the New Left* (New York: Vintage Books, 1985).
GIDDINGS, PAULA, *When and Where I Enter: The Impact of Black Women on Race and Sex in America* (New York: Bantam Books, 1984).
HULL, GLORIA T.; SCOTT, PATRICIA BELL; and SMITH, BARBARA, eds., *All the Women Are White, All the Blacks Are Men, But Some of Us Are Brave: Black Women's Studies* (New York: Feminist Press, 1982).

About war, peace, and gender, the best recent collection I know is:
HARRIS, ADRIENNE and KING, YNESTRA, eds. *Rocking the Ship of State: Toward a Feminist Peace Politics* (Boulder: Westview Press, 1989).
and still fresh after all these years:
WOOLF, VIRGINIA, *Three Guineas* (New York: Harcourt, Brace, Jovanovich Inc., 1938/1966).

All writers learn to write by reading, and there are a few essayists to whom I turn not only when thinking about words and sentences but when thinking about thinking—about the shape of an argument, about personal and political speech and their potentials and limitations.

Three of the greatest feminist essays of all time share these qualities: they dip and rise between the personal and political, the rational and the emotional, the earnest and the sarcastic, the polite and the outraged. They are all propelled by a ferocious anger at the injustices done to women and by a clarifying impatience for the release of female creativity, the freeing of female subjectivity:

DE BEAUVOIR, SIMONE, *The Second Sex* (New York: Vintage Books, 1974).

WOLLSTONECRAFT, MARY, *A Vindication of the Rights of Women* (1792) (New York: W. W. Norton and Co., 1988).

WOOLF, VIRGINIA, *A Room of One's Own* (1929, New York: Harcourt Brace Jovanovich/Harvest Books).

In grappling with *My Enemy, My Love,* I have turned as well to the feminist essayists of my own time, who are also grappling with the current issues of writing about women, men, and politics: how to be deeply cognizant of difference, yet speak beyond the idiosyncratic; to be authoritative yet not pretend to know it all; to race ahead incautiously, yet not fear to doubt; to come to conclusions, yet not close the door to further inquiry.

Not surprisingly, three of the writers whose work I admire most are also poets, who are accustomed to living with ambiguity. I name here only a few of their works.

RICH, ADRIENNE, *On Lies, Secrets, and Silence: Selected Prose 1966–1978* (New York: W. W. Norton & Co., 1979).

HOOKS, BELL, *Yearning: Race, Gender, and Cultural Politics* (Boston: South End Press, 1990).

———. *Talking Back: Thinking Feminist/Thinking Black* (Sept. 1989).

LORDE, AUDRE, *Sister Outsider: Essays and Speeches* (Freedom, CA.: Crossing Press, 1984).

Among the journalists and critics who have inspired me with their literacy, snarkiness, and perfect diction while thinking on their feet are Barbara Ehrenreich, Susan Jacoby, Jane O'Reilly, Ann Snitow, and Ellen Willis.

Index

About the Author

Judith Levine, a former contributing editor for *New York Woman,* writes for *The Village Voice* and many other national publications on women, sex, and politics. A longtime feminist activist and officer of the National Writers Union, she lives in Brooklyn, New York, and Hardwick, Vermont.